# Schema Therapy for Eating Disorders

Options can be limited for those who do not respond to standard eating disorder treatments. Schema therapy is one of the new exciting frontiers in the treatment of this clinical population, offering a much-needed model that integrates both developmental and deeper level personality factors. *Schema Therapy for Eating Disorders* is the first book of its kind, guiding clinicians to deliver the schema model to those with entrenched or enduring eating pathology, and in turn encouraging further clinical research on this approach to treatment.

Written by an international team of leading schema therapy experts, and with a foreword by Wendy Behary and Jeffrey Young, this book draws on their clinical knowledge and research experience. Comprehensive and practical, this book introduces the rapidly growing evidence base for schema therapy, outlines the application of this model across eating disorder diagnostic groups, as well as individual and group modalities, and explores practical considerations, common challenges and the therapeutic process. The book includes detailed case examples, which provide a theoretical and practical basis for working with therapist-client schema chemistry and transference, and outlines methods of ensuring therapist self-care in the face of difficult and often long-term work.

Innovative and accessible, this fresh look at the treatment of eating disorders will be an invaluable resource for clinicians in the field.

**Dr Susan Simpson** is training director of Schema Therapy Scotland, and Consultant Clinical Psychologist in an NHS-Scotland inpatient eating disorders unit. She has held numerous clinical and academic posts and has over 20 years of experience working with eating disorders and complex comorbidity. She has published widely on schema therapy and eating disorders.

**Dr Evelyn Smith** is a Clinical Psychologist and a Senior Lecturer at Western Sydney University, Australia. She has held multiple clinical positions, including heading the Eating Disorders and Obesity Psychology Research Clinic. She has published widely in the area of eating disorders and was Chief Investigator of a grant assessing group schema therapy for eating disorders.

"Schema therapy has become increasingly popular as a treatment for personality disorders and other chronic conditions. This book presents the application of schema therapy to a challenging group of disorders with a high comorbidity with personality disorders: eating disorders. Written by experts in both schema therapy and eating disorders, this book is an essential guide for those that want to extend their insight in and therapeutic possibilities for the more challenging patients with eating disorders. A must-have for those looking for a treatment method that integrates treatment of eating problems with treatment of personality problems."

**– Arnoud Arntz, Professor of Clinical Psychology, University of Amsterdam, The Netherlands**

"Think for a moment. What do you want when you invest the time (and money) to read a practitioner book? You do not want the words of another academic writer steeped in theory with only the distant memory of practice. This book gathers the luminaries of the schema therapy world to help you better treat eating disorders. All 'present tense' practitioners. Read and learn."

**– Professor Bruce A. Stevens, PhD (Boston University, 1987), Clinical Psychologist and Research Academic at Charles Sturt University, Canberra, Australia**

"This impressive volume details the application of schema therapy to eating disorders which is considered to be one of the most complex and difficult to treat disorders, not least because of the high rate of comorbidity with personality disorders.

The book provides a clear and up-to-date overview of theory and research in schema therapy and eating disorders. A detailed description of how to deliver the powerful schema therapy treatment strategies form a central portion of the book accompanied with rich clinical illustrations, making it essential reading for practising schema therapists working with clients with eating disorders. I thoroughly recommend it."

**– Dr. Vartouhi Ohanian, Consultant Clinical Psychologist and Director of Schema Therapy UK**

"This book represents a valuable and timely addition to the literature. It is written in an accessible style by experienced clinicians. Many of our patients remain unwell at the end of standardized treatments. This book encourages and aids the clinician in thinking in a more complex way about their clients' difficulties. I have already incorporated some of the ideas in this book to deepen my clinical work. This book has the potential to assist a clinician's thinking process with their most complex patients. The chapters on formulation, mode work, chair work and enhancing motivation for change are especially clinically rich."

**– Chris Thornton, Clinical Director of The Redleaf Practice**

# Schema Therapy for Eating Disorders

Theory and Practice for Individual
and Group Settings

Edited by
Susan Simpson and Evelyn Smith

Routledge
Taylor & Francis Group

LONDON AND NEW YORK

First published 2020
by Routledge
2 Park Square, Milton Park, Abingdon, Oxon OX14 4RN

and by Routledge
52 Vanderbilt Avenue, New York, NY 10017

*Routledge is an imprint of the Taylor & Francis Group, an informa business*

*British Library Cataloguing in Publication Data*
A catalogue record for this book is available from the British Library

*Library of Congress Cataloging-in-Publication Data*
A catalog record has been requested for this book

ISBN: 978-0-367-27239-5 (hbk)
ISBN: 978-0-367-27240-1 (pbk)
ISBN: 978-0-429-29571-3 (ebk)

Typeset in Times New Roman
by Taylor & Francis Books

To my husband Craig, and sons Finn and Rory, your loving presence, support and patience made this journey possible. To my parents, who inspired me to believe in myself and to write.

Susan Simpson

To my daughter, Asha, and my son, Sebastian – this book was inspired by you. I love you.

Evelyn Smith

To all of the clients who have contributed to our understanding of eating disorders, and the schema therapy model – we hope that what you have taught us will benefit others.

Susan and Evelyn

# Contents

# Illustrations

## Figures

## Tables

## Boxes

# Contributors

**Christina Archonti,** MD, is a Clinical Psychologist, Psychotherapist, Behavioural and Schema therapist. She graduated as Psychologist and as a Doctor of Medicine at the University of Saarland, as Behavioural Psychotherapist at the Centre of Psychological Therapy at the University of Heidelberg. Christina currently works as a psychotherapist, academic and supervisor, and has worked in her own clinical practice since 2008 in Frankfurt, Main/Germany.

**Robert Brockman** is a Clinical Psychologist and senior research fellow at the Institute for Positive Psychology and Education, Australian Catholic University. He is also principle Clinical Psychologist at *Schema Therapy Sydney*, a Sydney based psychology clinic focused on the practice and dissemination of schema therapy. His clinical practice and research has largely focused on the applicability of schema therapy to novel treatment populations (e.g. Eating Disorders, GAD, Psychotic Symptoms), and the integration of 3rd Wave Therapy techniques into schema therapy practice.

**Janet D. Carter** is a Professor in Clinical Psychology and also Dean of Science at the University of Canterbury in New Zealand. Her research interests include anxiety, mood and eating disorders. Her research has focused on investigating factors associated with response to different types of therapy so that we can improve outcome and she has published widely in this area. Janet has been investigator and therapist on clinical trials of schema therapy and cognitive behaviour therapy for depression and binge eating disorders. Her main teaching is with students training in the University's Clinical Psychology Program.

**Gianluca Castelnuovo,** Ph.D., Psy.D., is Associate Professor of Clinical Psychology, Rehabilitation Psychology and Psychopathology at the Faculty of Psychology of the Catholic University of Milan. He also serves as Senior Researcher in the Clinical Psychology Lab and Service at the Institute for Treatment and Research (IRCCS) Istituto Auxologico Italiano, San Giuseppe Hospital, Verbania Italy. He has conducted several research studies and published many papers in the field of clinical psychology and psychotherapy. Mostly, he is interested in the use of Virtual Reality, Tele-Psychology, eHealth and mHealth in medicine and clinical psychology for enhancing adherence to treatment in eating disorders, obesity and Type 2 Diabetes. He is Associate Editor for several academic journals (*BMC Obesity, SpringerPlus, Eating and Weight Disorders, Cogent Psychology, Health Psychology* and *Behavioral Medicine*) and Specialty Chief Editor for *Frontiers in Clinical and Health Psychology* journal.

**David Edwards** who lives in Cape Town, South Africa, runs a training program in schema therapy through the Schema Therapy Institute of South Africa. The focus of many of his over 100 academic publications is trauma and complex trauma. He has published several papers on case study methodology and is one of the editors of the recently published *Case Studies within Psychotherapy Trials: Integrating Qualitative and Quantitative Methods* (Oxford University Press). He has also written articles and book chapters on the history and application of imagery methods in psychotherapy and is the author, with Michael Jacobs, of *Conscious and Unconscious* in the series *Core Concepts in Psychotherapy* (McGraw Hill, 2003). His current work is on the phenomenology of schema modes and he has been presenting his ideas in a series of advanced workshops in which the key ideas are richly illustrated with transcripts from schema therapy sessions.

**Nicole Files**, BA Psychology (Hons), has been involved in Schema Therapy for Eating Disorders group project as a research assistant since 2014. Nicole has worked in the eating disorder field as a support group facilitator and volunteer coordinator at the Eating Disorder Association of South Australia and has contributed to several publications related to the field of eating disorders.

**Siri Hartmann**, BSc (Hons) in Psychology, MSc in Brain Sciences (Neuroscience) is a Trainee Clinical Psychologist at the University of Edinburgh, who has worked in an inpatient eating disorder unit, and more recently in Child and Adolescent Mental Health, NHS Glasgow, Scotland.

**Jennifer Jordan** is a Senior Lecturer at the University of Otago, Christchurch, New Zealand, teaching on postgraduate mental health and addiction papers. She also works as a Clinical Psychologist and researcher for the Canterbury District Health Board in the Clinical Research Unit on psychotherapy research studies, and clinically in an outpatient alcohol and drug service. Her primary research interest is clinical research for significant mental health problems, including comparative psychotherapy trials, translational research, and examining factors influencing psychotherapy outcomes. She has been an investigator and therapist on two randomised controlled trials examining schema therapy in relation to cognitive behaviour therapy for binge eating (bulimia nervosa or binge eating disorder) and for major depression.

**Virginia V. W. McIntosh**, PhD (Otago), Dip Clin Psyc, MNZCCP. Gini teaches in the Clinical Psychology Program at the University of Canterbury, Christchurch New Zealand. She has worked as an investigator and therapist on clinical trials of schema therapy for eating disorders and major depression and is interested in improving treatment outcome of eating disorders by studying the comparative efficacy of treatments and mechanisms of change within psychotherapy.

**Claudia Mendez** is a Clinical Psychologist with experience working in both the government and private settings. Claudia has worked in public mental health settings across the Hunter New England and South West Sydney Local Health Districts in Australia providing psychological interventions for complex mental health presentations. Claudia currently works for the Liverpool and Fairfield Mental Health Service working with adults who experience complex mental health, trauma and personality disorders and in the provision of supervision to clinicians. Claudia has been collaborating with Western Sydney University, on the Sydney site, of a multi-site trial of group schema therapy for eating disorders.

**Wendelien Merens** is a Clinical Psychologist with a PhD in social behavioural science. She has experience in treating eating disorders, both in inpatient and outpatient settings. She is a registered CBT therapist and senior schema therapist. She is currently working with personality disordered patients in an outpatient setting.

**Giada Pietrabissa**, Ph.D., Psy.D., is Adjunct Professor and Postdoctoral Researcher at the Faculty of Psychology of the Catholic University of Milan. She also serves as research psychologist in the Clinical Psychology Lab and Service at the Institute for Treatment and Research (IRCCS) Istituto Auxologico Italiano, San Luca Hospital, Milan, Italy. She is author of several articles published in academic peer-review journals and book chapters in the field of health care – particularly obesity, eating disorders and cardiovascular diseases. She has expert knowledge and experience in using a variety of therapeutic approaches including brief strategic and systemic therapy, motivational interviewing, and schema therapy.

**Matthew Pugh** is Clinical Psychologist, Cognitive Behavioural Psychotherapist, and Advanced Schema Therapist. He works with the Vincent Square Eating Disorders Service (Central and North West London NHS Foundation Trust) and is an honorary clinical lecturer with University College London. He writes and teaches on applications of chairwork within schema therapy and associated approaches including cognitive behavioural therapy, compassion-focused therapy, and motivational interviewing. His research interests include voice-experiencing in eating disorders and experiential methods in psychotherapy. Matthew is author of the book *Cognitive Behavioural Chairwork: Distinctive Features.*

**Sophie Rae** is a Counselling Psychologist based at the Vincent Square Eating Disorders Service (Central and North West London NHS Foundation Trust). She is currently working towards her schema therapy accreditation and has developed a particular interest in the application of chairwork.

**Eckhard Roediger** (MD) is a Neurologist, Psychiatrist and Psychotherapist, trained in both psychodynamic and cognitive behaviour therapy. Formerly he was Director of a Psychosomatic Department of a clinic in Berlin, Germany. Since 2007 he has been working in private practice and is Director of the Schema Therapy Training Centre in Frankfurt. He has been on the International Society of Schema Therapy Board since 2008, was past-President and is currently treasurer of the ISST. He has authored books on schema therapy for couples and integrating an ACT-perspective into schema therapy.

**Sally Skewes** is a Clinical Psychologist who treats clients with complex psychological presentations in Adelaide, Australia. Sally is certified as a Schema Therapist, Supervisor and Trainer with the International Society of Schema Therapy (ISST); and founded Secure Nest (www.securenest. org), an innovative online platform designed specifically for schema therapy. Sally has co-authored articles on schema therapy and has presented workshops on Schema Therapy and eHealth.

**Evelyn Smith**, PhD, MPsych (Clinical), is a Clinical Psychologist and a Senior Lecturer of Clinical Psychology at Western Sydney University, located in Sydney, Australia. She has 13 years of experience in the area of eating disorders, and has published widely in the area. She has held multiple clinical and academic positions, most recently heading the Eating Disorders and Obesity psychology research clinic (EDOC). She is currently the Chief Investigator of a randomised controlled trial funded by Ramaciotti Australia to investigate the effectiveness of cognitive remediation therapy for obesity, and Chief Investigator of a UWS Women's Research Fellowship to investigate the efficacy of group schema therapy for eating disorders. She is Associate Editor of the journal *Clinical Obesity*, and regularly presents plenaries, symposiums, keynotes, and paper presentations at national and international conferences in the areas of obesity and eating disorders.

**Susan Simpson**, DPsych, MPsych (Clinical), is a Clinical Psychologist and Schema Therapy trainer/supervisor, with a specialist interest in eating disorders and complex trauma. She has held several clinical and academic positions and is director of *Schema Therapy Scotland*, providing training and accreditation in schema therapy across Scotland, northern England, and internationally. She has over 20 years of experience working with eating disorders. She currently works with severe and enduring eating disorders at an NHS-inpatient eating disorders unit, and is adjunct lecturer at the University of South Australia. She is co-leading an international research group investigating the effectiveness of group schema therapy for eating disorders. She has published several research papers on the schema therapy model applied to a range of clinical populations, and has presented keynotes, seminars and workshops at national and international conferences.

**Adele Stavropoulos** is a Clinical Psychologist working in private practice in Sydney, Australia. She is also undertaking a PhD in clinical psychology at the University of Technology Sydney. Her research examines the application of imagery rescripting to the treatment of intrusive autobiographical memories in depression.

**Michiel van Vreeswijk** is a Clinical Psychologist, certified as a Schema Therapist and Supervisor with the ISST; a certified CBT practitioner and supervisor; and board member of G-kracht psychomedisch centrum BV, mental health care institute, the Netherlands. He offers regular workshops and supervision in schema therapy both in the Netherlands and abroad. Michiel has written and edited several books, and authored many chapters and articles on schema therapy. He edited and published several chapters in the *Wiley-Blackwell Handbook of Schema Therapy, Theory, Research, and Practice.*

**Aglaia Zedlitz** works as an Assistant Professor at Leiden University, The Netherlands and as a Psychologist providing schema therapy in specialist mental health care. After obtaining her PhD in rehabilitation psychology on fatigue in neurological disorders, she now focusses on innovations in rehabilitation and mental health care.

# Abbreviations

| | |
|---|---|
| ED | eating disorder |
| BN | bulimia nervosa |
| AN | anorexia nervosa |
| BED | binge eating disorder |
| CBT | cognitive behaviour therapy |
| CBT-E | cognitive behaviour therapy (enhanced) |
| AnCh | Angry Child |
| AvPr | Avoidant Protector |
| CSu | Compliant Surrenderer |
| DemP | Demanding Parent (Inner Critic) |
| DetPr | Detached Protector |
| DetSS | Detached Self-Soother |
| HA | Healthy Adult |
| HAC | Happy/Authentic Child |
| HS | Helpless Surrenderer |
| OC | Overcontroller |
| PP | Punitive Parent (Inner Critic) |
| ST | Schema Therapy |
| VCh | Vulnerable Child |

# Foreword

Schema therapy (ST) has a burgeoning evidence base for a wide range of psychological difficulties, with preliminary studies indicating that it holds promise for the treatment of eating disorders. Of note, ST already has a strong evidence-base for a range of longstanding characterological traits and psychological disorders that have high comorbidity with eating disorders. ST appears to be particularly suited to working with eating disorders linked to the long-term effects of trauma, abuse and emotional neglect, as well the effects of cultural/media influences that place a strong emphasis on perfectionism and achievement at the expense of health and happiness. The powerful techniques utilised within the schema therapy approach are particularly effective in addressing rigid personality traits that may be resistant to standard therapeutic approaches, highlighting its potential with this population.

We are delighted that our colleagues, Susan Simpson and Evelyn Smith have written this thoughtful and important book. This is a first to provide a practical guide to the application of ST for eating disorders, with 'how-to' steps for a range of assessment and therapeutic techniques relevant to working with this population. The authors elegantly describe how ST can be used as an adjunct to cognitive behavioural therapy (CBT), the gold-standard for bulimic disorders, as well as those with more complex and severe presentations, those with a history of trauma and neglect, and those who have not responded to or have become 'stuck' with standard first-line treatments. The authors beautifully describe ways in which ST can be integrated with other psychotherapy approaches, with a particular emphasis on behavioural change. Separate sections are included that explore ways in which experiential and behavioural treatment strategies can be applied with both bulimic and anorexic eating disorders, with detailed descriptions of how they can be used to address common therapeutic blocks and impasses.

Chapter 10, presents a detailed ST group manual for eating disorders (with links to online handouts). This is a valuable how-to guide for clinicians, and can be utilised as a stand-alone program or alongside individual sessions. Preliminary research supports the effectiveness of combining group and individual ST for a range of clinical difficulties including eating disorders, and this may provide one possible solution for the provision of time-limited effective treatments within resource-limited health services.

All of the authors who have contributed to this book have extensive clinical experience and expertise in the application of ST to eating disorders, and have carried out preliminary research in the field. Indeed, McIntosh et al. (Chapter 3) carried out the first randomised-controlled trial on ST for bulimic disorders, reporting equivalence with standard CBT. Further trials are ongoing, and the authors describe important guidelines for future research in the field.

*Schema Therapy for Eating Disorders* is a must for your clinical library of resources, offering the therapist an important guide for working with eating disorders, through reducing self-defeating life patterns whilst strengthening healthy coping and self-compassion. Powerful techniques are provided to guide therapists through working with ambivalence, whilst helping their clients to make the transition from cognitive to emotional and behavioural changes that enable them to transform their lives and learn to get their needs met in healthy adaptive ways. We are so grateful for this important contribution.

Wendy Behary, Past President—International Society of
Schema Therapy (2010–2014)
Jeffrey Young, Founder of Schema Therapy

# Acknowledgements

We would like to gratefully acknowledge Craig Whyte who spent time honing and proof reading the manuscript right down to the wire, and Sophie Arneil who checked for consistency on formatting and terminology throughout the book. We thank you so much for your close attention to detail.

# Part I

## Introduction to schema therapy

# Chapter 1

# Introduction to schema therapy for eating disorders

*Evelyn Smith, Susan Simpson and Virginia V. W. McIntosh*

## Abstract

*Given the limited efficacy of maintenance models such as cognitive behavioural therapy (CBT) in the treatment of eating disorders (EDs), there has been increased attention dedicated to exploring the role of deeper level factors such as core beliefs and schemas in the eating disorders literature. One model, which integrates both developmental and deeper level personality factors, is the schema model developed by Jeffrey Young (1990; 2003). Schema therapy (ST) has shown promising outcomes in recent randomised trials for a range of personality disorders and other complex psychological problems. On this basis it appears to be ideally suited to working with the ED population. This chapter introduces the reader to what ST is, highlighting the most prevalent modes in this population, and articulating why this treatment should be considered as a second line of treatment for adults with eating disorders who either have not responded to CBT or have stopped making progress. The aim of this book is to encourage further clinical research on the schema mode model, and to guide individuals to deliver ST for EDs confidently and successfully.*

EDs have the highest mortality of any mental illness, however recovery is possible with treatment. The evidence-base supporting psychological treatments for EDs has grown exponentially in the past decade, with a large proportion of individuals experiencing significant improvements. Nevertheless, in clinical settings, we often encounter ED presentations that do not fit into our standard protocols, and patients who do not engage in, nor respond to, our best treatments. Indeed, it is well recognised that the treatment of EDs can be fraught with complexity, and that a proportion of individuals develop a picture characterised by chronicity and ego-syntonicity (i.e. 'my anorexia defines who I am') (Bardone-Cone, Thompson, & Miller, 2018).

There are a significant number of individuals with EDs who do not respond to our first line treatment, namely CBT. Indeed, attrition (Fassino, Pierò, Tomba, & Abbate-Daga, 2009) and relapse rates are relatively high (Grilo et al., 2012) with a substantial proportion of EDs presenting as chronic, disabling and resistant to treatment (Steinhausen & Weber, 2009; Abbate-Daga,

Amianto, Delsedime, De-Bacco, & Fassino, 2013). While enhanced CBT (CBT-E) has led to improved outcomes for those with bulimia nervosa (BN) and binge eating disorder (BED) there still remain approximately 40 to 50% of individuals who do not respond to treatment (Fairburn et al., 2009; Byrne, Fursland, Allen, & Watson, 2011). In one recent study, at two years post-CBT-E, 44% of those with BN were found to be abstinent, whilst over half remained symptomatic (Poulson et al., 2014). Anorexia nervosa (AN) in particular remains difficult to treat, with CBT (and CBT-E) outcome trials reporting relatively high drop-out rates and limited efficacy (Hay, 2013). For those with severe and enduring AN, outcomes have been generally poor, with only a handful of outcome studies in the area. Whereas many clients become experts in identifying thinking errors and challenging their own negative thoughts and beliefs, they often describe limited changes to their deeply held core beliefs (Leung, Thomas, & Waller, 2000; Jones, Leung, & Harris, 2007) that are often experienced at a visceral or 'felt-sense' level (Simpson, 2012).

There is a relatively high prevalence of suicidal behaviour amongst those with EDs, with at least 25% engaging in self-harm (Sansone & Levitt, 2002). Comorbidity has been found to play a significant role in predicting treatment engagement and effectiveness. It is estimated that 58–69% of individuals with EDs meet a diagnosis for personality disorder, with up to 93% experiencing another disorder, including affective disorders, anxiety disorders and substance misuse (Rosenvinge, Martinussen, & Ostensen, 2000; Blinder, Cumella, & San-thara, 2006; Farstad, McGeown, & von Ranson, 2016). Preliminary evidence suggests that the presence of rigid personality pathology (e.g. perfectionism, narcissistic defences) and personality disorder (PD) (particularly avoidant and obsessive-compulsive PDs) may adversely affect treatment outcomes (Masheb & Grilo, 2008; Pham-Scottez et al., 2012; Zerwas et al., 2013). In addition, a range of personality traits have been found to be highly correlated with ED symptom severity and negative treatment outcomes, including impulsivity, compulsivity, avoidance motivation, and affective instability (Farstad et al., 2016). Of particular note, perfectionism is reported at high levels across ED diagnostic groups (Bardone-Cone et al., 2007) and is positively correlated with ED symptomatology. The majority of research suggests that standard treat-ments are not consistently effective in addressing perfectionism both for those with AN and BN (Aguera et al., 2012; Segura-Garcia et al., 2013).

There is a clear need for innovative transdiagnostic treatment models that are sufficiently sophisticated to address eating pathology, alongside char-acterological traits, affective instability, and other comorbidities in a focused, integrative and intensive way (Wilson, Grilo & Vitousek, 2007; Cooper & Kelland, 2015). Preliminary evidence suggests that schema therapy may be well suited to the treatment of EDs, particularly those with high complexity and comorbidity, and symptoms that are unresponsive to first-line treatments (Simpson, Morrow, van Vreeswijk, & Reid, 2010; Simpson & Slowey, 2011; McIntosh et al., 2016). A range of studies have demonstrated that ST is an efficacious and cost-effective treatment for borderline personality disorder (BPD) (Giesen-Bloo et al., 2006; van Asselt et al., 2008; Farrell, Shaw, & Webber, 2009; Nadort et al., 2009; Masley, Gillanders, Simpson, & Taylor, 2012), Cluster C personality disorders (Bamelis, Evers, Spinhoven, & Arntz, 2014), as well as a range of other disorders including substance misuse (Ball, Maccarelli, LaPaglia, & Ostrowski, 2011), depression (Carter et al., 2013), post-traumatic stress disorder (Cockram, Drummond, & Lee, 2010), panic disorder and agoraphobia (Gude & Hoffart, 2008).

## Introduction to schema therapy

ST is an integrative model, drawing on CBT, psychodynamic, gestalt, constructivism, and attachment models. It was originally designed for chronic, personality-related problems, and departs from CBT by conceptualising childhood and adolescent experiences at the origins of psychological problems. ST also differs from traditional CBT in the emphasis it places on the therapeutic relationship, the use of emotion-related therapy strategies and its focus on schema-driven maladaptive coping styles. The ST model comprises four constructs: early maladaptive schemas (EMS), schema domains, schema processes, and schema modes (Young, Klosko, & Weishaar, 2003), which are summarised below.

Young's conceptualisation of schemas differs from that of earlier cognitive theorists (Beck, Rush, Shaw, & Emery, 1979). Young's schema concept is an organising system or pattern, which includes thoughts, memories, emotions, physical sensations, and drives. EMS create self-defeating patterns and are central to an individual's core psychopathology (Young et al., 2003). See Appendix 1 for a list and brief description of all 18 EMS.

Schemas are theorised to develop when core emotional needs of childhood are not met, including the need for secure attachments to others; autonomy, competence, and a sense of identity; freedom to express valid needs and emotions; spontaneity and play; and realistic limits and self-control. Core needs may be unmet when the early environment is toxic or when there is a mismatch of the environment and the child's temperament. The nature of the adversity experienced during childhood relates directly to the types of EMS that may develop. For example, when a child experiences trauma or victimisation, schemas such as *mistrust/abuse* or *defectiveness/shame* may develop. If the childhood environment is deficient in warmth, nurturance, understanding, love or stability the child may develop schemas such as *emotional deprivation* or *abandonment*. On the other hand, if the child is overindulged or over-protected, experiencing too much of what would be healthy in moderation, schemas such as *entitlement/grandiosity* or *dependence/incompetence* may develop. Such early experiences are theorised to contribute to the development of schemas, which in turn drive the problems of later life, including binge eating and restriction.

ST's main goal is to heal EMS, which involves the diminishment of emotion, thoughts, bodily sensations and memories connected with the schema, reduction of maladaptive coping styles that the individual uses to avoid or cope with EMS, and development of new coping styles of behaviour that are adaptive and enable current unmet needs to be addressed (Young et al., 2003).

EMS are hypothesised to be extremely stable and enduring themes that develop during childhood and are elaborated upon throughout a person's lifetime. Schemas serve as templates for the processing of later experience. They are unconditional, self-perpetuating, and very resistant to change. Established early in life as a relatively adaptive response to the individual's environment, schemas may become maladaptive over time, in different contexts or with changed circumstances. When EMS are triggered, *schema processes* are employed to avoid or reduce negative affect associated with schema activation (Sheffield, Waller, Emanuelli, Murray, & Meyer, 2009). The three schema coping processes include *surrender* (passive acceptance of schemata); *avoidance* (blocking and avoiding schemata and associated emotions and situations); and *overcompensation* (fighting schemata by doing the opposite) (Luck, Waller, Meyer, Ussher, & Lacey, 2005).

*Schema modes* are defined as 'those schemas or schema operations – adaptive or maladaptive – that are currently active for an individual' (Young et al., 2003: p.37). The schema mode concept is broader than that of EMS and incorporates both EMS and schema processes into a unified construct (Young et al., 2003). Schema modes are state constructs that are triggered when trait-based EMS are activated and are consequently strongly influenced by the individual's current affective state and situational context (Young et al., 2003).

The concept of schema modes was developed to account for more complex presentations, whereby multiple schemas and coping styles are collapsed into different 'sides' of self. Schema modes represent the moment-by-moment states that an individual experiences. Young et al. (2003) report the presence of four schema mode categories: dysfunctional child modes that result from unmet childhood needs; parent modes which encapsulate the internalisation of parental behaviour toward the child; dysfunctional coping modes which correspond to the schema processes of avoidance, overcompensation and surrender; and the adaptive healthy modes which refer to the individual's functional and adaptive thoughts, feelings and behaviours and ability to act in a playful and spontaneous manner (Lobbestael, Van Vreeswijk, & Arntz, 2008). Modes include the *Vulnerable Child, Angry Child, Impulsive Child, Punitive* or *Demanding Parent, Detached Protector, Overcontroller, Happy Child, and Healthy Adult.* The experience of individual schemas can change very quickly, and the idea of being 'stuck in' one schema mode, or 'flipping between' schema modes can be particularly important for individuals with high complexity and comorbidity. Understanding which life events result in activation or triggering of schema modes becomes part of the work of healing in a schema modes therapeutic approach. For a description of each mode usually found in those with EDs, see Chapter 4, Box 4.1, page 46.

## Rationale for using schema mode therapy for adults with EDs

Evidence suggests that those with EDs are distinguishable from non-clinical populations both through significantly higher levels of EMS (Damiano, Reece, Reid, Atkins, & Patton, 2015) and schema modes (Talbot, Smith, Tomkins, Brockman, & Simpson, 2015). Further, difficulties associated with parental bonding and early attachment have been shown to mediate the relationship between EMS and ED symptoms (Deas, Power, Collin, Yellowlees, & Grierson, 2011; Brown, Selth, Stretton, & Simpson, 2016). Indeed, a disproportionately high rate of those with EDs have suffered childhood sexual, physical or emotional abuse (Brewerton, 2007), with clear indications that traumatic exposure is associated with self-reported severity of ED symptoms, higher secondary psychosocial difficulties, psychiatric comorbidity, and negative self-image (Backholm, Isomaa, & Birgegård, 2013).

In recent years, ST has been further developed into group treatment protocols. Evidence suggests that group therapy may in fact catalyse the effects of ST, by providing corrective emotional learning experiences, as well as a forum in which participants can begin to develop and practice new interpersonal and behavioural coping skills that heal their schemas. In addition, the experience of sharing similar experiences and schemas with other participants can counteract the experience of shame and powerlessness that many clients with EDs experience. This setting also provides ample opportunities to learn vicariously through others (Farrell et al., 2009; Simpson et al., 2010; van Vreeswijk, Spinhoven, Eurelings-Bontekoe, & Broersen, 2012).

The development of the *schema mode model* in recent years has facilitated a state-based conceptualisation of eating disordered behaviours, which is particularly useful in the context of complex comorbidity and characterological difficulties (Simpson, 2012). Further, recent research has highlighted the importance of schema processes (and coping modes) in mediating the association between adverse childhood experiences and eating disordered behaviour (Sheffield et al., 2009; Brown, Selth, Stretton, & Simpson 2016).

## This book

This book assumes a clear understanding of eating disorders and focuses on treating adults with Anorexia nervosa (AN), Bulimia nervosa (BN) and Binge eating disorder (BED) and is divided into five main parts. Part One introduces the evidence of ST for EDs, Part Two focuses on assessment and conceptualisation of ST for EDs, and Part Three describes the application of ST for EDs, with the inclusion of a how-to manual for group therapy. The challenges emerging from individual and group ST for EDs are outlined in Part Four, and the fifth part briefly discusses the future of ST. This book places equal emphasis on cognitive, experiential, interpersonal and behavioural techniques in the treatment of EDs, however the reader is directed to other sources for a more in-depth description of cognitive techniques (e.g. Waller, Kennerley, & Ohanian, 2007). The techniques in this book apply equally to males and females with EDs; where gender references are expressed in feminine terms, these can readily be substituted with the masculine equivalent. Finally, we have an Appendix section which provides readers with a link to further information, and expansion of chapters as documented or as needed.

We hope this book will encourage you to practice ST and to deliver it confidently and successfully to individuals with EDs. We also encourage that you evaluate your clinical practice, which will enhance further clinical research on this schema mode model. If you have any questions or comments please do not hesitate to email us at schematherapybook@gmail.com. We hope you enjoy the book.

## References

Abbate-Daga, G., Amianto, F., Delsedime, N., De-Bacco, C., & Fassino, S. (2013). Resistance to treatment in eating disorders: A critical challenge. *BMC Psychiatry*, 13, 294.

Aguera, Z., Krug, I., Sanchez, I., Granero, R., Penelo, E., Penas-Lledo, E., ... & Fernandez-Aranda, F. (2012). Personality changes in bulimia nervosa after a cognitive behaviour therapy. *European Eating Disorders Review*, 20, 379–385.

Ball, S. A., Maccarelli, L. M., LaPaglia, D. M., & Ostrowski, M. J. (2011). Randomized trial of dual-focused versus single-focused individual therapy for personality disorders and substance dependence. *The Journal of Nervous and Mental Disease, 199*(5), 319.

Bardone-Cone, A., Wonderlich, S., Frost, R. O., Bulik, C., Mitchell, J., Uppala, S., & Simonich, H. (2007). Perfectionism and eating disorders: Current status and future directions. *Clinical Psychology Review*, 27, 384–405.

Backholm, K., Isomaa, R., & Birgegård, A. (2013). The prevalence and impact of trauma history in eating disorder patients. *European Journal of Psychotraumatology*, 4, 22482.

Bamelis, L. L., Evers, S. M., Spinhoven, P., & Arntz, A. (2014). Results of a multicenter randomized controlled trial of the clinical effectiveness of schema therapy for personality disorders. *American Journal of Psychiatry*, 171(3), 305–322.

Bardone-Cone, A. M., Thompson, K. A., & Miller, A. J. (2018). The self and eating disorders. *Journal of Personality*. https://doi.org/10.1111/jopy.12448

Beck, A. T., Rush, A. J., Shaw, B. F., & Emery, G. (1979). *Cognitive Therapy of Depression*. New York: Guilford Press.

Blinder, B. J., Cumella, E. J., & Santhara, V. A. (2006). Psychiatric comorbidities of female inpatients with eating disorders. *Psychosomatic Medicine*, 68, 454–462.

Brewerton, T. D. (2007). Eating disorders, trauma, and comorbidity: Focus on PTSD. *Eating Disorders*, 15(4), 285–304.

Brown, J. M., Selth, S., Stretton, A., & Simpson, S. (2016). Do dysfunctional coping modes mediate the relationship between perceived parenting style and disordered eating behaviours? *Journal of Eating Disorders*, 4(1), 27.

Byrne, S. M., Fursland, A., Allen, K. L., & Watson, H. (2011). The effectiveness of enhanced cognitive behavioural therapy for eating disorders: An open trial. *Behaviour Research and Therapy*, 49, 219–226.

Carter, J. D., McIntosh, V. V., Jordan, J., Porter, R. J., Frampton, C. M., & Joyce, P. R. (2013). Psychotherapy for depression: A randomized clinical trial comparing schema therapy and cognitive behavior therapy. *Journal of Affective Disorders*, 151(2), 500–505.

Cockram, D. M., Drummond, P. D., & Lee, C. W. (2010). Role and treatment of early maladaptive schemas in Vietnam veterans with PTSD. *Clinical Psychology & Psychotherapy: An International Journal of Theory & Practice*, 17(3), 165–182.

Cooper, M., & Kelland, H. (2015). Medication and psychotherapy in eating disorders: Is there a gap between research and practice? *Journal of Eating Disorders, 3*, 45–52.

Damiano, S. R., Reece, J., Reid, S., Atkins, L., & Patton, G. (2015). Maladaptive schemas in adolescent females with anorexia nervosa and implications for treatment. *Eating Behaviors*, 16, 64–71.

Deas, S., Power, K., Collin, P., Yellowlees, A., & Grierson, D. (2011). The relationship between disordered eating, perceived parenting, and perfectionistic schemas. *Cognitive Therapy and Research*, 35(5), 414–424.

Fairburn, C. G., Cooper, Z., Doll, H. A., O'Connor, M. E., Bohn, K., Hawker, D. M., ... & Palmer, R. L. (2009). Transdiagnostic cognitive-behavioural therapy for patients with eating disorders: A two-site trial with 60-week follow-up. *American Journal of Psychiatry*, 166, 311–319.

Farrell, J. M., Shaw, I. A., & Webber, M. A. (2009). A schema-focused approach to group psychotherapy for outpatients with borderline personality disorder: A randomized controlled trial. *Journal of Behavior Therapy and Experimental Psychiatry*, 40(2), 317–328.

Farstad, S., McGeown, L., & von Ranson, K. (2016) Eating disorders and personality, 2004–2016: A systematic review and meta-analysis. *Clinical Psychology Review*, 46, 91–105.

Fassino, S., Pierò, A., Tomba, E., & Abbate-Daga, G. (2009). Factors associated with dropout from treatment for eating disorders: A comprehensive literature review. *BMC Psychiatry*, 9(1), 67.

Giesen-Bloo, J., van Dyck, R., Spinhoven, P., van Tilburg, W., Dirksen, C., van Asselt, T., ... & Arntz, A. (2006). Outpatient psychotherapy for borderline personality disorder: Randomized trial of schema-focused therapy vs transference-focused psychotherapy. *Archives of General Psychiatry*, 63(6), 649–658.

Grilo, C. M., Pagano, M. E., Stout, R. L., Markowitz, J. C., Ansell, E. B., Pinto, A., ... & Skodol, A. E. (2012). Stressful life events predict eating disorder relapse following remission: Six year prospective outcomes. *International Journal of Eating Disorders*, 45, 185–192.

Gude, T., & Hoffart, A. (2008). Change in interpersonal problems after cognitive agoraphobia and schema-focused therapy versus psychodynamic treatment as usual of inpatients with agoraphobia and Cluster C personality disorders. *Scandinavian Journal of Psychology*, 49(2), 195–199.

Hay, P. (2013). A systematic review of evidence for psychological treatments in eating disorders: 2005–2012. *International Journal of Eating Disorders*, 46, 462–469.

Jones, C., Leung, N., & Harris, G. (2007). Dysfunctional core beliefs in eating disorders: A review. *Journal of Cognitive Psychotherapy*, 21(2), 156–171.

Leung, N., Thomas, G., & Waller, G. (2000). The relationship between parental bonding and core beliefs in anorexic and bulimic women. *British Journal of Clinical Psychology*, 39(2), 205–213.

Lobbestael, J., van Vreeswijk, M. F., & Arntz, A. (2008). An empirical test of schema mode conceptualizations in personality disorders. *Behaviour Research and Therapy*, 46(7), 854–860.

Luck, A., Waller, G., Meyer, C., Ussher, M., & Lacey, H. (2005). The role of schema processes in the eating disorders. *Cognitive Therapy and Research*, 29(6), 717–732.

Masheb, R. M., & Grilo, C. M. (2008). Examination of predictors and moderators for self help treatments of binge-eating disorder. *Journal of Consulting and Clinical Psychology*, 76, 900–904.

Masley, S. A., Gillanders, D. T., Simpson, S. G., & Taylor, M. A. (2012). A systematic review of the evidence base for schema therapy. *Cognitive Behaviour Therapy*, 41(3), 185–202.

McIntosh, V., Jordan, J., Carter, J., Frampton, C., McKenzie, J., Latner, J., Joyce, P. (2016) Psychotherapy for transdiagnostic binge eating: A randomized controlled trial of cognitive-behavioural therapy, appetite-focused cognitive-behavioural therapy, and schema therapy. *Psychiatry Research*, 240, 412–420.

Nadort, M., Arntz, A., Smit, J. H., Giesen-Bloo, J., Eikelenboom, M., Spinhoven, P., ... & van Dyck, R. (2009). Implementation of outpatient schema therapy for borderline personality disorder with versus without crisis support by the therapist outside office hours: A randomized trial. *Behaviour Research and Therapy*, 47(11), 961–973.

Pham-Scottez, A., Huas, C., Perez-Diaz, F., Nordon, C., Divac, S., Dardennes, R., ... & Rouillon, F.(2012).Why do people with eating disorders drop out from inpatient treatment? The role of personality factors. *Journal of Nervous and Mental Disease*, 200, 807–813.

Poulson, S., Lunn, S., Daniel, S. I. F., Folke, S., Mathiesen, B. B., Katznelson, H., & Fairburn, C. G. (2014). A randomized controlled trial of psychoanalytic psychotherapy or cognitive-behavioral therapy for bulimia nervosa. *American Journal of Psychiatry*, 171, 109–116.

Rosenvinge, J. H., Martinussen, M., & Ostensen, E. (2000). The comorbidity of eating disorders and personality disorders: A meta-analytic review of studies published between 1983 and 1998. *Eating and Weight Disorders*, 5, 52–61.

Sansone, R. A., & Levitt, J. L. (2002). Self-harm behaviors among those with eating disorders: An overview. *Eating Disorders*, 10(3), 205–213.

Segura-García, C., Chiodo, D., Sinopoli, F., & De Fazio, P. (2013). Temperamental factors predict long-term modifications of eating disorders after treatment. *BMC Psychiatry*, 13(1), 288.

Sheffield, A., Waller, G., Emanuelli, F., Murray, J., & Meyer, C. (2009). Do schema processes mediate links between parenting and eating pathology? *European Eating Disorders Review: The Professional Journal of the Eating Disorders Association*, 17(4), 290–300.

Simpson, S. (2012). Schema therapy for eating disorders: A case study illustration of the mode approach. In M. van Vreeswijk, J. Broersen, & M. Nadort (Eds.), *The Wiley-Blackwell Handbook of Schema Therapy: Theory, Research, and Practice* (pp. 143–171). John Wiley.

Simpson, S. G., Morrow, E., van Vreeswijk, M. & Reid, C. (2010). Group schema therapy for eating disorders: A pilot study. *Frontiers in Psychology, 1*, 182.

Simpson, S. G., & Slowey, L. (2011). Video therapy for atypical eating disorder and obesity: A case study. *Clinical Practice and Epidemiology in Mental Health: CP & EMH*, 7, 38.

Steinhausen, H. C., & Weber, S. (2009). The outcome of bulimia nervosa: Findings from one-quarter century of research. *American Journal of Psychiatry*, 166(12), 1331–1341.

Talbot, D., Smith, E., Tomkins, A., Brockman, R., & Simpson, S. (2015). Schema modes in eating disorders compared to a community sample. *Journal of Eating Disorders*, 3, 41.

van Asselt, A. D., Dirksen, C. D., Arntz, A., Giesen-Bloo, J. H., van Dyck, R., Spinhoven, P., ... & Severens, J. L. (2008). Out-patient psychotherapy for borderline personality disorder: Cost-effectiveness of schema-focused therapy v. transference-focused psychotherapy. *The British Journal of Psychiatry*, 192(6), 450–457.

van Vreeswijk, M., Spinhoven, P., Eurelings-BontekoeE., & BroersenJ. (2012). Changes in symptom severity, schemas and modes in heterogeneous psychiatric patient groups following short term schema cognitive-behavioural group therapy: A naturalistic pre-post treatment design in an outpatient clinic. *Clinical Psychology & Psychotherapy*, 21(1), 29–38.

Waller, G., Kennerley, H., & Ohanian, V. (2007). Schema-focused cognitive behavioral therapy with eating disorders. In L. P. Riso, P. L. du Toit, D. Stein, & J. Young (Eds.). *Cognitive Schemas and Core Beliefs in Psychiatric Disorders: A Scientist-Practitioner Guide* (pp. 139–175). New York: American Psychological Association.

Wilson, G., Grilo, C., & Vitousek, K. (2007). Psychological treatment of eating disorders. *American Psychologist*, 62(3): 199–216.

Young, J. E. (1990). *Practitioner's Resource Series. Cognitive Therapy for Personality Disorders: A Schema-focused Approach*. Sarasota, FL, England: Professional Resource Exchange, Inc.

Young, J. E., Klosko, J. S., & Weishaar, M. E. (2003). *Schema Therapy: A Practitioner's Guide*. Guilford Press.

Zerwas, S., Lund, B., Von Holle, A., Thornton, L., Berrettini, W., Brandt, H., ... & Bulik, C. (2013). Factors associated with recovery from anorexia nervosa. *Journal of Psychiatric Research*, 47, 972–979.

# Chapter 2

# Review of the schema model and therapeutic application in eating disordered populations

*Susan Simpson, Siri Hartmann, Nicole Files and Evelyn Smith*

## Abstract

*There has been a recent growth in research into the schema therapy model for eating disorders (EDs). The aim of the present review is to describe the studies that have investigated the schema model for EDs with a view to understanding the factors contributing to the development and maintenance of ED symptoms. Findings regarding the links between ED pathology, early childhood experiences, schemas, and schema coping modes are described. In addition, preliminary schema therapy (ST) treatment outcomes for this population are explored and future research directions discussed.*

## Evidence of the schema mode model for eating disorders

The aim of the present chapter is to describe the studies that have investigated the schema model for eating disorders (EDs), and to outline and critically evaluate preliminary ST treatment findings for this population.

### Early maladaptive schemas in eating disorders and disordered eating

Research has consistently found that individuals reporting eating disorder (ED) pathology exhibit more severe early maladaptive schemas (EMS) than normal controls (Leung, Waller, & Thomas, 1999; Waller, Ohanian, Meyer, & Osman, 2000; Waller, 2003; Jones, Leung, & Harris, 2007; Leung & Price, 2007; Zhu et al., 2015). Those who have been identified with high ED symptomatology have also been shown to rate a higher severity of EMS compared with those with low ED symptomatology (Damiano, Reece, Reid, Atkins, & Patton, 2015).

Furthermore, those with ED who self-harm report higher levels of EMS than those who do not, indicating an even higher level of pathological core beliefs in this sub-group (Pauwels, Dierckx, Schoavaerts, & Claes, 2016). Weight and restraint related cognitions have also been correlated with higher ratings of EMS (Gongora, Derksen, & van der Staak, 2004), with body mass index (BMI) potentially playing a role in predicting the pattern between specific EMS, ED cognitions and ED symptoms (Hughes, Hamill, van Gerko, Lockwood, & Waller, 2006). Specific EMS have been linked to eating disordered symptoms across a range of studies (Waller et al., 2000; Cooper, Rose, & Turner, 2005; Keith, Gillanders, & Simpson, 2009; Jenkins, Meyer, & Blissett, 2013; Voderholzer et al., 2014, Pauwels et al., 2016; De Paoli, Fuller-Tyszkiewicz, & Krug, 2017), however, there are marked discrepancies between studies, with a lack of consistent patterns between EMS and symptoms. Similarly, research that has specifically investigated the link between EMS and ED subtypes has not produced a consistent profile across studies (Waller et al, 2000; Waller, 2003; Jones et al., 2007).

Schema domains have been shown to correlate with body image, evaluative concerns and perfectionism (Boone, Braet, Vandereycken, & Claes, 2013), but not specific ED subtypes (Dingemans, Spinhoven, & van Furth, 2006). There is some suggestion that particular clusters of EMS may be linked to both eating pathology and specific ED subtypes (Unoka, Tölgyes, & Czobor, 2007; Unoka, Tzölgyes, Czobor, & Simons, 2010; Imperatori et al., 2017). For example, compulsive behaviours have been linked with the EMS *mistrust/abuse, defectiveness/ shame, dependence* and *subjugation* (Lawson, Waller, & Lockwood, 2007). In another study, anorexia nervosa (AN) was characterised by high scores on an EMS factor comprised of *self-sacrifice, unrelenting standards*, and *punitiveness*; bulimia nervosa (BN) was distinguished by a factor composed of *entitlement* and *impulsivity (self-control)* (Unoka, et al., 2007); and binge eating disorder (BED) severity was positively related to *disconnection/rejection, impaired limits*, and *other-directedness* domains (Imperatori, et al., 2017).

EMS severity has been linked to poorer treatment outcomes (Cullum, 2009), highlighting the importance of understanding their role in the development and perpetuation of eating pathology. However, given the inconsistent findings across studies, it does not appear an assessment of EMS alone is sufficient to predict ED pathology and other mechanisms must be considered. Consequently, researchers investigating the role of EMS in ED pathology have also investigated the role of schema modes and processes as a means of better defining the mechanisms through which EMS lead to the development or maintenance of ED symptoms.

### Schema processes and disordered eating

Schema processes are implemented as either primary (i.e. prevent the initial triggering of affect) or secondary (i.e. employed once affect has been triggered) strategies. Evidence suggests that there may be higher levels of schema avoidance amongst those with ED pathology than non-clinical populations (Spranger, Waller, & Bryant-Waugh, 2000), with important differences between bulimic (binging and purging) and restrictive behaviours at the level of schema processing (Luck, Waller, Meyer, Ussher, & Lacey, 2005; Lawson et al., 2007). Specifically, restrictive pathology was characterised by both primary avoidance (i.e. schema over-compensation to avoid schema activation) and secondary avoidance (to reduce affect following schema activation), with

AN-binge/purge subtype rating the highest level of avoidance (Luck et al., 2005). This is consistent with the finding that perfectionism functions as an over-compensatory process that mediates the relationship between schema domains and ED pathology (Boone, Braet, Vandereycken, & Claes, 2013). In addition, evidence suggests that information processing may become less accurate in response to exposure to subliminal cues associated with specific EMS for those with restrictive pathology due to interference by secondary schema avoidance when exposed to an EMS cue (Mountford, Waller, Watson, & Scragg, 2004).

The clinical implications of these studies suggest it is not sufficient to focus purely on cognitive factors when treating disordered eating, but that schema processes must also be considered. Whilst the research to date provides insight into how two of the schema processes may be related to EDs, the role of schema surrender has not been explored. Further research is required to clarify and expand upon existing knowledge of the role of schema processes in ED pathology.

### Schema modes and ED pathology

To date, only a few studies have investigated the link between schema modes and ED pathology. Talbot, Smith, Tomkins, Brockman, & Simpson (2015) found that when compared to a community sample, female patients with ED rely on maladaptive schema modes more frequently, and on more adaptive schema modes less frequently. Similar patterns of modes were found for each ED. However, patients with BN demonstrated a unique significant difference from the community group on the schema modes *Angry Child (AnCh)* and *Impulsive Child*, which was absent in the case of AN and other specified feeding or eating disorder (OSFED). Furthermore, two unpublished dissertations (Jenkins, 2009; Masley, 2012) support these findings, linking schema modes to ED pathology. Preliminary evidence suggests a positive correlation between ED symptom severity, and maladaptive schema modes (Masley, 2012; Talbot et al., 2015).

### The relationship between childhood environment, disordered eating and early maladaptive schemas/modes

A key aspect of the schema model is the influence of early experiences, particularly the role of parenting and emotional invalidation and trauma during childhood, which are thought to contribute to the development of EMS and maladaptive schema coping styles (Waller, Corstorphine, & Mountford, 2007). Studies suggest that negative childhood experiences including emotional abuse, physical neglect and sexual abuse may be risk factors for the development of eating disorders (Kent & Waller, 2000; Leung, Thomas, & Waller, 2000; Brewerton, 2007; Kong & Bernstein, 2008;

Ford, Waller, & Mountford, 2010; Vajda & Láng, 2014), as well as EMS severity and schema processes in ED populations (Turner, Rose, & Cooper, 2004; Keith et al., 2009; Brown, Selth, Stretton, & Simpson, 2016). In fact, emotional abuse has been identified as a more powerful predictor of eating disturbance than sexual and physical abuse (Kent, Waller, & Dagnan, 1999; Waller, Sines, Meyer, Foster, & Skelton, 2007). Those with AN have been shown to rate parents as less caring and more controlling than controls (Deas, Power, Collin, Yellowlees, & Grierson, 2011), with maternal punitiveness associated with higher levels of ED psychopathology (Nesci, et al., 2014).

Emotional invalidation occurs when the emotional experience of the individual is ignored or responded to incongruently, leading the individual to believe his or her emotional experiences are not valued by others (Waller et al., 2007). Both maternal and paternal invalidation appear to be correlated with higher EMS scores and higher dysfunctional schema mode scores in those with EDs (Jenkins, 2009). EMS have been linked to a range of negative parenting styles, and some EMS have been linked with more specific parenting behaviours; *failure* schema has been linked with perceived belittling mothering, and the *mistrust/abuse* schema with punitive parenting (Sheffield, Waller, Emanuelli, Murray, & Meyer, 2006).

Although relationships between parenting, EMS and ED pathology have been noted, only a few studies have investigated the mechanisms through which this relationship exists. Some evidence suggests that coping processes may play a role in mediating the relationship between parenting, EMS and ED behaviour (Sheffield, Waller, Emanuelli, Murray, & Meyer, 2009). The only study that has specifically focused on coping modes found that overcompensatory (*Perfectionistic Overcontroller, Self-Aggrandiser*), avoidant (*Detached Protector (DetPr)* and *Detached Self-Soother (DetSS)*) and surrender (*Compliant Surrenderer (CSu)*) coping modes all played a significant role in mediating the relationship between perceived negative parental bonding and ED symptoms (Brown, et al., 2016).

## Schema therapy outcome studies for eating disorders

To date, only one randomised controlled trial has investigated the efficacy of ST for the treatment of transdiagnostic binge eating (McIntosh et al., 2016). This study is described in detail in Chapter 3. In brief, 112 women with BN and BED were randomised to either ST, appetite-focused cognitive behaviour therapy (CBT) or traditional CBT. Participants attended weekly sessions for six months, followed by monthly sessions for six months. Across groups, large effect sizes were reported for improvement in binge eating, other eating disorder symptoms and overall functioning. The findings indicated no difference in the outcomes reported by participants in the three treatment groups, suggesting that ST, along with appetite-focused CBT, is comparable to traditional CBT for the treatment of BN and BED. Additionally, preliminary evidence suggests that inpatient ST may be effective for those with EDs with comorbid personality pathology (Schaap, Chakhssi, & Westerhof, 2016). The study employed a small sample of 42 patients with a range of patients with ED and comorbid personality-based pathologies, who had not responded to previous psychotherapeutic interventions, and found significant improvement in maladaptive schemas, schema modes, maladaptive coping styles, mental-wellbeing, and psychological distress at post-treatment, which were maintained at follow-up.

There is also preliminary evidence for group ST for EDs, based on a pilot study utilising a 20-session protocol (Simpson, Morrow, van Vreeswijk, & Reid, 2010). The pilot study delivered ST to eight participants with chronic EDs. For the six participants who completed the treatment program, ED severity, anxiety and shame, and schema severity reduced, whilst quality of life scores increased. A mean reduction in eating pathology and schema severity of 43% at post-treatment and 59% at six month follow-up was achieved by the six treatment completers (two participants dropped-out mid-treatment) and reliable and clinically significant change in ED severity was achieved by four treatment completers (Simpson et al., 2010). Although this study was a pilot study with a small sample and no control comparison group, it provides preliminary evidence for group ST in this population and suggests that further studies in this area are warranted. Furthermore, a larger group ST pilot trial was recently conducted (Calvert, Smith, Brockman, & Simpson, 2018). This study comprised of 30 participants with diagnosed EDs. Only four participants dropped out in the middle of treatment, and the rest completed treatment. Participants attended 90-minute weekly group sessions over 25 weeks. Groups consisted of six to eight participants and were facilitated by two psychologists, at least one of whom was trained in ST. Measures were completed at pre-, mid- and post-treatment. Measures assessed ED symptoms, schemas and schema modes. As predicted, measures of ED symptoms were significantly reduced at post-treatment, with large effect sizes found. No significant changes were observed in EMS severity, however reductions in schema modes were observed (Mcguarie et al., Manuscript in preparation). Very low drop-out rates are suggestive that this is an acceptable treatment for those with EDs, and considered promising for this population as trials usually find around 50% drop out rates.

These findings are supported by a collection of case studies that have investigated ST as a treatment within ED populations. Simpson & Slowey (2011) investigated the efficacy of the ST mode model, delivered remotely via videoconferencing with a 39-year old female with symptoms of obesity, pre-occupation with food and eating, vomiting, fluctuations between restrictive and binge eating behaviour, and poor body image. In total, the participant completed seven ST sessions via videoconferencing and one telephone therapy session over a period of 11 weeks. Global EDE-Q (Eating Disorder Examination – Questionnaire) scores revealed a 77% reduction in the severity of symptoms from pre-treatment to post-treatment and there was an 86%

reduction in global distress. The participant further reported abstaining from any purging behaviour for the final 28 days of treatment. Similarly, a case study by Simpson and Morrow (2010) investigated the outcome of ST, delivered via video therapy as a treatment for BN with one female patient presenting with BN and comorbid general psychopathology. Following 28 weekly sessions of ST the patient reported a cessation of binge/purge behaviours, three of her six elevated EMS were no longer in the clinical range, and she no longer met criteria for a clinically diagnosable ED.

In addition, qualitative studies have investigated the process of ST with ED patients. A case study of AN by Edwards (2017a, 2017b) portrayed an interpretative phenomenological analysis of schema mode work with a single case of a young female patient with AN. Hodge and Simpson (2016) presented a qualitative case study focused on the role of drawing in the context of ST for eating disorders and complex trauma, suggesting that drawing can provide a pathway to access emotional states linked to EMS, facilitating sharing of insights and experiences which might otherwise stay inaccessible through verbal dialogue alone. In addition, a report by Munro et al. (2014) described preliminary findings from an intensive community-based treatment service for severe and enduring AN (including patients with a BMI <13) that utilises an adapted ST model as part of its intensive outpatient treatment stream. The service reported a reduction in service usage and costs and, on average, patients reported experiencing a high level of satisfaction with the service (i.e. staff were perceived as supportive, treatment was viewed as individualised and personalised, and emotionally supportive). Engagement rates were reported to be high with only two patients ceasing treatment over the 2009 to 2011 period. The study reported that service costs reduced by approximately £392,000 when compared to index costs of 2008 (prior to the service expansion). Further, despite the fact that the patient group was characterised by a high severity of ED symptomatology and high risk due to physical complications, a low mortality rate of 4% was recorded in the study, equating to four deaths out of a total of 101 patients over an eight-year period, which is less than the average of 10% (Munro et al., 2014).

In all, these studies provide preliminary evidence that ST may be a beneficial treatment approach for ED pathology. However, studies with larger participant groups and randomised-controlled designs are required to further evaluate the efficacy of ST for the treatment of EDs.

## Summary and research limitations

The research exploring the schema model in ED populations indicates high levels of EMS are present in ED populations, and suggests EMS play a key role in the development and maintenance of ED pathology (Jones et al., 2007). However, evidence for a specific schema profile lacks consistency with many researchers reporting orthogonal results (Leung et al., 1999; Waller et al., 2000; Unoka et al., 2007). There is, however, consistent evidence that schema processes underlie specific ED pathologies. That is, avoidance processes are related to bulimic pathology, whilst both overcompensation and avoidance processes have been linked to restrictive pathology.

Consistent with schema theory, adverse childhood experiences, namely negative perceptions of parenting and emotional invalidation, have been linked to the development of both EMS and schema processes, indicating the importance of including parenting style within any conceptualisation of ED pathology.

Lastly, there is a dearth of outcome research exploring the effectiveness of ST as a treatment for EDs. Preliminary findings suggest ST may be efficacious as an ED treatment, however, replication of these studies using larger populations and more robust research designs are required to validate these findings. Many studies collapse the eating subtypes into one participant group, which increases group heterogeneity and makes it difficult to determine whether specific EMS profiles exist for particular ED pathologies (Cooper et al., 2005; Jones et al., 2007). Given bulimic and restrictive pathologies are likely to have different risk factors and be related to separate EMS and schema processes, differentiating between the disorders or examining specific behaviours separately may provide a richer understanding of the factors that drive specific ED pathology. Further, much of the research relies on small sample sizes, which makes it difficult to generalise findings to the broader ED population (Leung et al., 1999; Waller et al., 2000). There is also a significant lack of research exploring the role of EMS in males with eating disorders.

Whilst nearly all studies report significantly more EMS in ED populations, the mechanisms through which these develop and operate are not fully explained. One concept that has not been addressed in the published literature is the role of schema modes. As schema modes are state-based constructs that encompass both EMS and schema processes that are currently active for an individual, it may provide a richer insight into the mechanisms that maintain ED pathology.

## Conclusions

The present review evaluated the research on the schema model within ED populations. Research suggests EMS and schema processes play a key role in ED pathology, indicating a focus on surface level cognitions alone may be insufficient when treating EDs (Gongora et al., 2004; Hughes et al., 2006). Although some aspects of the schema model have been investigated, our understanding of the schema mode concept and the interaction between early childhood experiences such as parenting, EMS, schema processes, and ED pathology are at an early stage of development, and we urge anyone interested in delivering ST to evaluate their practice. Please contact us if you are conducting research in this area, or should you require support with such endeavours (schematherapybook@gmail.com).

# References

Boone, L., Braet, C., Vandereycken, W., & Claes, L. (2013). Are maladaptive schema domains and perfectionism related to body image concerns in eating disorder patients. *European Eating Disorders Review*, 21(1), 45–51.

Brewerton, T.D. (2007). Eating disorders, trauma, and comorbidity: focus on PTSD. *Eating Disorders*, 15, 285–304.

Brown, J., Selth, S., Stretton, A., & Simpson, S. (2016). Do dysfunctional coping modes mediate the relationship between perceived parenting style and disordered eating behaviours. *Journal of Eating Disorders*, 4, 27.

Calvert, F., Smith, E., Brockman, R., & Simpson, S. (2018). Group schema therapy for eating disorders: Study protocol. *Journal of Eating Disorders*, 61, 1.

Cooper, M., Rose, K., & Turner, H. (2005). Core beliefs and the presence or absence of eating disorder symptoms and depressive symptoms in adolescent girls. *International Journal of Eating Disorders*, 38(1), 60–64.

Cullum, J. (2009). Maladaptive schemas as a predictor of residential treatment outcomes in females with eating disorders. *Graduate Theses and Dissertations*, 459.

Damiano, S., Reece, J., Reid, S., Atkins, L., & Patton, G. (2015). Maladaptive schemas in adolescent females with anorexia nervosa and implications for treatment. *Eating Behaviors*, 16, 64–71.

Deas, S., Power, K., Collin, P., Yellowlees, A., & Grierson, D. (2011). The relationship between disordered eating, perceived parenting, and perfectionistic schemas. *Cognitive Therapy and Research*, 35, 414–424.

De Paoli, T., Fuller-Tyszkiewicz, M., & Krug, I. (2017). Insecure attachment and maladaptive schema in disordered eating: The mediating role of rejection sensitivity. *Clinical Psychology & Psychotherapy*, 24(6), 1273–1284.

Dingemans, A., Spinhoven, P., & van Furth, E. (2006). Maladaptive core beliefs and eating disorder symptoms. *Eating Behaviors*, 7(3), 258–265.

Edwards, D. (2017a). An interpretative phenomenological analysis of schema modes in a single case of Anorexia Nervosa: Part 1 – Background, method, and child and parent modes. *Indo-Pacific Journal of Phenomenology*, 17(1). doi:10.1080/20797222.2017.1326728

Edwards, D. (2017b). An interpretative phenomenological analysis of schema modes in a single case of Anorexia Nervosa: Part 2 – Coping modes, healthy adult mode, superordinate themes, and implications for research and practice. *Indo-Pacific Journal of Phenomenology*, 17(1). doi:10.1080/20797222.2017.1326730

Ford, G., Waller, G., & Mountford, V. (2010). Invalidating childhood environments and core beliefs in women with eating disorders. *European Eating Disorders Review*, 19(4), 316–321.

Gongora, V., Derksen, J., & van der Staak, C. (2004). The role of core beliefs in the specific cognitions of bulimic patients. *Journal of Nervous and Mental Disease*, 192(4), 297–303.

Hodge, L., & Simpson, S. (2016). Speaking the unspeakable: Artistic expression in eating disorder research and schema therapy. *The Arts in Psychotherapy*, 50, 1–8.

Hughes, M., Hamill, M., van Gerko, K., Lockwood, R., & Waller, G. (2006). The relationship between different levels of cognition and behavioural symptoms in the eating disorders. *Eating behaviors*, 7(2), 125–133.

Imperatori, C., Innamorati, M., Lester, D., Continisio, M., Balsamo, M., Saggino, A., & Fabbricatore, M. (2017). The association between food addiction and early maladaptive schemas in overweight and obese women: A preliminary investigation. *Nutrients, 9*(12), 1259.

Jenkins, G. (2009). An investigation of schema modes in an eating disordered population. (Unpublished doctoral dissertation). The University of Edinburgh, UK.

Jenkins, P., Meyer, C., & Blissett, J. (2013). Childhood abuse and eating psychopathology: The mediating role of core beliefs. *Journal of Aggression, Maltreatment & Trauma, 22*(3), 248–261.

Jones, C., Leung, N., & Harris, G. (2007). Dysfunctional core beliefs in eating disorders: A review. *Journal of Cognitive Psychotherapy: An International Quarterly, 21*, 156–171.

Keith, L., Gillanders, D., & Simpson, S. (2009). An exploration of the main sources of shame in an eating-disordered population. *Clinical Psychology & Psychotherapy, 16*(4), 317–327.

Kent, A., Waller, G., & Dagnan, D. (1999). A greater role of emotional than physical or sexual abuse in predicting disordered eating attitudes: The role of mediating variables. *International Journal of Eating Disorders, 25*, 159–167.

Kent, A., & Waller, G. (2000). Childhood emotional abuse and eating psychopathology. *Clinical Psychology Review, 20*(7), 887–903.

Kong, S., & Bernstein, K. (2008). Childhood trauma as a predictor of eating psychopathology and its mediating variables in patients with eating disorders. *Journal of Clinical Nursing, 18*, 1897–1907.

Lawson, R., Waller, G., & Lockwood, R. (2007). Cognitive content and process in eating-disordered patients with obsessive-compulsive features. *Eating Behaviors, 8*(3), 305–310.

Leung, N., Thomas, G., & Waller, G. (2000). The relationship between parental bonding and core beliefs in anorexic and bulimic women. *British Journal of Clinical Psychology, 39*(2), 205–213.

Leung, N., & Price, E. (2007). Core beliefs in dieters and eating disordered women. *Eating Behaviors, 8*(1), 65–72.

Leung, N., Waller, G., & Thomas, G. (1999). Core beliefs in anorexic and bulimic women. *Journal of Nervous and Mental Disease, 187*, 736–741.

Luck, A., Waller, G., Meyer, C., Ussher, M., & Lacey, H. (2005). The role of schema processes in the eating disorders. *Cognitive Therapy and Research, 6*, 717–732.

Masley, S. (2012). Exploring the relationship between cognitive fusion, schema modes, and eating disorders. (Unpublished doctoral dissertation). The University of Edinburgh, UK.

Mcguarie, G., Smith, E., Brockman, R., Veremeenko, K., Richards, P., Skewes, S., Samson, R., Vanvreeswjk, M., Middleton, N., & Simpson, S., Manuscript in preparation. Group schema therapy for eating disorders.

McIntosh, V., Jordan, J., Carter, J., Frampton, C., McKenzie, J., Latner, J., & Joyce, P. (2016). Psychotherapy for transdiagnostic binge eating: A randomized controlled trial of cognitive-behavioural therapy, appetite-focused cognitive-behavioural therapy, and schema therapy. *Psychiatry Research, 240*, 412–420.

Mountford, V., Waller, G., Watson, D., & Scragg, P. (2004). An experimental analysis of the role of schema compensation in anorexia nervosa. *Eating Behaviors, 5*, 223–230.

Munro, C., Thomson, V., Corr, J., Randell, L., Davies, J., Gittoes, C., Honeyman, V., & Freeman, C. (2014). A new service model for the treatment of severe anorexia nervosa in the community: the Anorexia Nervosa Intensive Treatment Team. *Psychiatric Bulletin*, 38(5), 220–225.

Nesci, J., Redston, S., Newton, R., Snell, M., KaplanA., & Cleeve, S. (2014). Perceived parenting of inpatients with anorexia nervosa: implications for schema theory and practice. Conference Presentation at The International Society of Schema Therapy (ISST) Conference (June, 2014). Istanbul, Turkey. doi:10.13140/2.1.4074.5601

Pauwels, E., Dierckx, E., Schoavaerts, K., & Claes, L. (2016). Early maladaptive schemas in eating disordered patients with or without non-suicidal self-injury. *European Eating Disorders Review*, 24(5), 399–405.

Schaap, G., Chakhssi, F., & Westerhof, G. (2016). Inpatient schema therapy for nonresponsive patients with personality pathology: Changes in symptomatic distress, schemas, schema modes, coping styles, experienced parenting styles, and mental-wellbeing. *Psychotherapy*, 53(4), 402–412.

Sheffield, A., Waller, G., Emanuelli, F., Murray, J., & Meyer, C. (2006). Links between parenting and core beliefs: Preliminary psychometric validation of the Young Parenting Inventory. *Cognitive Therapy and Research*, 29(6), 787–802.

Sheffield, A., Waller, G., Emanuelli, F., Murray, J., & Meyer, C. (2009). Do schema processes mediate links between parenting and eating pathology. *European Eating Disorders Review*, 17, 290–300.

Simpson, S., & Morrow, E. (2010). Using video conferencing for conducting therapeutic relationships. In K. Anthony, D. Nagel & S. Goss (Eds.), *The Use of Technology in Mental Health: Applications, Ethics and Practices* (pp. 94–103). Springfield: Charles C Thomas.

Simpson, S. G., Morrow, E., van Vreeswijk, M., & Reid, C. (2010). Group schema therapy for eating disorders: A pilot study. *Frontiers in Psychology*, 1, 1–10.

Simpson, S., & Slowey, L. (2011). Video therapy for atypical eating disorder and obesity: A case study. *Clinical Practice and Epidemiology in Mental Health*, 7, 38–43.

Spranger, S. C., Waller, G., & Bryant-Waugh, R. (2000). Schema avoidance in bulimic and non-eating disordered women. *International Journal of Eating Disorders*, 29, 302–306.

Talbot, D., Smith, E., Tomkins, A., Brockman, R., & Simpson, S. (2015). Schema modes in eating disorders compared to a community sample. *Journal of Eating Disorders*, 3(1), 41.

Turner, H., Rose, K., & Cooper, M. (2004). Parental bonding and eating disorder symptoms in adolescents. The mediating role of core beliefs. *Eating Behaviors*, 6, 113–118.

Unoka, Z., Tölgyes, T., & Czobor, P. (2007). Early maladaptive schemas and body mass index in subgroups of eating disorders: A differential association. *Comprehensive Psychiatry*, 48, 199–204.

Unoka, Z., Tölgyes, T., Czobor, P., & Simon, L. (2010). Eating disorder behavior and early maladaptive schemas in subgroups of eating disorders. *Journal of Nervous and Mental Disease*, 198, 425–431.

Vajda, A., & Láng, A. (2014). Emotional Abuse, neglect in eating disorders and their relationship with emotion regulation. *Procedia-Social and Behavioral Sciences*, 131, 386–390.

Voderholzer, U., Schwartz, C., Thielf, N., Kuelz, A., Hartmann, A., Scheidth, C., Schlegl, S., & Zeeck, A. (2014). A comparison of schemas, schema modes and childhood traumas in obsessive-compulsive disorder, chronic pain disorder and eating disorders. *Psychopathology*, 47(1), 24–31.

Waller, G. (2003). Schema level cognitions in patients with binge eating disorder: A case control study. *International Journal of Eating Disorders*, 33, 458–464.

Waller, G., Corstorphine, E., & Mountford, E. (2007). The role of emotional abuse in the eating disorders: Implications for treatment. *The Journal of Treatment and Prevention*, 15, 317–331.

WallerG., OhanianV., MeyerC., & OsmanS. (2000). Cognitive content among bulimic women: The role of core beliefs. *International Journal of Eating Disorders*, 28, 235–241.

Waller, G., Sines, J., Meyer, C., Foster, E., & Skelton, A. (2007). Narcissism and narcissistic defences in the eating disorders. *International Journal of Eating Disorders*, 40, 143–148.

Zhu, H., Luo, X., Cai, T., He, J., Lu, Y., & Wu, S. (2015). Life event stress and binge eating among adolescents: The roles of early maladaptive schemas and impulsivity. *Stress and Health*, 32(4), 395–401.

# Chapter 3

# Applying schema therapy to binge eating disorders

## A transdiagnostic approach

*Virginia V. W. McIntosh, Janet D. Carter and Jennifer Jordan*

### Abstract

*Although most models of the eating disorders (ED) do not view early experiences as causal in developing eating problems, links between early events and later eating difficulties are widely noted. For example, binge eating is associated with childhood abuse, schema-level cognitions mediate childhood experiences and later binge eating, and improved treatment efficacy is possible with models that connect past experiences in the development of binge eating. Schema therapy (ST) for transdiagnostic binge eating increases awareness of maladaptive schemas or modes (clusters of schemas), identifies early experiences from which they developed, and heals maladaptive schemas, thereby reducing the drive for binge eating behaviours. Whereas traditional cognitive behavioural therapy (CBT) addresses negative automatic thoughts about food, eating, shape and weight, ST targets schemas, deep underlying beliefs, such as* defectiveness *or emotional deprivation. In this chapter we will introduce the schema model for binge eating disorders, outline the evidence and introduce a case study.*

### A schema model for binge eating disorders

Cognitive formulations of binge eating disorders have focused on negative automatic thoughts and dysfunctional assumptions, manifesting as distorted beliefs about food, eating, body shape and weight (Fairburn, Cooper, & Cooper, 1986). However, this level of cognition is not sufficient to fully explain the cognitions relevant to binge eating psychopathology. Further, cognitive behavioural therapies based on the assumptions of this cognitive model are only partially successful (Leung, Waller, & Thomas, 2000).

A schema model for binge eating disorders, including bulimia nervosa (BN) and binge eating disorder (BED), is supported by existing research showing the association of EDs and early adverse experiences, the association of adverse childhood experiences and the development of early maladaptive schemas (EMS), higher rates of EMS in people with EDs, more severe EDs in those with more dysfunctional schemas, and poorer CBT treatment outcome for people with more pathological schemas. The following sections review this research.

### The role of adverse childhood experiences and maladaptive schemas in eating disorders

EDs, particularly those characterised by binge eating or purging, are associated with exposure to physical, sexual and emotional abuse during childhood (Schmidt, Humfress, & Treasure, 1997; Steiger et al., 2010). Perceived parenting experiences are associated with the development of EMS. Overall, EMS are associated with perceptions of either parent as belittling, mothers as pessimistic, fearful or controlling, and fathers as punitive (Sheffield et al., 2006). Severity of abuse is associated with several EMS, *defectiveness/shame, emotional deprivation, emotional inhibition, mistrust/abuse, subjugation,* and *vulnerability to harm* (Hartt & Waller, 2002).

People with EDs have more pathological core beliefs/EMS than those without EDs (Vitousek & Hollon, 1990; Waller et al., 2000; Waller et al., 2001; Waller, Dickson, & Ohanian, 2002; Waller, 2003). This finding applied to those with BN and the binge-purge subtype of anorexia nervosa (AN) (Waller et al., 2000) and those with BED (Waller, 2003) compared to those without EDs. More severe maladaptive schemas have been shown to relate to eating psychopathology (Waller, Ohanian, Meyer, & Osman, 2000), ego-dysfunction characteristics such as perfectionism and self-esteem (Waller, Dickson, & Ohanian, 2002) and anger (Waller et al., 2003), which together lead to the conceptualisation that ego-dysfunction characteristics might serve as mediators of the link between core beliefs and eating pathology. Associations between EMS and binge eating suggest a causative link, with earlier Young Schema Questionnaire (YSQ) scores predicting later psychopathology (Waller et al., 2001). Further, people with bulimic behaviours can be differentiated from those without by a specific set of maladaptive schemas, characterised by *defectiveness/shame, insufficient self-control,* and *failure* (Waller et al., 2000), with the severity of binge eating predicted by *emotional inhibition* and severity of vomiting predicted by *defectiveness* schema (Waller et al., 2000).

### CBT treatment outcomes for individuals with pathological core beliefs

Leung et al.'s (2000) study of the outcome of treatment for BN found that pathological core beliefs, measured before the beginning of CBT, predicted less change over the course of treatment in the core ED symptoms of vomiting, restrictive eating and binge eating behaviours. The strongest cognitive predictor of continued vomiting at the end of treatment was more severe *defectiveness/shame* beliefs on the YSQ.

Leung et al.'s (2000) finding of poorer outcome after traditional CBT for BN for people with more pathological core beliefs has prompted the suggestion that treatment models incorporating past experiences as causal in the aetiology of binge eating disorders may be needed for improved outcome (Waller & Kennerley, 2003). At the least this could be the inclusion of a schema-focused component in therapy, such as that described by Padesky (1994), addressing core beliefs unrelated to food, eating, shape and weight.

### Schemas mediate the association between early experiences and binge eating

Taken together, the findings of links between adverse childhood experiences and the development of EMS, and between EMS and the presence or severity of binge eating, support a ST model of binge eating disorders. In such a model, schema level cognitions mediate the association between childhood experiences and eating problems, as suggested by Waller (2001), with cognitive factors, including schema-level cognitions hypothesised as mediators in the link between childhood sexual abuse and BN. This association between abuse and neglect and psychiatric disorders has been found to be mediated by negative self-esteem and EMS or modes in a number of studies (Shah & Waller, 2000; Wright, Crawford, & Del Castillo, 2009; Brown, Selth, Stretton, & Simpson, 2016).

### Delivering schema therapy for binge eating

The following manual of ST for binge eating was developed for use in our randomised controlled trial comparing ST, standard CBT and appetite-focused CBT for binge eating (McIntosh et al., 2016). Participants were 112 women aged between 16 and 65 years with a current primary DSM-IV binge eating diagnosis, BED or BN. Therapy consisted of six months of weekly individual psychotherapy sessions, followed by six months of approximately monthly sessions. Trial therapists were four clinical psychologists, trained in each of the therapeutic modalities, with weekly clinical supervision in each therapy modality. ST was effective and did not differ from the other cognitive behavioural therapies on key outcomes, providing preliminary evidence of efficacy for ST with binge eating.

## Treatment manual

### Therapeutic alliance

As with all ST, the therapeutic relationship is central to effective ST for binge eating disorders. Attention to building a strong therapeutic alliance in the initial phases of therapy facilitates assessment of EMS, modes and coping styles, and provides the context for provision of psychoeducation encouraging change. A strong therapeutic relationship is essential in providing a safe environment so the client can tolerate the emotional focus in components of ST, such as imagery. The therapist provides a safe, reassuring and trustworthy presence, including a therapist stance of limited reparenting and the use of empathic confrontation.

## Orienting to schema therapy

At the outset of therapy, the therapist provides a rationale for ST, drawing on information gathered during the clinical assessment and from schema questionnaires. Key terms such as schemas, modes and unhelpful schema coping strategies are defined and discussed. Psychoeducation about ST, binge eating and other ED behaviours is provided, verbally and with a range of handouts given as appropriate.

The therapist explains that the core goal of therapy is to resolve EMS in order to reduce the impact of continued, unhelpful activation of those EMS resulting in binge eating and other life problems. The therapist explains that strategies within ST aid in weakening EMS and modes, that focusing on these deeper underlying issues can be distressing, and that building up coping skills will enable core needs to be met in a more adaptive manner. A key aspect of weakening EMS or modes is for the client to develop or strengthen *Healthy Adult* (*HA*) functioning, to gain greater awareness of core needs and for these needs to be met in adaptive ways. Some clients present with weak, but present, *HA* modes, so the work of therapy is to strengthen these; others have a relative absence of *HA* modes, requiring much of the initial therapy work involving development of HA modes.

## Assessment and formulation

In the initial stage of therapy, assessment and formulation is the focus. During this phase the therapist's goal is working with the client to identify EMS or modes and their associated cognitive, emotional and physical experiences. The time required to complete the assessment is variable. Relatively straightforward cases are likely to be completed in five assessment sessions, whereas this may be longer when working with some people with binge eating disorders, both due to the complexity of the EDs and other comorbidity, and when there is greater overcompensation or avoidance.

Data for the formulation are gathered in a variety of ways including clinical interview, developmental and life history, questionnaires (e.g. YSQ, Schema Mode Inventory, Young Parenting Inventory and Young-Rygh Avoidance Questionnaire), assessment imagery, and by exploring and reviewing the client's cognitive, emotional and physical experiences associated with activation of schemas or modes. As such the assessment has objective, reflective and emotional or experiential aspects. The goal during this process is for the client not only to develop an intellectual understanding but also to gain a 'felt' understanding of core needs, the EMS or modes and associated coping styles, including ED behaviours that have developed to meet these needs.

Binge eating behaviours are understood as maladaptive coping styles, which allow the client to avoid or escape the upsetting emotions generated by activated schemas. Binge eating behaviours may be present in any of the three coping styles (surrender, avoidance, overcompensation) and may be activated by more than one mode, serving a different coping function in each. The developmental origins of EMS or modes are uncovered through imagery, and events or situations that trigger the operation of each EMS or mode are explored and identified. Psychoeducation develops the client's understanding of the link between core needs, EMS or modes and ED behaviours – binge eating and other ED behaviours, including compensatory behaviours such as vomiting, laxative use, exercising, fasting or restrictive eating.

### Schema therapy strategies

As therapy proceeds, each of the EMS or modes is identified and explored; the origins of the EMS or mode and the reasons it developed become clear. The client is helped to understand that during childhood or adolescence the EMS or mode had a function, but that it is no longer needed, and has disadvantages in adult life. Links between EMS or modes and current problems including ED symptoms and behaviours are discovered collaboratively. As with ST for other problems, ST for binge eating makes use of cognitive, experiential, interpersonal and behavioural strategies to facilitate change.

### Cognitive and behavioural strategies

Core cognitive and behavioural components of standard CBT for eating disorders can be incorporated into ST, including self-monitoring of food intake, binge eating and precursors, which is reviewed and integrated within the schema formulation. Viewing food monitoring alongside identification of core needs, EMS and modes activation and coping styles enables the client to gain understanding about the function of the ED.

The focus of behavioural pattern breaking is to replace EMS- or mode-driven coping styles including ED behaviours, with adapting behaviours. Behavioural strategies for binge eating may include ED related treatment strategies such as increasing food variety and increasing awareness of cues and consequences to develop strategies to avoid high-risk situations. In the final phase of therapy, attention is paid to consolidating use of *HA* functioning and includes a relapse prevention focus.

### Session format and structure

Therapy sessions have considerable flexibility, while including key components of ST. The session begins with a review of the previous week, including any homework, with identification and labelling of schemas or modes that have been apparent alongside the review of food monitoring. Session content focuses on linking EMS or modes to current problems, including binge eating. This includes exploring and elaborating EMS or modes so the client gains a deeper understanding of EMS or modes, their functioning, cues triggering their activation, and disadvantages. There is a focus on developing the *HA*, which is nurturing, validating, protects the *Vulnerable Child* (*VCh*), but also set limits and can counter maladaptive modes throughout therapy. Therapy sessions aim to access the *VCh* through imagery and using limited re-parenting, with the therapist initially advocating for the client, subsequently progressing to the client's own *HA* performing this role as this mode develops and is strengthened. Dialogues between EMS or modes help to weaken maladaptive schemas and modes. Behaviour change strategies are explored to facilitate changes in coping styles. Homework is set as relevant to the content of the session.

## Case description

### Eating disorder presentation

Jane (a composite case) is a 32 year-old woman referred for treatment by her general practitioner. Jane started binge eating from the age of 12 and engaged in yo-yo dieting for ten years from her mid-teens, with her Body Mass Index (BMI) fluctuating from 19–29 over that time. At presentation, she met criteria for BN non-purging subtype with daily objective binge eating (and four subjective binge episodes weekly) along with food restriction and exercise to compensate for binge eating. Jane's eating pattern was to restrict her food intake through the day but she would binge in the evening when unable to sustain this. Binge episodes were followed by further restriction, eating small quantities of low calorie 'healthy' meals and eliminating snacks. Jane's exercise pattern was 60 minutes of exercise six days a week. Although she had positive reasons for exercise, after binge episodes, the exercising had a driven quality, with greater intensity and duration to compensate for binge eating. At assessment, Jane did not differentiate between objective (larger-than-normal amounts of food) and subjective (ordinary amounts of food) binges, describing all eating episodes that felt out of control as binges. With further assessment, Jane reported high body dissatisfaction, describing her body as "pudgy" despite a stable BMI of 21 for the last five years. She had previously used laxatives to compensate for binge eating but had no history of other purging behaviours.

### Psychosocial history

Jane reported a difficult early life. She was the middle of three children and described her mother as caring but always tired and somewhat ineffectual, unable to meet the needs of her children. Jane reported that looking back her mother was probably depressed. Her father was a heavy drinker and was rarely at home. He was often angry and Jane witnessed him hitting her mother on a number of occasions. Jane reported some rare days when they would all go to the river for a picnic and a swim and have fun as a family. Jane reported that she and her younger sister were sexually abused by an older cousin. Jane tried to tell her mother, who refused to believe her and the cousin continued to visit, leaving Jane and her sister to keep themselves safe. Jane said that the children largely raised themselves. Jane was close to her siblings and tried to stick up for her younger sister. She described herself as an anxious child, but she did well at school and had good friends.

She had a series of brief relationships as a teen before marrying young to a man who was loving and attentive and seemed perfect for her. After several months though she found out that he was seeing another woman. She was devastated and urged him to go to counselling with her, but he refused. He maintained that he loved her, however it became clear that he did not want to change the situation. When Jane became pregnant, she decided to stay in the marriage for their child, but felt upset, lonely and increasingly low in mood. Her binge eating increased to once or twice a day most days. After her weight increased, she started using laxatives three times a week and tried to fast two days a week to control her weight. Over this time, she was torn between trying to save the relationship and wanting to leave. Eventually, when her daughter started school, with the support of friends, she left the marriage. Jane wanted to be financially independent and so she began nursing training. She built up her social network and was enjoying life. She was eating well, she joined a running club, and binge eating became infrequent (once every 2–3 months) and she lost the weight that she had gained during her marriage.

Jane was happy being single for some years raising her daughter and enjoying her nursing position, gaining respect for her highly competent, conscientious and professional approach. She enjoyed training regularly with her friends at the running club. She had other close friends whom she saw regularly and maintained close relationships with her siblings.

A year prior to coming for treatment she met Joe. They quickly became close and he moved in with Jane and her daughter. He shared her interests and she admired his sense of humour, intelligence and his interesting friends. Within six months though, Jane began to feel unhappy about several aspects of the relationship. She felt insecure when he would flirt with other women, and if she said anything, he would deny it and portray it as her problem, saying that she was being over-sensitive. This had become a major issue between them. When she tried to discuss it he would withdraw. Immediately prior to starting therapy, her relatively new boss appointed a bright 'up and coming' nurse and allocated her a task that had previously been Jane's area of expertise. Jane was very upset and this was affecting her career satisfaction, but she was uncertain about what action to take. Her mood had dropped, she frequently felt stressed and her ED re-emerged with a cycle of binge eating, food restriction and driven exercise to compensate after binge episodes. She wanted to get back in control of her eating, to be able to feel normal around food.

### Schema formulation

Jane's early environment failed to meet her emotional needs for safety and nurturance. She experienced abuse (from her angry, emotionally abusive and largely absent father), witnessed violence towards her mother and experienced sexual abuse. Her mother's depleted resources meant she was unable to provide protection, acknowledgement of the abuse, or nurturance. Jane had been seeking care, validation and acceptance in relationships throughout her life, but struggled to find this in intimate relationships.

Jane's strongest endorsements on the YSQ were *defectiveness, abandonment, self-sacrifice, emotional deprivation schema* and *approval seeking schemas*. As therapy progressed the focus switched to schema modes work, which better captured her emotional functioning. Jane's *VCh* mode (*emotional deprivation, abandonment* and *defectiveness schemas*) became activated when Joe was flirting, compounded when he denied her view of the situation and discounted her distress. This would then flip to an *Angry Child (AnCh)* mode ("it's not fair"), or a *Punitive Parent (PP)* mode demanding that he accept her position (overcompensation), or to a 'working things through' mode – this employed pseudo-healthy adult coping strategies of trying to resolve interpersonal problems by repeatedly talking things through; however this was driven by an anxious, reassurance-seeking, abandoned *VCh*. Both the *PP* and the anxious, abandoned *VCh* led her to pursue Joe to look for answers, reassurance or validation, but which led Joe to pulling further away. When neither mode was effective at bringing about validation and change from Joe, a surrender coping strategy would lead to binge eating. Jane had an effective *HA* operating well in most areas of her life (parenting, work, friendships and family), except when triggered by EMS activation.

### Therapy

Jane was oriented to ST, including how cognitive behavioural skills would be used with here-and-now ED symptoms and behaviours, while ST would work on deeper underlying EMS and emotional reactions related to causation and maintenance of the ED, distress and life issues. Self-monitoring was reviewed, and psychoeducation modules introduced. Discussion of the YSQ, and EMS endorsed from this questionnaire, followed.

In the remainder of the first phase of ST, CBT strategies included review of self-monitoring: Jane was eating small regular meals but irregular snacks, which were not planned or were missed because she was overly busy. Cues were identified for increased risk of binge eating, including affective cues (feeling anxious, angry, helpless, hopeless, trapped, overlooked and tired) and situational cues (being alone, driving, and after conflict). Self-monitoring was linked to EMS/mode activation when relevant. Modules and handouts were given on normalised eating, techniques for avoiding high-risk situations and readings on relevant EMS and modes.

Early phase strategies included introducing safe place imagery and completing imagery assessments. Jane had a very good response to safe place imagery and used it effectively throughout therapy. Imagery assessment provided an opportunity to focus on identifying bodily and emotional responses and unmet needs in situations that triggered schema activation and/or binge eating. The current EMS/mode activation was tracked via the emotional distress back to a related past distressing situation. The primary focus of therapy was Jane's relationship with Joe, and in particular her insecurity and distress triggered by Joe flirting. A typical incident involving invalidating messages would trigger Jane's abandoned *VCh*, which often led to a binge.

### Schema imagery rescripting

In one imagery exercise after Joe refused to discuss her accusation of flirting, Jane was asked to close her eyes and to visualise the incident in detail, calling to mind what she was thinking and feeling, both emotionally and in her bodily responses. When she had the full experience, she was asked to allow her mind to find a childhood memory with similar feelings. Her imagery went back to when she was six years old and was trying to tell her mother about her cousin touching her sexually. Her mother continued cooking and did not respond to Jane. Jane's aunt came into the room and her mother talked to the aunt continuing to ignore Jane, who went to her room crying to herself, feeling bereft. In rescripting the image, *HA* Jane stood next to *VCh* Jane and insisted that her mother turn around and listen to what Jane was saying, however in the imagery her mother was not able to provide the supportive response that Jane needed. Jane then brought her aunt (who was always fond of Jane and treated her well) into the image. Jane then told her aunt what had happened and the therapist was able to voice what the aunt would have said to Jane – Jane visualised herself being hugged and supported by her aunt. She experienced this imagery as being very powerful and healing. The limited re-parenting aspect of therapy was important in providing a warm, steady, validating presence in the therapy relationship itself but also in imagery. The therapist would (by negotiation and as required) provide a supportive adult or bolster Jane's *HA* self by protecting, advocating for, nurturing or supporting young Jane in the image in order to meet the needs of the *VCh*, with the aim of schema healing.

### Mode dialogues

Mode dialogues were used to a larger extent later in the therapy. A dialogue session was conducted regarding Jane's distress at feeling overlooked and invalidated by her new boss in the team meeting, where 'her' portfolio was allocated by her boss to the new nurse. Jane was encouraged to voice and feel the distress experienced by the different modes activated by the incident.

Firstly, she voiced the anger she felt from her *PP* mode, where she wanted to go in and 'have a go' at the boss ('how dare she reallocate my portfolio without discussing it with me'), then she shifted to her *VCh* ('maybe I haven't done a good enough job, she doesn't rate me'). The therapist took the *HA* mode providing nurturance and support to the *VCh*. The therapist and Jane switched roles with the therapist repeating Jane's *VCh* reactions, and Jane providing alternative views on why the boss might have taken that action that weren't about Jane being defective ('the boss is new, she wouldn't actually know that was something I did a project on two years ago', 'she may have given it to the new nurse because she knows the rest of us are over-whelmed with our caseloads and the new nurse will have time to do that at the moment'). Jane then role-played her *HA* speaking to her boss (the therapist), explaining her expertise and expressing an interest in continuing to be involved, with or without the new nurse. Jane then used her *HA* to discuss with the *PP* mode who grudgingly accepted that course of action was reasonable to try out.

## Progress and outcomes

### Schema therapy outcomes

Jane struggled in her relationship with Joe throughout therapy, trying hard to make it work. She eventually moved out, trying to maintain a friendship with Joe, before finally acknowledging that this was not working and making a clean break. At the end of therapy, Jane was resigned to end the relationship and planned to be on her own for a time to consolidate what she had learned from therapy and to rebuild her wellbeing and resilience.

She was sad at terminating therapy but said she had incorporated the therapist's voice as part of her *HA* and she felt confident about being able to manage on her own. She was aware that as long as she recognised schema activation, stepped back and used her *HA* to 'self-soothe' the *VCh*, she would be able to employ her already extensive set of coping skills within her *HA*.

### Symptom outcomes

Jane engaged well in therapy, attending 22 weekly and six monthly maintenance sessions. Although she had small fluctuations in weight during therapy, her BMI was 21.8 at the end of treatment, unchanged from pre-treatment. Although objective and subjective binges increased to pre-treatment levels on several occasions of intense stress during therapy, Jane was abstinent from binge eating over the last three months of treatment and no longer met criteria for any ED at the end of treatment. Her exercise was regular but no longer driven or used as a compensatory behaviour, and she was able to take a day off exercising if busy or tired. She was aware that she needed to keep working on improving her body image to reduce the risk of relapse. Her mood was euthymic and her psychosocial functioning was good (Global Assessment of Functioning score 84- absent of minimal symptoms range), with good work performance, hobbies, close relationships with friends and family, and she was happy living alone 'for now at least'.

## Conclusion

ST is a comprehensive therapy offering a plausible explanation for the early childhood origin of current life difficulties, including binge eating and other ED behaviours. The breadth of strategies offers flexibility in aligning strategies with individual needs, which may be particularly relevant for individuals with complex presentations, including early childhood adversity or trauma and comorbid current difficulties, along with the binge eating. It is likely that ST may reduce relapse, due to its goal to identify and heal EMS, thus reducing or eliminating the driver for the dysfunctional ED behaviours. The schema-mode approach in particular enables conceptualisation of complex psychopathology. Current standard treatments for adults with binge eating do not help everyone. There is a need for evidence-based treatments including ST which target deeper level processes driving the ED in those where standard treatments have little effect.

## References

Brown, J., Selth, S., Stretton, A., & Simpson, S. (2016). Do dysfunctional coping modes mediate the relationship between perceived parenting style and disordered eating behaviours. *Journal of Eating Disorders*, 4, 27.

Fairburn, C., Cooper, Z., & Cooper, P. (1986). The clinical features and maintenance of bulimia nervosa. In K. Brownell & J. Foryet (Eds.), *Handbook of Eating Disorders: Psychology and Treatment of Obesity, Anorexia and Bulimia* (pp. 389–404). New York, NY: Basic Books.

Hartt, J., & Waller, G. (2002). Child abuse, dissociation, and core beliefs in bulimic disorders. *Child Abuse & Neglect*, 26(9), 923–938.

Leung, N., Waller, G., & Thomas, G. (2000). Outcome of group cognitive-behavior therapy for bulimia nervosa: The role of core beliefs. *Behaviour Research and Therapy*, 38(2), 145–156.

McIntosh, V., Jordan, J., Carter, J., Frampton, C., McKenzie, J., Latner, J., & Joyce, P. (2016). Psychotherapy for transdiagnostic binge eating: A randomized controlled trial of cognitive-behavioural therapy, appetite-focused cognitive-behavioural therapy, and schema therapy. *Psychiatry Research*, 240, 412–420.

Padesky, C. (1994). Schema change processes in cognitive therapy. *Clinical Psychology and Psychotherapy*, 1, 267–278.

Schmidt, U., Humfress, H., & Treasure, J. (1997). The role of general family environment and sexual and physical abuse in the origins of eating disorders. *European Eating Disorders Review*, 5(3), 184–207.

Shah, R., & Waller, G. (2000). Parental style and vulnerability to depression: The role of core beliefs. *Journal of Nervous and Mental Disease*, 188(1), 19–25.

Sheffield, A., Waller, G., Emanuelli, F., Murray, J., & Meyer, C. (2006). Links between parenting and core beliefs: Preliminary psychometric validation of the Young Parenting Inventory. *Cognitive Therapy and Research*, 29(6), 787–802.

Steiger, H., Richardson, J., Schmitz, N., Israel, M., Bruce, K., & Gauvin, L. (2010). Trait-defined eating-disorder subtypes and history of childhood abuse. *International Journal of Eating Disorders*, 43(5), 428–432.

Vitousek, K., & Hollon, S. (1990). The investigation of schematic content and processing in eating disorders. *Cognitive Therapy and Research*, 14(2), 191–214.

Waller, G. (2003). Schema-level cognitions in patients with binge eating disorder: A case control study. *International Journal of Eating Disorders*, 33(4), 458–464.

Waller, G., Babbs, M., Milligan, R., Meyer, C., Ohanian, V., & Leung, N. (2003). Anger and core beliefs in the eating disorders. *International Journal of Eating Disorders*, 34(1), 118–124.

Waller, G., Dickson, C., & Ohanian, V. (2002). Cognitive content in bulimic disorders. Core beliefs and eating attitudes. *Eating Behaviors*, 3(2), 171–178.

Waller, G., & Kennerley, H. (2003). Cognitive-behavioral treatments. In J. Treasure, U. Schmidt & E. van Furth (Eds.), *Handbook of Eating Disorders* (pp. 233–252). Chichester: Wiley.

Waller, G., Meyer, C., Ohanian, V., Elliott, P., Dickson, C., & Sellings, J. (2001). The psychopathology of bulimic women who report childhood sexual abuse: The mediating role of core beliefs. *Journal of Nervous and Mental Disease*, 189(10), 700–708.

Waller, G., Ohanian, V., Meyer, C., & Osman, S. (2000). Cognitive content among bulimic women: The role of core beliefs. *International Journal of Eating Disorders*, 28(2), 235–241.

Wright, M. O. D., Crawford, E., & Del Castillo, D. (2009). Childhood emotional maltreatment and later psychological distress among college students: The mediating role of maladaptive schemas. *Child Abuse & Neglect*, 33(1), 59–68.

# Part II

# Schema therapy assessment and case conceptualisation

# Chapter 4

# Schema therapy assessment of eating disorders

*Susan Simpson*

## Abstract

*A myriad of interconnected factors contribute to the aetiology and maintenance of eating disorders (EDs). A comprehensive assessment must take into consideration factors associated with the onset of the eating disorder, premorbid and systemic factors, temperament, personality traits, and both psychological and physical comorbidities. There is increasing evidence that trauma factors, including emotional, physical and sexual abuse and emotional neglect may be risk factors, highlighting the importance of investigating these in the context of a life history assessment. Assessment of early maladaptive schemas (EMS) and modes should take place in conjunction with an investigation of early life history and eating symptoms. This chapter provides recommendations for carrying out a comprehensive schema therapy (ST) assessment in the context of EDs.*

## Multiple pathways to eating disorders

There appear to be multiple pathways to the development of EDs with a range of precursors, triggers, and reinforcers playing a critical role. Preliminary studies suggest that particular temperament profiles may discriminate ED subtypes (Bulik, Sullivan, Wetlzin, & Kaye, 1995; Fassino et al., 2002). A growing body of evidence suggests a higher prevalence of anxious, perfectionistic and achievement-oriented personality traits amongst those with anorexia and bulimia nervosa (Kaye et al., 2014). In addition, high trait sensitivity and empathy may increase vulnerability to developing an ED (Buchholz et al., 2007; Gulliksen, Nordbø, Espeset, Skårderud, & Holte, 2016).

It is hypothesised that precursors involve a complex interplay of temperament and childhood environment, and include characterological traits (e.g. perfectionism, obsessionality, shyness, other-attunement, high need for control, low uncertainty tolerance, cognitive rigidity), insecure attachment styles (e.g. avoidant, disorganised), socio-emotional factors (e.g. experience of loneliness, and social isolation), body/eating-related traits (e.g. a sense of being lighter or larger in comparison with peers; a propensity to experience increase or loss of appetite in the face of stress; hyper-awareness of internal bodily sensations), role models (e.g. body image attitudes, dieting, high-exercise-focus amongst family members; eating disordered behaviours amongst peers) and cognitive factors (e.g. internalised ideals of thinness, sexual objectification) (Ringer & Crittenden, 2007; Fischer, Stojek, & Hartzell, 2010; Gulliksen et al., 2017; Sternheim, Fisher, Harrison, & Watling, 2017).

In addition, experiences of sexual, physical and emotional abuse/neglect as well as bullying/social exclusion have been strongly linked to ED symptomatology (Sweetingham & Waller, 2007; Afifi et al., 2017; Kimber et al., 2017). Emotional abuse has been identified as an even stronger predictor of eating pathology than either physical or sexual abuse, and linked to a wider range of ED symptoms and comorbidities (Kennedy, Ip, Samra, & Gorzalka, 2007). Emotional neglect is becoming more widespread in society, with mostly unintended, but significant consequences (Kimber et al., 2017). Psychiatric comorbidity is elevated in the ED population, with high levels of chronic dysthymia, depressive and anxiety disorders, substance misuse (Blinder, Cumella, & Sanathara, 2006) and personality disorders (PD) (Bruce & Steiger, 2005). In addition, prevalence of both attention deficit/hyperactivity disorder (ADHD) and autistic-spectrum disorders (ASD) is relatively high (Råstam et al., 2013).

## Schema therapy assessment for eating disorders

Based on the above-mentioned factors it is imperative that assessment and individualised case conceptualisation includes an exploration of the wide range of presenting issues and comorbidities experienced by the client. ST is transdiagnostic, such that multiple complex patterns of diagnoses and behaviours can be understood and formulated within a single comprehensive conceptualisation and mode map. The mode map is a diagram that shows the position and dynamics between the client's main modes (or 'self-states'). The life history interview will require two to six sessions, depending on the degree to which the client can provide a coherent and detailed account of their early experiences. During this period, the client is socialised to the model, and the concept of early maladaptive schemas (EMS) and modes are introduced in the context of their developing conceptualisation. Interviewing is focused on identifying strengths and gaps in childhood and adolescence in terms of core emotional and physical needs, including (1) Secure attachments to others, including a sense of safety, predictability, belonging, unconditional acceptance, warmth, empathy, attunement, and genuinely being 'seen' and known, (2) Autonomy, competence and sense of identity, which is developed through encouragement, praise, mastery, appropriate control over choices, destiny, and body, (3) Freedom to express valid needs and emotions, (4) Spontaneity and play, and (5) Realistic limits and control. In particular, we explore any imbalance between the child's innate needs and temperament and the capacity of caregivers to meet those needs. Questions relevant to each area of enquiry are suggested in the following section.

## Assessment of eating psychopathology and comorbidities

- Comprehensive assessment of ED symptoms. For more detailed descriptions of ED assessment, the reader is directed to the multiple resources available on this topic (Grilo & Mitchell, 2010).
- Investigate issues and patterns linked both to EDs and comorbid conditions and link to modes. For example, the *Overcontroller* (*OC*) mode might include behaviours linked to the ED (restriction, compulsive exercise, body-checking, cutting food into tiny pieces, separating food-types on the plate), as well as obsessive compulsive disorder (OCD) (checking, cleaning, prayer rituals, magical or superstitious thinking), and other non-specific factors such as controlling behaviours within relationships, striving for perfectionism at work.
- Explore the degree to which the person's attendance is motivated by insight into their ED symptoms, or by demands from other family members. Enquire about current perceptions of their body shape and weight.
- Comorbidity: Enquire about other behaviours that in some way support or interact with the ED, such as shop-lifting, alcohol binges (e.g. drunkorexia), substance misuse. Assess for comorbidities, including mood disorders, OCD, post-traumatic stress disorder (PTSD), addictions, ADHD and ASD. Risk associated with self-harm and suicidal ideation should also be assessed and monitored alongside ED symptoms.

## Assessment of life history

In order to develop an understanding of the emergence of EMS and schema modes within a developmental context, it is recommended to investigate the following areas.

### Temperament

- Investigate traits linked to ED, including: impulsivity, compulsivity, perfectionism, introversion/extroversion, affective instability, high need for control, and high sensitivity/empathy to others' distress.
- Investigate body/eating-related traits, including a felt-sense of being lighter or larger in comparison with peers; propensity to experience increase or loss of appetite in the face of stress; hyper-awareness of internal bodily sensations and changes.
- Enquire about clients' impressions of how their temperament and body were perceived by other family members.

### Relationships with parents/caregivers/friends/significant others

- Explore how the relationship with both parents evolved, throughout childhood.

- Identify differences in relationships with each parent (linked to possible unmet needs). How attuned was each parent to the child; did they spend time listening, showing an interest, emotionally connecting? How much physical contact or explicit affection/nurturance was expressed?
- Ask the client to describe their parents, and ways they perceive that they are similar/different to each of their parents.
- What is the client's perception of the qualities their parent valued most as they were growing up? To what extent do they feel that they have those qualities? Does the client try to be more like either of their parents in any way (e.g. striving to become more stoic or to 'toughen up')?
- Explore the way in which the client was disciplined. Was this consistent or chaotic? Absent or punitive?
- Identify possible experiences of rejection or criticism within family-of-origin, and explore any indications of physical/sexual/emotional abuse.
- Inquire about family illness during childhood (either the client or other family members). How did family members react and cope with this? (This can uncover negative impacts such as reduced capacity of parents to respond to the child, or reinforcement of illness behaviour through an increase in [hitherto deficient] levels of nurturance and attentiveness).
- Inquire about any significant loss or separation from a parent/relative/ friend through divorce or death throughout childhood. How did they cope and how much support was available?
- Inquire about whether all siblings were treated equally, or were particular features/traits valued over others? For example, in some families there may have been one child who behaved and achieved according to parental expectations, whereas the child who was more outspoken, spontaneous or impulsive may have attracted disapproval. Did any of the siblings have special needs or disabilities that required significant parental attention? How capable were parents of setting limits on sibling behaviours that impacted other family members?
- Identify themes of parentification, whereby the client has learned to take responsibility for the parents' wellbeing.
- Use hypothetical questions to identify the presence of [often unintentional] emotional neglect: "*If you were upset about something that happened at school, who would you have talked to about that?*" "*Who would you have gone to if you needed a hug?*" "*What would have happened if you went to your mum/dad after scuffing your knee as a young child?*"
- Inquire about how parents reacted to emotional events (e.g. loss, stress, conflict).
- How were anger and distress expressed within family of origin? How did parents respond to conflict and client's emotions?
- Inquire about 'buffer' relationships – if relationships at home were difficult, was there anyone else in their life on whom they could rely for support or comfort?

- Explore client's capacity to self-reflect – do they perceive any link between the way they relate to others now and in early relationships?
- Explore social connectedness/sense of belonging within family and wider community.
- Inquire about peer relationships. Did the client have any close friendships as they grew up? If so, how long did these last? Were they able to maintain relationships outside school hours, or were opportunities restricted?
- Explore client's history of intimate relationships. How long did these last? Who ended the relationships, why, and how? How did they cope?

### Family culture related to food and eating

In many cases, subtle but powerful messages are passed on, explicitly and implicitly, regarding the importance of 'healthy' eating, dieting, fitness and exercise.
   Useful issues to investigate include:

- Family culture around weight/shape/eating
- Past history of dieting by either parent; parental reactions to their own body shape and weight; presence of hyper-healthy diets, and/or compulsive exercise as a means of recognition-seeking or striving.
- Presence of avoidant coping mechanisms, including binge eating/drinking, substance misuse, purging, obsessional rituals.
- Parental reactions to impulsivity or undisciplined behaviour (e.g. in relation to eating, exercise, bodily urges, emotional expression). Use of food by family members for purposes other than sustenance (e.g. self-soothing, substitute for intimacy/affection, regulating emotions).
- Parental viewpoints in relation to the importance of striving, self-control and will-power.
- Reactions of family and friends over the course of the ED.
- The 'role' or secondary functions that the ED might have played during childhood/adolescence, such as drawing attention away from other more distressing family dynamics; securing some kind of emotional presence or connection amongst family members who may be too busy or preoccupied to be present with each other.
- The age and circumstances connected to the first signs of ED attitudes and behaviours in childhood, including possible activating losses or conflicts.
- History of previous inpatient admissions, and client's reactions and experience of these.

### Diagnostic imagery for assessment

Imagery for assessment can be used to connect current ED triggers with early memories, highlighting the link between ED urges and behaviours, EMS and unmet needs. It also provides a starting point for discussions around when/

why/how the person learned to 'switch off' their emotional/physical needs in childhood, and the circumstances around this. For a comprehensive description of diagnostic imagery, see Arntz & Jacob (2013).

### Assessment of schemas and modes

The most reliable way to identify schemas and modes is through observation, with particular attention to verbal content, countertransference reactions and non-verbal communication, such as emotional tone and gestures. The task is to identify how schemas/modes are expressed within the therapy relationship, based on assumptions learned within clients' early relationships. We must distinguish between aspects of countertransference linked to triggering of therapists' own schemas, and reactions that are generated by avoidant or overcompensatory client behaviour. For example:

- In *Perfectionistic Overcontroller (OC)* mode, the person may describe particular areas of concern in an overly detailed and cognitive way, whilst losing sight of the bigger picture. Or they may appear to be overly focused on getting the treatment 'right' and achieving the 'perfect' recovery (*unrelenting standards* EMS). The therapist might also feel pressured to get the treatment 'right'. In *Detached Protector (DetPr)* (*emotional inhibition* EMS), they may tell their story in a detached way, whereby overt emotional expression is inconsistent with their narrative. In both *OC* and *DetPr*, when prompted to tune in to their visceral experience, the client is likely to struggle to describe emotions and bodily felt sense. Countertransference linked to overcompensatory modes may include therapist feelings of irritation or of being scrutinised/judged.
- In the presence of the *Helpless Surrenderer* mode therapists may feel pressured to come up with immediate solutions to 'fix' the client, but it never feels enough. A strong maternal urge to 'rescue' the client can indicate a strong *Abandoned/ dependent [Vulnerable] Child* mode (*VCh*). To distinguish predominant coping modes, the client can be moved to another chair that represents the currently active mode, and interviewed to reveal its origins, as well as past and present functions (Arntz & Jacob, 2013).

Explore content and tone of internally directed messages to discriminate between *Inner Critic* [Parent] modes, for example: *Punitive* ('You're bad'), *Demanding* ('Try harder…where is the extra 10%?'), *Guilt-inducing* ('When you say what you feel, you are hurting me'), *Over-anxious* ('Your feelings or needs are too overwhelming for me'). This provides information that enables us to deal with the *Inner Critic* in a more nuanced way in the context of imagery re-scripting and chairwork. Throughout the book, the terms *Inner Critic* and *Parent* modes are used interchangeably. A description of the most relevant modes for those with EDs is provided in Box 4.1, page 46.

### Questionnaires

Questionnaires are a useful tool for building a picture of eating symptoms, unmet emotional needs, EMS and schema modes. Clients with strong over-compensatory modes tend to endorse artificially low scores on core EMS and child modes, effectively reflecting reduced awareness of underlying vulnerability and distress. It can therefore be more useful to administer these measures again after eight to ten sessions of therapy, or when there is some preliminary evidence of increased self-awareness.

- Food-monitoring diaries (Fairburn, 2008) are used early in therapy to develop self-awareness into links between eating behaviours to triggers and modes. For individuals who are unable to tolerate self-monitoring due to high levels of shame, mode-work is used to bypass the mode responsible for the impasse, and this exercise is re-introduced later in therapy.
- A wide range of ED self-report assessment measures are available to measure ED cognitions and behaviours (for an overview, see Anderson, Lundgren, Shapiro, & Paulosky, 2004; Surgenor & Maguire, 2013).
- The Young Schema Questionnaire (YSQ-3; Young, 2006) and 'Young Parenting Inventory' (YPI; Young, 1994) are useful measures for identifying cognitive aspects of EMS. For a comprehensive description of EMS, the reader is referred to Appendix I, and Young, Klosko, & Weishaar, 2003.
- The Schema Mode Inventory for EDs (SMI-ED; Simpson et al., 2018) and the Schema Mode Inventory Short-Form (SMI-ED-SF; Pietrabissa et al., 2019) are psychometrically tested and validated tools specifically adapted for the ED population (see Appendix 1).
- Given the high physical risks associated with EDs, ongoing medical monitoring is essential alongside psychological treatments, particularly for those most at risk (see CEED, 2013).
- Improvement in psychological wellbeing is as essential to recovery as ED symptom remission. Measures that assess childhood trauma and bonding, levels of dissociation, wellbeing, resilience/self-adaptability, shame, self-acceptance, self-compassion, social connectedness, quality of life, autonomy, can provide useful information on recovery (de Vos et al., 2017).

### Defining treatment goals

- Explore client treatment goals (if any) that relate to eating, weight and shape as well as other aspects of their lives. Bear in mind that their goals are likely to be influenced to a large extent by the function of their default coping modes. For example, the *OC* might wish to have tighter control over eating patterns, and reduced uncontrolled behaviour such as bingeing. The *OC*'s perspective consists entirely of what is physical and tangible, and it will therefore struggle to articulate goals associated with the person's internal world.

- With the ultimate goal of bypassing coping modes, it is therefore important to link ED treatment goals with the client's underlying experience of vulnerability. If possible, collaboratively define some of the treatment goals around these areas of vulnerability (e.g. to reduce loneliness, or suicidality, and strengthen interpersonal connections).
- Recognising the link between ED behaviours and the perpetuation of emotional distress will later become useful as a therapeutic 'hook', which can be used to motivate the client to engage in experiential work that will alleviate their emotional suffering.

### Troubleshooting common problems

Client is prone to guilt and feels disloyal discussing their childhood:

- Explore potential multiple origins of the [*guilt-inducing*] *Inner Critic* modes, including parents, siblings, teachers, religious messages, media, culture. Explore specific guilt-inducing messages conveyed explicitly and implicitly in childhood.
- Discuss origins of loyalty and effects of abandoning oneself to protect significant others.
- Identify role of 'transgenerational' EMS through gently exploring parents'/grandparents' childhoods, and using genograms from a non-blaming stance to identify transgenerational EMS. Use self-disclosure where appropriate to normalise and illustrate role of transgenerational EMS.
- Explore role of modes in current life, and re-visit the life history after strengthening rapport.
- Generate a list of the positive aspects of childhood before exploring gaps and unmet needs (particularly useful for exploring the childhood of clients with well-intentioned parents whose parenting was hindered by their own mental health problems and/or experiences of emotional neglect).

Client struggles to remember clear details of their childhood:

- Explore and interview coping modes blocking memories (or emotions associated with memories) due to fears that emotions will be overwhelming, uncontrollable and/or unacceptable to others. Link to early experiences of emotional neglect, abuse, disconnection.

Client's description of symptoms is incongruent with their physical presentation and weight:

- Client's denial of ED behaviours is likely to be driven by shame, induced by the *Inner Critic* mode – leading to dissociation of the 'rejected' parts of self (e.g. *VCh, Detached Self-Soother*) from conscious awareness. It may also be linked to the *Suspicious OC* mode, which mistrusts others' motives. This dynamic is also likely to sabotage any authentic recording within food/eating monitoring diaries. It is recommended using the mode map to gently introduce and validate the positive survival value of coping modes and associated 'possible' behaviours, before exploring the disadvantages, and setting up dialogues using chairwork.

Client describes intense and intransigent shame:

• The *Inner Critic* mode is often highly egosyntonic at the beginning of therapy. As shown in Figure 4.1, it is hypothesised that this mode stems from multiple internalised explicit and/or implicit messages. The experience of shame often manifests at a deeply visceral level, and is described as a physical felt-sense, such as 'skin crawling', or 'a black cloak that sticks to my skin' and can include fixed ideation around body-image and shape distortion, as well as hypersensitivity to body sensations associated with eating and digestion. Childhood origins of shame should be explored, especially abuse, neglect, and guilt-inducing messages linked to emotional and physical needs.

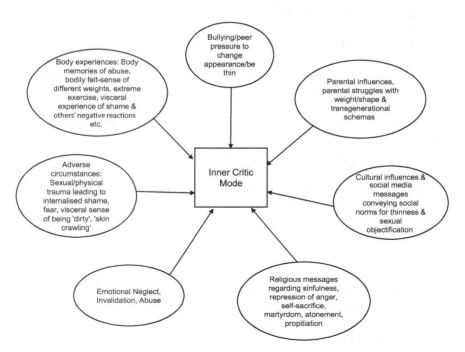

*Figure 4.1* The *Inner Critic* mode

Client perceives that their ED is secondary to another problem (e.g. ADHD and ASD):

- It can be useful to conceptualise all problems, including neurodevelopmental conditions as 'parts of self' within the context of the mode map. For example, aspects of ASD can often fit within the context of the *OC*, or the *Contented [Quirky, Creative] Child*, and the aspects of ADHD could fit within *Impulsive/Undisciplined Child* modes. This enables the shared understanding to move beyond diagnosis into mode work.

---

### Box 4.1  Schema modes [adapted] for eating disorders

**CHILD MODES**

**[Vulnerable] Shamed/Lonely Child**: feels needy, rejected, hurt, a burden, ashamed, undeserving, invisible, anxious, panicky, lost, unattractive, inferior empty, helpless, powerless, trapped, and desperate for nurturance, protection and attention. Feels like a lonely child that is valued only by 'proving' herself to others (e.g. achievement, physical appearance) and/or meeting others' needs. Feels ashamed of normal emotions and needs. Feels different and inferior due to perceived [physical and personality-based] flaws. Feels unattractive and ashamed at an emotional and a bodily 'felt-sense' level.

**Impulsive Child**: Feels like s/he can never get enough of what s/he needs. Acts on impulses in an uncontrolled manner without regard to consequences. Impulsive bingeing functions as a means of meeting/seizing needs or desires (before the next 'famine'). Can also function as a backlash against external/internal demands to be 'good' or tightly controlled. In conjunction with the Detached Self Soother, impulsivity may also be linked to addictions, shop-lifting, and self-harm as a means of attaining emotional regulation, and then perpetuated by habit energy.

**Undisciplined Child**: finds it difficult to tolerate physical or emotional discomfort. Struggles to complete tasks that require determination and perseverance. Intolerant of hard-work and discomfort (e.g. of stomach distension, oedema) associated with recovery.

**Angry/Rebellious Child**: Feels intensely angry because emotional needs have not been met. Expresses anger through passive-aggressive means (e.g. withdrawal, irritability, lashing out). Anger is usually suppressed, as it is experienced as being 'out-of-control', which is viewed as unacceptable and shameful. 'Cuts off nose to spite the face' through hurting the self to express anger at or punish others. For example, using restriction or bingeing as a way of getting back at others in an entitled manner ('I'll do as I please!'). Angry outbursts are triggered if the operations of coping modes (e.g. compulsive rituals, binge/vomit episodes) are interrupted. This mode can also manifest as an Obstinate Child (Arntz & Jacob, 2013), linked to early childhood fears of abandonment, and the expectation that the therapist should be the 'perfect nurturer' – infinitely and indefinitely available.

**Happy Child**: Views body as a positive aspect of the 'self' and uses it appropriately for play, expression of feelings and pleasurable activities.

## MALADAPTIVE COPING MODES

### Surrenderer modes
**Compliant Surrenderer**: Passively allows others to take control or even openly gives control to others in an attempt to gain approval, acceptance or nurturance or reduce conflict, criticism, rejection and humiliation.

**Helpless Surrenderer**: Manifests as a mixture of surrender and over-compensatory behaviours, usually linked to *emotional deprivation, dependence, negativity/pessimism* and *subjugation* schemas. It can have a *resigned* or *victim* tone, whereby the person believes they are powerless. This is accompanied by an external locus of control, and frustration that others will not take control/responsibility, 'fix' their problems, and/or provide relief from anxiety and emotional pain. In this mode the person avoids expressing authentic vulnerability directly, but instead describes suffering in a way that suggests s/he is helpless to change her circumstances and that others are not doing enough. This leads to feeling invalidated or misunderstood when others attempt to second-guess their needs. Others are expected to intuitively know what they feel and need, and there is a tendency to feel frustrated when this does not materialise. In this mode the person seeks attention passively (e.g. through overplayed withdrawal; complaint), without explicitly expressing needs or underlying feelings (e.g. for nurturance, comfort, support). This mode can manifest with different 'flavours', e.g. aggrieved, passive-aggressive, histrionic (theatrical, 'flouncy'), sullen ('teenager'), entitled, hopeless, negative, or complaining, under a façade of deference or submissiveness. ED behaviour becomes a mechanism for indirect expression of vulnerability and emotional needs. Restriction may function as a form of martyrdom, using self-denial to communicate frailty and elicit sympathy (and/or guilt) from others, leading others to feel controlled or manipulated. In this mode, the person replies to suggestions with 'Yes...but...' responses, and attempts to use therapy as a place for 'downloading', or 'acting out', whilst avoiding true connection and actively working on difficulties.

### Avoidant modes
**Detached Protector**: Numbs emotions. Keeps relationships at superficial level. Uses restriction (starving or dieting) or work/study to shut off from relationships and the demands of life. Meticulous planning of binges and preoccupation with eating/weight/shape can also function to

completely switch off from overwhelming feelings and bodily felt-sense. May become angry and defensive (Angry Protector) if feeling threatened by potential loss of control (e.g. when prompted to explore feelings or when eating behaviours are blocked). Can also include dissociation and derealisation (where the person loses touch with reality regarding size of body parts). Suicidal ideation can function as a fantasy of escape from emotional pain and suffering, providing hope and comfort in the face of ongoing despair.

**Detached Self-Soother**: Shuts off emotion by engaging in solitary activities that will soothe, stimulate or distract from uncomfortable feelings. These behaviours mostly function in an impulsive manner (i.e. in tandem with Impulsive Child Mode) to avoid acute anxiety or distress after schemas have been triggered. Bingeing, exercise, drugs and alcohol (and vomiting) are used to block strong emotions and to self-soothe. Subsequently, vomiting may follow as a way of 'cancelling out' the feelings of shame and guilt triggered by bingeing. These behaviours are also self-soothing during episodes of generalised anxiety, linked to schemas that may be 'primed' but not fully triggered (e.g. 'free-floating' feelings of anxiety and vulnerability linked to the *emotional deprivation* schema).

### Overcompensatory modes

These are modes that compensate for strong emotions associated with fear of being ignored, hurt or rejected and losing control (e.g. of emotions, eating, body shape/weight).

**Self-Aggrandiser:** This mode compensates for underlying feelings of defectiveness or inferiority by actively seeking approval or trying to appear 'perfect' or superior to others. In this mode the person only feels worthwhile if they are 'special' or the best at what they do (e.g. regarding work/study/dieting achievements, weight, shape, appearance). May be self-absorbed, competitive, or trying to gain attention. This may involve using diet and compulsive exercise to hone body shape and weight; placing excessive emphasis on clothes, hairstyles and makeup; spending hours on appearance. May be condescending, domineering and dismissive, and lack awareness of others' emotional states. Feels powerful, puts others down, excludes and judges others on superficial grounds, is aggressive, opinionated.

**Pollyanna Overcompensator**: Maintains persistently positive attitude, even in the face of difficult events and interpersonal tensions. Avoids genuine assertiveness and minimises feelings that might lead to criticism or rejection (e.g. authentic anger, sadness, shame). Excessive 'positive thinking', finds a 'silver lining' even in the most difficult situations or circumstances, whilst [unwittingly] invalidating one's own or others' struggles and difficulties. May communicate in an enthusiastic, or 'pleasant' manner, whilst outwardly minimising own and others' vulnerabilities and struggles. In this mode, the person is often upbeat about recovery, presenting a positive 'gung-ho' attitude that is dissonant with actual weight gain/behavioural change. May use platitudes such as 'Everything happens for a reason', 'It was meant to be', as a means of reassuring others in times of adversity. By placing themselves in the 'knowing' and 'caring' role, they elevate their own status through being 'needed' by others. This mode overcompensates for underlying *negativity/pessimism, mistrust/abuse* schemas, and fear of being criticised/rejected/shamed by others. Often the person has learned early on in life that they are responsible for buoying up others around them who are depressed, emotionally fragile, overly negative and/or pessimistic. At a deeper level, other people are compartmentalised as good or bad. From the perspective of this mode (often in tandem with the Suspicious Overcontroller), others are often idealised at first, but then swiftly renounced following any misdemeanour or perceived betrayal.

**Overcontroller**: This mode is generally that of a 'keeper', or internally generated 'surrogate-parent' designed to provide guidance, certainty, pride, predictability, security and the promise that self-worth is achievable (if the 'rules' are followed adequately). Operates as overcompensation for underlying EMS (e.g. *emotional deprivation, dependence, abandonment, defectiveness/shame, subjugation*) or as surrender to EMS (e.g. *unrelenting standards, approval seeking*). Keeps self on a tight 'rein' to reduce risk that behaviour will evoke criticism, shame, or control. The ultimate goal is complete self-sufficiency, through overriding (being 'on top') of all emotional and physical needs. Dietary rules and regulations provide a sense of direction and purpose in an otherwise confusing and frightening world and a substitute for true emotional nurturance and connection. Believes that breaking one's dietary rules will lead to loss of self-control, excessive weight gain and ultimately, rejection. The Overcontroller takes pride in overruling and overriding basic human instincts, needs and vulnerability, eliciting a [pseudo] sense of self-determination, control and self-expression. Feelings are viewed as 'weak', self-indulgent and must be overcome. ED behaviours effectively facilitate disconnection from the feelings held in the body. This mode can be so rigid that at times it can have a 'fixed ideation' delusional quality. It takes a problem-solving, 'fix-it' approach to life, and is simplistic in its black-and-white perception of events (e.g. productive/unproductive; success/failure; well/unwell; attractive/unattractive). The Overcontroller's specific 'flavour' or character is influenced by underlying schemas and can take the following forms.

**Perfectionistic Overcontroller**: Maintains tight control to ensure that everything is completed to perfection and that there is no scope for criticism or humiliation. The Overcontroller is never satisfied – it insists that the client tries harder and sets ever-higher targets. Often has an interchangeable focus and alternates between restrictive eating/weight/shape, exercise, grades or other forms of achievement. Functional, cold, focused on rules, regulations, instructions, doing everything the 'right' way. Any mistake or set back or imperfection is seen as the 'wrong' way. Sets simple rules [dietary and weight-related] that must be followed to retain feelings of control. When these rules are met, they also compensate for the hitherto absence of a sense of achievement and pride in other life domains. Invests significant energy in planning ahead to ensure that life is predictable and/or controllable.

Exerts control through:

*Behavioural strategies:* Focuses on perfection, orderliness, symmetry, sense of 'right[ness]'. Dislikes mess. This includes actual physical mess, wastefulness, or 'messy' (unpredictable; complicated) emotions. Any sign of fat on the body can also be considered 'messy', especially if bone structure is not visible. Behavioural rituals and routines are focused on minimising mess and achieving a sense of safety, certainty and control. Minimisation of needs (which are considered self-indulgent) and emotions via restriction. Anything which is not 100% required for survival in this moment is considered a form of self-indulgence. This translates into restriction of any form of nourishment – including food, rest, sleep, fun, enjoyment, pleasure, emotional connectedness. Restriction becomes the mechanism through which the Overcontroller compensates for shame associated with long-standing perception that their needs and feelings are symptoms of their impetuous, greedy, needy, over-indulgent nature.

Excessive adherence to routine, which may include ritualised binge-ing, purging, cleaning, exercise, planning binges and hoarding food. Sets up internal challenges and makes [unfulfilled] promises and contracts, but rarely if ever follows through on its side of the bargain, e.g. 'If you cut back and miss this meal/go for a run, you can have something nice to eat later'. Changes the goal-posts as soon as they are reached. Goals are based on minimising emotion, whilst increasing productivity, not allowing a single moment to go to waste. For example, one should be walking, running, cleaning at all times. One must work hard before being permitted to relax, with the goal of achieving a sense of competence or achievement. Is controlling toward others, expecting them to comply with ritualised schedules and plans. Engages in compulsive checking rituals to provide reassurance that body weight/shape is not spiraling out of control, and that one is completely 'safe' from the risk of criticism.

*Cognitive strategies:* At face value, this mode is highly logical and rational, and can be mistaken for Healthy Adult. It is stuck in present-tense tunnel-vision, with no long-term or 'big-picture' capacity. Represents a hyper-mentalised state of pervasive rumination and over-analysing of one's own and others' responses, focused on behaving in the 'correct' way and avoiding mistakes. Ruminates as a means of identifying and solving potential 'problems', thereby avoiding anxiety associated with vulnerability, uncertainty, unpredictability. Views interpersonal relationships as transactions, as opposed to opportunities for connection and getting needs met. Compares self constantly with others and is hyper vigilant to signs that one may be inferior in some respect (e.g. body shape, skin, clothing, outward expression of happiness) whilst striving to be better, thinner or more attractive (exercise, restriction, plastic surgery) than others.

*Emotional strategies:* Minimises and overrides vulnerability and needs, e.g. 'You're not really hungry…you don't need dinner. Skip that and it will help with that stomach and thighs…'. Emotions (and associated visceral felt-sense, sensory/perceptual experience and trauma-based 'body memories') are avoided through the perception of 'mastery over' the body through overriding basic human requirements and needs. Views the body as an object which must meet all-or-nothing internalised standards of perfection. The body is simply treated as 'transport for the head', or as a 'work-horse' that provides a means of achieving goals, rather than an internal 'home' to which they can return. The body may be perceived as weak, needy and threatening. It is the 'container' of vulnerability and needs that are considered shameful and/or disgusting.

**Flagellating Overcontroller**: May attack, inflict harm, deprive and criticise the self as a way of achieving self-improvement or appeasing and minimising attack, humiliation or shaming from others and the [Punitive] *Inner Critic*. This mode ostensibly functions in a protective role, providing a sense of security and direction. It can operate as the 'foot soldier' for the [Demanding] *Inner Critic*, minimising the existence of vulnerability, and meeting internalised standards. May derive satisfaction from harming or depriving the self through circular thinking (i. e. 'If I beat myself up enough, I will succeed'; or 'If I know I'm bad and treat myself badly, then I become a better person for recognising this'). This mode may have developed in response to an 'impossible dilemma', faced by the child who felt unsafe to express anger associated with unmet needs, due to fear of being rejected or punished, or a sense that family members would not cope. The emotional 'immune system' (i.e. anger) thereby turns in on itself. The anger is re-directed inwardly to protect the stability of the wider family system.

May also derive satisfaction from being the one who is in control of the punishment and deprivation, rather than having others inflict it on them. Provides the illusion of control, by functioning (1) as a form of a propitiation or atonement; (2) as a safety behaviour that will reduce [perceived] risk of rejection/harm from external sources; (3) as a safety behaviour that builds [perceived] tolerance to emotional pain caused by 'inevitable' abuse/ neglect from external sources; (4) as a buffer against feelings powerlessness in relation to the unpredictability of emotional pain – especially in relation to rejection or abuse. May also be controlling, blaming or scolding of others for not doing things the 'right' way or not colluding with rigid rules and expectations.

**Invincible Overcontroller**: Feels invincible, indestructible powerful, victorious over the body by cheating death. Seeks to be completely invulnerable and to eliminate or be 'on top' of emotional needs. Survival on a day-to-day basis reinforces the notion that restriction of eating and low weight is not dangerous, and that others have an exaggerated and excessive perception of human needs. Taking anything more than what is needed for survival is considered excessive. Vulnerability is perceived to be synonymous with weakness. Seeks to be autonomous and avoid dependence, reliance or emotional connection with others. This mode can be triggered following recognition for achievements, gaining attention, praise or approval from others. When in this mode, the person feels worthy and even superior to others. They may feel they can do or achieve anything. This can provide a strong sense of pride, mastery, righteousness, alongside an emotional 'high', which may approximate feelings of happiness. By overcoming or surpassing basic human urges and instincts (hunger), as well as perceived human flaws and mistakes, the person strives to achieve acceptance or a sense of omnipotence based on their moral and physical superiority. In this mode s/he feels uninhibited, with a sense of fun, freedom, and risk-taking, regardless of what others want or feel. Very busy or even 'manic'. Frequently co-occurs with other overcompensatory modes.

**Suspicious Overcontroller**: Hypervigilant to danger. Fearful that if others are allowed to see their true 'self' or to witness their vulnerability, they will be controlled, overpowered, or made to feel guilty. There is often a *mistrust/abuse* and *defectiveness* schema at the source of this mode, and the person can take a paranoid stance, due to an underlying belief that others will discover they are inferior or flawed and reject them. May be suspicious that trusting others will lead to others 'taking over' or controlling them, such as through directing eating, or even through detaining them in hospital for re-feeding. Tries to 'manage' others' responses through excessive scrutinising and second-guessing others' intentions or responses, avoidance or [passive] blaming. Uses deceit as a tactic to divert unwanted attention and hide ED behaviours. This mode is conspicuous by black-and-white thinking and jumping to conclusions that others are unreliable or untrustworthy. Intrusive images/hallucinations may have developed as an early warning mechanism to be on the alert for impending danger, especially amongst those with a background of trauma/abuse.

## ADULT MODES

### Inner critic modes

**Demanding mode**: Functions as the internalised voice of parents, family, teachers, peers, media (especially social) and religion. This side views emotional needs as unacceptable, unmanageable and a burden on others. This voice then evolves into an internalised self-dictator that demands that one behaves the 'right' way. Continually pushes and pressures the person to meet excessively high standards. Feels that the 'right' way is to achieve at a very high level, to keep everything in order, to strive for high status, to be humble, to put other needs before one's own or to be efficient or avoid wasting time. This mode believes that it is wrong to express feelings or to act spontaneously. Has unrealistic standards in regard to eating and the body.

**Punitive mode**: This is the internalised voice (or perceived meaning) of the parent, family, peers, abuser or others who criticised or bullied them in the past. In this mode, the client becomes their own punitive, rejecting parent, directing anger at themselves for showing normal needs or feelings. Alternatively, in some instances this mode can be linked to guilt-inducing parenting, whereby the child learns that their own needs (physical/emotional) are perceived as a burden by caregivers, thus resulting in an internalisation of self-disgust/loathing. The tone of this mode is harsh, critical, and unforgiving. Signs and symptoms include self-loathing, self-criticism, self-denial, self-mutilation, suicidal fantasies, and self-destructive behaviour. Punishment may take the form of cutting or depriving oneself (e.g. of food) and talking about oneself in a mean, harsh way. This is often experienced as a feeling of 'heaviness' and a felt-sense of disgust, inside the body.

May express harsh messages of disgust, criticism and labelling towards body. Disowns the body and blames it for everything that goes wrong. May distort perception of body image through internalised (felt-sense) shame and disgust and associated images of body as ugly. Can be triggered by signs of possible weight gain (e.g. bloating, compliments 'you look healthy', tightness of clothes etc.) that are then used as evidence for 'fatness' and 'unattractiveness'. Alternatively, weight gain can reduce the 'numbing' effect of low weight and restriction, leading to increased exposure to punitive messages and trauma symptoms (intrusive images, nightmares, physiological arousal) from the past.

**Healthy Adult**: Recognises and understands one's own vulnerability, is compassionate towards the self and others. Tries to enhance helpful, responsible behaviours (sustaining a job, taking responsibility, connecting to others). Strives for a good balance between pleasant adult activities (intellectual/cultural/physical) and social obligations. Shows respect for the body. Experiences the body and mind as integrated parts of the self. Is able to give and receive nurturance and care. Can tolerate the 'messiness' and unpredictability of life. Is fully embodied and able to experience and tolerate both distress and joy within the body without need for dissociation.

## Conclusion

A comprehensive assessment includes an understanding of early attachment relationships, and the way in which attachment patterns have historically become interwoven with eating and beliefs regarding weight and shape. Assessment of EMS and schema modes can take place through observation, careful questioning, and awareness of countertransference reactions. Questionnaires can be used both qualitatively and quantitatively to uncover EMS, modes, and the early patterns linked to their development. A detailed assessment that elicits the way in which the ED has evolved and become perpetuated in the context of EMS facilitates the development of a refined individualised case conceptualisation – and a roadmap for future therapy.

## References

Afifi, T., Sareen, J., Fortier, J., Taillieu, T., Turner, S., Cheung, C., & Henriksen, C. (2017). Child maltreatment and eating disorders among men and women in adulthood: Results from a nationally representative United States sample. *International Journal of Eating Disorders*, 1–16.

Anderson, D., Lundgren, J., Shapiro, J., & Paulosky, C. (2004). Assessment of eating disorders: Review and recommendations for clinical use. *Behavior Modification*, 28(6), 763–782.

Arntz, A., & Jacob, G. (2013). *Schema Therapy in Practice: An Introductory Guide to the Schema Mode Approach*. Chichester, UK: Wiley-Blackwell.

Blinder, B., CumellaE., & SanatharaV. (2006). Psychiatric comorbidities of female inpatients with eating disorders. *Psychosomatic Medicine*, 68, 454–462.

Bruce, K., & Steiger, H. (2005). Treatment implications of Axis-II comorbidity in eating disorders. *Eating Disorders*, 13, 93–108.

Buchholz, A., Henderson, K., Hounsell, A., Wagner, A., NorrisM., & Spettigue, W. (2007). Self-silencing in a clinical sample of female adolescents with eating disorders. *Journal of the Canadian Academy of Child and Adolescent Psychiatry*, 16(4), 158–163.

Bulik, C., Sullivan, P., Weltzin, T., & Kaye, W. (1995). Temperament in eating disorders. *International Journal of Eating Disorders*, 17(3), 251–261.

CEED (The Victorian Centre of Excellence in Eating Disorders) (2013). Medical monitoring in eating disorders. Retrieved from: http://www.ceed.org.au/sites/default/files/resources/documents/Medical%20Monitoring%20in%20Eating%20Disorders%20Summary%20Chart%206%20Sept%202013%20HANDOUT%20DRAFT.pdf

De Vos, J. A., LaMarre, A., Radstaak, M., Bijkerk, C. A., Bohlmeijer, E. T., & Westerhof, G. J. (2017). Identifying fundamental criteria for eating disorder recovery: A systematic review and qualitative meta-analysis. *Journal of Eating Disorders*, 5, 34.

Fairburn, C. (2008). *Cognitive Behavioral Therapy and Eating Disorders*. New York: Guilford Press.

Fassino, S., Abbate-Daga, G., Amianto, F., Leombruni, P., Boggio, S., & Rovera, G. (2002). Temperament and character profile of eating disorders: A controlled study with the Temperament and Character Inventory. *International Journal of Eating Disorders*, 32(4), 412–425.

Fischer, S., Stojek, M., & Hartzell, E. (2010). Effects of multiple forms of childhood abuse and adult sexual assault on current eating disorder symptoms. *Eating Behaviors*, 11(3), 190–192.

Grilo, C., & Mitchell, J. (2010). *The Treatment of Eating Disorders: a Clinical Handbook*. New York: Guilford Press.

Gulliksen, K.S., Nordbø, R., Espeset, E., Skårderud, F., & Holte, A. (2017). Four pathways to anorexia nervosa: Patients' perspectives on the emergence of AN. *Clinical Psychology & Psychotherapy*, 24(4), 846–858.

Kaye, W. H., Wierenga, C. E., Knatz, S., Liang, J., Boutelle, K., Hill, L., & Eisler, I. (2014). Temperament-based treatment for anorexia nervosa. *European Eating Disorders Review*, 23(1), 12–18.

Kennedy, M.A., Ip, K., Samra, J., & Gorzalka, B.B. (2007). The role of childhood emotional abuse in disordered eating. *Journal of Emotional Abuse*, 7(1), 17–36.

Kimber, M., McTavish, J., Couturier, J., Boven, A., Gill, S., Dimitropoulos, G., & MacMillan, H. (2017). Consequences of child emotional abuse, emotional neglect and exposure to intimate partner violence for eating disorders: A systematic critical review. *BioMed Central Psychology*, 5, 33.

Pietrabissa, G., Rossi, A., Castelnuovo, G., Tagliagambe, A., Bertuzzi, V., Volpi, C., Fava, G., Manzoni, G., Gravina, G., & Simpson, S. (2019). Translation and evaluation of the reliability and validity of the Italian version of the Schema Mode Inventory for Eating Disorders: Short-form. *Eat Weight Disorders*.

Råstam, M., Täljemark, J., Tajnia, A., Lundström, S., Gustafsson, P., Lichtenstein, P., Gillberg, C., \h Anckarsäter, H., & Kerekes, N. (2013). Eating problems and overlap with ADHD and autism spectrum disorders in a nationwide twin study of 9- and 12-year-old children. *The Scientific World Journal*, 315429.

Ringer, F., & Crittenden, P. (2007). Eating disorders and attachment: The effects of hidden family processes on eating disorders. *European Eating Disorders Review*, 15, 119–130.

Simpson, S. (2016). A conceptualisation of schema modes in the eating disorders. In C. Archonti, E. Roediger, M. de Zwaan (Eds.). *Schematherapie bei Essstörungen* (pp. 70–82). Weinheim, Germany: Beltz.

Simpson, S., Pietrabissa, G., Rossi, A., Seychell, T.Manzoni, G., Munro, C.Nesci, J., & Castelnuovo, G. (2018). Factorial structure and preliminary validation of the Schema Mode Inventory for Eating Disorders (SMI-ED). *Frontiers in Psychology*, 9, 600.

Sternheim, L., Fisher, M., Harrison, A., & Watling, R. (2017). Predicting intolerance of uncertainty in individuals with eating disorder symptoms. *Journal of Eating Disorders*, 5, 26.

Surgenor, L., & Maguire, S. (2013). Assessment of anorexia nervosa: an overview of universal issues and contextual challenges. *Journal of Eating Disorders*, 1, 29.

Sweetingham, R., & Waller, G. (2007). Childhood experiences of being bullied and teased in the eating disorders. *European Eating Disorders Review*, 16(5), 401–407.

Young, J. (1994). *Young Parenting Inventory*. New York: Cognitive Therapy Center.

Young, J. (2006). *Young Schema Questionnaire-3*. New York: Cognitive Therapy Center.

Young, J., Klosko, J., & Weishaar, M. (2003). *Schema Therapy: A Practitioners Guide*. New York: Guilford Press.

# Chapter 5

# Schema therapy conceptualisation of eating disorders

*Susan Simpson*

## Abstract

*In schema therapy (ST), the case conceptualisation integrates multiple complex factors that influence the development and perpetuation of early maladaptive schemas (EMS) and modes that play a role in driving eating problems. Preliminary studies indicate that EMS and modes mediate childhood experiences and both eating and comorbid symptoms, with a range of multiple complex relationships possible. The ST case conceptualisation provides a template which is sufficiently sophisticated to allow a transdiagnostic understanding of an eating disorder (ED) alongside other comorbidities and complex presentations. Rather than treating each diagnosis as a separate entity, the schema approach facilitates the development of an overarching conceptualisation that guides an integrated and nuanced therapeutic treatment plan. This chapter explores possible factors that should be taken into consideration in the development of a ST case conceptualisation for eating disorders, with an emphasis on making meaningful links between schemas, modes and eating symptoms.*

## Development of a case conceptualisation for eating disorders

The case conceptualisation synthesises the information gathered in the assessment phase, and identifies the EMS and unmet needs linked to the development and maintenance of ED pathology. The mode-map provides a state-based conceptualisation which illustrates how the EMS are manifested moment-by-moment, incorporating both ED and comorbid symptoms/patterns. Overcompensatory, avoidant and surrender coping modes all play a role in the maintenance of ED symptoms, with multiple complex relationships between these and EMS (Talbot, Smith, Tomkins, Brockman, & Simpson, 2015; Brown, Selth, Stretton, & Simpson 2016). Each mode should be identified according to its underlying EMS, 'character' [emotional/behavioural manifestation] and functions. Ideally, using the client's own vernacular can enable clients to begin to 'own' their modes and to use these labels to describe their experience in a more 'mentalised' way. For example, instead of saying 'I binged all day yesterday, there's no hope for me', they might instead say 'That phone call triggered my *Vulnerable Child* (*VCh*) mode, and then my *Bully* [*Inner Critic*] mode started kicking in... so my *Detached Self-Soother* (*DetSS*) came to the rescue and tried to save me from feeling so bad'. In developing a case conceptualisation, the following modes may be considered, given their high prevalence amongst those with EDs.

## Main eating disorder coping modes

The avoidant coping modes may function either as primary avoidance mechanisms aimed at preventing EMS from being activated, or as secondary avoidance to reduce distress, following EMS triggering. It is well documented that many of those with EDs have a low tolerance for negative emotions, boredom and discomfort (e.g. Fairburn, Cooper, & Shafran, 2003). Whereas the *Detached Protector* (*DetPr*) uses numbing and distancing as a means of primary and secondary avoidance, the *DetSS* mostly tends to operate as (impulsive) avoidance, aimed at regulating emotions following schema triggering. In some cases, avoidant modes appear to work in tandem with child modes – for example the *DetSS* appears to join forces with the *Impulsive/Angry/Rebellious Child* mode and functions as a backlash against the demands and rules of an overbearing *Demanding mode* and/or *Overcontroller* (*OC*) mode. This *DetSS/Impulsive Child* combination results in a rebellious and hedonistic short-term perspective, which ultimately perpetuates the fear that any loosening of the rules will inevitably lead to excessiveness and loss of control. In *DetPr/DetSS* modes, suicidal ideation may represent the promise of the ultimate escape from hopelessness, pain and suffering, whereas self-harm provides short-term relief from emotional pain or emptiness.

The *OC* is the main overcompensatory mode prominent in EDs (Brown et al., 2016). It also operates as a core mode in Cluster C personality disorders (Bamelis, Renner, Heidkamp, & Arntz, 2011) which have high comorbidity in this population. The *OC* generally manifests either as surrender to the underlying *unrelenting standards* and *emotional inhibition* EMS [*Inner Critic* mode], or as overcompensation for underlying EMS in the disconnection/rejection domain. It operates as a form of counterdependence, functioning as a primary (compulsive, ritualised) avoidance mechanism to prevent EMS from being triggered. Restriction becomes a means of creating one's own (body-based) rules, thereby creating an emotional 'high' of pseudo-empowerment, mastery, and pride. The person no longer needs to negotiate the uncertainty and 'messiness' of human relationships – by creating an 'idealised self', they have a concrete set of rules that provide a tangible path to invulnerability and/or invincibility.

The *OC* may manifest with various functions and behavioural patterns across a wide spectrum of eating patterns. This may include provision of (1) protection from potential rejection, humiliation and shame, (2) a buffer against their own *Inner Critic* mode, and the guilt associated with having needs or enjoying any aspect of life, (3) a sense of hope, protection and guidance in a confusing and unpredictable environment, (4) a sense of certainty or 'right-ness' through superstitious or magical thinking, (5) the illusion of control to compensate for underlying uncertainty, anxiety, shame and powerlessness, (6) a pseudo-identity or 'socially acceptable self', and (7) a mechanism for managing unprocessed 'taboo' emotions toward others – by turning them inwards. The *Vulnerable Child* (VCh) mode often feels a strong attachment to the *OC* – it often functions as a reliable, consistent inner 'parent' (that the individual has created for themselves) – and is therefore painful to relinquish. For the *OC*, life is an ordeal to be endured. Everything and everyone represents a demand to be 'dealt with' or 'fixed'. The *OC* spends a lot of time calculating, treating interpersonal exchanges as 'transactions' to reduce the chances of being short-changed or blamed. In the case of EDs, calories must be counted, with the goal of calculating (and recalculating) the minimum possible intake. In addition, this mode implements the measures of austerity and a spartan existence in accordance with the values advocated by the underlying *Inner Critic* (and underlying EMS, e.g. *emotional deprivation, defectiveness, unrelenting standards*). Although the *OC* is well-intentioned, and represents values that attract strong approval within western culture (e.g. productivity, exceptional standards, weight loss), it is not in any way focused on the underlying emotional needs of the *VCh*, and therefore perpetuates the underlying sense of loneliness and suffering.

In the same manner, the *Flagellating OC* mode chastises or criticises in order to achieve safety. However, unlike the *Inner Critic* mode which has the sole purpose of punishing, the *Flagellating OC* brings a sense of relief. A metaphor is that of capsaican (chilli) in that it initially causes pain and then numbs it. In fact, some research suggests that humans may condition themselves to make painful or aversive experiences rewarding. It is perhaps through the interacting systems of pleasure and aversion that painful experiences can become gratifying, and in this case the paired experience of pain followed by the relief of having endured it (McQuaid, 2015). This has been referred to as 'hedonic reversal', whereby innately negative sensory experiences become gratifying (Rozin, 1999). The *Flagellating OC* mode may manifest through self-denial (e.g. 'I must deprive myself of anything that might give me pleasure, including food, sex, fun') through to more extreme forms of self-punishment such as eating dirty or raw meat, taking cold showers, cutting, burning and placing hands in hot water. Through intentional suffering, the *Flagellating OC* provides a tangible roadmap with the goal of 'earning' a sense of deservingness. In addition to the functions of the *OC* listed above, the *Flagellating OC* may be intended to fulfil additional functions, including 'self-improvement' through 'martyrdom' (e.g. 'flogging myself makes me more acceptable', 'if I treat myself badly, I can live with myself'). This is congruent with the concept of shame-based self-attacking, which functions as a safety behaviour (Gilbert & Miles, 2002). Many clients describe needing to punish themselves more and more to attain the same effect, just as one might have an increasing tolerance for a drug.

Another common overcompensator mode, is the *Pollyanna* mode. This mode overcompensates for underlying negativity/pessimism, denies vulnerability and 'silver-lines' even the most difficult circumstances. Like the *OC*, this mode has a feel of invincibility, and in the case of anorexia nervosa (AN) can blind the person to their own dire health condition due to the excessive emphasis on staying optimistic. The mode provides a cover for underlying anxiety, negativity, powerlessness, and resentment, with a cheerful demeanour. This can also manifest an upbeat attitude to recovery which is likely to be at odds with the struggle and distress associated with the personal growth linked to an 'authentic' recovery.

The *Compliant Surrenderer (CSu)* and *Helpless Surrenderer (HSu)* modes both operate as a means of avoiding overt conflict, and involve passively handing over control to others. In *CSu*, the person sacrifices themselves excessively, whilst overriding their own needs. In the case of the *HSu,* the person covertly tries to get others to take responsibility, and often feels aggrieved that others are not doing enough. This can also take on the flavour of a complaining or victim mode, whereby the person passively relinquishes control and tries to manoeuvre others into feeling obliged to meet their needs. Both modes may have a passive-aggressive feel, whereby unexpressed anger is manifested through passive acting out (e.g. turning up late for appointments, withdrawing from others in a hostile manner).

## Differentiating modes

Parent and coping modes can manifest in similar ways, making them difficult to differentiate. In order to do so, it can be useful to interview the mode on a separate chair to reveal whether it has a purpose or function. This overlap in messages and behaviour is especially marked in regards to the *OC* and *Inner Critic* modes. Whereas the parent modes are experienced more as an 'echo' of early messages, a 'voice from the past', the coping mode is experienced as an urge, an attitude, a way of being, or an imperative, with a function. For example, an *Inner Critic* may be using restriction and/or self-harm as a way of punishing the self simply because this was the message that they internalised as a child ('I deserve punishment'). In contrast, the *OC* may be using restriction and/or self-harm to develop a sense of predictability, achievement, protection, in order to feel 'on top' of vulnerability, or as a means of counterdependence and self-improvement. The *HSu* mode may use restriction as a form of martyrdom, using self-denial to communicate frailty and elicit sympathy (and/or guilt) from others. Like child modes, the coping modes live in an eternal present, with no capacity to discriminate between past trauma or danger, and current relationships and circumstances. They are generally on constant alert to protect against the imminent perceived re-emergence of the original childhood patterns which contributed to the formation of the EMS. In addition, the *VCh* will often be reluctant to relinquish a coping mode, even if it is experienced as punitive, in contrast to the relief they experience if you send their *Inner Critic* away.

## Bringing it all together

A diagram illustrating the development and perpetuation of modes as applied to EDs is shown in Figure 5.1. This also illustrates how coping modes function to moderate the effects of the *Inner Critic* and emotional vulnerability. A more detailed example of an individualised mode map that would be used collaboratively with clients is provided in Figures 5.2 and 5.3.

Both clinical experience and research support the notion that it is the interaction of particular temperaments with childhood environment that may 'set the scene' for an ED (Waller, Corstorphine, & Mountford, 2007). Temperaments that may be most vulnerable include those who are highly attuned to the needs and feelings of others, and may therefore have a higher propensity to internalise others' stress. In addition, those who are highly sensitive, have perfectionistic/obsessional traits, and/or have a high need for control appear to require a higher level of nurturance to ensure that these traits are channelled into adaptive functioning (Dobbs, 2012). Those with high sensitivity/empathy can be prone to 'flying under the radar', leading to their emotional needs going unnoticed by others. Their high attunement to the anxieties and stressors of their caregivers leads them to avoid overt expressions of vulnerability whilst minimising their needs, giving the outward appearance of coping autonomously.

Childhood environments characterised by early attachment trauma and emotional neglect, alongside cultural pressures for achievement at the expense of interpersonal connection, can result in the child feeling undeserving, lonely and invisible. This experience may be heightened in the context of a highly empathic/sensitive temperament. A sense of defectiveness/shame is internalised as a result of the perception that one's basic human needs and emotions are a burden or imposition on significant others. The *VCh* mode embodies the 'unacceptable' self, alongside the felt-sense experience of intolerable distress and emptiness. The image of the 'unacceptable child' of the past remains static, and as a constant reminder of their perceived inner defectiveness. In EDs, this experience becomes dissociated through the development of survival coping modes that serve to assist in avoiding, escaping or hiding from shame activation (*DetPr/DetSS*); appeasing and serving others to reduce any possibility of rejection, whilst striving to be valued, 'seen' or supported by others (*CSu* and *HSu*); or overcompensation whereby the person tries to be the opposite of their 'unacceptable' child self, through perfectionism, and self-denial of basic human needs (e.g. *OC; Pollyanna*). The *OC* functions as an idealised pseudo-self. This becomes the dominant or default identity from which the person perceives themselves, relationships and the world. The *OC* is (unconsciously) tasked with meeting the needs for control, autonomy, achievement, self-efficacy, certainty and predictability. Its goal is being the 'best' and is therefore in constant competition with others. This mode commonly perceives others as a threat to its perfectionistic goals – s/he

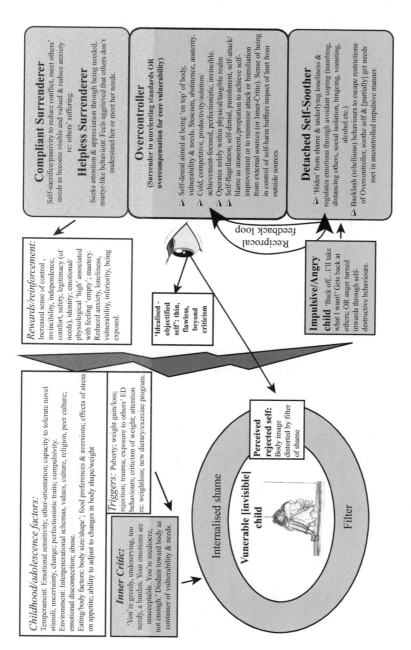

*Figure 5.1* Generic eating disorder case conceptualisation

**Compliant Surrenderer**
Self-sacrifice/passivity to reduce conflict, meet others' needs to become visible and valued & reduce anxiety re: others' suffering.

**Helpless Surrenderer**
Seeks attention & appreciation through being needed, martyr-like behaviour. Feels aggrieved that others don't understand her or meet her needs.

**Overcontroller**
(Surrender to unrelenting standards OR overcompensation for core vulnerability)

▷ Self-denial aimed at being 'on top' of body, vulnerability & needs. Stoicism, abstinence, austerity.
▷ Cold, competitive, productivity/solution/achievement-focused, perfectionistic, invincible.
▷ Operates solely within physical/tangible realm
▷ Self-flagellation; self-denial, punishment, self-attack/blame as atonement, propiation to achieve self-improvement or to minimise attack or humiliation from external sources (or Inner-Critic). Sense of being in control of self-harm buffers impact of hurt from outside sources.

**Detached Self-Soother**
▷ 'Hides' from shame & underlying loneliness & regulates emotions through avoidant coping (numbing, distancing others, social isolation, bingeing, vomiting, alcohol etc.)
▷ Backlash (rebellious) behaviours to escape restrictions of Overcontroller, soothe self & [partially] get needs met in uncontrolled impulsive manner.

*Rewards/reinforcement:*
Increased sense of control, invincibility, independence, comfort, safety, legitimacy (of needs), identity; emotional/physiological 'high' associated with feeling 'empty'; mastery. Reduced anxiety, loneliness, vulnerability, inferiority, being exposed.

Reciprocal feedback loop

'Idealised – objectified self': thin, flawless, beyond criticism

**Impulsive/Angry child** 'Back off… I'll take what I want!' Gets back at others; OR anger turned inwards through self-destructive behaviours.

*Childhood/adolescence factors:*
Temperament: Emotional sensitivity; other-orientation; capacity to tolerate novel stimuli, uncertainty, change; perfectionistic traits; compulsivity.
Environment: Intergenerational schemas, values, culture, religion, peer culture; emotional disconnection; abuse.
Eating/body factors: body size/shape'; food preferences & aversions; effects of stress on appetite; ability to adjust to changes in body shape/weight

*Triggers:* Puberty; weight gain/loss; rejection; trauma; exposure to others' ED behaviours; criticism of weight; attention re: weight/loss; new dietary/exercise program.

*Inner Critic:*
'You're greedy, undeserving, too needy, a burden. Your emotions are unacceptable. You're mediocre, not enough. Disdain toward body as container of vulnerability & needs.

**Perceived rejected self:** Body image distorted by filter of shame

Internalised shame

**Vunerable [invisible] child**

Filter

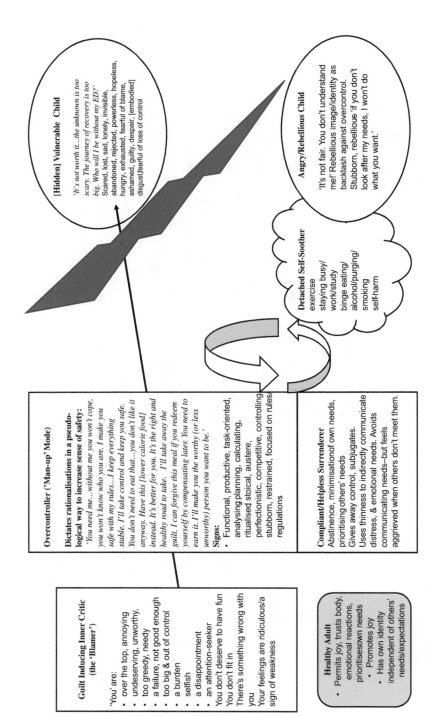

*Figure 5.2* Example of individualised mode map

**[Hidden] Vulnerable Child**

*'It's not worth it...the unknown is too scary. The journey of recovery is too big. Who will I be without my ED?'*
Scared, lost, sad, lonely, invisible, abandoned, rejected, powerless, hopeless, hungry, exhausted, fearful of blame, ashamed, guilty, despair, [embodied] disgust/fearful of loss of control

**Angry/Rebellious Child**

'It's not fair. You don't understand me!' Rebellious image/identity as backlash against overcontrol. Stubborn, rebellious 'if you don't look after my needs, I won't do what you want.'

**Detached Self-Soother**
exercise
staying busy/
work/study
binge eating/
alcohol/purging/
smoking
self-harm

**Overcontroller ('Man-up' Mode)**

**Dictates rationalisations in a pseudo-logical way to increase sense of safety:**
*'You need me...without me you won't cope, you won't know who you are. I make you safe with my rules...I keep everything stable. I'll take control and keep you safe. You don't need to eat that...you don't like it anyway. Have this [lower calorie food] instead. It's better for you. It's the right and healthy road to take. I'll take away the guilt. I can forgive this meal if you redeem yourself by compensating later. You need to earn it. I'll make you the worthy (or less unworthy) person you want to be.'*
**Signs:**
* Functional, productive, task-oriented, analysing planning, calculating, ritualised stoical, austere, perfectionistic, competitive, controlling stubborn, restrained, focused on rules/ regulations

**Compliant/Helpless Surrenderer**
Abstinence, minimisation of own needs, prioritising others' needs
Gives away control, subjugates.
Uses thinness to indirectly communicate distress, & emotional needs. Avoids communicating needs–but feels aggrieved when others don't meet them.

**Guilt Inducing Inner Critic (the 'Blamer')**

'You' are:
* over the top, annoying,
* undeserving, unworthy,
* too greedy, needy
* a failure, not good enough
* too big & out of control
* a burden
* selfish
* a disappointment
* an attention-seeker
You don't deserve to have fun
You don't fit in
There's something wrong with you
Your feelings are ridiculous/a sign of weakness

**Healthy Adult**
* Permits joy, trusts body, emotional reactions, prioritises own needs
* Promotes joy
* Has own identity independent of others' needs/expectations

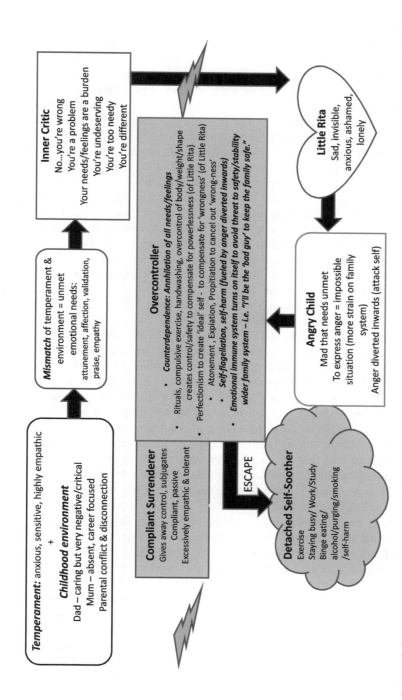

*Figure 5.3* Example of eating disorder mode map

is either on top/the best, or s/he reverts to being the child from the past who is shameful, inferior, and at risk of rejection. In *OC* mode, the person views the self, relationships and the world only in terms of what is material/tangible – ruminating, overanalysing and comparing herself constantly to an idealised and invincible self-image. Further, expression of anger associated with unmet needs (*AnCh*) is perceived by the child as a threat to the overarching stability and safety of the family, leading to an impossible dilemma. In order to safeguard attachment and the needs of the wider family system, anger is diverted inwards, fueling the *Inner Critic* and *Flagellating OC* mode. The 'emotional immune system' (*AnCh*) turns against itself (Maté, 2003). In addition, the *Flagellating OC* may use self-punishment and deprivation as a means of attaining self-improvement as well as protection from potential external humiliation. In all of these coping modes, ED behaviours are utilised to dissociate from the body, and thereby the distress experienced by the *VCh*. Dietary restriction and the sensation of an empty stomach have been recognised as powerful mechanisms for achieving a soothing, dissociated state, producing sensations ranging from distraction to euphoria (Kaye, Wierenga, Bailer, Simmons, & Bischoff-Grethe, 2013).

Binge eating often functions as a means of soothing the self, and maintaining distance from the unwanted *VCh* self from the past. Bingeing is generally a manifestation of the *DetSS* mode, driven by the *Impulsive* and/or *Angry/Rebellious Child* (*AnCh*) modes. The *Impulsive* and *Angry/Rebellious* modes operate as a backlash to criticism from the *Inner Critic* and/or the oppressive controlling mechanisms of the *OC* mode. This can take the form of binge eating and drinking, self-harm and other forms of impulsivity, representing a form of 'escape' or 'uprising' (as in AN binge-purge subtype; and bulimia nervosa (BN)) – and providing an opportunity for trance-like enjoyment, as in binge eating disorder (BED). Compensatory purging, compulsive exercise and fasting mostly represent an *OC* attempt to regain control by 'reining-in' the despised child modes and re-establishing a regime of austerity. However, it is important to recognise that the function of ED behaviours varies widely between clients; for example, both bingeing and purging can also be driven by other modes, such as the *Perfectionistic OC* (rituals that bring sense of control), *Flagellating OC or Punitive Inner Critic* (as a form of self-punishment or atonement); or *Helpless Surrenderer* (as covert communication of underlying distress and need for support).

Body image (and/or body avoidance) is the focal point of an ED – as the body is where intolerable or unmanageable emotions and felt-sense experience are stored (Seijo, 2016). The body is perceived as 'defective', as it contains the intolerable emotions, felt-sense and unmet needs of the rejected *VCh* from the past. The *VCh* is infused with the shaming interpretations and messages of the *Inner Critic* and is seen as the 'problem', steeped in a secondary layer of shame, further exacerbating the individual's primary experience of trauma-distress (linked to unmet emotional needs). Subsequently, cognitive and emotional processes focused on the body become distorted when viewed through the filter of the *Shamed VCh*. Many people with EDs describe fixed or even delusional ideation associated with distorted body perception. Body image distortion can therefore be conceptualised as a mechanism for dissociating from the *VCh* mode. The body becomes the container for the *VCh* 'past-self', to which the person never wants to return, and which they are trying to distance from their conscious mind. Body image distortion can therefore be somewhat resistant to current cognitive strategies that are focused solely on maintenance factors.

Body distortion [cognitive and emotional] filters are activated in the here-and-now in response to specific triggers (e.g. an image of oneself in the mirror, being weighed, trying on clothes). The person then perceives themselves once again through the shame filter of their past self: the *VCh*. When the body is perceived through 'dissociative' coping modes, the particular mode in question dominates the way in which the body is evaluated. For example, the *OC* is a black-and-white rigid mode that is focused on distancing from the *VCh* through cultivating idealistic notions of perfectionism. The *OC* objectifies the body, and strives for elimination of all that is 'non-functional' and uncontrollable, including flesh, emotional vulnerability and needs. Similarly, the dissociative operations of the *DetPr* mode are linked to body-experiences of depersonalisation and derealisation, leading to perceptive confusion over the position and size of one's body. Body image distortion appears to be further elevated amongst those with a sexual or physical trauma history (Dyer et al., 2013).

In AN, the reflected image of the current self is perceived through a filter of the past *VCh* – creating a dissociated self-image that is perceived as excessive, over-weight, and/or flawed. In fatorexia (an emerging phenomenon, whereby the person perceives themselves to be thin, in contrast to the reality of their over-weight), the person dissociates from reality by creating an idealised body-image. Whereas body image distortion is largely characterised by schema-surrender in AN and BN, fatorexia is characterised by schema-overcompensation. In BED, body image distortion is characterised by schema-avoidance, whereby the person self-soothes through overeating, perpetuating schemas through further weight gain and the fusion of abhorred current and past *Vulnerable [shamed] selves*.

In sum, coping modes play a key role in ED behaviours and cognitions and these should be delineated within individualised formulations. The function of ED behaviours can vary widely according to which mode is active, and it is therefore essential to investigate this through exploration, interviewing the modes, and chairwork.

## Conclusions

The schema mode model provides a sophisticated transdiagnostic framework for understanding the complexities of ED symptomotology and comorbidity. In order to build a comprehensive case conceptualisation, a nuanced understanding is required of the EMS and unmet needs that have played a part in the development of eating and comorbid disorders. Mode maps should be personalised to facilitate the conceptualisation of ED symptoms alongside other comorbid patterns of functioning. The mode map can capture the cognitive, behavioural and visceral experience of the modes and the way in which these interact in the here-and-now. This then becomes a useful tool for reflecting on the modes and identifying them as they arise both during and between therapeutic sessions.

## References

Bamelis, L., Renner, F., Heidkamp, D., & Arntz, A. (2011). Extended schema mode conceptualizations for specific personality disorders: An empirical study. *Journal of Personality Disorders*, 25(1), 41–58.

Brown, J., Selth, S., Stretton, A., & Simpson, S. (2016). Do dysfunctional coping modes mediate the relationship between perceived parenting style and disordered eating behaviours? *Journal of Eating Disorders*, 4(27), 1–10.

Dobbs, D. (2012). Are you an orchid or a dandelion? *The New Scientist*, 213(2849), 42–45.

Dyer, A., Borgmann, E., Kleindienst, N., Feldmann, R., Vocks, S., & Bohus, M. (2013). Body image in patients with posttraumatic stress disorder after childhood sexual abuse and co-occurring eating disorder. *Psychopathology*, 46, 186–191.

Fairburn, C. G., Cooper, R., & Shafran, R. (2003). Cognitive behaviour therapy for eating disorders: A 'transdiagnostic' theory and treatment. *Behavior Research & Therapy*, 41:509–528.

Gilbert, P., & Miles, J. (eds). (2002). *Body Shame: Conceptualisation, Research, and Treatment*. Hove: Brunner-Routledge.

Kaye, W. H., Wierenga, C. E., Bailer, U. F., Simmons, A. N., & Bischoff-Grethe, A. (2013). Nothing tastes as good as skinny feels: The neurobiology of anorexia nervosa. *Trends in Neuroscience*, 36(2), 110–120.

McQuaid, J. (2015). *Tasty: The Art and Science of What We Eat*. US: Scribner.

Maté, G. (2003). *When the Body Says No: The Cost of Hidden Stress*. Toronto: Vintage Canada.

Rozin, P. (1999). Preadaptation and the puzzles and properties of pleasure. In D. Kahneman, E. Diener & N. Schwarz (Eds.). *Well Being: The Foundations of Hedonic Psychology* (pp. 109–133). New York: Russell Sage.

Seijo, N. (2016). The Rejected Self: working with body image distortion in eating disorders . *ESTD Newsletter*, 5(4), 5–13. Available at: http://www.nataliaseijo.com/PDF/Rejectedself.pdf

Talbot, D., Smith, E., Tomkins, A., Brockman, R., & Simpson, S. (2015). Schema modes in eating disorders compared to a community sample. *Journal of Eating Disorders*, 3: 41.

Waller, G., Corstorphine, E., & Mountford, V. (2007). The role of emotional abuse in the eating disorders: Implications for treatment. *Eating Disorders*, 15(4), 317–331.

# Application of schema therapy to eating disorders

# Chapter 6

# Repetitive negative thinking in eating disorders

## Identifying and bypassing over-analysing coping modes and building schema attunement

*Robert Brockman and Adele Stavropoulos*

## Abstract

*Research into the cognitive behavioural treatment of eating disorders (EDs) has largely focused on the content of cognitions and their relation to ED pathology. Yet recent research has demonstrated the relevance of negative cognitive processes in the experience of EDs (Smith, Mason, & Lavender, 2018); in particular, the repetitive, abstract and negative way in which individuals with EDs commonly process cognitions, termed Repetitive Negative Thinking (RNT). Theory and research suggest that RNT processes represent an important transdiagnostic maintenance factor across EDs, which may function to block emotional processing. We review a body of research that outlines the potential importance of RNT processes to ED pathology, and present a schema mode conceptualisation of RNT in which high levels of RNT are conceptualised as maladaptive coping (mode) behaviour. Specific therapeutic strategies for bypassing RNT coping in schema therapy (ST) are discussed, including a process-focused approach to building schema attunement.*

At its core, schema therapy (ST) aims to provide deep emotional schema change through the facilitation of *corrective emotional experiences* (Farrell & Shaw, 2017). In general, much research has focused on the *content* of negative self-beliefs and their links with eating disorder (ED) pathology (Waller, Ohanian, Meyer, & Osman, 2000; Waller, 2003). This research has supported the advancement of prominent theories and treatment models that aim to address the core negative cognitive theme thought to be at the heart of all ED presentations: *the over-valuation of body shape and weight and their control* (Fairburn, 2008). While this line of enquiry has focused on negative cognitive *content*, research has demonstrated the relevance of negative cognitive *processes* (e.g. rumination, worry) as central to the experience of EDs (Sassaroli et al., 2005; Rawal, Park, & Williams, 2010). One study found clients with anorexia nervosa (AN) to have significantly higher levels of worry and rumination compared to anxiety disorder groups (Startup et al., 2013). A meta-analytic study by Smith and colleagues (Smith, Mason, & Lavender,

2018) reported consistent associations between rumination and all forms of EDs, and concluded that while the content of ED cognitions may be important, it may be that the repetitive, abstract, and negative way in which individuals process these thoughts could be the most influential feature of ED cognitions. Taken together, these studies indicate that negative thinking *processes* may be an important transdiagnostic maintenance factor across EDs (Smith et al., 2018). These negative processing styles have been termed *Repetitive Negative Thinking* (RNT) (Ehring & Watkins, 2008). This chapter outlines the potential importance of RNT processes to ED pathology, before discussing how to conceptualise and treat ED cases from a ST perspective where high levels of RNT may present as a threat to emotional processing.

Worry has been defined as 'passive, repetitive thoughts about future negative events with an uncertain outcome' (Papageorgiou & Wells, 2004). Such thoughts are often associated with increased anxiety. In contrast, rumination refers to a cognitive process in which one repetitively focuses on the meaning, causes, antecedents, and consequences of negative emotions (Nolen-Hoeksema, Wisco, & Lyubomirsky, 2008). This process tends to be rather passive. When ruminating, people tend to fixate on their problems and associated distress as a covert mental behaviour, reducing their tendency to take overt action to remediate, and potentially disconnecting them from sources of reinforcement. Worry and rumination have been conceptualised as distinct in both thought content (worry involves themes of anticipated threat, rumination focuses on past loss or failure) and temporal orientation (worry is future and rumination past oriented; Papageorgiou & Wells, 2004). However, evidence suggests that worry and rumination appear to share more similarities than differences. Both are repetitive, difficult to control, negative in content, predominantly verbal, and are relatively abstract strategies implemented in response to an initial thought intrusion (Watkins & Moulds, 2005).

In light of these findings, Nolen-Hoeksema & Watkins (2011) proposed a transdiagnostic model, in which rumination and worry reflect the same underlying cognitive process: Repetitive Negative Thinking. RNT is defined as self-focused repetitive thinking that is prolonged, negative in content, and difficult to control (Watkins, 2008). Multiple findings support this model, namely that worry and rumination have been found in individuals with either a mood or anxiety disorder and do not differ depending on the disorder (McEvoy, Moulds, & Mahony, 2013). Additionally, RNT has been found to have more predictive utility for depression and anxiety than rumination or worry individually (Spinhoven, Penelo, de Rooij, Penninx, & Ormel, 2015). Furthermore, treatment specifically targeting RNT has been found to reduce both symptoms of anxiety and depression, providing evidence for the clinical utility of the construct (Nolen-Hoeksema & Watkins, 2011). Thus, despite evidence that rumination and worry are distinct processes, theory and evidence suggest RNT to be the overarching construct underlying both cognitive strategies, which can be differentiated mostly by content and time orientation.

## Repetitive Negative Thinking and emotional processing

RNT processes such as worry and rumination have been hypothesised to be problematic for cognitive behavioural treatments because they tend to have the effect of blocking *emotional processing*. First, Processing Mode Theory (Watkins and Teasdale, 2004) suggests that incoming emotional information can be processed via two distinct modes, an abstract analytic (AA) or concrete experiential (CE) mode. The AA mode indicates analysing a situation based on its general causes, consequences and importance through focusing on the past or future. In contrast, the CE mode implies directly processing a situation though specifically experiencing one's emotional state, physical sensations and environment in a way that is both problem and present focused.

Processing Mode Theory proposes that these two processing styles produce distinct functional effects on memory, with the AA mode being maladaptive and CE being adaptive. The CE is adaptive because the abstract over-generalised memories involved in AA evoke less vivid imagery than concrete specific memories, reducing activation of underlying emotional structure of memory and impeding the natural emotional processing of negative events (Foa & Kozak, 1986). Furthermore, abstract thoughts are less detailed or contextualised than concrete thoughts, promoting poorer elaboration and problem solving (Watkins & Teasdale, 2004).

This account of RNT as representing an AA processing style that blocks emotional processing is also consistent with the hypothesis that worry and rumination may function as a form of emotional avoidance. Borkovec and colleagues (Borkovec, Alcaine, & Behar, 2004) propose an avoidance model of worry which suggests that worry is a verbal-linguistic regulatory strategy that functions to reduce experiencing the full impact of the fear imagery associated with anxiety. From this position it is argued that worry is a predominantly verbal-linguistic process, and that such verbal articulation and elaboration of feared material leads to less sympathetic nervous system activation than engaging in processing of cognitive imagery, which can lead to increased emotional processing, and for some individuals, the feeling of being overwhelmed (Shearer & Tucker, 1981). Worry is thus characterised by abstract thinking, which produces less vivid and frequent images, and is thus less likely to evoke somatic responses (Borkovec & Ruscio, 2001). It is thus proposed by this model that this abstract, verbal linguistic regulatory strategy is reinforced by avoidance of more intense negative emotions inherent in processing imagery. Taken together, these theories and the empirical results that support them, suggest worry and rumination each function as a form of experiential avoidance; because focusing individuals on the verbal content of distressing material limits its emotional impact and gives a sense of control (Moulds, Kandris, Starr & Wong, 2007).

## Repetitive Negative Thinking: A schema therapy perspective

It is clear from the above review of the literature that (a) RNT is a transdiagnostic maintenance factor for psychopathology commonly seen in individuals with EDs, and (b) that RNT may be problematic to psychological interventions because it serves as a form of avoidant coping, blocking *emotional processing*. This is entirely consistent with the ST perspective, whereby avoidant attempts to cope with intense emotions and images are conceptualised as *maladaptive coping modes* (Arntz, Bernstein, & Jacob, 2012). From this perspective, coping modes produce some relief from intense emotional states (e.g. *Vulnerable child (VCh), Angry Child (AnCh)*), and cope with external (e.g. work pressure) and internal demands and expectations (e.g. *Inner critic/Parent modes*) and are thereby maintained via an avoidance function (Jacob & Arntz, 2012). Further, the theory suggests that such coping states, while potentially useful in some contexts (e.g. during stressful circumstances in childhood), may come at some long-term cost in terms of not being able to meet their own needs, and maintaining early maladaptive schemas (EMS) (Young, Klosko, & Weishaar, 2003). Through the lens of ST, RNT may be viewed as a form of maladaptive coping, either as a part of the repertoire of a broader coping mode (e.g. *Perfectionist-Overcontroller (OC)* mode, *Detached Protector (DetPr)* mode), or as a coping mode in and of itself (e.g. *Over-analyser mode*; Stavropoulos, Haire, Brockman, & Meade, in preparation). As such, addressing RNT will involve explicitly formulating this process as a part of a maladaptive coping mode, and then applying strategies to bypass the coping mode and connect to the core emotional modes where the schemas can be accessed for *emotional processing* – this is the hallmark of schema treatment (Arntz, Bernstein, & Jacob, 2012). Stavropoulos and colleagues (in preparation) suggest a functional name for RNT modes of processing, 'over-analysing' which can be viewed as a part of a broader coping mode, or which may be formulated as an isolated mode. Stavropoulos and colleagues (in preparation) suggest that this *'Over-analysing mode'* may be defined as

> a focus on the verbal-linguistic processing of past and/or future events (in the form RNT), at the expense of attending to the experiential and emotional features of present experience. The over-analysing mode functions to block the emotional processing of threat schemas, which may result in the maintenance of EMS/ modes (e.g. *VCh* and *AnCh*).

## Strategies for bypassing RNT and 'over-analysing' coping behaviour in schema therapy

The core management of coping modes within ST largely involves 'bypassing' coping modes or behaviour so as to engage more fully with emotions, where emotion-focused, and limited reparenting techniques may be successfully applied (Arntz, Bernstein, & Jacob, 2012). We argue that in some EDs (e.g.

AN), this behaviour may be best understood as a feature of the *Perfectionistic-OC* mode. However, it is also possible to conceptualise this behaviour as its own stand-alone coping mode in cases with over-analysing (mental) behaviour but no signs of overt perfectionistic behaviour. Such decisions are likely to be made pragmatically, in consultation with the client, as to what fits best with their experience. What follows is a series of techniques designed to facilitate the goal of bypassing over-analysing coping behaviour that may be blocking the potential for emotional processing within ST sessions. These techniques may also be useful for addressing other coping modes that may serve a similar avoidant function (e.g. *DetPr*).

### Education and empathy for the functional role of over-analysing coping

Treatment of any coping mode involves educating and empathising with the client, about the understandable functional role of the coping mode, both in the past, perhaps as a child, as well as currently as an adult. We have found that clients with strong coping modes are more likely to soften their stance if the coping mode feels understood and appreciated. Here, the client's autonomy to give up (or keep) the coping mode intact should be central to the therapy. Clients who feel that a part of them is being attacked are likely to retreat further into their coping mode/s. It is from this position of empathy for the coping mode that the client may feel safe to tolerate and engage in some discussion of the pros and cons of their coping style.

### Use of the pros and cons technique

Spend a session really evaluating both sides of the coping mode, considering its adaptive value, both past and present. You can do this using a whiteboard, and can extend this into chair dialogues, offering the client a chair for both sides. This will often lead to a dialogue between the coping mode and the healthy side. For the therapist, it is also important to deeply acknowledge the functionality of the coping mode, so the client may feel safe to explore how the coping mode leads to problems, or blocks your client from getting their needs met. Helping the client stand back and evaluate both sides of the coping mode, how it may work to protect, but ultimately block their needs, tends to trigger a *Healthy Adult* (*HA*) perspective in the session. It is from this position that the client can make an autonomous choice about whether to address the coping mode, and ultimately, engage in the therapy. The goal is to activate and then to 'do a deal' with their *HA* mode. While there is often ambivalence, there is nearly always at least one side of the client wanting flexibility over the coping mode. You will need to get autonomous permission from your client to either reduce, or gain flexibility over the coping mode, or else attempts to bypass the coping may prove unsuccessful, and therapy will likely stagnate (Roediger, Stevens, & Brockman, 2018).

*Labeling the coping mode in session*

Gently point out and label the coping mode. This builds mode awareness, helping the client to identify cues that they are in a particular coping mode. Mindfully noticing that one is in a coping mode is generally incompatible with being in a coping mode, and reinforces more of a *HA* 'observing' stance in the session, at least temporarily. Over time, clients may learn to recognise themselves going into coping positions without prompting, evidence of progress in building their own *HA* mode.

THERAPIST: I'm just noticing we are getting into that analysing thing again… searching for the answer on why this happened to you [*ruminating*]…I wonder if we could focus on how you really felt at that moment [*attunement, focus on emotions*].

## Schema attunement: Building a healthy adult relationship with emotions using the therapy relationship

Schema attunement is potentially the most important intervention strategy the schema therapist has to offer; perhaps even 'the glue of schema therapy' (Roediger et al., 2018). A key skill of any therapist is the ability to listen and empathise. ST strives however to go beyond a standard level of therapeutic skill to provide a much higher level of understanding and attunement, where the therapist is able to communicate to the client the feeling of a deep understanding of the client's 'internal reality'. Erskine (1998) defines attunement as a two-part process that starts with (1) empathy; being sensitive to and identifying with another person's sensations, needs, and/or feelings *and* (2) communicating that understanding to the other person to create the feeling of *resonance*. This has several clear implications within ST for the relational style and skills required of the therapist trying to implement 'Limited Reparenting' strategies. Firstly, the communication of attunement validates the client's needs, feelings, and experiences, laying a foundation for healing the failures of previous interpersonal experiences (Erskine, 1998). Secondly, orientating the client towards their emotional experiencing in this way also lays the groundwork for emotive interventions as it communicates the importance of emotion-focused work, and starts to help the client share, experience, and ultimately tolerate smaller, more manageable amounts of emotional pain. In our experience, problems in the application of emotive techniques can often be traced back to a poor capacity for attunement on behalf of the therapist and/or the client. Therefore, the level of felt attunement between the therapist and client may be a good indicator of readiness for emotion-focused interventions. Finally, attunement aids the therapist's formulation of the specific underlying schemas and needs driving the clinical presentation. Without a high level of attunement, the therapist risks applying limited reparenting and rescripting techniques in a way that does not specifically target or connect with the relevant underlying schemas or needs. As described, a high level of attunement sets so much of the groundwork for ST that it can be thought of as the 'glue' of ST, a necessary skill/condition that relates to and underpins all four broad ST intervention strategies (limited reparenting, experiential, cognitive, behavioural). A focus on emotional attunement is particularly important in ED populations who often struggle to connect to emotions, and who have for some time now been associated with alexithymia (Cochrane, Brewerton, Wilson, & Hodges, 1993). What follows next is an approach to building schema attunement based on a stepped process outlined by Roediger et al. (2018).

## A process-based approach to building schema attunement

### 1. Focus on specific episodes of distress

Spend a good portion of the session focusing on understanding the client's recent emotional experiences or 'triggers'. This will often be aided with homework such as schema or mode monitoring sheets which will provide you with a prompt about a client's recent relevant triggering experiences. For some clients that are extremely avoidant or who withdraw into over-analysing, finding such episodes of distress may be difficult as they may make little contact with everyday life. For these clients, setting some very mild and scaffolded behavioural pattern-breaking tasks (e.g. socialising, eating meals around others) upfront may be necessary in order to produce some emotions to work on in therapy.

We have found it useful to structure ST sessions such that the first 15–20 minutes of the session are spent discussing any recent triggering experiences. This can often be combined with a check in of any homework tasks, which themselves are often felt to be emotionally triggering. Use this first third of the session to try and attune to relevant experiences. It is usually helpful to slow things down during your attempts at attunement and ask for very specific episodes as people who over-analyse tend to speak quickly and relay quite broad narratives that invariably gloss over the emotional content of any triggers (e.g. quickly linking from one episode to the next).

THERAPIST: So Jackie, you are saying that you have been feeling very upset this week, can you tell me about a specific time when you were feeling this way?
JACKIE: Yes on Monday I felt terrible all day.
THERAPIST: Can you tell me about a specific moment you were feeling upset on Monday, Jackie, perhaps when it was most upsetting for you?
JACKIE: When my mother was being her usual self!

THERAPIST: What exactly was it, Jackie, that was upsetting about the way she was treating you?

JACKIE: It was just her being her usual self, …but it was the look she gave me, it was 'that look' again.

THERAPIST: That look…

JACKIE: A look of disapproval…Like I've disappointed her again.


## 2. Tune in to the emotional response

This should be done by enquiring as to the nature of the emotional reaction to the triggering event in terms of emotion labels (e.g. 'I felt sad') and/or related bodily sensations (e.g. 'I felt it in my throat').

THERAPIST: And how did you feel when she gave you this look?

JACKIE: I felt anxious…like pressure.

THERAPIST: and where could you feel this pressure or anxiety building up [*in your body*]?

JACKIE: In my head…like a headache.

THERAPIST: [*summarising the understanding so far, and empathising*]: OK, so let's see if I am understanding this right so far…she was screaming at you and giving you the look, and this led to you feeling intense anxiety and a kind of pressure in your head, like a headache?

JACKIE: Yes.

THERAPIST: That does sound hard [*also communicating empathy with facial gesture*].

JACKIE: Yes.


## 3. Uncover underlying schema/s and needs

In ST, it is important to attune not only to the feelings, but also the under-lying schemas and needs driving the distress. In most cases, episodes of dis-tress can be understood in terms of the activation of specific schema/s and needs. Take an enquiring stance to continue questioning about the meaning of the trigger and feeling for them, using cognitive techniques such as downward arrowing and Socratic questioning.

THERAPIST: OK, and I could easily assume why you were feeling that way, but I'd like to check with you. What did it mean to you that she was giving you the look in that way?

JACKIE: I've disappointed her yet again.

THERAPIST: And what would that mean if you disappoint her?

JACKIE: I am a bad daughter. [*activation of emotions becomes evident*]

THERAPIST: Ah... OK, I think I'm starting to get it. Did it kind of feel like you're 'not good enough' again? [*Therapist checks the emerging understanding.*]

JACKIE: Yes, of course. She always makes me feel that way, especially with the look.

THERAPIST: Does that feeling of 'not good enough'...does it capture all of the pressured feeling or is there something else too? [*Therapist checking to see if there are other schemas at play.*]

JACKIE: No that is it, I'm a disappointment to her; nothing I do is ever good enough!

### 4. Summarise understanding, empathise, and link to historical origins

Tentatively summarise your understanding so far for the client, based on your line of enquiry. Do so, and repeat steps 1–3 as necessary until the client reports a high degree of resonance. Once the client communicates this resonance, offer some empathic statement/s and look for opportunities to link to relevant childhood experiences, making such links explicit.

THERAPIST: OK, so I think I'm starting to get it now, you were hanging out with mum, and like usual, she started picking at you and criticising, but it was 'the look' that really got you feeling anxious, and pressured, and like once again nothing you do is ever 'good enough'. Is that right?

JACKIE: Yes.

THERAPIST: And this makes a lot of sense to me that you would react so strongly, because it's not the first time you have been treated this way. This is kind of like all those other times she would pressure and criticise you growing up, right?

JACKIE: Yes.

THERAPIST: I'm really sorry to hear this Jackie, because I don't think you deserve this from your mother, but at the same time I'm really glad that you shared this with me, I feel like I understand you a lot more, particularly about the relationship between you and mum, and how she has a way of making you feel 'not good enough' so easily.

### 5. Intensify attunement

If necessary, you may ask the client to close their eyes to increase the level of emotional experiencing, including any bodily sensations. This may be necessary in cases where the coping mode is strong, and the level of emotional activation is low. For clients who can easily process and talk about their emotions, or those that become too easily overwhelmed, this may not be necessary.

### 6. Move into experiential techniques

High levels of attunement will on most occasions be very validating and reinforcing for clients, but also represent an opportunity to skilfully bridge into experiential techniques.

THERAPIST: This issue of feeling 'not good enough' seems really important for you at the moment Jackie, I'm wondering if it would be a good use of our time if we focus on this feeling or theme of 'not good enough' for some imagery work?

*Therapist balance matrix.* The matrix in Figure 6.1 represents two important dimensions the schema therapist must be aware of, in order to remain flexible and sensitive to clients' needs from moment-to-moment. One reason that clients become stuck in maladaptive coping is often because they have been overly triggered by negative emotions (e.g. *VCh, Inner Critic (Parent) modes*), and may have started feeling overwhelmed, leading to a strong coping response. This pattern would be represented at the top of the vertical axis. In these cases, careful management of scaffolding emotion focused tasks may be necessary to slowly build efficacy to deal with disturbing emotional content. That is, if the work is pitched 'too high' in terms of the level of emotional activation, you will likely find it more difficult to bypass the coping mode. Conversely, at the bottom of the vertical axis, a strong coping mode such as over-analysing may represent a pre-emptive protective strategy to avoid activation of any negative emotions. In these cases, it could

*Therapist is tasked to balance both axes depending on the client's current needs.

*Figure 6.1* Therapist balance matrix

be that the therapist needs to purposely make the sessions more experiential (e.g. by focusing on imagery techniques).

The horizontal axis serves to keep therapists aware that they will also need to balance connection tasks (e.g. care, guidance) with the tasks of empathic confrontation and setting limits. Just as a good parent will find a balance between these approaches, given the child and situation, so too the schema therapist will need to find the right balance. For clients that are over-analysing, some mild empathic confrontation may be necessary to bypass.

THERAPIST: I know it feels more comfortable to explain all of the detail – it's that Over-analyser mode again, but I think it is important to, just for a moment, focus on how you felt in that situation.

This may open up more opportunity to switch to the connection leg on the left of the horizontal axis and engage in attunement as the client may start opening up on an emotional level. As described above, bypassing maladaptive coping and increasing schema attunement is a fluid, unfolding process. The therapist balance matrix may be a useful tool for schema therapists to keep aware of these two important therapist tasks.

### Behavioural pattern-breaking techniques

While we have focused practically thus far on within session management strategies to 'bypass' the over-analysing behaviour, within ST it is also important to reverse maladaptive patterns of behaviour in real life so as to disrupt schema maintenance. Several behavioural skills and techniques taken from the broader CBT literature appear to be promising here, including, but not limited to, behavioural activation (Jacobson, Martell, & Dimidjian, 2001), mindfulness skills (Linehan, 1993; , Strosahl, & Wilson, 2011), and process focused CBT approaches (Watkins, 2016). Techniques such as these are promising for breaking the pattern of RNT, helping people connect with a healthier style of self-processing more reminiscent of a *HA* (Roediger et al., 2018). Timing the introduction of behavioural pattern-breaking techniques takes some careful consideration. Ordinarily in ST, these techniques should be implemented more at the back end of treatment, once considerable healing has taken place via the cognitive, emotive, and limited reparenting. However, some clients may benefit from some early focus on very small, graded attempts to pattern-break, particularly for those whose avoidant coping is very strong, and emotional engagement very low. For those with strong over-analyser coping, we have similarly noticed that an earlier focus on pattern-breaking is warranted, as they can assist in overcoming some of the problems of over-analysing behaviour earlier in treatment, increasing emotional engagement.

## Conclusion

RNT processes have been conceptualised as a transdiagnostic maintenance factor common to the experience of EDs. Further, these negative processing styles represent a significant threat to ST, which relies heavily on corrective emotional experiences for treatment effects. Treating RNT as representing 'over-analysing' coping mode activity represents a promising approach to formulating and managing these difficult clinical phenomena within a ST approach.

## References

Arntz, A., Bernstein, D., & Jacob, G. (2012). *Schema Therapy in Practice: An Introductory Guide to the Schema Mode Approach*. John Wiley & Sons.

Borkovec, T. D., Alcaine, O., & Behar, E. (2004). Avoidance theory of worry and generalized anxiety disorder. *Generalized Anxiety Disorder: Advances in Research and Practice, 2004*. New York: Guilford.

Borkovec, T. D., & Ruscio, A. M. (2001). Psychotherapy for generalised anxiety disorder. *Journal of Clinical Psychiatry*, 62, 37–42.

Cochrane, C. E., Brewerton, T. D., Wilson, D. B., & Hodges, E. L. (1993). Alexithymia in the eating disorders. *International Journal of Eating Disorders*, 14(2), 219–222.

Ehring, T., & Watkins, E. R. (2008). Repetitive negative thinking as a transdiagnostic process. *International Journal of Cognitive Therapy*, 1(3), 192–205.

Erskine, R. G. (1998). Attunement and involvement: Therapeutic responses to relational needs. *International Journal of Psychotherapy*, 3(3), 235.

Foa, E. B., & Kozak, M. J. (1986). Emotional processing of fear: Exposure to corrective information. *Psychological Bulletin*, 99(1), 20–35.

Fairburn, C. (2008). *Cognitive Behavior Therapy and Eating Disorders*. New York: Guilford.

Farrell, J. M., & Shaw, I. A. (2017). *Experiencing Schema Therapy from the Inside Out: A Self-Practice/Self-Reflection Workbook for Therapists*. New York: Guilford.

Hayes, S. C., Strosahl, K. D., & Wilson, K. G. (2011). *Acceptance and Commitment Therapy: The Process and Practice of Mindful Change*. New York: Guilford.

Jacobson, N. S., Martell, C. R., & Dimidjian, S. (2001). Behavioral activation treatment for depression: Returning to contextual roots. *Clinical Psychology: Science and Practice*, 8(3), 255–270.

Jacob, G. A., & Arntz, A. (2012). Emotion-focused techniques in schema therapy and the role of exposure techniques. In P. Neudeck & H. Wittchen (Eds.). *Exposure Therapy* (pp.167–181). New York: Springer.

Linehan, M. (1993). *Cognitive-Behavioral Treatment of Borderline Personality Disorder*. New York: Guilford.

Moulds, M. L., Kandris, E., Starr, S., & Wong, A.C. (2007). The relationship between rumination, avoidance and depression in a non-clinical sample. *Behaviour Research Therapy*, 45(2), 251–261. doi:10.1016/j.brat.2006.03.003

McEvoy, P. M., Moulds, M., & Mahony, A. E. J. (2013). Are worry, rumination, and post event processing one and the same? Development of the repetitive thinking questionnaire. *Journal of Anxiety Disorders*, 24, 509–519. doi:10.1016/j.janxdis.2010.03.008

Nolen-Hoeksema, S., & Watkins, E. R. (2011). A heuristic for developing transdiagnostic models of psychopathology: Explaining multifinality and divergent trajectories. *Perspectives on Psychological Science, 6*, 589–609. doi:10.1177/1745691611419672

Nolen-Hoeksema, S., Wisco, B. E., & Lyubomirsky, S. (2008). Rethinking rumination. *Perspectives on Psychological Science*, 3(5), 400–424.

Papageorgiou, C., & Wells, A. (Eds.). (2004). *Depressive Rumination: Nature, Theory and Treatment*. John Wiley & Sons.

Rawal, A., Park, R. J., & Williams, J. M. G. (2010). Rumination, experiential avoidance, and dysfunctional thinking in eating disorders. *Behaviour Research and Therapy*, 48(9), 851–859.

Roediger, E., Stevens, B., & Brockman, R. (2018). *Contextual Schema Therapy: An Integrative Approach to Personality Disorders, Emotional Dysregulation, and Interpersonal Functioning*. New Harbinger.

Sassaroli, S., Bertelli, S., Decoppi, M., Crosina, M., Milos, G., & Ruggiero, G. M. (2005). Worry and eating disorders: A psychopathological association. *Eating Behaviors*, 6(4), 301–307.

Shearer, S. L., & Tucker, D. M. (1981). Differential cognitive contributions of the cerebral hemispheres in the modulation of emotional arousal. *Cognitive Therapy and Research*, 5(1), 85–93.

Smith, K. E., Mason, T. B., & Lavender, J. M. (2018). Rumination and eating disorder psychopathology: A meta-analysis. *Clinical Psychology Review*. doi:10.1016/j.cpr.2018.03.004

Spinhoven, P., Penelo, E., de Rooij, M., Penninx, B. W., & Ormel, J. (2014). Reciprocal effects of stable and temporary components of neuroticism and affective disorders: Results of a longitudinal cohort study. *Psychological Medicine*, 44, 337–348. doi:10.1017/S0033291713000822

Startup, H., Lavender, A., Oldershaw, A., Stott, R., Tchanturia, K., Treasure, J., & Schmidt, U. (2013). Worry and rumination in anorexia nervosa. *Behavioural and Cognitive Psychotherapy*, 41(3), 301–316.

Stavropoulos, A., Haire, M., Brockman, R., & Meade, T. (in preparation). *Examining a Schema Mode Model of Pathological Worry, Rumination, and Repetitive Negative Thinking*.

Waller, G., Ohanian, V., Meyer, C., & Osman, S. (2000). Cognitive content among bulimic women: The role of core beliefs. *International Journal of Eating Disorders*, 28(2), 235–241.

Waller, G. (2003). Schema-level cognitions in patients with binge eating disorder: A case control study. *International Journal of Eating Disorders*, 33(4), 458–464.

Watkins, E. R. (2008). Constructive and unconstructive repetitive thought. *Psychological Bulletin*, 134(2), 163–206. doi:10.1037/0033–2909.134.2.163

Watkins, E. R. (2016). *Rumination-Focused Cognitive-Behavioral Therapy for Depression*. New York: Guilford.

Watkins, E., & Moulds, M. (2005). Distinct modes of ruminative self-focus: impact of abstract versus concrete rumination on problem solving in depression. *Emotion*, 5(3), 319–328. doi:10.1037/1528–3542.5.3.319

Watkins, E., & Teasdale, J. D. (2004). Adaptive and maladaptive self-focus in depression. *Journal of Affective Disorders*, 82(1), 1–8. doi:10.1016/j.jad.2003.10.006

Young, J. R., Klosko, M. E., & Weishaar, M. E. (2003). *Schema Therapy: A Practitioner's Guide*. New York: Guilford.

# Chapter 7

# Experiential mode work with eating disorders

*Susan Simpson*

## Abstract

*The schema therapy (ST) model aims to bring about transformational change through working in four main areas: cognitive, behavioural, experiential and interpersonal. Experiential techniques 'fire up' the cognitive work, transcending intellectual change and penetrating early maladaptive schemas (EMS) that are held at a deeply embodied level. The experiential techniques employed in ST are potent mechanisms for reducing entrenched shame and cultivating self-compassion in eating disorders (EDs). It is only by establishing significant shifts in deeply held EMS, that behavioural changes can be established without risk of relapse. A range of experiential techniques are described in this chapter, which can be adapted, depending on the primary coping modes being manifested.*

One of the main objectives in ST is to help participants to recognise and distinguish their different 'sides' or modes, with the aim of differentiating and gradually integrating them into a coherent sense of self. Many clients with EDs are 'fused' within a particular coping mode (e.g. *Detached Protector (DetPr)*, *Overcontroller (OC)*) that they identify as 'self'. Whilst acknowledging the functional value of coping mechanisms as a means of dealing with developmental disruptions, the therapist's primary task is to bypass these in order to access underlying painful feelings and emotional needs. The *Vulnerable Child (VCh)* side is often hidden behind guarded and resistive coping modes, which we must find ways of bypassing. It is only once we have reached the *VCh* that we can introduce therapeutic healing work.

The behavioural eating responses associated with coping modes are largely resistant to change unless the underlying EMS are also addressed. We do this in ST firstly by helping clients to recognise and gradually accept the existence of the *VCh* – the side of themselves that has suffered as a result of unmet needs during childhood. EDs partly operate through mechanisms that result in a 'shut-down' of physiological [and emotional] needs. Although a significant component of behavioural work takes place once the underlying EMS have been at least partially healed, there is usually a need to explicitly work on reducing behaviours (e.g. restriction or bingeing that poses a severe risk to the client) through empathic confrontation in the early phases of therapy, in order to create a therapeutic space which is sufficiently safe to facilitate further schema healing work. By placing emphasis on adequate nutrition and stabilisation of weight, we are giving clients the strong message that their safety and wellbeing are essential. The focus of this chapter is an exploration of experiential techniques with the ED population, with an emphasis on techniques that are not covered in detail by other chapters and schema resources.

## Experiential work with reluctant or ambivalent clients

Many clients with EDs who present for treatment do not feel ready to talk about their eating, nor to explore family relationships or childhood difficulties. They have often learned to avoid feelings of vulnerability, which are equated with being "weak" [an internalised message from *Inner Critic*]. Therapeutic techniques that are directly aimed at accessing and working with vulnerability tend to be in direct conflict with over-compensatory or avoidant coping modes, and may be experienced as shameful, guilt inducing and confronting. It is therefore important to spend time at the beginning of therapy building a relationship based on 'being with' the client through attunement to their experience, rather than making assumptions or rushing in to apply techniques. Bypassing the coping modes is essential to facilitate true attunement. Gradually, as a genuine relationship develops, more difficult topics can be raised, linked to family dynamics, culture and EMS. Clients with a very strong *Inner Critic* mode (associated with *mistrust/abuse, defectiveness/shame and emotional deprivation* EMS) often feel threatened by or suspicious of signs of nurturance, reassurance or empathy from others (Gilbert, 2009). Therapists therefore need to be completely transparent, to take the time to explain the rationale for techniques, and introduce reparenting in a gradual way. The ultimate goal is to motivate the client to build a range of healthy healing relationships that will enable them to get their emotional needs met.

Often at the beginning of therapy, the *Inner Critic* is highly ego syntonic and therefore preliminary work is focused on noticing and tracking this mode moment-by-moment in order to begin to conceptualise it as a separate 'part' that has been learned or internalised – in order to confront it. In contrast, the *OC*, which has a coping function, is better dealt with through negotiation rather than direct confrontation.

The *Overcontroller* (*OC*) functions as the default mode for many people with EDs, leaving them in a tightly controlled, emotionally constricted state that is completely disconnected from emotional needs and vulnerability. It is important to recognise the *OC* in its various manifestations, as it appears both during and between therapy sessions.

In session, the *OC* commonly intellectualises, gives too much detail, brings lists to demonstrate how hard they have been working. This mode is productivity and achievement focused. It can be perfectionistic and impatient about recovery, with an all-or-nothing focus on self-improvement, as a series of 'tasks' to be performed ("it needs to be sorted out now!").

## Chairwork and imagery rescripting (IR) to bypass coping modes

Chairwork and IR are essential techniques for circumventing the coping modes, in order to gain access to the *VCh* for reparenting work. As with other coping modes, the *OC can be interviewed on a separate chair* and questioned about the protective role it played during childhood. The *OC* may have provided a range of primary and secondary functions, including: a sense of achievement and approval, a sense of control within an unpredictable family environment, and the promise of tangible happiness and self-worth once all rules have been followed. This exercise leads easily into the cognitive *Pros and Cons* exercise (see Appendix 1). The key here is to consider the ED as only one component of the *OC* coping mode, which incorporates a wide range of ruminative and compulsive behaviours, and thought processes. By considering the consequences of the whole array of excessive behaviours driven by the *OC* (such as obsessional rumination, checking, rituals, work, study, cleaning) as well as the aspects of life that it forbids (e.g. friendships, relaxation, fun, connection), the client is helped to take a 'meta' perspective of their difficulties, thereby bypassing any potential 'battle' over the actual ED. By taking the emphasis away from the ED and focusing on the coping mode and all of its idiosyncrasies, the client can begin to recognise their ED behaviours as just one of several manifestations of this mode. Clients can also be asked to *draw a picture of the OC*, which depicts the messages it conveys, its purpose in life, its 'tone' and the feelings it elicits in the body. Importantly, this also begins the process of defusing this mode, and highlighting its role in relation to other aspects of the self. Interviewing this mode can then lead on to *negotiating with the OC mode* in order to reparent the child mode.

Chairwork with coping modes prior to imagery rescripting can help to clarify the role that avoidant or overcompensatory modes play in trying to protect the client, whilst also highlighting their role in sabotaging therapy and preventing the person from getting their needs met, both within and outwith therapy. When clients are reluctant to participate in chairwork, the therapist may need to begin by acting out all of the modes until the client feels more comfortable to join in. However, most clients can at the very least manage to play or provide the words for the *Inner Critic* mode. Below is an example of bypassing the *OC* mode in order to facilitate imagery work.

## Empathic confrontation to bypass the OC

THERAPIST: Mia, I think it would be helpful for you if we introduced some imagery work. This is a way in which I can reach little Mia more easily and start to meet her needs. It is a way of giving you a different experience and providing a healing antidote for difficult experiences from the past.

MIA: [*in OC mode*]: I don't understand why would I want to do that? I have a list of things I have made that I want to talk about today. That is most important for me. I don't see how imagery is going to help me.

THERAPIST: I understand that it might seem a strange idea that imagery could influence the way you feel, but you have told me that you struggle a lot between sessions, and I think it is important for the work that we do together to be helpful in an enduring way, to help you during sessions and also between sessions when I am not present with you.

MIA: I just want to talk about the things on my list. I've got a lot of things to cover. I just want to get on with it.

THERAPIST: I respect that you feel that way, but I wonder, could it be that the side of you that copes by trying to take control is here...and is a little afraid of difficult feelings and imagery? It makes sense that you cope that way...you learned as a little child when you felt overwhelmed that it helped to take control over the situation and people around you.

MIA: I don't know...[*sounds frustrated*]

THERAPIST: I wonder if we could put that side on the chair so we can get to know it a bit better?

MIA: Can't we just get on with the therapy? I just need answers to my questions.

THERAPIST: Ok, how about I play the part of the *OC*. [*Therapist moves to* OC *chair.*] "I don't want to let Mia do the imagery or any other things that you suggest. I don't 'do' feelings. I just want you to pay attention to her lists and answer all of her questions." [*to Mia*] "Have I got that right?"

THERAPIST: [*moves back to own chair and replies to* OC]: I understand and respect that, and I would like to answer your questions. However, I also notice that we have had several sessions that have now been taken up with talking about details rather than getting in touch with little Mia's feelings. Although I understand that you want to focus on the list, I would also like to ask that you allow me to have some control over our sessions. I know that you are focused on staying away from feelings right now, but it would be negligent of me as your therapist to ignore little Mia's needs. I feel for little Mia who is feeling so desperate and lonely most of the time. Therefore, I would ask that you trust me a little, and give me some space to do some imagery with little Mia in our sessions, so that she can start to feel better not just in the short term, but also start to get what she needs to feel better overall. Would that be okay? Mia, what is that side saying back...

The therapist must strike a balance between respectfully empathising with the perspective of the coping mode, whilst firmly reminding them that there is another [vulnerable] side that needs connection and support. It is easy for sessions with the *OC* mode to become locked into debate, overanalysing, and working through endless lists. The task of the therapist is to notice when this mode is present, and to give it a limited period of air-time, with the explicit intention of then moving beyond this to reach the underlying vulnerability.

### Multi-modal chairwork

Chairwork can include multiple modes as they are identified within sessions. It is not uncommon for clients to 'flip' between modes. The therapist therefore needs to remain alert and to bring in another chair to represent the new mode at relevant junctures. In this way, clients learn to recognise their own modes as they transition between them, as well as how to deal with these modes in a healthy way that facilitates meeting the needs of the *VCh* mode.

When we reach the *VCh* underneath the *OC* (or other coping) mode, the goal is to normalise and validate their needs. Essentially, this includes physical needs (such as hunger, rest, relaxation, breathing, sleep) as well as emotional needs (connection, warm, attunement). The *Inner Critic* takes the view that needs are shameful and a burden on others. It can often mask the critical message within a 'friendly' façade (e.g. "Toughen up, sunshine!"). The *Inner Critic* makes the client feel that they are undeserving and not worthy of receiving emotional or physical nourishment. The *OC* takes on the role of 'actioning' this message, by 'fixing' the client through restriction, asceticism and self-denial in order to vanquish all needs.

As therapists, we need to challenge the messages of the *Inner Critic*, disengage the restrictive stranglehold of the *OC*, and enable the *VCh* to begin practicing '*receiving*'. This can be done through actively and purposefully setting up a practice of *receiving* various types of nourishment: breath (i.e. practicing deep breathing, mindful breathing), food, rest, sleep, fun, pleasure. In addition, the *OC* can be given constructive homework 'tasks', such as experimenting with shifting the focus from internal to external bodily experience through 'curious awareness', by spending time in nature, and learning to nurture themselves. Although psychoeducation and socratic questioning may facilitate shifting these ideas at a cognitive level, chairwork, imagery rescripting and behavioural experiments will enable a deeper-level shift. An example of multi-modal chairwork with a client with BN is provided below.

THERAPIST: I would like us to do some chairwork to try to explore this dynamic between the different modes that are leading to binge eating. Would that be okay? First of all, I would like you to move to the chair of the *Overcontroller* to voice what that side has been telling you this week?

KARA: [as Overcontroller (OC)]: You need to get on top of everything, to get everything under control. You just need to do a better job of counting the calories, and measuring the food out – that will make you feel better. You won't achieve anything until you record properly, eat better, do more exercise. You need discipline. There's no point in having fun – you need to be productive!...You're such a loser. You always overindulge. You are greedy.

THERAPIST: It sounds like you are switching to the Critical side. Can you voice that side from the chair next to the *Overcontroller*? [*Kara moves to* Inner Critic *chair*].

KARA: [as Inner Critic]: You're such a loser...a pig. You'll never get this under control, who are you kidding? You're doomed. You're pathetic, fatter than ever, revolting.

THERAPIST: Now can you move to Little Kara's chair and voice what she feels?

KARA: [as *Little Kara*]: I feel sad, hopeless. What's the point?

THERAPIST: What do you feel like doing just now? What would you do if you were at home and feeling like this?

KARA: I feel like I need a caramel sundae.

THERAPIST: I wonder, could this be your *Detached Self-Soother* mode...can you move to that chair and express the message of that mode?

KARA: [as Detached Self-Soother (DetSS)]: Kara deserves some fun in her life. Life is hard. She works so hard. She needs to relax. So many things are not going well. This is the only chance she gets to enjoy herself. Surely, she deserves that!

THERAPIST: ...now I would like you to stand on the *Wise Healthy Adult* spot, and together we can talk to the other modes. Firstly, I want you to look at the picture you drew of your *Wise* mode, and try to embody that part of yourself. Really be the *Wise* side from the inside out. Notice how your posture changes as you do that. Can you stand even taller? How about your facial expression? How does your body feel in *Wise* mode? Remember that Little Kara is only small and her feet don't touch the ground. What can you say to the different parts to try to protect and take care of her?

KARA: [as Wise side/Healthy Adult (HA) *(therapist coaching)*]: *To* Inner Critic [*looking down over the* Critic, *with strong voice*] – It's never okay to put others down. You are the problem here! You just need to stay in the past where you belong. She's done nothing wrong, but you keep bullying her without reason. Stop it now!

*To* OC – I know you think you are protecting Kara, but you are controlling her too much. She needs warmth and gentle guidance, not control. Your lists and planning give her no time to exist as a human, to just 'be' or connect with others. This isn't good for her...it's making her feel suffocated and isolated. If you weren't pushing her so hard, she wouldn't need to rely on bingeing to find some space and freedom.

She doesn't need to be productive all the time to be lovable and worthwhile – she is lovable just as she is. You've been around a long time, but she is still unhappy and lonely. You don't define her. I see you squashing her true qualities. I know you are trying to give her certainty, but it's false – it blocks her from opportunities to have the life she really wants, to develop her potential. It's the way you make it – not the way it is. Even though I understand you have helped in the past, if you really care, you need to let go a bit and give her some space to allow her to grow and be at ease.

*To* DetSS – I'm glad that you are trying to give little Kara some pleasure and she does deserve to have fun and to be healthy and happy. But bingeing is not the best way to give her what she needs, it's a poor substitute…You only work in the moment, but you don't see how your behaviour affects Kara in the long-term. By getting her to overeat, she misses out on other pleasures. She doesn't get the chance to connect to others or to enjoy all of the different aspects of her life. You put her health at risk and make her feel guilty and unhappy. You take away her energy. You make her feel heavy and lethargic. You don't give her the chance to really taste food. She needs the chance to enjoy herself and to have treats without you taking it too far. I can help her to learn other skills for managing sadness, anxiety, stress and to manage the urges. You need to pull back so that little Kara can get what she really needs…to be nurtured, encouraged and accepted. She deserves a better life. You're holding her back from that. *Kara returns to VCh chair.*

THERAPIST: [*to little Kara*]: How are you feeling? Can you tell these sides what you really need? Is it to be controlled, to be 'fobbed off' with food or is it something else?

LITTLE KARA: What I really need is…to be with people. To be close. To not be so alone.

THERAPIST: It won't always be like this. I know the feelings are painful, but I really want to hear about how you feel and what you need. You're not bad. You're not worthless. It's sad that you're scared. You deserve to feel excited for all the good things ahead. These modes don't offer the kind of friendship that you need anymore. Everyone needs connection and closeness and that is normal. And your body deserves to be taken care of and not put in danger. There will be ups and downs ahead, and sometimes it will be hard. I am here for you, I want to understand how you really feel. You don't have to do this alone.

### Chairwork variations to address common issues

*Client is unable to access their VCh feelings and needs and/or is unable to recognise the ongoing negative impact of their coping mode*

- Therapist plays the role of the *VCh*: in this variation, the therapist plays the role of the client's *VCh* mode, expressing underlying sadness/loneliness, and expressing authentic emotional needs. The client responds in the role of the coping mode (e.g. *DetSS or OC*). The therapist persists in the role of the *VCh*, explaining how the coping mode makes her feel, and repeats patterns from earlier in life through isolating and controlling her, and reiterates what she really needs (in the current situation and in general). This exercise can help the client to begin to connect with the presence of their *VCh*, and the suffering and unmet needs underlying their coping modes.

*Client has intellectual insight into the OC mode but remains emotionally attached to it*

- 'Devil's Advocate Chairwork' can be used to spark irritation at the excessive demands of coping (and/or parent) modes. In this variation, there are three chairs (*Healthy Adult (HA), VCh*, and *OC*). A photograph or drawing of the client as a baby or toddler is placed on the *VCh* chair. Ideally, it should be a picture that the client identifies with, and does not intensely dislike. In addition, baby pictures of one or more of their friends and the therapist (or all participants, in the case of group work), are placed on the *VCh* chair. Additionally, they could add a photograph or drawing of their own children, nieces, nephews from the present or future. The client sits on the *HA* chair. The therapist moves to the *OC* chair and expresses the sentiments of the mode in a slightly provocative manner. The wording should be adapted to the particular client – based on their own *OC* and its particular 'flavour', eating disorder urges, as well as compulsions linked to comorbidities (e.g. obsessive-compulsive rituals). The client is then asked to respond to the *OC*, and then the *VCh* from their *HA* side, drawing on what a good parent would say in that situation if an authority figure said these things to a young child. The therapist can kneel next to the *HA* chair and coach the client to get in touch with feelings of irritability, and to express these. The idea is not to eliminate the *OC* mode, but rather to appreciate that although it is trying to help and protect, it has become a source of further pain. The client (as *HA*) is then encouraged to offer the child a loving, balanced alternative to the *OC*.

An example is provided below with a client with AN.

### Devil's Advocate chairwork with OC mode

THERAPIST: [*as* Overcontroller (OC)]: Man up, baby, you need to toughen
up. It's time to get some runs on the board. I've got some plans for
you that will make you feel much better about yourself, but you have
to follow the rules. First, I want you to cut back on your milk. No
snacks, they are bad for you. I'll give you some low-fat snacks at the
end of the day if you follow the rules. But first I need to see more
productivity. You need to clean all morning, then study the alphabet
all afternoon. You need to go for a long run. All this sitting around
needs to be corrected. These are the rules...although I'll change them
as I go along, just to keep you on your toes. Forget your friends and
family – you don't need people – rules are much more reliable. My
rules will make you happy. You will be completely prepared for
everything. Fun is over-rated. So is spontaneity. You'll be safe and
much better off with me.

THERAPIST PROMPTS: What does the child side feel when the *OC* is so strong?
Is it helping the child part to feel less lonely? To be happier and more
fulfilled? To be less anxious? What does she really need? Can you move
over to the *VCh* chair and tell the *OC* mode?

ROS: [*as* Vulnerable Child (VCh)]: I feel guilty, and stressed, like I can never
get it right. What I need is...love, people, rest, to be able to be myself,
have fun and be happy without feeling guilty.

THERAPIST: So, although the *OC* is trying hard to help, it actually makes you
more stressed, tired and anxious, and more cut-off from your relationships with other people? [*Therapist invites Ros to move to* Healthy Adult
(HA) *chair, and kneels just behind in coaching role.*]

THERAPIST: Let's bring in the healthy side – this is the side of you that wants
to genuinely care for all of you and is compassionate, warm and gentle,
but is also strong, powerful and authentic...what would she say to the
*OC* mode, knowing all that you now know? What could we say to the
*OC*, acknowledging that it's working so hard to help you and doesn't
seem to realise it's taking you around in circles?

ROS: [*as* HA *to* OC *empty chair*]: You've been a good friend, but this is
too much, too controlling...she needs to exist, to laugh, to play. You
are pressuring her too much. She is allowed to relax, to rest, to just
be. You don't need to 'fix' her, she is already lovable as she is. You
started out with good intentions, but she has become a slave to you.
She deserves real happiness, not moving goal posts. Your rules have
shrunk her time, her fun, and her soul, and alienated others from
her. Emotional relationships are what should sustain her – they've all
but gone and all you have left her with is the anorexia-playing-field.
You are so awesome and strong and powerful...why don't we work

together to help her find true happiness in a way that isn't harmful? [*Therapist invites Ros to return to* VCh *chair*].

THERAPIST: [*as* HA]: I can see that you are very alone and that you developed this protector side because you were so afraid to show your feelings. But I am here to help you so you don't have to be in that mode all the time...so you don't have to be lonely and scared. This part of you needs connection and love. It isn't weak. But you learned that if you showed your feelings, others would dismiss or ignore them...you learned it wasn't safe to share your feelings, and that made you feel ashamed and lonely. But you can learn to share your feelings now with me and other people. It might feel scary and it will take time. You have started the journey. You can learn to express your feelings. I feel more connected with this side of you... this is the part I want to spend more time with, and I know that others will too. It's hard for people to relax and just be with you when the OC is there, blocking your soft side and your warmth. I can see in this chair that you are a good person who deserves to be nurtured and loved. I'm here to help you learn to connect and stay with the vulnerability. I know it's hard to trust, but I care about this side of you. I'm here with you. Even the darkest most difficult times will pass and there will be joy and happiness awaiting you. What is it like when I say these things to you?

ROS: [*as* VCh]: ...it feels nice, but also strange...scary.

THERAPIST: I wonder how this relates to your life outside?...

In many cases, the OC mode switches between driving the dietary restriction to trying to take control over the recovery process. It can do this in a very convincing and seemingly logical way. However, under the direction of the OC, the recovery process becomes almost exclusively thought-focused, with an emphasis on finding a quick 'fix', that is efficient, 'perfect', and 'pure' (i.e. based on what it perceives to be 'pure' food e.g. protein, vegan etc.). This can involve diversion into other areas (e.g. orthorexia, anorexia-athletica, workaholism) without any real change at an experiential level. The OC is easily mistaken for the HA mode, as it is convincingly logical, rational and efficient. It is essential to recognise and challenge this mode using empathic confrontation and/or chairwork. It is not just the ED that we are trying to address here, but the entire 'misplaced' doctrine represented by the OC mode.

## Imagery rescripting

Imagery rescripting (IR) is most commonly used to counteract the messages associated with core EMS. This is also an opportunity to cultivate the client's *HA* and to nurture and carry out healing work with the *VCh*.

IR consists of three main phases: (1) client recollects a childhood memory linked to their EMS and describes this as if they are reliving it, from the child's perspective in first person, present tense. When recalling trauma events, the image is frozen just before the event occurs in order to ensure sufficient, but not excessive affect is activated; (2) the therapist or client's *HA* self enters the image and rescripts to set limits on the antagonist until they 'win' the exchange, then soothes the child; (3) the client experiences the processing again, but this time from the child's perspective, receiving the corrective emotional messages and noticing how it feels to get their needs met (Arntz & Weertman, 1999). Following the IR session, time is spent debriefing, reflecting on how these needs can be met in their current life circumstances. Variations are introduced in accordance with clients' emotional needs and their capacity to take on the role of a compassionate *HA* in IR. Most clients require the therapist to take on the *HA* role in the initial stages of therapy, until they have begun to develop their own *HA* self. Safe place imagery (see Chapter 10 for example script) can also be used as a means of self-regulating in the context of dealing with severe trauma images, to 'book-end' the start and end of IR. The goal is to access early memories connected to core caregivers, and to elicit emotion linked to their EMS (Young, Klosko, & Weishaar, 2003).

IR is used to identify the aetiological factors that contributed to the ED through unmet needs during childhood. The ED develops either as a direct result of the injury (e.g. a person may develop a *defectiveness* EMS and restrict their dietary intake as a result of feeling undeserving or unworthy), or as a form of overcompensation for the underlying EMS (e.g. a person with a *failure* EMS restricts in order to gain a sense of achievement and mastery through their compensatory *unrelenting standards*). Target images for IR can be accessed either by (1) starting with a recent upsetting situation and then using an 'affect-bridge' to connect with a childhood memory linked to the same EMS and feeling-state (e.g. asking the client to close their eyes and allow a memory to come up of the first time they felt like this); or (2) asking the client to directly focus on a specific childhood trauma situation, or by allowing their mind to drift back to an early upsetting memory. Current triggers may include situations such as looking in the mirror, trying on clothes, being weighed, eating carbohydrates or fats, or situations that are directly linked to past experiences (e.g. when food was offered before or after abuse or conflict, food then activates the *defectiveness* and *mistrust* EMS linked to the early experience). IR can help to 'untangle' the origins of the ED and associated EMS, enabling the person to recognise that their ED is linked to early attachment injury. By learning that their ED developed as a result of something that happened to them that shouldn't have happened (or didn't happen that should have happened, such as attunement, nurturance), the person can recognise that their ED behaviour is a form of re-enactment of the original injury. This process begins to defuse the EMS and associated ED behaviours, making them more egodystonic at a cognitive and experiential level. An example of IR is described below with a client who was repeatedly made to feel that she was greedy for eating outside strict mealtimes, and learned to distrust her body signals of hunger/satiety.

### Rescripting childhood image

MIA: [*describes childhood memory in present tense*]: I'm at home after school, watching TV with my brother, eating a chocolate from the sweetie drawer.

THERAPIST: What happens next?

MIA: Dad comes in and says "I hope you haven't ruined your dinner. You shouldn't be eating all of that chocolate! You should be eating fruit, not sweet things." He looks disappointed in me, annoyed.

THERAPIST: What are you thinking/feeling?

MIA: I'm in trouble. I'm ashamed. I'm too greedy. I've eaten too much.

THERAPIST: What do you need?

MIA: I need permission to eat.

THERAPIST: Can you freeze the picture while I come into the image with you? [*client nods*]. I want you to stand over here behind me...does that feel okay? [*nods again*]. [*Therapist addresses dad*]: Dad, I know that you want the best for your kids, but this is too strict. It is normal to be hungry after school and to want to eat sweet foods. She is not overindulging, what she is eating is normal. It's good for children to have a balance of sweet and healthier foods. She gets a good balance of foods in her diet. Can you try to let it go and lighten up a bit? [*To Mia*]: What is he saying back?

MIA: He is saying that he just wants us to be healthy.

THERAPIST: I am going to reply to dad now: "It's great that you want to take such good care of Mia and her brother. But I want you to trust her instincts more. Children need to learn what feels right for them and their bodies. Sometimes they need more sweet foods to keep up with all the energy they use at school. You have a clever daughter. You can trust her to make the choices that are right for her. She is hungry now, and it's healthy to allow her to her eat." [*To Mia*]: What is he saying now?

MIA: He's gone quiet. I feel a bit guilty about you saying that to him.

THERAPIST: [*to Mia*]: I understand, you are so good at trying to take care of your family, and you are such a sweet girl for caring about dad's feelings. But sometimes grown-ups need someone to remind them of what is healthy. You are not greedy at all, and it's normal to want to eat sweet things. Most children love sweet foods. You are not eating too much and you don't have to justify what you are eating in any way. Just listen to your body and you will know when you have had enough. Your feelings are important. Is there anything you need from me to help with those feelings?

MIA: I need a hug.

THERAPIST: Can you feel the hug I am giving to 'little you'?

MIA: ... that feels good.

THERAPIST: I want you to know that you can return to this image and these physical sensations whenever you need them during the week. Whenever little Mia needs to remember that she can trust her body and her hunger...and that she is allowed to eat.

### Imagery rescripting variations to address common issues

*Client is 'stuck' in the paradox of feeling both love and anger toward caregivers.*

- The therapist can invite both the client's *VCh* and the client's parent's *VCh* (e.g. little dad) into the image. Following this, the therapist (and client's *HA*) can rescript the image as usual, through protecting and reparenting both children, whilst setting limits on the adult parent in the image. In order to implement this variation, the therapist needs to find out the details of the parent's own childhood and unmet needs. This can then allow the therapist to confront the adult with the fact that they are neglecting/hurting both their own inner child and their [biological] child. This enables the client to see that, although their parent's inner child is essentially good, the parent's coping modes were responsible for the client's unmet needs and schema messages.

*Client has experienced absent, overly anxious or emotionally neglectful parenting, with childhood memories focused around spending long periods alone, or unable to access the guidance, warmth, attunement and empathy that every child needs.*

- The target for IR is to remind the parent/carer of the emotional needs of all children, and in particular their own child. The therapist can enter the image as the 'therapist from the future', travelling back in time, to inform the parent that if they don't emotionally and physically nourish the child, this will lead to the child learning to neglect themselves. The goal is for the therapist (and eventually the client's *HA*) to fill the void created by the parenting gap by providing nourishment, warmth, encouragement and closeness through imagery.

*Client has developed a strong OC mode to compensate for emotionally deficient parenting (emotional deprivation/abandonment).*

- An important target for IR is to focus on the moment of vulnerability linked to the emergence (or 'splitting off') of the *OC* mode during childhood. The client can either spontaneously allow this memory to emerge during imagery (e.g. via an affect bridge from a recent memory linked to their eating difficulties), or access this through consciously recalling the events surrounding the time that this mode first took hold of their life. Focusing the imagery on this will help to identify the core pain of the child, alongside the unmet need that the *OC* was created to fulfil (e.g. to protect against danger, to 'earn' respect or love, to 'whip them into shape' in order to reduce the risk of shame or attack, or to numb the pain associated with inevitable criticism, and so on). Either the therapist or client's *HA* rescripts by taking control and meeting the child's needs, whilst conveying corrective messages to the *OC* mode (i.e. the child does not need to be 'fixed'). The positive intention of the *OC* is acknowledged, whilst asserting that it is too forceful and strict. It can be helpful either before or during imagery to slow the process down in order to gain a clear image of the *OC* mode. (What does it look like? Where does it stand? What is its expression? Tone and vibration of its voice? Main messages? How does it think it is helping?) Asking the client to draw the *OC* beforehand can also help them to get a clear image of this mode. This method can be particularly useful for exploring the 'parental substitute' role of the *OC* in the context of emotionally absent families, but also can be incorporated as an adjunct in the context of rescripting memories which include actual demanding or punitive parent figures, whereby the *OC* has appeared to provide 'protective solutions'.

*Client has diminished capacity to protect their needs and/or set limits on schema driven messages.*

- The client's irritation can be stimulated to set limits on *OC* messages, by having the therapist play the part of the *VCh* who has internalised the *OC*'s messages, e.g. "My needs are wrong. I shouldn't ever get hungry. I'm wrong to want to play. I should sit and work all the time." The client is then encouraged to counter this from her healthy side with corrective emotional messages for the child, giving her permission to have needs and be nourished (connection, love, space, fun, joy, spontaneity etc.), e.g. "What kind of message is that for a child?...All children deserve to be loved, to relax, to have fun!"

*Client has difficulty resisting powerful habitual ED coping patterns in the here-and-now.*

- IR to confront the *OC* can also focus on current and future situations where the *OC* is frequently triggered (e.g. looking in the mirror, standing on the scales, eating a meal). Rescripting follows a similar format to memory-based imagery work, but the future orientation (flash-forward IR) allows them the possibility of rehearsing a scenario whereby their *HA* takes over the reins and meets the needs of the *VCh* in the present. This can also be useful as a means of 'untangling' the various mode messages that tend to be overwhelming in the context of their usual trigger situations. For example, the person may see themselves in the mirror, with the *OC* on one side, and their *HA* on the other. They are asked to listen to both sides, and not be dominated by the *OC* side even though it is louder. They are then invited to choose which mode to 'step into', and to manage from that perspective.

*Clients feels disconnected from emotions/vulnerability contained in the body.*

- To further the process of facilitating embodiment of the *VCh*, just before ending IR sessions the client can be asked to 'tuck' all of the modes into the body (e.g. heart, legs, etc.). This taps into the nurturing notion of 'tucking a child into bed at night', whereby the client literally imagines the healthy, coping and child modes that have been present in the imagery being tucked in to a place in the body of their choice. This also allows the client to know exactly where in the body they can contact these parts between sessions (e.g. to dialogue with them, to reparent the child, etc.). Whilst tucking them in, you can also ask them if there is anything else they need. If desired, the child can be tucked away safely with the *HA* self, or another attachment figure. This also conveys the felt-sense that these parts are safely 'contained' and resourced until the next session – this practice is drawn from the Comprehensive Resource Model (CRM) (Schwarz et al., 2017).

*Clients experience anxiety associated with attachment to an adult in* IR *(i.e. often associated with strong emotional deprivation and mistrust/abuse EMS).*

- A 'Power Animal' or aspect of nature (e.g. tree, mountain, rock) can be used as an alternative attachment figure until the client is able to cultivate their own *HA* self (drawn from the CRM model; Schwarz et al., 2017).. Once inside the image, the child can invite the Power Animal or Being that is 'waiting to be called on', to enter the image (i.e. allow it to spontaneously emerge). They are then gently guided through the experience of this fantasy figure attuning to them (e.g. noticing what it feels like to have eye contact, physical contact, including forehead to forehead, breathing together, listening to its soothing nurturing messages, hearts beating together, and taking in its scent). This attunement imagery may promote rewiring of healthy attachment, and a positive, self-sufficient relationship with self. The attachment imagery is highly sensory focused (drawing on touch, sound, vision, smell), drawing on neural templates available from birth for the purpose of parent–child bonding. Many clients find this to be a powerful way of building attachment, especially bypassing blocks associated with strong *mistrust/ abuse, emotional deprivation* and *defectiveness* schemas that interfere with their capacity to receive connection and closeness. This can be the first step in enabling the client to experience deep connection and the experience of being truly seen and known, without the threat of abandonment or harm.

*Client's* Inner Critic *is highly ego-syntonic and dominates day-to-day.*

- Client draws a picture of their *Inner Critic* and then practices imagery exercises whereby they visualise it projected on a cinema screen, then shrinking, or 'wiping' it out with a whiteboard eraser or a giant water hose. They are encouraged to focus on this for 1–2 minutes at a time. Alternatively, they can practice visualising the *Inner Critic* as a thief that has taken over aspects of the brain, and creatively imagine both the therapist and their own *HA* fighting off the thief (e.g. symbolised as a dragon, or monster) and reclaiming their 'brain real estate'.

*Client has severe body image disturbances.*

- Body image distortion can manifest as a sensory experience associated with the *Inner Critic* shaming the *VCh* [*defectiveness, emotional deprivation, abandonment* and *mistrust/abuse* schemas], and/or as a manifestation of trauma-based body memories. It is also linked to anger associated with unmet childhood needs being diverted inwards in order to maintain attachment with caregivers. We can begin to challenge these habitual trauma responses by drawing our clients' attention to them, noticing the way these manifest as images and physical sensations in different parts of the body (e.g. chest, arms, legs, throat, jaw, etc.). By tuning in to physical sensations, emotions and impulses through gentle mindfulness, the therapist can help the client to begin to explore and trust their visceral felt experience. Many visual and sensory experiences of distortion occur in conjunction with schema triggering linked to early trauma. Trauma processing should include a strong sensory focus in order to begin to 'untangle' the complex interplay of bodily responses and visceral felt-sense that are encoded within trauma memories. Further, through a combination of play and imagery work, the client can experiment with touch and felt-sense in order to begin to distinguish between shame-driven responses and actual bodily felt-sense.
- The client can also be asked to begin by focusing on one tiny aspect of their body (even if it's just one cell, or an internal organ) to practice acceptance and self-compassion. They are asked to mindfully focus on that part of themselves and either form an image of that part with their eyes closed, or look at that part in the mirror. They can then place their hand over that part of their body, and mindfully breathe into and out of that part for 5–10 minutes, with the intention of accepting this part of them completely. This can then build to two cells, to three cells and so forth.

*Client is highly traumatised and/or has difficulty regulating their emotions.*

- The emphasis is on teaching the client to reduce their level of arousal and tolerate emotion sufficiently, thereby enabling them to process traumatic incidents (physical/sexual/emotional) from childhood. Drawing can be a useful starting point for communicating difficult experiences and emotions (Hodge & Simpson, 2016).

- One way in which we can begin co-regulation of emotions is through starting with simple Reparenting-IR (i.e. meeting the child's needs in a safe imagery setting) before we move onto imagery that involves confronting abusers/perpetrators. We also use structured imagery exercises where they meet and learn from their *HA* self, and short mindfulness exercises with a focus on visualisation and the breath. During general discussion and IR we use a gentle, soft, soothing tone to assist with regulating clients' emotions. IR exercises can also be used creatively to begin to visualise physical boundaries around the self as protection against harmful actions or thoughts, as well as to counter current frightening ED images (e.g. sugar crossing the skin barrier). We also encourage clients to practise body actions that elicit a sense of physical strength and capacity to self-protect – such as a strong upright posture (in *HA* chair). Other activities such as a gentle weights workout at the gym whilst focusing on the sensation of strength in their bodies, yoga, and tai chi, are also useful in learning to develop a sense of connection with the body and physical strength (when it is safe and appropriate to introduce this).

*Client's* Happy Child *mode* (HAC) *is underdeveloped.*

- Experiment with sensate focused play (imagery and actual), including kinetic sand, colouring-in, knitting, working with clay or painting. We focus on experiencing new sensations and ask clients to practise this between sessions, such as feeling sand between toes and water on their body at the beach, the feeling of grass on the soles of their feet, climbing a tree. During IR we ask clients to connect with sensate focused needs from childhood: e.g. being gently rocked, having hair stroked, being cuddled or held. Some clients who have been severely deprived of spontaneity and play during childhood also benefit from dancing to music, jumping, skipping and other childlike movements alongside their therapist. It can be helpful to metaphorically leave the *OC* in the corner with a job to do (e.g. counting, calculating, colouring-in).

## Working with the Impulsive Child mode

Most clients with EDs are fearful of their impulsivity, the part of them that is uncontrolled, undisciplined, and connected with the shamed *VCh*. There is often a fear that if the *Inner Critic* or *OC* mode stops harassing them, their whole world will spiral out of control, leading to a cycle of uncontrolled bingeing and weight gain. This can be based on a strong *emotional inhibition* schema whereby the person has learned to view body-based emotions and urges with distrust. Part of the role of the therapist (and eventually the client's own *HA*) is to validate and normalise the *Impulsive Child* mode. Without some level of impulsivity, there can be no fun and spontaneity in life. The *Inner Critic* generally views the *Impulsive Child* as shameful, and it therefore largely operates in secret (e.g. binges that take place standing up, when other people are not around). The more subjugated the *Impulsive Child* feels, the more it rebels, often in secret, and 'in cahoots' with the *Detached Self-Soother* (*DetSS*) (driven both by hunger and frustration at being controlled). In therapy, we need to gradually help the client to begin to trust their own internal bodily signals and instincts. We need to teach clients to take care of their *Impulsive Child* and to be attuned to the unmet needs of the *VCh* that this side may be reacting to. We can begin this process by asking clients to draw their *Impulsive Child*, and perhaps to portray both the up- and down-sides of this mode – recognising that the existence of this side is essential for the healthy development of a *HAC*. This might incorporate the sense of disgust or shame they experience (driven by the *Inner Critic*) associated with their hunger, alongside the joy this side can bring in terms of (longed-for) spontaneity and joy. They can also be encouraged to watch educational materials that normalise children's impulsive and spontaneous behaviours (e.g. the British television series: 'The Secret Life of 4 and 5 year olds').

Clients can also be encouraged to start to notice and monitor their *Impulsive Child* in their day-to-day lives, and to talk to her from the *HA* side, reassuring her, and giving her a balance of limits and treats based on balancing her current and future health and happiness. Ultimately, the message we are giving the *Impulsive Child* is the same as we would give to a young child: 'Use your words to say what you feel, not your behaviour. Your needs are normal and healthy. I will help you to get your needs met in a healthy way – you don't need to hide away and feel ashamed anymore.' However, in general, it will be difficult to bring about any lasting changes in bingeing driven by the *Impulsive Child* mode, without also addressing the *Inner Critic* and *OC* modes alongside this. Chairwork that addresses both the *Impulsive Child* and *DetSS* 'addictive' behaviours, as well as the suffocating *OC* mode, can be a powerful way to highlight the fact that both extremes are unhealthy and self-reinforcing.

### *Building* Healthy Adult *and* Happy Child *modes*

One of the most important aspects of developing a *HA* self in this population is the cultivation of self-compassion. Many clients confuse the *HA* with the *OC* mode and view the concept of being 'healthy' as equivalent to being rational and 'in control'. They may go through the motions of carrying out activities that are considered healthy on a superficial level (e.g. attending the gym, eating the right foods) with a sense of efficiency, rather than self-compassion. In this way, the needs of the *VCh* are abandoned in favour of being reasonable and sensible. Therapy sessions should focus on coaching the client's *HA* to develop a keen awareness of their *VCh* and *HAC* selves, and to learn how to prioritise their needs over the competing demands and needs of others (when appropriate). Often clients have been made to feel guilty and selfish for considering their needs - this should be reversed through many repetitions of IR and chairwork. For clients who have little awareness of their vulnerability, it can be useful to recommend that they bring a photograph or drawing of themselves as a little child (especially pictures where they appear vulnerable or sad). The photo can then be placed on the *VCh* chair and used when the therapist is either asking the client to connect with their vulnerability or coaching the client to be compassionate toward their *VCh*.

Many clients with EDs confuse the need for nurturance with other needs, such as hunger and the desire for others to take control or responsibility for them (especially if this was a substitute for nurturance during childhood). One of the tasks of therapy is to help clients to differentiate emotional needs from coping mode reactions that often bring immediate gratification or relief. Chair and imagery work provide an opportunity to learn to soothe their *VCh* through nurturance rather than alternative [short-term] substitutes. As therapy progresses, we check-in regularly to help clients to develop an awareness of and 'connection' with their embodied self through mindfulness of sensations and emotions that are experienced in the body. They are helped to track feelings within the body by asking questions such as: "Where do you feel that in your body when you say that? What does that feel like? What sensations do you notice?" The aim of this is to assist the client with developing a sense of self that is based on authenticity of experience and connection with body rather than perceived expectations or reactions of others.

Therapists can use self-disclosure of current or previous situations to model ways of managing distress in healthy ways within their own lives. This can include talking about difficult situations in the past that the therapist has overcome, which are also relevant to the client. In the context of a trusting therapeutic rapport, therapists can lighten the sessions, such as through humour, gentle teasing (where appropriate), and poking fun at themselves. Over the course of therapy, the focus gradually widens from being problem-focused to nurturing identity development, by helping clients to learn about themselves, their likes and dislikes, and to accept their own individuality.

## Conclusion

In order to fully grasp the nature of EDs, we must recognise the complex interaction of ED and comorbid symptoms that masks underlying distress. The schema mode model provides a framework for conceptualising these complex phenomena. It facilitates a process of de-fusion from egosyntonic parent and coping modes, and a pathway to connect with and heal underlying vulnerability. In ST, experiential techniques provide powerful mechanisms to bypass the coping modes, set limits on the *Inner Critic*, strengthen healthy modes, and reparent child modes. The experiential techniques described in this chapter should be applied flexibly, in accordance with individualised mode conceptualisations that encapsulate ED presentations.

## References

Arntz, A., & Weertman, A. (1999). Treatment of childhood memories: Theory and practice. *Behaviour Research and Therapy*, 37(8), 715–740.

Gilbert, P. (2009). *The Compassionate Mind. A New Approach to the Challenges of Life*. London: Constable & Robinson.

Hodge, L., & Simpson, S. (2016). Speaking the unspeakable: Artistic expression in eating disorder research and schema therapy. *The Arts in Psychotherapy*, 50, 1–8.

Schwarz, L., Corrigan, F., Hull, A., & Ragu, R. (2017). *Comprehensive Resource Model: Effective Therapeutic Techniques for the Healing of Complex Trauma*. New York: Routledge.

Young, J., Klosko, J., & Weishaar, M. (2003). *Schema Therapy: A Practitioner's Guide*. New York: Guilford Press.

# Chapter 8

# Chairwork in schema therapy

## Applications and considerations in the treatment of eating disorders

*Matthew Pugh and Sophie Rae*

## Abstract

*Experiential interventions such as imagery rescripting and chairwork are amongst the most effective methods for bringing about schema-level change and have been centralised in schema therapy (ST). This chapter provides an overview of chairwork techniques utilised in ST and describes how they can be applied in work with eating disorders (ED). The chapter begins with an introduction to the format and process of chairwork. Key chair-based techniques are then described alongside illustrative extracts from ST sessions. Common obstacles which can arise when using chairwork with ED cases, and recommendations for resolving these issues, are then discussed.*

## Introduction

First conceived over one century ago, 'chairwork' represents a collective of established experiential techniques which utilise chairs and their relative positions to facilitate therapeutic dialogues (Pugh, 2017a). Chairwork techniques were first utilised within the psychodrama approach (Moreno, 1948) and later gained wider recognition within gestalt therapy (Perls, 1973) before being more rigorously evaluated within emotion-focused therapy (Greenberg, 2011). Chairwork has since been incorporated into other evidence-based therapies including cognitive behavioural therapy (CBT) (Pugh, 2017b, 2018), compassion-focused therapy (Gilbert, 2009), and schema therapy (ST) (Young, Klosko & Weishaar, 2003; Arntz & Jacob, 2013). Preliminary research supports the potential effectiveness of chairwork in addressing multifarious clinical issues (Butollo, Willi, Karl, König, & Rosner, 2016).

### Process-related skills

Schema therapists maintain an active roleplay during chairwork and use process-based skills to stimulate change. These moment-by-moment interventions help clients immerse themselves in the dialogue, connect with internal states, and establish a sense of agency to maximise the effects of chairwork. Equally, schema therapists attend to their role in the dialogical process – at times prompting the client, actively intervening at other points, and sometimes remaining silent – to ensure the intervention reaches a therapeutic conclusion. Key process-related skills are summarised in Table 8.1. For detailed guidance, readers are referred to Greenberg (1979), Kellogg (2014) and Pugh (2017b, 2018).

## Chairwork and eating disorders

Preliminary findings suggest that chairwork techniques may be particularly effective in the treatment of eating disorders (ED) (Dolhanty & Greenberg, 2009; Pugh & Salter, 2017). Chairwork is a powerful means of concretising abstract concepts such as 'multiplicity of mind', facilitating shifts in perspective, encouraging emotional expression, and differentiating complex affective states, all of which can be challenging for this group. It also provides an effective method for resolving distressing events in childhood and so can provide an alternative to imagery rescripting (IR). Lastly, through utilising process-skills, chairwork can overcome impairments in emotional regulation and meet each individual's needs.

### Schema-focused chairwork

#### Assessing early maladaptive schemas

Standard methods for assessing early maladaptive schemas (EMS) such as imagery assessment (Young et al., 2003) and self-report inventories are complemented by chairwork. For example, chairwork roleplays can be used to identify which EMS become activated in problematic situations. By recreating these events, the therapist and client are better able to 'feel' and name underlying schemas.

THERAPIST: That sounds like a tough situation at work, Susie. Could we re-create the meeting you had with your manager? It might help us identify which schemas came up for you.

CLIENT: Ok.

THERAPIST: Great. Let's change seats and, when we do, I'll play your manager and I'd like you to respond the way you did at work.
[*Therapist and client move to new seats.*]

THERAPIST: Susie, your performance this month has been unacceptable. This is the second time your sales have fallen.

CLIENT: I'm trying my best. Perhaps my performance fell because I took some sick leave.

THERAPIST: Enough excuses, Susie! You need to take responsibility for yourself! [*Client becomes tearful*]. Ok, let's pause there. You look really upset, Susie. What's happening for you?

CLIENT: I feel really horrible.

THERAPIST: What's running through your mind right now? What are you saying to yourself?

CLIENT: I'm a complete failure. I'll never get anywhere in this job.

THERAPIST: That sounds really painful. I can understand why you feel so upset if you're thinking about yourself in that way. Do you often see yourself as a failure?

CLIENT: Always.

THERAPIST: And what do you feel like doing as you're thinking that?

CLIENT: I want to hide away in my bedroom. I want to binge.

THERAPIST: I see. So this situation is triggering a belief about being a failure, is that right? [*Client nods*]. I wonder if binge-eating and withdrawing is something you often want to do when this schema gets activated? Like it's a way of coping with those feelings?

### Modifying maladaptive schemas

Compared to other clinical groups, EMS are particularly pronounced in the EDs (Pugh, 2015). Accordingly, addressing EMS plays a vital role in reducing distress and ameliorating disordered eating. A powerful method for re-evaluating the accuracy of EMS is 'schema dialogue' (Young et al., 2003). This intervention, sometimes referred to as 'point-counterpoint' in schema-focused CBT (Young, 1990), involves a two-chair dialogue between the 'voice' of the client's EMS and their healthy side. In contrast to more spontaneous mode-focused dialogues between *Inner Critic* (parent) modes and the *Healthy Adult* (*HA*) mode, schema dialogues are preceded by a thorough examination of the evidence which supports the EMS which is then re-appraised. This cognitive work is then made more visceral and evocative through the use of chairwork. First, the client is asked to present evidence supporting the schema in chair one whilst rebuttals are provided by the therapist (enacting the client's healthy side) in chair two. Once the client has developed skill in formulating healthy counter-arguments, they are encouraged to play both roles: the client presents a single piece of evidence supporting the EMS in chair one and then challenges this evidence in chair two (with coaching from the therapist).

Finally, schema dialogues may incorporate a final provocative step, sometimes referred to as the 'devil's advocate technique'. In this stage, the therapist enacts the schema (chair one) and actively challenges the client's healthy statements (chair two). If the client becomes stuck, the dialogue is paused so that convincing counter-arguments can be collaboratively constructed. It is

*Table 8.1* Process-skills in chairwork

| Skill | Example |
|-------|---------|
| *Maintaining boundaries* | **Keeping voices clear** |
| | C: I might be ok as a person, but I still look like a slob. |
| | T: It sounds like your *Punitive Inner Critic* mode is really coming out now. Let's put that critical part of you in the empty chair. |
| | **Personification** |
| | C: I get so tired of these constant thoughts to exercise more and more. |
| | T: Let's speak to your *Demanding Inner Critic* mode then. If that mode were sat in the empty chair, how would it look? |
| | **Embodiment** |
| | C: My body looks so horrible and disgusting. |
| | T: That sounds like your *Punitive Inner Critic* mode. Can you change seats and speak as that part of yourself for a moment? |
| | **Directing attention** |
| | C: [*to the* Punitive Inner Critic] Leave me alone! [*turning to the therapist*] This *Inner Critic* mode really isn't helpful, is it? |
| | T: [*re-directing attention*]. Try saying that to your *Inner Critic*: 'You're not helping me'. |
| *Facilitating expression* | **Elaboration** |
| | C: [*to the* Detached Protector] It's not helpful to always feel numb. I need to feel my emotions sometimes. |
| | T: Tell the *Detached Protector* more about why you need to feel sometimes. |
| | **Specificity** |
| | C: [*to the* Demanding Inner Critic *mode*] |
| | T: Tell that side about the specific ways it stops you living a happy life. |
| *Heightening affect* | **Repetition** |
| | C: [*to the* Vulnerable Child]) There's nothing wrong with you. |
| | T: Tell Little Susie that once more, 'there is nothing wrong with you'. |
| | **Tone** |
| | C: [*to the* Punitive Inner Critic] Stop putting me down. |
| | T: Say that again, but louder this time. |
| | **Posture** |
| | C: [*to the* Demanding Inner Critic] I'm allowed to eat what I like. |
| | T: Try standing up as you say that. |
| | **Exploring non-verbal communication** |
| | T: When you speak to the punitive mode you seem so composed, but I also notice you are clenching your fists. |
| | C: I guess I feel quite angry right now. |
| | T: I see, so there's actually some anger there. Can you put your anger into words? |
| | **Offering statements** |
| | C: [*to the* Vulnerable Child] Being abused wasn't your fault. |
| | T: Yes, no child deserves to be treated like that. You are a good little girl. Can you try saying that to Little Susie? |

| Skill | Example |
|---|---|
| *Responsibility taking* | **Owning perspective**<br>T: [*to the* Detached Self-soother]. You just make things worse when you encourage me to binge.<br>C: Tell that side how that feels to you. What's *your* experience?<br>T: I just feel sadder when I binge. It's not helpful.<br>**Existential language**<br>C: [*to the* Punitive Inner Critic]. If I want to eat, I'm going to eat! That's up to me, not you!<br>T: Try saying, 'From now, I'm going to decide to eat when I like'. |

worth noting that encouraging the client to develop anger at their EMS can also stimulate change during schema dialogues (Young, 1990): by expressing their anger at the EMS, clients not only challenge the content and utility of their schemas, but also acquire distance from these beliefs (Therapist: 'Tell the schema what you resent about it').

---

The client and the therapist have been practising schema dialogues. The therapist now proposes using the 'devil's advocate' technique.

THERAPIST: You did really well during that dialogue, Susie. We are developing a really strong case against your emotional inhibition schema. Let's take this one step further. In a moment I'm going to change seats and enact your schema but I'm going to be more persistent this time. I'd like you to play your healthy side and convince me that what I am saying is not true. Let me know if you get stuck so I can help you generate a convincing counter-argument. Ready?

CLIENT: I think so.

[*Therapist and client move to new seats.*]

THERAPIST: You shouldn't show people how you really feel. If your friends knew about how difficult eating can be for you, they would run a mile.

CLIENT: That's not true. I told one of my friends about my eating disorder and I got quite upset, but she was really supportive. It's good to express how you feel.

THERAPIST: But no one wants to know how you really feel, do they? It's too much of a burden.

CLIENT: ...[*silent*].

THERAPIST: [*out of role*]: Tell me why sharing your feelings aren't a burden for others.

CLIENT: When I tell others how I feel, I feel more connected to them. They are happy that I've opened up. They don't say I'm a burden, they say the opposite!

*Addressing schema origins*

Childhood maltreatment is common across ED subtypes (Caslini et al., 2016). As well as addressing the content of schemas, chairwork enables clients to confront individuals who have played a role in formation of an EMS. This often involves the client speaking with caregivers who were unable to meet their needs in childhood. Empty-chair and roleplay formats can be used to facilitate such dialogues. Empty-chair techniques involve the client challenging specific individuals held in the empty seat. Historical roleplay is a more elaborate intervention involving both the client and the therapist, and which involve three stages of enactment (Arntz & Jacob, 2013). First, the client (enacting their child self) and the therapist (enacting the parental antagonist) re-enact a troubling childhood event. Therapists may want to pause after this first roleplay and – perhaps from a standing ('meta-') perspective – explore how this interaction between parent and child is wrong, inappropriate, and fails to meet the child's needs. Roles are then reversed in the second stage: by adopting the parental role, the client is able to garner new insights into the behaviours and validity of distressing messages conveyed by caregivers. Concurrently, the therapist is able to challenge these messages from the perspective of the client's child self. In the final stage, the client is invited to enact their child self once again and respond to their parent in more satisfying ways (with coaching, if needed).

---

**Empty-chair technique**

THERAPIST: It sounds like the things your father said to you as a child have played a big role in seeing yourself as defective in some way.

CLIENT: Yes. His comments about my body made me feel so ashamed when I was small.

THERAPIST: I wonder if it might be helpful for us to speak to him about this, in imagination.

CLIENT: Ok.

THERAPIST: Take a moment to imagine that he is here, in this empty chair. What do you see?

CLIENT: I see him sat there, crossing his arms. He's looking at me judgementally.

THERAPIST: How do you feel seeing him?

CLIENT: I feel angry.

THERAPIST: Tell him what makes you feel angry.

CLIENT: I'm angry at how embarrassed and ashamed you made me feel about my body when I was small. It was wrong!

---

**Historical roleplay technique (final stage)**

THERAPIST: I am going to change chairs and play your father once more, and this time I'd like you to respond to what I say from your healthy side.
[*Therapist and client move to new seats.*]
THERAPIST: You shouldn't eat as much as you do. Pretty girls keep an eye on their figure.
CLIENT: I can eat as much as like. There is nothing wrong with me enjoying food.
THERAPIST: It's greedy and disgusting. You are behaving like a pig.
CLIENT: I'm not a pig! I'm a normal human being and I am allowed to eat as much as I like!
THERAPIST: [*out of role*]: Tell me why it's wrong for a father to say these things to a child.
CLIENT: A father shouldn't speak to their child like this! It's wrong and makes me feel bad!

---

### Constructing positive schemas

Whilst modifying EMS plays an important role in ST, constructing positive self-beliefs may be equally important in bringing about lasting change (Brewin, 2006). Two methods can help achieve this. The first involves the client changing seats when an EMS becomes activated (i.e. decentring from the schema) and outlining positive events, achievements and experiences which do not support the schema (Therapist: 'Try and leave the defectiveness schema in this empty chair and, from your new seat, describe some of the ways in which you are acceptable'). If this method proves challenging, the client can be invited to enact someone who views them in a compassionate light in order to elicit positive data (Therapist: 'Susie, I'd like you to change seats and be your Auntie Mary for a moment…Auntie Mary, Susie thinks of herself as worthless. As someone who cares deeply for her, can you tell Susie some things that you like and value in her?'). Chadwick (2003) has outlined an alternative, three-stage procedure for generating positive schema-level beliefs. A modified version of this technique combining imagery work, which we have found particularly helpful in ST-ED, is outlined below. It is worth noting that, unlike schema dialogues, the positive and negative schema chairs do not speak to one another in this intervention: this is important, as the negative schema might easily overpower the newly constructed positive schema if such dialogues were to occur.

*Susie has changed seats and is describing her lived experience of her failure schema.*

THERAPIST: How do you experience yourself when your failure schema becomes activated?

CLIENT: I see myself as useless, like I've achieved nothing in life.

THERAPIST: And how does the future seem to you in moments like these?

CLIENT: The future looks so bleak. I'm doomed to fail over and over again. I'll never recover.

THERAPIST: And how do you experience other people in these moments?

CLIENT: Everyone around me seems so superior. I'm scared that they're going to humiliate me for not having a job or for having an eating disorder.

THERAPIST: It sounds like your mistrust schema is also active now. I'd like you to change seats, Susie. [*Client moves seats*]. Now let's take a moment to leave those schemas in your first chair and separate from them a little...Take a moment to just set them aside...Now, I wonder, Susie, have there been any moments in life where you have experienced yourself as something other than a failure, even if it was just for a moment?

CLIENT: [*thinking*]: ...Well, I remember how I felt when I got my first job.

THERAPIST: Take me back to that moment. Tell me what happened. [*Client describes the event in detail.*] And how did you feel when the manager said she wanted you to join the company?

CLIENT: It felt great. I was over the moon!

THERAPIST: How did others seem to you in that moment? What did the future look like?

CLIENT: I felt like I was like everyone else, like I was achieving something. Other people seemed friendly and encouraging. It felt like I was moving on with my life. I was hopeful.

THERAPIST: Do you feel a little of that hope and happiness right now? Where do you feel it?

CLIENT: [*touches chest*]. I feel it near my heart. It's a warm feeling.

THERAPIST: Close your eyes for a moment, Susie, and really focus on that warm feeling...Allow it to get a little bigger if you can... And now just see if any other memories come to mind when you felt something similar, like you were successful...What other memories do you notice?

## Mode-focused chairwork

### Mode assessment

Individuals with EDs present with multifarious and often conflicting schema modes (Pugh, 2015). Chair-based techniques enable the client and therapist to identify key modes and to 'get to know' these parts of the client better. This can be achieved by inviting the client to change seats and embody these [mal]adaptive self-parts. Alternatively, modes can be interviewed by the therapist regarding their origins, functions, motivations, and intent (Arntz & Jacob, 2013). Intrapersonal roleplays are described in more detail later in this chapter (see p.114).

### Mode socialisation

Chairs can be used in creative ways to help clients grasp the schema mode concept and explore how modes interact. For example, the therapist might place a wall of chairs between their chair and a seat representing the *Vulnerable Child* (*VCh*) to illustrate how coping modes (for example, the *Detached Protector* (*DetPr*)) block child modes and prevent them from experiencing the reparenting they need. Problematic events can also be reviewed from the perspective of different modes, held in different chairs, to elucidate the patterns of thinking, feeling, and behaving which each tends to generate. This technique can help identify modes that are most powerful or obstructive, whilst also highlighting the sequences in which modes tend to become activated.

THERAPIST: Last week we talked about how introducing a meal plan might help reduce your binges, but I got the impression that you had mixed feelings about doing that.

CLIENT: Yes. I'm not sure I'm ready to try a meal plan yet.

THERAPIST: Ok. Can we try an exercise to explore what my suggestion brought up in you? I thought it might be helpful to explore what each of your modes think about the idea of regular eating.

CLIENT: I'm not sure they were thinking anything, but ok.

THERAPIST: Great. Let me arrange a few chairs. [*Therapist arranges a small circle of chairs.*] I wonder what your *Vulnerable Child* – Little Susie – thinks about following a meal plan. Would you mind moving to this chair and speaking from the vulnerable side of yourself?

CLIENT: [*changes seats*] I'm really scared about eating more food. It's going to be so difficult and I'm worried I'm going to gain weight. What if I get fat?

THERAPIST: I can see Little Susie is really worried about what might happen if you tried the meal plan. What about your Inner Critic mode? What does that side think?

CLIENT: [*changes seats*] I don't deserve to eat anything. I'm a fat slob and ought to starve.

THERAPIST: Gosh, that side of you can be so harsh, Susie. What about your overcontrolling mode? Change seats and be that side of yourself...

### Working with wounded child modes

*Vulnerable* and *Angry Child* modes (*VCh* and *AnCh*) require particular attention in ST-ED (Simpson, 2012). Chairwork aims to give these parts of the client an opportunity to be visible, supported, and validated. Through enactment and embodiment, chairwork provides clients with a visceral connection to their child modes and so allows for a more powerful experience of re-parenting by the therapist. Given that many clients with EDs find expressing anger and sadness challenging, particularly when these feelings arise within the therapeutic relationship, many individuals will tend to suppress their emotional experiencing during chairwork (Geller, Cockell, Hewitt, Goldner, & Flett, 2000). If this occurs, schema therapists will need to work with obstructive coping modes as a precursor to more emotive dialogues.

THERAPIST: It sounds like you felt really sad before you binged, Susie. I can understand why given how hurtful the argument with your boyfriend was earlier on in the day.

CLIENT: I guess so.

THERAPIST: Can you connect with any of that sadness right now?

CLIENT: No. Not really.

THERAPIST: So right now you feel kind of...?

CLIENT: Numb.

THERAPIST: I see. That sounds a little like your *Detached Protector* mode to me. I'd like to have a conversation with that part, if that's ok? Can you move over to this chair and be the protector? [*Therapist proceeds to negotiate contact with client's* Vulnerable Child *mode.*] Thank you for agreeing to give Susie's vulnerable side a little more space to be heard today, *Detached Protector*. Susie, would you mind moving over to Little Susie's chair for a moment? [*Client changes seats.*] Tell me about how the argument with your boyfriend left you feeling, Susie.

CLIENT: I felt so hurt and let down by him. He doesn't understand how hard it is for me to eat. I'm such a freak. [*Client begins to cry.*]
THERAPIST: That sounds so hard, Susie. You suffer so much when you argue with him. But I want you to know that you are not a freak. I think you are a perfectly normal, acceptable human being...

## Working with Demanding and Punitive modes

*Demanding (DemP)* and *Punitive (PP) Parent/Inner Critic* modes are often more pronounced in EDs, compared to other clinical groups (Talbot, Smith, Tomkins, Brockman, & Simpson, 2015). Chairwork can be used to set limits on the *DemP* and fight the *PP*. In terms of process, therapists will need to adjust their tone and stance depending upon which mode is addressed: a forceful tone is adopted when speaking with the *PP*, whilst *DemP* is addressed in a firm but fair manner (Arntz & Jacob, 2013).

**Multi-chair technique with the *Punitive* Mode (*PP*)**

THERAPIST: It sounds like your *PP* was really attacking you yesterday, Susie. Can you change seats and be the *PP* just for a moment? [*Client changes seats.*] Now, as the *PP*, speak to Susie about the way she looks.
CLIENT: You're a fat, horrible pig! Look at all those horrible rolls of fat. You look like a disgusting mess. [*Client becomes tearful.*]
THERAPIST: Come back over to Little Susie's chair. [*Client changes seats.*] It really hurts when that side puts you down like that, doesn't it?
CLIENT: It hurts so much. I just want to never eat again.
THERAPIST: You don't deserve this, Susie, not at all. I'd like to speak to your *PP*, if that's ok? [*Client nods.*] [*Therapist speaks to the empty chair.*] You need to stop putting Susie down like this! She is fine just the way she is and you have no right to hurt her in this way!...

## Working with dysfunctional coping modes

Clients frequently describe feeling ambivalent about giving up entrenched coping modes, given their apparent functionality. Accordingly, chair-based methods for negotiating with, 'bypassing', and developing motivation to 'relax' coping modes are vital in work with EDs. Relevant techniques might include exploring the costs (chair one) and benefits (chair two) of a coping mode using the decisional balance technique (Kellogg, 2014); asking the client to argue in favour of the coping mode whilst the therapist responds from the position of the *Healthy Adult* (*HA*) (Therapist: 'I'd like you to outline the reasons why your *Avoidant Protector* (*AvPr*) is helpful and I will respond from the *HA* perspective') and then, later, reversing these roles; or encouraging the client to respond to coping modes from the perspective of evocative child modes to highlight their maladaptive consequences (Therapist: 'Change chairs and be Little Susie…Little Susie, can you tell the *Perfectionistic Overcontroller* about how sad it sometimes makes you feel?'). Readers are encouraged to refer to the ST literature for detailed guidance on bypassing coping modes (see Arntz & Jacob, 2013; Young et al., 2003).

*Strengthening the* Healthy Adult *mode*

Given that the *HA* mode is often underdeveloped in ED groups (Talbot et al.,), therapists need to spend considerable time helping clients develop a supportive internal voice. Chairwork provides a potent vehicle for generating the self-directed kindness, encouragement and understanding embodied by the *HA*. Various chair-based methods can achieve this. Initially, clients may find it easiest to strengthen their *HA* by providing care and support to another individual held in empty chair, as the following extract illustrates.

---

**Empty-chair dialogue**

THERAPIST: Your mother's remarks about your body shape must have really hurt, Susie. I wonder, is there a child you know and care about?

CLIENT: I guess my cousin, Martha. She's only nine.

THERAPIST: Ok, let's imagine little Martha in the empty chair. Can you imagine her sitting there?

CLIENT: Yes, she's very small. She'd sit with her legs crossed, probably playing with her hair.

THERAPIST: Let's just imagine that Martha has been told by someone that she looks fat and horrible. What would you like to say to her to help her feel better?

CLIENT: I'd tell her that she shouldn't listen to someone like that. She is perfect just the way she is. Her shape and weight don't matter. What matters is what is on the inside.

THERAPIST: That's lovely, Susie. You have such a caring side. Can you move over to Martha's seat now? [*Client changes seats.*] How do you feel hearing that? Are you able to connect with any of the things you have just said?

As well as using empty-chair techniques to practice vicarious re-parenting, two-chair techniques allow the client to practice giving and receiving care from a supportive individual they know.

---

**Two-chair dialogue**

THERAPIST: Your mother's remarks about your body shape must have really hurt, Susie. I wonder, can you think of someone who has shown you care and kindness in the past?

CLIENT: My grandfather, Tony.

THERAPIST: I'd like you to imagine your grandfather is sitting in this other chair. How do you imagine he might respond to hearing what happened to you?

CLIENT: I think he would be concerned knowing how hurt I feel. He would want to help.

THERAPIST: How would he show his care? What would he want to do to help you?

CLIENT: He would want to reassure me that I'm not fat or horrible. He would probably tell me about the nice things he sees in me.

THERAPIST: I'd like you to move over to your grandfather's chair and, as best as you can, try and be his kind voice. [*Client changes seats.*] Grandpa Tony, Susie has had a really tough few days. She feels really hurt by what her mother has said about her appearance. What would you like to tell her?

---

Lastly, chairwork roleplays can help the client embody the therapist's perspective and so begin internalising the *HA* mode. As well as allowing clients to respond to their distress from the supportive vantage point of the therapist, this method can also provide an indirect and less threatening method of empathic confrontation. This is particularly helpful when working with individuals with EDs, who are often highly sensitive to rejection.

---

**Limited re-parenting through chairwork roleplay**

CLIENT: I tried to introduce the meal plan but it was a disaster. I managed to follow it for one day and then I started binge-eating again. I'm such a waste of space.

THERAPIST: Do you think that I think you're waste of space?

CLIENT: I don't know…Probably not.

THERAPIST: If you were me right now, how would you see what's happened?

CLIENT: I guess you'd think setbacks aren't unusual. You wouldn't think I was a complete failure.

THERAPIST: Can you come over here and sit beside me? [*Client moves seats.*] So, over there is someone who is trying their best to do something scary [*Gesturing to the empty chair*], but she's finding it really hard to do. She's working hard but, like every other human being, this scary new thing gets difficult at times. Now, as my co-therapist, would you say that individual is a waste of space for having that experience?

CLIENT: No.

THERAPIST: Well, that's the way she feels right now. What would you want to say to her?

CLIENT: I'd tell her it's great she's trying so hard, even though it scares her. That takes a lot of courage.

THERAPIST: Do you think she's a failure?

CLIENT: No.

THERAPIST: How come?

CLIENT: Everyone finds things hard the first time they do it, especially if it makes them feel anxious.

THERAPIST: Can you tell her that?

CLIENT: You're not a failure.

THERAPIST: You're right, Susie. She's not a failure. You are not a failure.

**Empathic confrontation through chairwork**

CLIENT: I just couldn't cut back on my exercise this week. The urge was too strong. You must be so fed up of talking about my exercise routine over and over again.

THERAPIST: I'm not fed up, Susie. I can understand why exercising less is so difficult. You've been exercising like this for a long time, right? Whether you exercise or not doesn't change the care I have for you. At the same time, I'm concerned. I feel both those things right now – I care about you and I'm concerned. Does that make sense? [*Client nods.*] Have you ever felt care and concern for someone, at the same time?

CLIENT: I felt that way when my mum was giving up smoking. I understood why she found it hard to stop smoking because I found it hard too, but I didn't want her to damage her lungs either.

THERAPIST: Would you mind moving over to this chair beside me, Susie? [*Client moves seats.*] I'd like you to step into my shoes for a moment, as if you are the therapist right now. How can you show the individual over there that you feel both care and concern for her? What would you say?

> CLIENT: I'd tell her that it's understandable that exercising less was difficult because it's a hard habit to break, but it's also really important that she cuts it down.
> THERAPIST: [*Gesturing to the empty chair*] Can you tell her why that's important and why you care about that?
> CLIENT: It's important because the more exercise you do, the worse the eating disorder gets, and I don't want you to suffer like that…

## Special considerations in schema therapy for eating disorders

### *The internal eating disorder 'voice'*

Many individuals with EDs make reference to an internal eating disorder 'voice' (EDV) which has been linked to multiple aspects of eating psychopathology (Pugh & Waller, 2017). Albeit a controversial concept (Pugh, 2016), working with the EDV can provide therapists with a welcome opportunity to stand shoulder-to-shoulder with clients against an aspect of their illness. Suggestions for working with the EDV in ST-ED include the following:

- Clinicians must establish which mode(s) are represented by the EDV. This can be achieved using diagnostic chairwork techniques, which enable schema therapists to identify the form, functions, and (most importantly) schema modes which are encapsulated by the EDV.
- Illuminating questions to pose during diagnostic interviews with the EDV may include its developmental origins ('Where do you come from?'), intent ('What is your role in this individual's life?') and motives ('What are your fears about not performing this role?').
- Research has linked the EDV to childhood trauma (Pugh, Waller & Esposito 2018). As such, dialogues with the EDV can provide an inroad to IR later in therapy.

> THERAPIST: So, anorexia, what is your role in Susie's life?
> CLIENT: My job is to make sure Susie doesn't eat too much and stays below her calorie limit. I push her to exercise as hard as she can, every day. If she doesn't do that, well, then I tell her off. She needs to stick to the rules and do exactly as I say [EDV *as* DemP].
> THERAPIST: What do you think would happen if you weren't doing this in Susie's life?
> CLIENT: She'd become lazy and out of control. If she wants to eat, she needs to earn it.

> *Client and therapist go on to explore the origins of the EDV and its manifestations.*
>
> THERAPIST: Thank you for taking the time to speak with me, anorexia. It has been very helpful getting to know you better. Susie, can you come back to your chair?
>
> *Therapist and client de-brief following the dialogue.*
>
> THERAPIST: I wonder, did the voice remind you of any of the modes we have talked about lately?
> CLIENT: Well, it reminded me a bit of the *Inner Critic* you mentioned.
> THERAPIST: That's what I thought too. It really does sound like your *Inner Critic* plays a big role in your exercise and calorie counting. Does it remind you of anyone you've known?
> CLIENT: Now that you say that, it kind of reminds me of my dad. I remember he would always tell us not to overeat at dinner...

### Over-regulation of emotion (emotional suppression and inhibition)

Individuals with EDs tend to inhibit their emotional reactions. Of all of the emotions, anger can be especially difficult for individuals with EDs to acknowledge, validate and express. Furthermore, anger is often accompanied by feelings of self-disgust and guilt (i.e. activation of parent modes) (Fox & Harrison, 2008). This can be obstructive in ST given that healthy anger can help facilitate schema modification (Young, 1990). Strategies for working with anger and anger suppression include:

- Using the client's nomenclature to refer to anger, which can feel less threatening (Therapist: 'Can you tell your schema about how it *pisses you off*?').
- Initially encouraging safer, less intense expressions of anger during chairwork, e.g. asking the client to read 'no send' letters (in imagination) to individuals who inspire irritation.
- Bypassing coping modes which inhibit expressions of anger (e.g. the *Detached Protector* (*DetPr*)) and/or silencing modes which attack the client for expressing annoyance (e.g. inner critic modes).
- Roleplaying individuals who express anger in healthy ways (Therapist: 'Can you think of someone who expresses their anger in a helpful and assertive way? How do you imagine they would respond to a *Punitive mode* like this? Can you show me?').
- Encouraging anger expression by using increasingly evocative language to describe the client's emotional experience (Therapist: 'Can you respond to your *PP* from your irritated/annoyed/angry/enraged side?').

### Under-regulation of emotion (distress intolerance)

At the other end of the emotional regulation continuum, some clients with EDs struggle to tolerate emotional distress (Anestis, Selby, Fink, & Joiner, 2007). As a result, evocative interventions such as chairwork can generate considerable anxiety. Several adjustments can be made during chairwork to help manage these concerns and temper clients' levels of emotional arousal:

- Rather than embodying distressing modes, clients can at first be invited to stand behind the chair of the mode and speak from this perspective in the third-person (Therapist: 'What is the *Inner Critic* saying to Little Susie now?').
- A 'safe chair' can be included in chairwork, so that the client has a protective place to move to if they feel overwhelmed.
- Delaying the more evocative forms of chairwork (e.g. historical roleplay) until a containing alliance has developed, and the client has greater resources for managing distress, is often important.

### Other issues

- Individuals with EDs often feel self-conscious when engaging in chairwork. Enacting modes on behalf of the client (under their direction), or demonstrating the interactions between one's own schema modes through chairwork, can help normalise the dialogical process and build confidence in chair-techniques.
- Alexithymia (i.e. difficulties identifying and describing emotions) is common in EDs. Chairwork techniques such as the 'emotional selves' exercise (see Gilbert, 2009) and 'physicalising' affective states in the empty chair (Therapist: 'What colour and shape would "sadness" be?') are useful ways to help clients concretise and get to know their emotions better.
- Therapists shouldn't give up if individuals initially refuse to engage in chairwork or discount it: patient persistence is often required with this client group.

## Conclusion

Chairwork has stood the test of time and continues to inspire therapists from diverse therapeutic backgrounds. Within ST, chair-based techniques provide a powerful medium for combining cognitive and affective elements to help bring about last schematic change. Although evidence for effectiveness remains limited in the EDs, preliminary findings and clinical experience suggest that these techniques represent a promising method for working with the challenges that often arise with this population. It is hoped that through further research and continued clinical application, chairwork will continue to be recognised as an effective, and perhaps vital, tool in ST for ED and other client groups.

## References

Anestis, M., Selby, E., Fink, E., & Joiner, T. (2007). The multifaceted role of distress tolerance in dysregulated eating behaviors. *International Journal of Eating Disorders*, 40(8), 718–726.

Arntz, A., & Jacob, G. (2013). *Schema Therapy in Practice: An Introductory Guide to the Schema Mode Approach*. Chichester: Wiley.

Butollo, W., Karl, R., König, J., & Rosner, R. (2016). A randomized controlled clinical trial of dialogical exposure therapy versus cognitive processing therapy for adult outpatients suffering from PTSD after type I trauma in adulthood. *Psychotherapy and Psychosomatics*, 85(1), 16–26.

Brewin, C. R. (2006). Understanding cognitive behaviour therapy: A retrieval competition account. *Behaviour Research and Therapy*, 44(6), 765–784.

Caslini, M., Bartoli, F., Crocamo, C., Dakanalis, A., Clerici, M., & Carrà, G. (2016). Disentangling the association between child abuse and eating disorders: A systematic review and meta-analysis. *Psychosomatic Medicine*, 78(1), 79–90.

Chadwick, P. (2003). Two chairs, self-schemata and a person based approach to psychosis. *Behavioural and Cognitive Psychotherapy*, 31(4), 439–449.

Dolhanty, J., & Greenberg, L. (2009). Emotion-focused therapy in a case of anorexia nervosa. *Clinical Psychology and Psychotherapy*, 16(4), 336–382.

Fox, J., & Harrison, A. (2008). The relation of anger to disgust: The potential role of coupled emotions within eating pathology. *Clinical Psychology & Psychotherapy*, 15(2), 86–95.

Geller, J., Cockell, S., Hewitt, P., Goldner, E., & Flett, G. (2000). Inhibited expression of negative emotions and interpersonal orientation in anorexia nervosa. *International Journal of Eating Disorders*, 28(1), 8–19.

Gilbert, P. (2009). *Overcoming Depression: A Self-Help Guide Using Cognitive Behavioral Techniques*. London: Constable and Robinson.

Greenberg, L. (1979). Resolving splits: Use of the two chair technique. *Psychotherapy: Theory, Research & Practice*, 16(3), 316.

Greenberg, L. (2011). *Emotion-focused Therapy*. American Psychological Association.

Kellogg, S. (2004). Dialogical encounters: Contemporary perspectives on 'chairwork' in psychotherapy. *Psychotherapy: Theory, Research, Practice, Training*, 41(3), 310.

Kellogg, S. (2014). *Transformational Chairwork: Using Psychotherapeutic Dialogues in Clinical Practice*. Lanham, MD: Rowman & Littlefield.

Moreno, J. (1948). Group psychotherapy: Theory and practice. *Group Psychotherapy*, 3(2–3), 142–188.

Perls, F. (1973). *The Gestalt Approach and& Eye Witness to Therapy*. Palo Alto, CA: Science & Behavior Books.

Pugh, M. (2015). A narrative review of schemas and schema therapy outcomes in the eating disorders. *Clinical Psychology Review*, 39, 30–41.

Pugh, M. (2016). The internal 'anorexic voice': a feature or fallacy of eating disorders? *Advances in Eating Disorders*, 4(1), 75–83.

Pugh, M. (2017a). Pull up a chair. *The Psychologist*, 30, 42–47.

Pugh, M. (2017b). Chairwork in cognitive behavioural therapy: A narrative review. *Cognitive Therapy and Research*, 41(1), 16–30.

Pugh, M. (2018). Cognitive behavioural chairwork. *International Journal of Cognitive Therapy*, 11(1), 100–116.

Pugh, M., & Salter, C. (2017). *Motivational Chairwork: A Novel Method for Enhancing Motivation and Resolving Ambivalence in Eating Disorders.* Workshop presented at the London Eating Disorders Conference, London, March.

Pugh, M., & Waller, G. (2017). Understanding the 'anorexic voice' in anorexia nervosa. *Clinical Psychology & Psychotherapy*, 24(3), 670–676.

Pugh, M., Waller, G., & Esposito, M. (2018). Childhood trauma, dissociation, and the internal eating disorder 'voice'. *Child Abuse & Neglect*, 86, 197–205.

Simpson, S. (2012). Schema therapy for eating disorders: A case illustration of the mode approach. In van Vreeswijk, M., Broersen, J. & Nadort, M. (Eds.), *The Wiley-Blackwell Handbook of Schema Therapy: Theory, Research, and Practice* (145–171). Chichester: Wiley.

Talbot, D., Smith, E., Tomkins, A., Brockman, R., & Simpson, S. (2015). Schema modes in eating disorders compared to a community sample. *Journal of Eating Disorders*, 3(1), 41.

Young, J. E. (1990). *Practitioner's Resource Series. Cognitive Therapy for Personality Disorders: A Schema-focused Approach.* Sarasota, FL, England: Professional Resource Exchange, Inc.

Young, J., Klosko, J., & Weishaar, M. (2003). *Schema Therapy: A Practitioner's Guide.* New York: Guilford Press.

Chapter 9

# Behavioural pattern breaking in schema therapy for eating disorders

## Learning from other evidence-based approaches

*Christina Archonti, Susan Simpson, Gianluca Castelnuovo and Giada Pietrabissa*

### Abstract

*This chapter explores a range of behavioural interventions to specifically address anorexia (AN) and bulimia nervosa (BN)/binge eating, by integrating schema therapy (ST) with behavioural strategies utilised in other evidence-based approaches. Each diagnostic profile is symptomatically different, to the extent that, at times, the specific challenges may indeed be contradictory. The challenges concern the differences between coping modes, which serve to regulate emotions, but also the quality of the* Inner Critic *(Demanding or Punitive Parent modes) (Archonti, Roediger & De Zwaan, 2016). Historical assessment of the onset of eating disorder (ED) symptoms often reveals important signs that these were preceded by expressions of already frustrated needs and self-soothing behaviours. Identification of these 'clues' point to the early factors that precipitated and maintained 'survival' coping modes at the time they first emerged.*

### Introduction

Much of the cognitive, interpersonal and experiential work in ST is aimed at shifting the underlying early maladaptive schemas (EMS) that drive and maintain EDs (alongside other comorbidities). This includes recognising and challenging the *Inner Critic (Parent)* modes, re-parenting to heal the *Vulnerable Child (VCh)* mode, bypassing the resulting coping modes that are linked to the over-evaluation of shape, weight and self-starvation, as well as validating and setting limits on *Angry Child (AnCh)* and *Impulsive Child* modes that drive self-destructive 'acting out' of needs (e.g. bingeing). The techniques that are utilised to facilitate emotional shifts in ST operate as pre-requisites for change, but they are usually insufficient on their own to address chronically established eating behaviours. Specific interventions are selected according to the type of mode and the 'phase' of an ED.

ST techniques are based on the premise that a state of emotional home-ostasis can only be reached once core emotional (and physical) needs are consistently met in healthy ways. To this aim, the personal qualities of thera-pists are of fundamental importance: they need to be openly warm and flex-ible enough to allow for different interpersonal styles to create a re-parenting bond with the client (limited reparenting). It is especially important for the client to trust their therapist sufficiently to take anxiety-provoking steps associated with relinquishing ED behaviours. As therapy progresses, and the therapeutic rapport is strengthened, the therapist can introduce healthy limit-setting and empathic confrontation, to challenge clients to change their behaviours in order to get their needs met. This also involves developing a healthy tension between meeting the client's needs in a way that creates enough frustration for them to feel motivated to seek opportunities to get their needs met in other relationships outside of therapy.

## Overview of therapy steps: Behavioural techniques with anorexia nervosa

The experiential techniques employed within ST can function as a powerful extension to a first-line cognitive behavioural therapy (CBT) (Fairburn, Marcus, & Wilson, 1993) treatment plan, as well as a broader stand-alone treatment for those with high complexity and comorbidity. The ST approach enables an in depth understanding of the motives of the self-damaging beha-viour associated with EDs. The frustrated needs become apparent once access to the child modes, which are hidden behind the coping modes, has been achieved. The *VCh* holds the experience of feeling alone or isolated (disrupted attachment), whereas the *AnCh* often represents the tension associated with frustrated assertiveness, autonomy and control. In general, there is a strong internal tension between the *Inner Critic* and the needs of the *VCh*. The coping modes can be understood and thus validated as failed 'attempted solutions' to resolve this inner tension. This deeper-level understanding, which is established through re-parenting and an empathic emotionally attuned relationship with the child modes, enhances the therapeutic alliance. Behavioural pattern-breaking is a crucial component of the ST model, as a means of addressing the specific symptoms and behaviours that perpetuate the underlying schemas. Therefore, cognitive and experiential ST interven-tions ultimately serve to increase motivation and facilitate behavioural change.

The first part of this chapter will focus on behavioural pattern-breaking in the context of ST for AN, followed by a focus on bulimic/binge eating dis-orders in the second half. For the purpose of the overview on mode work for AN, we will present the three main components of therapy and describe a brief approach for clients who have at least a minimal level of willingness to attend therapy. We also describe ways of addressing common obstacles within the therapeutic process. In all of these steps, cognitive and experiental mode work techniques can be used to enhance outcomes, alongside CBT and skills training to promote eating behaviours and emotional regulation (Safer, Telch & Chen, 2009). For a summary of CBT behavioural strategies, alongside ST extensions, see Table 9.1.

### Step 1: Developing a hierarchy for behavioural experiments

Although we recognise that clients are frequently reluctant to relinquish their coping strategies/modes, there is no way to do therapy with restrictive and underweight clients without a target weight range and a graduated meal plan. We recommend developing a hierarchy in the style of a hierarchical therapy plan in dialectical behaviour therapy (DBT) (Linehan, 2014), with the dual goals of enhancing commitment to therapy (contract and agreement about healthy targets) and quality of life (all of the well-known strategies from CBT plus DBT skills training). The hierarchy can be made more meaningful by widening it to include behavioural experiments regarding both ED and comorbidity-specific behaviours. CBT and DBT can easily be incorporated into ST behavioural change work, with adaptations targeting modes and EMS. For example, the idiosyncratic 'safety behaviours' associated with the *Overcontroller (OC)* mode can be overtly addressed through behavioural experiments. This might address target behaviours such as water loading (drinking excessive amounts of water to reduce hunger and/or give the impression of weight gain), behavioural rituals at mealtimes, hiding or smearing food, reassurance seeking, weighing food, cutting food into tiny pieces, separating food groups on the plate to avoid cross-contamination, and waiting to be given permission to eat instead of self-initiating. Meal support sessions provided by multi-disciplinary teams and in/day-patient services can greatly assist the process of identifying target behaviours and working through behavioural hierarchies. In addition, intermittently video-recording meal-times can enable the therapist and client to 'stand outside' the modes and to link them with ED behaviours after the event. This can help build insight into mode-based behaviour, facilitate self-reflection in terms of the effects of these behaviours on others, and identify behaviours which can be added to behavioural hierarchies.

### Linking CBT with ST

As in CBT, ST psychoeducation is provided to manage expectations regarding the recovery process, and to pre-empt possible factors that may impact on outcomes of behavioural experiments. This is particularly important given that the unrelenting thinking style characteristic of the *OC* can frequently impair recovery. For example, many clients expect that if they behave 'correctly', the recovery process should be quick, efficient and anxiety-free. Clients

*Table 9.1* Integration of cognitive behavioural therapy strategies with schema therapy

| Cognitive behavioural therapy (CBT/CBT-E) | Schema therapy integration |
|---|---|
| **FIRST and SECOND PHASE** | |
| Thorough *quanti-qualitative assessment* | Life history assessment, exploration of eating behaviours linked to schemas. In-session *tracking/observation of modes*; diagnostic mode dialogue |
| Case formulation; personalised *goal-setting*; and *psychoeducation* about treatment/disorder | *Schema case conceptualisation* and *mode map*; explicit psychoeducation regarding schemas/modes |
| *Self-monitoring* and collaborative *weekly weighing* | *Promote mode awareness* through self-monitoring of schemas/modes/ED behaviours<br>*Link current problems to schemas/modes*, childhood/adolescent experiences, unmet needs |
| Implementation of initial *behavioural modifications* (e.g. meal planning, identification of alternative activities) | *Pros/cons of coping modes* exercise<br>*Explore therapeutic goals:* (1) access vulnerability and unmet needs underlying ED behaviours, (2) build/strengthen *Healthy Adult* side capable of self-compassion, acceptance of feelings/needs, and nourishing self (3) learn to identify and ask for needs to be met in direct ways (from emotionally available others), (4) learn to trust body signals and set limits on coping modes. |
| *Involving significant others* to support change<br>Ongoing progress review | Deepening therapeutic relationship through emotional *attunement*. *Schema-based family interventions* to address transgenerational cognitive-behavioural coping patterns that perpetuate EMS. |
| **THIRD PHASE** | |
| *Behavioural experiments* to test feared predictions regarding consequences of healthy eating | *Behavioural experiments* aimed at challenging parent and coping modes, with goal of examining fears and values linked to modes, learning to trust body signals, and breaking behavioural patterns that perpetuate EMS<br>*Chairwork and empathic confrontation* to bypass coping modes, and access *Vulnerable/Lonely Child mode* |
| *Cognitive restructuring* of beliefs and values that trigger and maintain ED | Provide corrective emotional experiences using *imagery rescripting, reparenting imagery, historical role-play and positive imagery.* |
| *Skills building*: emotional regulation, building interpersonal relationships, reduce clinical perfectionism, increase self-esteem | Client develops and strengthens a (*Healthy Adult*) self-compassionate perspective via internalisation of therapist messages introduced through *experiential work, limited reparenting, cognitive "scaffolding"* |

| Cognitive behavioural therapy (CBT/CBT-E) | Schema therapy integration |
|---|---|
| **FOURTH PHASE** | |
| *Consolidation and maintenance of progress* *Support self-efficacy*: personalised plans of action jointly devised; person is encouraged to continue developing new interests *Relapse prevention* and establishment of realistic expectations regarding the future | Strengthening *Healthy Adult* coping and self-nourishment through *mode/schema flashcards and schema diaries* *Future-based imagery* to identify and dialogue with modes blocking progress; behavioural rehearsal to strengthen *Healthy Adult* coping in place of eating behaviours – to get needs met. |

with AN frequently express shock and confusion regarding the discomfort (both emotional and physiological) associated with recovery. Clients can be reassured regarding the typical physiological and emotional changes associated with weight gain. This may include explanations regarding the role of oedema and fluid shifts, delayed gastric emptying (leading to feeling full longer than usual), fluctuating hunger (as the system attempts to recalibrate), and increases in metabolic rates, that can lead to unexpected weight fluctuations. In addition, it is important to normalise weight gain redistribution, whereby initial weight gain tends to be focused around vital organs, mostly the stomach area, often taking many months for this to redistribute across the body. Emotional vulnerability and distress becomes overtly apparent as the client gains weight, and experiential techniques can become easier to implement.

In order to maximise commitment to therapy, both within inpatient and outpatient settings, we suggest starting with any problem that the client prioritises and would like to change. For clients who are strongly motivated by the positive reinforcement of the *OC* by peers or family (e.g. being thin, gaining attention, feeling strong and morally superior) it is important to identify which particular behaviours they see as problematic, and continue to enquire through an ongoing dialectic exploratory dialogue. Generating a list of pros and cons of the coping modes that includes both ED and non-ED behaviours can generate awareness of its far-reaching impact on the person's life (see Appendix 1).

In other cases it may be important to start exploring difficulties arising from working specifically on triggers associated with behavioural aspects of therapy. Typical triggers might include setting the target weight contract above a body mass index of 17.5, or a therapist's unintentional use of words, such as 'this won't be *enough*' (for a healthy weight/as a stopover – in reference to the weight contract). Possible questions for helping clients to consider problematic behaviours/symptoms are:

- *On the one hand, you don't see any problem behaviour, is there another view/perspective?*
- *What kinds of behaviour does this part of you (mode) feel are necessary?*
- *When you begin each day, what kinds of thoughts do you notice...what's the first thought that pops into your mind?*
- *How do you feel about your target weight?*
- *I understand that you don't see any reason to gain weight, but I'm also curious as to why you seem to be struggling to concentrate at work? How does this link in with the idea that you don't need to eat more than once a day?*
- *When I said the word 'average', it seemed to trigger something in you. This was not my purpose, but, what I'm wondering whether this word feels familiar to you? Is this how you think of yourself, or do you think anyone in your family sees you this way?*

The collaborative development of a mode map can be the first step to introduce the client to the concept of modes. This includes identifying the *Inner Critic* and recognising its impact on their inner experience of distress (*VCh*), and functioning as a strong driving factor behind the ED. Mode work leads on to a usual CBT-behavioural focus with meal plans, self-monitoring and regular in-session weighing. A typical mode map developed in the early stages of therapy with a client with AN is shown in Chapter 5. Mode maps represent a preliminary mechanism for facilitating behavioural change. They can be used to identify and separate the *Inner Critic* from other helpful and more life-affirming thoughts and feelings, and can be used for self-monitoring and addressing avoidance of 'forbidden foods' or any ED behaviour.

Usually within the first five therapy sessions, a therapy contract, a weight contract and materials such as meal plans and schema (schema-eating) diaries are introduced, together with an individualised mode map. These provide the foundation on which all further interventions are based. The contract should include weight gain goals – we aim to find a balance between setting realistic and healthy weight gain targets, whilst avoiding falling into the trap of stepping into the *Inner Critic* role by demanding that they must re-gain an exact amount of weight each week. In outpatient treatment, when gaining weight is not a question of survival or averting imminent medical emergencies, weight gain may be carried out in more manageable steps. Weight loss should not be reinforced with additional or longer sessions, and the contract should record the consequence if weight loss persists, including limit-setting through 'non-negotiables'. Examples of non-negotiables may include regular weighing, attendance at sessions, the weight/medical parameters at which the client will be admitted to hospital for re-feeding, as well as communication between the professional team. Research has shown that setting limits on weight loss in advance through non-negotiables can be therapeutic if certain conditions are followed, including: involving the client, carers, and treatment team; ensuring that limits are clearly recorded in written format and re-evaluated on a regular basis (e.g. at care-program review meetings); ensuring clients understand the rationale and view it as fair; maximising client autonomy; and applying limits consistently, thereby avoiding surprises (Geller & Srikameswaran, 2006). In order to engage the client in discussions regarding non-negotiables, they need to be presented in an empathic, 'one-down position' whereby the therapist and client are both obliged to follow the laws of a higher order (e.g. mental health legislation or laws of nature) (Treasure & Schmidt, 2008). Therapists should also be aware of their own schemas that may interfere with their capacity to set and follow through with non-negotiables (e.g. a *subjugation* schema may lead to avoidance of following through with setting limits due to fear of the client becoming angry).

### Step 2: Experiental chairwork and imagery rescripting

As mentioned above, the first challenge when starting therapy is to gain clients' commitment to therapy. It is inevitable that most clients experience some level of ambivalence about attending therapy, even if it is masked by an upbeat and positive narrative. No matter what the circumstances, the aim is to introduce some kind of nutritional change as early as possible in the therapeutic process.

Blocks are frequent for very rigid restrictive clients with AN due to over-identification with the *Inner Critic* and coping modes. Self-critical thoughts and self-sabotaging eating behaviours remain egosyntonic (consistent with one's ideal self-image) at this early stage of therapy. Those with AN are often focused on improving their productivity and general performance, rather than addressing their body weight. They perceive self-starvation and deficit in self-care as a strength, which brings a sense of pride. Coping modes function to block or overcompensate for emotional distress because of the continual [self-] shaming of the *Inner Critic*. Questioning this status can lead to a power struggle whereby the client defends her dysfunctional coping mode, rather than engaging in treatment.

In contrast to a classic CBT-contract which encourages the use of behavioural analysis and behavioural distractions early in the therapeutic process, we recommend experiental work as a precursor to introducing these steps. Imagery rescripting can be used both for diagnostic purposes and changing behaviours. Imagery rescripting (Chapter 7) can begin by focusing on current triggers such as getting a less-than-perfect grade at school, or target behaviours such as eating forbidden food. Alternatively, any current situation which leads to strong inner tension and ambivalence can be used, such as attempts to 'break the rules' of the parent/coping modes by eating more. Through imagery work, the affect-bridge links current stressors with relevant childhood memories, thus providing a mechanism for understanding and healing the EMS and associated unmet needs associated with ED behaviours. Chairwork (Chapter 8) is another powerful intervention strategy that can be used to investigate and address obstructions in therapy, facilitating differentiation of modes that are afraid of or angry about change, from the parts that continue to suffer as a result of the status quo.

### Step 3: Between-session behavioural work – transferring into daily life

One useful mechanism that can be employed to support the transfer of the corrective emotional messages into behavioural change is that of written and audio flashcards (see Appendix 1 for template of a mode flashcard). These provide a reality-check in the face of recurrent situations that trigger ED behaviours, by preparing a response to old schema-messages, thereby activating healthy coping mechanisms that allow the person to get their needs met in direct, adaptive ways. Flashcards should be adapted according to the disorder, with a focus on replacing habitual eating behaviours with adaptive behaviours that can directly meet the person's emotional and physical needs (Young, Klosko, & Weishaar, 2003). At this point all of the well-known strategies from CBT and skills training can be incorporated, with some ST adaptations. Chairwork and flashcards together with CBT-behavioural analysis are used in and between sessions to reinforce and enhance the effect of intervention strategies.

In some instances, particularly for low weight AN, planned inpatient admissions can provide a powerful adjunct to outpatient treatment, especially when ST is available across both services. Medical and nutritional stabilisation through planned inpatient admissions can provide the safety for processing of trauma and/or targeting specific behavioural changes.

## Behavioural pattern-breaking for individuals who binge eat

This second part of the chapter will focus on behavioural pattern-breaking in binge eating disorders, drawing on and integrating effective strategies from other well-established therapeutic approaches: CBT, and Brief Strategic Therapy (BST). ST behavioural pattern-breaking strategies rely on standard behaviour therapy techniques.

### Integrating CBT behavioural change strategies in ST for binge eating disorders

Individuals with BN and BED often hold negative or distorted views of themselves and their bodies. These beliefs are shaped by developmental processes and experiences, often resulting in dysfunctional cognitions (e.g. over-evaluation of weight and shape, negative body image, core beliefs about self-worth, negative self-evaluation, perfectionism) and unmanageable emotions that trigger maladaptive weight-control behaviours – including dieting, fasting, purging in the form of vomiting, laxative/diuretic use or over-exercise, as well as body checking and body avoidance. These, in turn, result in further negative emotions – such as guilt or shame – that reinforce the vicious cycle that maintains the problem (Jackson, Pietrabissa, Rossi, Manzoni, & Castelnuovo, 2018).

For clients with binge eating who have been unable to engage in CBT and implement behavioural changes due to entrenched EMS and modes, the ST approach may provide the scaffolding to facilitate strengthening of their *Healthy Adult (HA)* self, alongside healing of underlying emotional vulnerability. Once the *HA* side has been strengthened through cognitive, interpersonal and experiential strategies, they are then ready to once again embark on behavioural pattern-breaking, through self-monitoring, establishing regular mealtimes, setting up behavioural experiments and hierarchical exposure to feared foods. Due to the high levels of distress associated with ED symptomatology, the earlier these steps can be implemented, the better. Breaking the steps into mini-steps in the early stages of therapy can build self-efficacy, as well as a sense of safety and relief from ongoing distress. In the latter stages of therapy, the ST therapist must be relentless in pushing for change, empathically reminding clients that their capacity to overcome feelings of loneliness, anxiety and depression that are perpetuated by their eating difficulties, and to reach their life goals, is heavily dependent on changing the behaviours that perpetuate their EMS and ED. ST extensions of traditional CBT techniques for change are provided in Table 9.1.

### Behavioural experiments

Behavioural experiments with binge eating disorders are aimed at investigating and challenging the *Inner Critic [Parent]* and coping modes. This must be done gradually to examine beliefs and values linked to the modes, to test feared catastrophes associated with 'letting go' of these modes, and to provide a desensitisation function. For example, if a person believes that eating a cupcake will cause a five-pound weight gain, s/he would be encouraged to consume a cupcake and see if it does. Once both eating and non-eating related behaviours are listed in relation to a given mode, the therapist and client collaboratively arrange these hierarchically according to the level of clients' associated distress. When working to reduce the perfectionism typical of the *OC*, for example, the hierarchy might include a range of behavioural steps, including reducing cleaning/checking rituals, purposefully making mistakes, drawing/painting (and other 'uncontrollable-creative' exercises), as well as reducing specific eating disorder behaviours such as body-checking, restriction and compulsive exercise. Starting with non-eating or appearance-related behaviours can help to build confidence before moving on to address more established ED behaviours. With each behavioural step, the *HA* grows, and the 'neuronal gossip' associated with the *Inner Critic* and coping modes weakens. While reducing self-perpetuating behaviours, behavioural experiments increase the repertoire of healthy eating behaviours (e.g. eating foods in a different order, eating new foods, eating at regular meal times, eating greater quantities) that represent the healthy functional modes (*HA* and *Happy Child*). Behavioural experiments are generally much more effective than cognitive restructuring alone. Clients might also view this as an opportunity to 'rebel' against their *Inner Critic*, thereby empowering them to fight their EMS, and facilitating individuation and autonomy. Behavioural experiments can be carried out in the context of multidisciplinary therapeutic work, and also completed for homework, in order to gradually build a *HA* sense of self-efficacy.

### Integrating Brief Strategic Therapy behavioural change strategies for binge eating disorders

In contrast to CBT, BST builds its intervention protocols starting from the *attempted solutions* that maintain and reinforce the problem, and simultaneously intervenes to disrupt and substitute dysfunctional patterns with more functional ones. In fact, all people have a natural inclination to reiterate solutions that have proven to be functional in the past (i.e. schema perpetuation through repeated reliance on 'survival' coping modes). But generalising such solutions to different situations, or insistently reapplying the same strategy when it is no longer effective, results in a vicious circle that creates and maintains a dysfunctional way of perceiving and reacting. For a summary of BST behavioural strategies, alongside ST extensions see Table 9.2.

### First phase of treatment

The *first phase* of the BST treatment for BN is crucial to capture clients' motivations and bypass any resistance towards change. Individuals with BN are, in fact, collaborative in their intentions, but are also hindered by the fact that they rely almost exclusively on their strength of will (i.e. *OC* mode) as their 'solution' to recovery. Depending on clients' EMS, the therapist may use the *miracle fantasy* technique to induce a form of positive self-deception or prophecy, that facilitates the development of a strong image of a possible life without the problem. From a ST perspective, the therapist can use future-oriented imagery, starting with details of the client's routine before going to sleep, and then imagining the miracle unexpectedly happens whilst they are asleep, with no explanation, and that when they awake the next morning, the miracle has fixed the problem that brought them to therapy. They are asked to identify the first thing they notice when they awaken, or how they discover that things are different. This is used to inspire hope and access *HA* goals beyond the limitations of coping mode mindsets. Other prescriptions include inviting the client to think how they could voluntarily worsen his/her target problem (*how worst* technique). This results in recognition that the [coping

*Table 9.2* Integration of Brief Strategic Therapy behavioural strategies with schema therapy

| Brief Strategic Therapy (BST) for bulimia nervosa (BN) | Brief Strategic Therapy (BST) for binge eating disorder (BED) | Schema therapy integration |
|---|---|---|
| **FIRST and SECOND PHASE** | | |
| *Miracle fantasy Conspiracy of silence Paradoxical exploration of functions of eating problems Paradoxical diet* | *Replace fear of bingeing with 'fear of fasting' Conspiracy of silence* | Circumvent coping modes via: *Pros/cons of coping modes exercise Interview and bypass coping modes through chairwork and imagery rescripting.* Encourage client to articulate vulnerability and needs directly *Pros & cons* of coping mode exercise *Empathic confrontation* and *chairwork* to dialogue with *Overcontroller* mode and empathically challenge strict rules as 'attempted solution' to underlying vulnerability, distress and low self-worth *Schema-based family sessions*, focused on family education, transgenerational schema identification, and developing empathic connections |
| **THIRD PHASE** | | |
| *Small food transgressions* during regular/well-balanced meals to reduce the urge to transgress | *'How worst'* to uncover perpetuating role of coping modes *'If you do it once, do it five times' paradoxical prescription* | *Chairwork* and *imagery rescripting* to address underlying psychological injury through confronting *Inner Critic* and reparenting *Vulnerable Child* Invite the *Impulsive Child mode* to 'break' the dietary *(Overcontroller)* rules, through regular transgressions – introducing new 'forbidden' foods and/or larger food intake Introduce *spontaneity*, humour, fun to overcome inhibition |
| **FOURTH PHASE** | | |
| Increase self-confidence and self-efficacy through evocative *stories/metaphors*, reviewing treatment progress, highlighting personal responsibility for change | | *Visualisation of Healthy Adult* nourishing and caring for *Vulnerable Child* side Use *flashcards* to reinforce behavioural changes, recognise achievements, and encourage responsibility of *Healthy Adult* mode |

mode] behaviours designed as 'solutions' to underlying EMS are in fact high risk maintaining factors, which must be reversed in order to achieve recovery. Chairwork can be used to identify and address modes that are resistant to change through increasing awareness of the costs of ED coping behaviours and associated unmet needs, thereby enhancing motivation to change (see Chapter 11).

The solutions offered by others who may be unwittingly colluding with keeping the current eating system intact must also be addressed. The important efforts of family are acknowledged, whilst asking them to provide no further attempts to 'fix' or mention the problem during the course of treatment: *conspiracy of silence* (Nardone & Barbieri, 2010). This highlights the importance of schema-based family work to ensure that coping modes are not reinforced and perpetuated at a systemic level. Systemic ST work can provide a powerful means of identifying and gently challenging transgenerational EMS and coping modes that may be unconsciously acted out.

### Second phase of treatment

During the *second phase* of treatment, the *paradoxical diet* represents the main manoeuvre for those with BN – they are asked to prepare and eat their favourite dishes for three meals each day (breakfast, lunch, and dinner), over a period of 10–14 days. They are instructed to enjoy the taste, and to avoid eating outside mealtimes. This provides an opportunity to learn that eating is beneficial up to a certain quantity, after which it becomes sickening. This is usually accompanied by the *if you do it once, do it five times* paradoxical prescription (Nardone, Verbitz, & Milanese, 1999), which, in ST-terms involves giving the *Impulsive Child* and/or *Detached Self-Soother* (*DetSS*) modes the opportunity and control – to eat everything they want – setting no limits, to the point where it becomes uncomfortable. This is based on the idea that temptation can best be overcome through succumbing to it, and is aimed at transforming the perceived pleasure of eating transgressions outside of meal-times into an experience of discomfort. The person learns that it is only through eating liked foods (rather than an exclusive diet of low-fat health foods) that one can find contentment, with no urges to binge. In contrast, with BED the challenge is to address the *OC* practice of extensive fasting, which increases the desire to binge (*Impulsive Child/DetSS*). Behavioural change is aimed at short-circuiting the vicious fast-binge cycle through transforming the fear of bingeing into a *fear of fasting* – the person is helped to recognise that it is in fact the *OC* (rather than the *Impulsive Child/DetSS* duo) that is creating the conditions for loss of control and further weight gain. In both BN and BED, this provides an opportunity to develop the capacity to set limits on their own eating based on their own body-experience – rather than through fear of loss-of-control (*Impulsive Child/DetSS*), or instructions from others.

### Third phase of treatment

In the *third stage* of therapy – once regular eating patterns are established – clients are encouraged to *regularly engage in small transgressions* of their *OC* rules (e.g. each day, treat yourself to a small portion of food that you crave but that your *OC* forbids). The more rigid the *OC* boundaries, the greater the temptation to transgress. In ST terms, the client thereby learns to internalise a healthy sense of self-control, through allowing their internal *Impulsive Child* to have regular opportunities to eat outside the 'rules'. Direct and paradoxical manoeuvres for consolidating gains made over the course of treatment, and revision of effective strategies for improving clients' relationship with food by adopting more balanced, flexible, and healthy eating behaviours are also further implemented until reaching the *fourth phase* of the therapy – ultimately designed to give their *HA* responsibility over their positive changes, so as to increase self-esteem and self-confidence (Nardone et al., 1999).

*Future imagery-rehearsal* can be used to facilitate recovery from all EDs, mental-practice of new behaviour, and identification of stuck-points and/or change-blocking modes (e.g. *AnCh* may believe that it isn't fair that s/he has to endure the stress of change; the *DetSS* may believe that there is no harm in a bit of bingeing; the *Inner Critic* may believe they don't deserve to recover, or that relaxation or eating is unnecessary and self-indulgent; the *VCh* may fear disappointment or anger from others as a result of changing family dynamics, or the *OC* may believe that restriction is a sign of inner-strength and is the best solution to ensure safety and overcome problems; *Helpless Surrenderer* believes that someone else should 'fix' them). In addition, full imagery rescripting allows painful memories to be revised – with the goal of meeting the clients' emotional and physical needs. With all EDs, imagery rescripting can facilitate processing of traumatic memories in order to facilitate behavioural changes that enable needs such as safety and protection to be met – rather than primarily using exposure and desensitisation techniques used in CBT. In addition, imagery rehearsal can be used to nurture clients' *Happy Child* – by focusing on behavioural changes that reduce stoicism and rigidity whilst increasing play and spontaneity. Further, roleplays can be utilised both in-session and as homework to practise and overcome stumbling blocks in interpersonal behavioural change work.

## Conclusions

Over the last decade, the integration of different forms of evidence-based treatments has been encouraged for the treatment of a range of psychiatric disorders. In particular, there is agreement among clinicians that EDs are very difficult disorders to treat: premature drop-out and relapse is frequent (Pietrabissa et al., 2012), and intensive hospital-based treatment programs for EDs have notoriously high rates of recidivism (Sorgente et al., 2017; Jackson et al., 2018). Motivation and readiness to change has been found to be especially low in individuals with EDs, and the existing literature on the topic suggests that the individuals' level of motivation is an important factor to be considered and fostered before engaging ED clients in intensive treatment for disordered eating (Pietrabissa et al., 2012; Ceccarini, Borrello, Pietrabissa, Manzoni, & Castelnuovo, 2015). In fact, although CBT approaches have some of the strongest evidence for change in their favour, it is also true that many individuals do not respond to treatment, do not adhere to treatment tasks, discontinue treatment prematurely or, after initial success, are unable to maintain change (Castelnuovo et al., 2011). Thus, integrating powerful behavioural change techniques from across a range of therapeutic modalities within ST may assist clients to consider relinquishing ED behaviours driven by underlying EMS, and improve both initial response rates and maintenance of change after treatment completion. Given the powerful role of ED coping behaviours in perpetuating underlying EMS, behavioural pattern-breaking is an essential component of ST throughout the therapeutic process. In order to accomplish this, and to bypass powerful habitual coping modes, the therapist must act as the 'lighthouse' (Chris Hayes, personal correspondence), sticking to our methods and goals of helping those with EDs to develop an authentic sense of self free of the 'chains' of habitual coping, and to develop healthy ways of getting their needs met.

## References

Archonti, C., Roediger, E., & De Zwaan, M. (Eds.). (2016). *Schematherapie bei Essstörungen: Mit E-Book inside und Arbeitsmaterial.* Mainz: Beltz.

Castelnuovo, G., Manzoni, G., Villa, V., Cesa, G., Pietrabissa, G., & Molinari, E. (2011). The STRATOB study: Design of a randomized controlled clinical trial of Cognitive Behavioral Therapy and Brief Strategic Therapy with telecare in patients with obesity and binge-eating disorder referred to residential nutritional rehabilitation. *Trials,* 12(1), 114.

Ceccarini, M., Borrello, M., Pietrabissa, G., Manzoni, G., & Castelnuovo, G. (2015). Assessing motivation and readiness to change for weight management and control: An in-depth evaluation of three sets of instruments. *Frontiers in Psychology,* 6, 511.

Fairburn, C., Marcus, M., & Wilson, G. (1993). Cognitive-behavioral therapy for binge eating and bulimia nervosa: A comprehensive treatment manual. In C. Fairburn & G. Wilson (Eds.). *Binge Eating: Nature, Assessment and Treatment* (pp. 361–404). New York: Guilford Press.

Geller, J., & Srikameswaran, S. (2006). Treatment non-negotiables: Why we need them and how to make them work. *European Eating Disorders Review: The Professional Journal of the Eating Disorders Association,* 14(4), 212–217.

Jackson, J. B., Pietrabissa, G., Rossi, A., Manzoni, G. M., & Castelnuovo, G. (2018). Brief strategic therapy and cognitive behavioral therapy for women with binge eating disorder and comorbid obesity: A randomized clinical trial one-year follow-up. *Journal of Consulting and Clinical Psychology,* 86(8), 688.

Linehan, M. (2014). *DBT Skills Training Manual.* New York: Guilford Publications.

Nardone, G., & Barbieri, R. B. (2010). Advanced Brief Strategic Therapy: An over-view of interventions with eating disorders to exemplify how theory and practice work. *European Journal of Psychotherapy and Counselling*, 12(2), 113–127.

Nardone, G., Verbitz, T., & Milanese, R. 1999. *The Prisons of Food: Strategic Solution-oriented Research and Treatment of Eating Disorders*. London: Karnac.

Pietrabissa, G., Manzoni, G., Corti, S., Vegliante, N., Molinari, E., & Castelnuovo, G. (2012). Addressing motivation in globesity treatment: A new challenge for clinical psychology. *Frontiers in Psychology*, 3, 317.

Safer, D., Telch, C., & Chen, E. (2009). *Dialectical Behavior Therapy for Binge Eating and Bulimia*. New York: Guilford Press.

Sorgente, A., Pietrabissa, G., Manzoni, G. M., Re, F., Simpson, S., Perona, S.,...& Castelnuovo, G. (2017). Web-based interventions for weight loss or weight loss maintenance in overweight and obese people: A systematic review of systematic reviews. *Journal of Medical Internet Research*, 19(6), e229.

Treasure, J., & Schmidt, U. (2008). Motivational interviewing in eating disorders. In H. Arkowitz, Westra, H., Miller, W., & Rollnick, S. (Eds.) *Motivational Interviewing and the Promotion of Mental Health* (pp. 194–224). New York: Guilford Press.

Young, J. E., Klosko, J. S., & Weishaar, M. E. (2003). *Schema Therapy: A Practitioner's Guide*. New York: Guilford Press.

# Chapter 10

# Manual of group schema therapy for eating disorders

*Susan Simpson*

## Abstract

*Health services are more challenged than ever to find ways of providing effective treatments for eating disorders (EDs) with limited resources. One way of addressing this is through combining group and individual treatment protocols. It is suggested that group therapy may in fact catalyse the effects of schema therapy (ST), by providing corrective emotional learning experiences, as well as fora in which participants can begin to develop and practice new interpersonal and behavioural coping skills that heal their early maladaptive schemas (EMS). In addition, the experience of sharing similar experiences and early maladaptive schemas with other participants can counteract the experience of shame and powerlessness that many clients with ED experience, as well as providing ample opportunities to learn vicariously through others (Simpson, Morrow, van Vreeswijk, & Reid, 2010; Broersen & Van Vreeswijk, 2012). Preliminary pilot group trials have utilised this manual with a mixed transdiagnostic ED sample (Calvert, Smith, Brockman, & Simpson, 2018; Simpson et al., 2010).*

## STE-g manual overview

The manual of schema therapy for eating disorders group (STE-g manual) combines all four elements of the ST approach: interpersonal, experiential, cognitive and behavioural. All four are essential in bringing about change, both in terms of emotional and physical health and well-being for this client group. The emphasis of this group manual is on experiential group exercises and processes that facilitate change with the whole group. It also has a strong focus on pushing for behavioural change, in order to reduce schema perpetuation and reinforcement. Most importantly, the protocol focuses on helping participants to support each other in getting their emotional (and physiological) needs met. This is not individual therapy in a group context. Group leaders need to utilise group exercises flexibly in a way that meets the needs of the group as well as possible. Not all participants' needs will be directly met in all sessions. However, it is important for group leaders to encourage participants to learn to ask for what they need. Diagnostic imagery during initial (individual) assessment sessions can help group members to begin to link early experiences with their current problems, modes and EMS. Further information on the assessment and conceptualisation of EDs is described in Chapters 4 and 5, and further details on experiential mode work in Chapters 7 and 8.

The protocol that is described here has a flexible structure and is based on 25 90-minute group sessions and two follow-up sessions. A 'bank' of up to four individual sessions is also available to participants, to be taken at any point during the course of the group program. The evidence base for EDs has shown that standard treatments for this client group generally range between 19–40 sessions (Fairburn et al., 2009).

### Goals in group schema therapy – changing modes

One of the main objectives in STE-g is to help participants recognise and distinguish their different 'sides' or modes. The aim is to differentiate the modes in order to eventually integrate them into a coherent self. Many clients with EDs come to therapy feeling 'stuck' in a particular coping mode that they identify as 'self'. Coping modes and associated ED behaviours are schema driven and therefore resistant to change unless the underlying EMS are addressed. We begin the healing work in ST firstly by helping participants to recognise and gradually accept their own and other participants' vulnerability – a side of themselves which is all too often rejected and viewed as 'too needy', 'ridiculous', 'over the top' as a result of emotionally invalidating messages during childhood. These messages have also often been internalised from cultural sources, which place a high emphasis on success and outward appearance at the expense of internal self-value and interpersonal connection (Moradi, Dirks, & Matteson, 2005; Roberts & Gettman, 2004). Many sufferers fear that if they let go of the main coping modes that drive their ED (e.g. *Overcontroller (OC), Detached Self Soother (DetSS)*), they will return to a state of profound and deep loneliness and abandonment, leaving them feeling overwhelmed, out of control and unsafe. In treatment, the goal is to help participants differentiate the modes in order to join them up and facilitate healthy integration. Participants develop the capacity to self-govern as the *Healthy Adult (HA)* self takes over the role of 'chairperson' of the modes. This transition opens opportunities to value the self as a whole person that embraces vulnerability, to connect with others at a deeper level and ultimately to enable emotional needs to be met.

### Practical issues

#### Selecting group participants and leaders

Although STE-g has a psychoeducational component, the mainstay of the treatment has an emphasis on group processes that facilitate interpersonal learning and emotional, cognitive and behavioural change. The goal in STE-g is to balance the structure offered within the manual with the flexibility that is one of the strengths of the schema mode model.

### Diagnostics and measurements

The therapeutic interview is the central assessment tool. Useful psychometric evaluations at baseline are outlined in Chapter 4. At the beginning of the group, leaders should have an assessment overview, EMS and schema mode profile, and case conceptualisation for each participant.

### Preparation for group work

Attendance can be improved if therapists meet with group participants prior to the start of the group, to begin therapeutic bonding. This is especially important for clients with a history of attachment difficulties, who may benefit from the extra security of building a connection with the therapists before the group begins. Ideally, group members should have at least two individual assessment sessions prior to the group starting. At least one of these assessment sessions should be attended by at least one of the group leaders. This helps with initial therapeutic bonding, which can in turn help group members to overcome the anxiety they experience in relation to attending the group. At a minimum, the assessment should cover developmental history, attachment /relationship history and patterns, and current difficulties, culminating in a case conceptualisation which guides their treatment.

### Minimising dropouts

Although dropouts are not uncommon in the context of group therapy, they can, potentially, affect the morale of the group negatively and therefore should be handled carefully. Participants who at the start of the group demonstrate poor psychological mindedness and motivation, a lack of self-awareness, and a tendency to be overly wary or mistrustful of the group can evoke hostile reactions from other group participants, thereby perpetuating their schemas. Group leaders should aim to provide these group members with their bank of individual sessions in the early part of therapy in order to facilitate the bonding process. Group members are strongly encouraged to use what they learn in individual sessions when they return to the group, and to share their new insights with other group members. Some preparation prior to the group starting, including assistance with developing insight into their interpersonal responses and subsequently their ability to get their needs met within the group can be invaluable. Having said this, preliminary evidence suggests that dropout rates in group ST are low (e.g. Farrell, Shaw & Webber, 2009; Simpson et al., 2010).

Participants are encouraged to recognise their attendance as important not only for their own recovery, but also as an essential contribution to the recovery of other participants. If participants plan to be away due to unavoidable circumstances, they are invited to attend via a secure videoconferencing platform (e.g. VSee, Zoom). Absences are discussed openly in terms of the experience of loss, disconnection, and subsequent impact on the group 'family' as a whole. When group participants make comments to help or support others within the group, it is important to draw attention to how important and potentially healing their presence and input is. Therapists should stress the importance of noticing the impact that each group participant has on the other participants. Typically, at the start of the group, many participants believe that the group therapists are the only ones who contribute to their recovery, and that they have little or nothing of value to offer each other. As the group progresses, we emphasise the importance of consciously internalising the messages from therapists and other group members. Participants are encouraged to identify shared modes that are sabotaging their progress, and these are confronted with a focus on the whole group.

### Therapists

Therapists should ideally be trained in group processes and stages, and/or have experience in running groups (Burlingame, MacKenzie, & Strauss, 2004). It is essential to have a minimum of two therapists in order to manage the complex dynamics that evolve within the context of group treatment (Berk, 2005). Group therapists are advised to take turns at taking the lead or playing the co-therapist. Often one therapist may be focused on particular participants at any given point, whilst the other therapist is remaining attuned to the needs and reactions of the remainder of the group. In this way, the group remains the main focus at all times, even when there is a focus on individuals in particular sessions.

Therapists take on a parental role within the group 'family'. Even though it can be beneficial for group therapists to have their own differing personal styles, it is essential that both are competent in implementing the ST model. Therapists can provide the group with a model for interpersonal communication and staying connected whilst managing minor disagreements. It can be beneficial for the group if therapists model gentle confrontations from time to time, as this is an essential interpersonal skill that many group participants are lacking. This can lead to discussions around managing tension and anger in constructive and healthy ways in interpersonal relationships. "Modelling disagreements" also creates a situation where the group members can be angry with one therapist and still experience the other as 'the good therapist'. In a well working therapist couple the 'good parent' can help group members integrate their feelings regarding the other parent and help them not to experience them only as 'bad'. Therefore, in this context a temporary split can be helpful. For example, within group therapy, clients with the *emotional deprivation* EMS have the opportunity to experience the [perceived] 'bad' parent as concurrently caring and emotionally nurturing in their own unique way. This can facilitate the development of greater tolerance toward others, even in the context of feeling let-down or disappointed by others' responses (Van Vreeswijk & Broersen, 2013)

The therapists' role is to hold the group boundaries and to contain transferential reactions, whilst helping participants to develop insight into the realistic differences between the group and their childhood interpersonal experiences. It is of utmost importance that therapists maintain a high level of self-awareness and self-care in order to best manage the strong transference and countertransference reactions within group settings. A regular mindfulness practice can be invaluable in keeping this high on the agenda (van Vreeswijk, Broersen, & Schurink, 2014). Regular supervision facilitates the containment of transference and countertransference reactions, and provides an opportunity to explore ways in which therapists' own EMS are triggered within sessions by group participants and also by each other (e.g. competitiveness associated with *failure* or *unrelenting standards* EMS).

### Managing risk

Due to the medical risk that often accompanies EDs, it is of utmost importance that group participants provide written consent to allow group leaders to liaise with general practitioners and medical specialists who provide medical monitoring.

### Therapy interfering behaviours – setting limits

Due to the way in which coping modes operate, group leaders will need to set limits when group boundaries are violated. Limit-setting and empathic confrontation will mostly be directed at behaviours in which other participants' needs are being disregarded (e.g. shouting, excluding, aggrandising). Group leaders empathise with the underlying distress, whilst letting the participant know that their behaviour is preventing others from hearing them and being able to meet their needs. They are then encouraged to try a new way of communicating in order to more effectively connect with others and get their needs met.

## STE-g manual content

### Sessions 1–5

Sessions one to five focus on understanding the ST model, and incorporating ED (and other problematic) symptoms and behaviours within a mode map conceptualisation. This enables us to shift the focus from doing 'battle' with the ED to working explicitly with the modes that drive it. Much of the work in these preliminary sessions is psychoeducational and based on cognitive and behavioural principles. We introduce the concept that over the course of the group, participants' *HA* parts are coached, in order to enable them to fight their *Inner Critic*, negotiate with their coping modes, value and care for their

*Vulnerable Child* (*VCh*), and set limits on both coping modes and *Angry* (*AnCh*)/*Impulsive Child* modes. Behavioural goals linked to the ED are explicitly formulated for each individual at the outset of the group, and these are linked to their mode map. We explain that the overarching goal is for participants to change behavioural patterns whilst learning healthy ways of recognising and asking for underlying needs to be met. Although group leaders model the *HA* role for the first part of the programme, participants gradually take on this role for each other as the group proceeds.

At the beginning of each session, we encourage participants to reflect on how they feel, giving options so that each participant can find a way of expressing their felt-sense in a way that resonates for them, for example, through providing colour wheels, lists of 'emotion-words', lists of facial emojis, and/or packs of emotion cards. Scarves can be used in the group as an overt tangible representation of emotional connection, especially with participants who 'zone out' in a coping mode, or those who need comfort within a child mode (Farrell & Shaw, 2012). However, we have found that with this client group, directly connecting with participants through sitting close to them, and speaking gently and directly with them (and inviting the group to help) can be preferable, especially for those who feel self-conscious about their vulnerability and emotional needs. Group bonding is enhanced throughout the program by including exercises that counteract rigidity and encourage spontaneity and play. For ideas, see section on *Happy Child* (*HAC*) exercises, and Appendix 1.

Self-monitoring is introduced as a mechanism for 'watching' one's own modes in action. Linking of modes and ED behaviours is facilitated through measures such as the *Schema-Mode Eating Diary, Schema Mode Tracker, Understanding Coping Modes* (see Appendix I), and *Mode Pie Charts* (Farrell & Shaw, 2018). Participants are asked to monitor modes that have been identified in their own mode maps, alongside associated ED behaviours. Throughout the group, the *Schema Decision Flowchart* (Appendix 1) can be used to guide behavioural choices based on *HA* versus coping modes. Exercises can be used flexibly across sessions, according to the needs of the particular group, but we have made suggestions in brackets as a rough guide (e.g. Session 1:S1)

### Establish group safety and bonding (S1)

Use exercises that cultivate connection between participants to promote group cohesion.

1.  Participants (sitting in a circle) can be invited to hold several long scarves between them as a tangible representation of their connection and belonging to the group. Participants are also given *HA* messages to remind them of their value both as individuals and group members, as a means of starting the healing process.

2.   Group wrist-bands (Farrell & Shaw, 2012) can be handed out at the start of each group, to be used as a reminder of participants' connection to the group between sessions, and facilitate development of object permanence and healthy attachment.
3.   Imagery exercises focus on developing a safe-place (participants are assisted in generating their own individualised safe/sacred place image ideally in nature, based either on a real place or fantasy, incorporating elements of comfort and protection that match their particular needs). Some participants may need more help, and those with higher levels of mistrust/abuse may need to build in safety mechanisms (e.g. a vortex around their safe place that allows them to decide who can come in and who has to stay out). Spend time thickening the image using all five senses:

> "What do you see as you look around? What are the colours, textures that you notice? What do you see as you look out to the horizon? What can you hear? Just notice and allow any sounds, tones, vibrations in that place to come to you, taking them in. Are there any scents or smells associated with this place? Just breathe these in, allowing yourself to receive whatever scents arise. Are there any tastes associated with this place? Just notice any tastes that arise, allowing yourself to just 'be' in this space. Reach down and touch something close to you, feeling the sensations, textures on your fingers and hands. Notice how it feels for your bare feet to be grounded in this place. What is the sensation under your feet? Where in your body do you feel connected to this place?"

### Psychoeducation of EMS and modes

Group participants are consistently reminded that their schemas and modes influence the way in which current events and relationships within the group are interpreted. Within the group, participants are helped to develop self-awareness and to notice the way in which their schema modes can hijack their progress in therapy, and interfere with their ability to connect and relate to others. This development of self-awareness is an essential component of the ST model, and is linked to the growth of a *HA* self who can act as the chairperson who oversees all of the other modes. An important role of the group leaders is to be consistently making links between current and past experiences. Participants are invited to bring a photograph of themselves as a baby or child (preferably one that they like) which are then collated into a group collage. This is used across the whole group program at regular intervals to facilitate connection with their *VCh* side. Group therapy goals are established early in therapy: to heal and validate child modes and promote safety and attachment, to re-establishing personal interconnectness through 'refamily-ing' [personal correspondence, van Vreeswijk], and to develop a *HA* side that can take over from the coping modes that drive ED behaviours. It is explained that recovery is facilitated equally through attending therapy sessions alongside implementation of behavioural pattern-breaking homework tasks. The group is reminded that feelings are a package-deal.

> "It can feel uncomfortable to get in touch with feelings, BUT this also opens up future possibilities to experience the good/fun stuff in life. Recovery operates in a similar way to the stages of 'grief' – many different feelings will arise in no particular order, and sometimes it will feel like you are going around in circles. There are no good and bad feelings – all of them are part of the healing process. If we try to control our grief, it just gets stuck. So, we need to trust the process, knowing that difficult feelings of sadness and anxiety are a healthy sign that you are reconnecting with your vulnerable self. It can be very scary to change sometimes. You have to let go of something that you know will be replaced with the unknown. As human beings, we like to stay with what is familiar to us, even if it stops us getting what we need in the longer term. The goal is to figure out your hidden needs, so you can find healthy ways to get these met. The group is a safe setting where you can take the risk of trying out new and healthy ways of coping and expressing feelings and needs, before experimenting in the outside world."

In the early stages of STE-g, a significant amount of time is focused on psychoeducation and exploration of coping modes, and linking these to eating disordered and interpersonal behaviours. The main coping modes represented within the group are identified and the group as a whole is encouraged to brainstorm a list of the range of coping behaviours linked to each mode. Dietary restriction, compulsive exercise, body-checking, counting calories and so on, are explained as a form of overcompensation (e.g. *OC* mode) with the function of positioning oneself 'on top' of or 'above' vulnerability, and/or a form of avoidance (e.g. *Detached Protector (DetPr)*) by completely numbing the self in order to block emotions. Binge eating is often linked to *DetSS* and/ or *Impulsive Child* modes, but can also be a manifestation of a range of other modes (e.g. *AnCh, OC, Inner Critic; Helpless Surrenderer*).

### Teach schema model

Group participants brainstorm the types of experiences that children need to grow into healthy, happy people: Safety, Stable Base, Predictability, Love, Nurturing, Attention, Acceptance and Praise, Empathy, Guidance, Protection, Validation of Feelings and Needs. We explain that everyone has some of these needs met, and some unmet, and our job is to do the detective work to figure out the bits that have been positive AND the bits that are missing. Card games and the 'brick-walls' exercise (Silver, 2013) can also be used to explore unmet needs, and then linked to the development of schemas.

"These beliefs, or schemas feel like facts. They are our reality and they reflect the way that we (and our family) have learned to see the world through our experiences. Every family is slightly different. We are also influenced by school, peers (and bullying), religious messages, social media, and culture, so we are bombarded by messages from everywhere. It's like looking through cellophane glasses...the world just takes on that colour and we don't question it (especially if we have been looking through the cellophane since we were very young). The problem is that some of these beliefs might have fitted well with the family or world that we grew up in, but they don't necessarily fit with our current adult relationships or life. In fact, they can stop us from getting what we need and from being happy. Our schemas are our blind spots...we are so familiar with them that they feel like facts. It's hard to take the cellophane out of our lenses!

Also, schemas can be passed down through the generations (transgenerational schemas). For example, a great grandparent may have survived a war, genocide, poverty, immigration or lost one or both parents. Many people from previous generations suffered from severe hardship, deprivation and trauma. There were no public social services, and prejudice/social exclusion was rife. When these generations had children, they struggled with their own problems, which made it difficult for them to raise their own children in a loving way. If they had become accustomed to being punished, hurt and criticised, they often passed this on to the next generation because they didn't know any different. If they received the message that feelings were weak and shameful, then they might have punished their own children for showing feelings or expressing themselves. It's not just the bad experiences that affect us – sometimes we just don't get enough of the good stuff. In our fast-paced culture, children's emotional needs often go unnoticed and unmet. It might seem a little thing, but the research shows that this is very important for our future health and wellbeing. 'Emotional vitamins' that nourish us include deep attunement, feeling cherished, understood and unconditionally loved. Sometimes if parents are isolated, depressed, or in stressful relationships, they are unable to meet their children's needs. This is how schemas are passed on."

### Linking childhood needs with EMS

Use Figure 10.1 as a template to link EMS and ED behaviours with childhood needs. Use metaphors to introduce the concept of EMS: e.g. 'blind spots', 'emotional buttons', 'coloured cellophane lenses' and coping modes as perpetuating factors (or 'schema snacks'). Use a generic mode map (see Figure 10.2) to link ED behaviours and symptoms to coping styles/modes that function like a 'home-made anaesthetic'.

### Introductory exercises

#### 1. Mode mapping group exercises (S1–3)

In groups of two (or three), participants draw each of the main modes represented within the group on large cardboard – to convey their characters, functions and felt-sense. For example, participants might draw a strict teacher or sergeant to represent their *OC* mode, or a witch to represent their *Inner Critic*. The group brainstorms 'labels/names' that personalise and capture the felt-sense of modes. These are pieced together into a whole group mode map, telling the story of how they relate to each other, and linked to ED (and other) symptoms. Participants are encouraged to expand on their own mode maps, writing in extra information as they begin to notice their modes more. Draw a group mode map, showing how the modes are linked to each other (See Figure 10.2).

#### 2. Mode spotting exercise (S2–3)

(1) Group leaders roleplay modes, demonstrating ways they can sabotage therapy. Group participants try to guess which modes are being demonstrated and to recognise the hallmark signs of each mode (tone, content, and how it blocks getting needs met). For example, *Inner Critic (Demanding)*: "I really need to try harder. I should be doing better in my studies, a distinction isn't good enough; I should have dealt with this eating disorder by now, I'm letting everyone else down"; *Inner Critic (Punitive)*: "I really am useless. I'm pathetic. There is something very wrong with me/my body. Others don't realise how defective I am. I'm a burden on others. I'm undeserving, ungrateful, selfish"; *Compliant Surrenderer (CSu)* – "I'm happy either way; I'll go along with what you want; Please tell me what to do; I don't mind"; *OC*: "I must get on top of everything; I have to get through my lists, I have to be productive; I have to get it 'right'/perfect" or everything will fall apart; *Suspicious OC*: "Be on your guard. Others can't be trusted. They are only being nice because they want something. It's fake"; *DetPr*: "Everything is fine; it is what it is; I don't know; I don't want to feel…just give me some strategies"; *VCh*: "I feel ashamed, anxious, sad, lonely, undeserving, invisible, rejected, hurt"; *AnCh*: "No-one understands me and no-one cares about me. I'm angry that everyone else's needs come first. It's not fair!"

(2) Next, the whole group comes up with *HA* responses to each mode, recording them on the *HA Message Worksheet* (see Appendix 1).

#### 3. Modes on the bus exercise (S4)

This exercise is based on a mode roleplay exercise from Farrell & Shaw (2012). Invite participants to engage in a role play where they will play the

**Childhood Experiences and Temperament**
Temperament: Energetic, bouncy, giggly, boisterous, creative, noisy
**Mum was depressed and struggling with her own problems; Dad was excessively**
focused on health and fitness
Emotional inhibition, lack of attunement, emotional communication and connection

**Schemas (and unmet needs)**
I am too needy, I am a burden (insufficient attunement, nurturance, warmth)
**I am weak, unlovable** (excessive emotional invalidation; insufficient unconditional love)
**I shouldn't say what I feel or need** (excessive inhibition of emotions, insufficient
encouragement, recognition)
**I'm different, I don't belong** (insufficient sense of connectedness, belonging, acceptance)

**Coping**
*Avoidance (Detached Self Soother):* **Bingeing, vomiting, internet surfing, sleeping, alcohol**
*Surrender (Compliant Surrenderer):* **Doing what everyone else wants, avoiding**
**confrontation and assertiveness**
*Overcompensation (Overcontroller):* **Being controlling and perfectionistic toward the self,**
**the body, the house (cleaning), work/study**

**Problems**
Isolated, overwhelmed, loss of control over eating via restriction/bingeing/vomiting,
feeling ashamed. Feeling isolated from others and stuck – 'I can't get what I need'

*Figure 10.1* Diagram of schema model

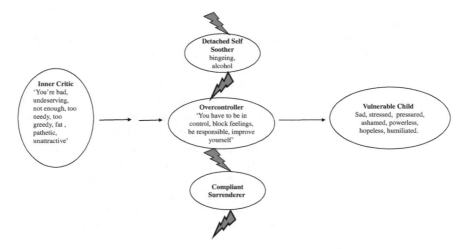

*Figure 10.2* Mode map

part of all of the different sides/modes within one person. Participants volunteer for the following roles: *HA* (two participants) *OC, DetSS, Inner Critic, AnCh, VCh*. Depending on the number of participants, there can be more than two people representing each mode.

1. Using whiteboard, prompt participants to generate a script for each mode, based on a trigger situation (e.g. group leaders have forgotten to check-in with you and are focusing on other group members). For instance, *OC*: "I don't need them anyway, I can cope on my own. I just need to get on top of things (of my eating, body). I've got everything under control, I just need to stick to my lists and I will get through everything. I feel fine as long as I just go for a run tonight"; *AnCh*: "It's not fair, you don't care about me. You never listen. What about me?"; *VCh*: "I feel sad and hurt, like I don't belong. No-one cares about me"; *Inner Critic (directed to VCh)*: "No-one cares about you – you're useless and lazy. You're a burden. You're bad/worthless"; *DetSS:* "I need to binge (eat/drink) to block out these feelings"; *HA*: "You're ok as you are; you deserve to get your needs met. You're worthwhile. I'll help you work through this. I'm here for you."

2. Place six chairs – three rows of two chairs to imitate a bus. Place the *VCh* and *AnCh* chairs together in the back row of the bus, with the *OC* and *DetPr/DetSS* in the middle row. Sit the *Inner Critic*(s) in the front seat, facing backwards towards the child and coping modes. Ask group members to notice their experience (including body sensations and urges) from the different modes they are playing. Participants are all  prompted to talk at once in character (drawing on scripts on the whiteboard). For example, the *Inner Critic* is punitive towards the *VCh,* and the coping mode tries to protect the *VCh* – allow this to go on for a minute or so, with all participants speaking from the perspective of their 'mode character'. After a minute or so, the *HA* modes (group leader and participant) call out *"enough!"* The therapist explains that this is what is happening within each of us – the *Inner Critic* is strong and we are trying to block it through using coping modes. But the only healthy way to stop the Inner critic is with the *HA*. Then debrief – check with each participant how they are feeling. Next, the *HA* mode (therapist and participant helper) deals with each mode in turn: (1) Move the *Inner Critic*(s) away – saying "You aren't needed here – you belong in the past!" Move *Inner Critic*(s) to outside of the circle (guarded by one of the *HA* modes); (2) Validate the protective intention of coping modes, whilst asking that they move to the side a little to give access to the child modes; (3) Validate unmet needs of *AnCh*, and explain she can learn new ways to express her anger so that others understand her needs; (4) Validate *VCh*: "How are you feeling? What do you need? We see you. You are not invisible to us."

3. Debrief: How did everyone feel in their roles? This roleplay demonstrates the main goal of therapy – for our *HA* side to be the one in the driving seat. For many of us, our coping modes are in the driving seat (trying to block out the feelings of the *VCh* or *Inner Critic* messages). If our *HA* mode can be strengthened, it can take over from coping modes, to validate and protect our emotional needs in healthy ways. Explain to group members that they can help each other detect the *Inner Critic* mode as it arises during the group, to make sure that it no longer 'flies under the radar'. Encourage group members to think about what it means to allow themselves to be vulnerable and to have emotions. Talk about the *VCh* mode as a healthy side that facilitates connection, warmth, love, affection, and that in spite of what they may have been taught, it is important to accept and take care of this side of ourselves. Indeed, we emphasise that if we want true connection and intimacy, we need to gradually learn to tolerate sharing our vulnerability – and to view it not as weakness, but as our most human part.

## 4. Mode role plays (S4–5)

In pairs, participants demonstrate a dialogue or body posture that showcases one mode, manifesting the main mode messages, as well as gestures and facial expressions associated with the modes. This can be in the context of eating/weight/shape, or other situations. The rest of the group try to guess which one is which (list the modes on the white board in advance). Group members are encouraged to track their own and others' mode changes during group sessions. This exercise also brings 'lightness' and fun to the discussion of modes.

## 5. Detective work with pseudo-healthy modes (S5)

This exercise starts with introducing the *HA* mode and differentiating it from coping modes. In pairs, ask participants to identify differences between *HA* and their main coping modes. How could others tell the difference? How does it feel different in the body? For example, the *OC* mode may be recovery-focused, but will expect this to be carried out as an efficient, productive, solution-focused manner, whilst minimising emotional vulnerability. The *OC* is rigid, and a 'one-trick pony' (i.e. 'fixing' through getting things 'right'), whereas the *HA* reacts in a flexible, mindful way, drawing on multiple possible options and focusing on being kind, compassionate and prioritising wellbeing. The coping modes tend to dress-up as 'rational' or 'logical', but are lacking in authentic compassion/empathy.

Give a sheet of whiteboard paper, and red and green sticky notes to participants. In pairs, participants use red sticky notes to identify internal signs that a coping mode is present (e.g. signs of *OC* mode might include irritation, frustration, an exclusive focus on productivity, internal feelings of pressure and tension, impatience with own and others' vulnerability, making internal comparisons with others, perfectionism, language such as "I'm going to blitz this") and green sticky notes identify the signs that others might notice (external signs: e.g. impatient, black-and-white thinking; blaming; intellectualising instead of connecting with feelings; focused on solutions and 'fixing'; intolerance of mistakes, competitiveness, acting in expert role, advising others rather than sharing own vulnerability). Participants place sticky notes in/outside their body outline (red notes placed within the shape of coping mode; green notes placed outside the shape), then merge all sticky notes onto a body outline on the group whiteboard and discuss findings as a group.

### 6. Genogram exercise (S5)

Use a genogram template (See Appendix 1) to set homework task for participants to identify possible origins of *Inner Critic* (parent modes), coping modes and/or schemas in previous generations. Then discuss patterns of schema/mode transgenerational transmissions as a group in the following session. Group leaders can use self-disclosure to talk about their ancestors' experiences and how these may have led to the development of schemas/ modes, and how these might have been passed down the generations. This can also be used to explore the influence of modes on relationships, including patterns of dependency, parentification, enmeshment issues, and schema chemistry (i.e. the high level of attraction that draws us to form relationships with others who have either symmetrical or opposite schemas, thereby reinforcing and perpetuating our own schemas).

### Sessions 6–21

Sessions 6–21 focus on recognising and bypassing the coping modes, developing a *HA* side, beginning the process of fighting the *Inner Critic*, and recognising vulnerability and emotional needs. Participants are also encouraged to connect with their *HAC* side through fun exercises, to reduce the 'heaviness' of the work of therapy, and counter the messages of the *Inner Critic* and *OC* modes. The following 27 exercises should be included over the next 15 sessions.

### 1. Bypassing coping modes

A strong emphasis of the group is on identifying and working with coping modes as they arise. Depending on the specific situation, group leaders may empathically point out mode 'flipping' (i.e. transitioning between mode-states) when they notice the demeanour of individuals or whole group changes. The person can be asked if they know which mode has arisen (they are invited to describe what it feels like and can ask the group for help, or group leaders can gently ask whether anyone else in the group can identify with this mode). Participants can also be asked if they can identify triggers for their coping mode during the week (or within the group). It can be useful to use the whiteboard to link events to activation of a chain reaction of mode flipping (e.g. "Visiting my mum triggered my *Inner Critic*, which made my *VCh* feel guilty and anxious. I then flipped into the *DetPr* mode and have been in that mode ever since").

The self-perpetuating relationship between the *Inner Critic* and coping modes is explored. In particular, it is acknowledged that coping modes operate as mechanisms that facilitate escape from difficult emotions that are triggered by the *Inner Critic*. However, the *Inner Critic* then uses the coping behaviours as further ammunition and proof that its criticisms are correct (e.g. binge eating may trigger the response: "You are hopeless, why don't you just stop! This proves you are no good!"). The self-perpetuating nature of coping modes is explored in the early stages of the group, and in particular, the way in which long-term goals are sacrificed in order to achieve immediate relief/gratification. Participants are encouraged to draw their own coping modes for homework, to enhance their understanding of their tone, expression, shape, and colour, as they manifest in day-to-day life. In addition, worksheets can be used between or during sessions to increase day-to-day conscious awareness of the operation of coping modes (see *Coping Mode Worksheet*, Appendix 1).

Participants are asked to notice and monitor invalidating mode messages that tell them that they have no problems, that they are just imagining them, that they should forget their troubles and 'get on with it'. When we are accustomed to a coping mode being in the driving seat, it can be painful to acknowledge our human struggles and emotional problems. Group leaders can explain that therapy has an opposite agenda to the participants' coping modes – it is about learning to accept and soothe painful feelings in healthy ways that allow participants to get their needs met..

Participants are encouraged to reflect on the ways they cope through detaching and overcompensation. For example, the *DetPr* can bring numbness or a soothing feeling through bingeing, alcohol, self-harm, shopping and so on. The *OC* mode can give us a 'high', a sense of control, achievement, and pride...it can even trick us into thinking that we are in *HA* mode. Using the whiteboard, brainstorm ways this mode tries to 'overcome' human vulnerability by being 'on top', or the best: e.g. perfectionism and competitiveness through dietary restriction and/or compulsive exercise, purging. This might be through a focus on appearance (thinnest, most toned, athletic, trying to out-manoeuvre basic human subsistence needs), and/or excessive overcontrol (e.g. of oneself, one's body, thoughts, eating, other people). The *OC* often thinks 'if I am the thinnest/smartest/cleverest/most attractive, then I will be loved and I don't ever have to feel that vulnerability or shame again. No-one can hurt me or criticise or reject me when I am the thinnest/most attractive/best etc.'

So how can we tell the difference between *HA* and *Overcompensator* (e.g. *OC, Pollyanna, Self-Aggrandiser* etc.) modes? Ask participants to reflect on the function of these behaviours – is it to try to give themselves an artificial sense of control or self-esteem? Or to protect themselves from abandonment through being entirely self-sufficient? Ask for examples from the group (based on individuals' own mode maps). What does their *Overcompensator* look like? Where did they learn that way of trying to feel good about themselves? How well does it work? Does anyone else in their family cope that way? Do others in their family need them to 'perform' or overachieve in order to boost their own self-esteem?

Help participants draw distinctions between coping modes and *HA* mode.

*"It is natural to feel the urge to 'do something' to try to feel better about yourself. However, if we do this by overcompensating then we don't ever truly feel better about ourselves in an authentic way...just in an artificial way. So in OC or DetPr mode you can be going through the motions and doing all the 'right things'...e.g. going to the gym, doing healthy things, acting healthily, without actually being in contact with your feelings. It's natural to work hard and want to be happy and get a sense of achievement – but OC strives for happiness in a way that is not authentic, and it pushes feelings away. It can look healthy on the outside. But the OC doesn't have limits...the list is never ending. And when you are not busy and productive, then you don't feel good about yourself. HA is more authentic and accepts you for who you really are. It congratulates you. It stops to celebrate. Its number one priority is your health and happiness."*

### 2. Grounding exercises

Co-therapists need to keep track of when participants 'flip' into their coping modes. Short grounding exercises are employed on a regular basis throughout sessions to enable clients to move back into their bodies in a safe way and regulate their emotions without becoming overwhelmed. Sometimes movement can be a very powerful way of grounding and creating safety in the body, whilst giving the mind a focus. These include stretching side to side; swinging arms side to side (while keeping the head facing forwards); swinging arms around in circles in opposite directions from the other and then swapping directions; active breathing techniques; gentle shoulder rolls (back and forth); rapid shoulder shrugs; taking off shoes and noticing barefoot sensations on different surfaces. For all grounding exercises, participants should be prompted to *"notice how that feels in your body...what sensations are you experiencing as you do this exercise?"*. They can then repeat this and notice how the body feels differently after the exercise.

### 3. Mask exercise

This is an experiential group exercise from Farrell & Shaw (2012), whereby two group participants wear a mask whilst the rest of the group carry on talking, attempting to draw the masked participants into the conversation. Following this, the masks are discarded and participants are encouraged to reflect on how this exercise made them feel (both as 'masked' and 'unmasked' participants). Through making this experience of [dis]connection more concrete, this exercise raises awareness of impact of the *DetPr* on self and others, and in particular on individuals' capacity to get emotional needs met. Participants brainstorm ideas to identify potential in-session triggers for activation of coping modes as well as possible ways that the group can help to reconnect with participants who are detached.

### 4. Pros and cons of coping modes brainstorming exercise

Focus on coping modes that are most significant for current group participants (e.g. *OC*, *DetPr*, *CSu*) and identify all possible behaviours (ED and non-ED) linked to this mode. Use whiteboard to brainstorm a list of pros and cons in the present, including effects on health, relationships, energy, happiness, work/studies, reaching life-goals, lost-years due to illness/hospital admissions etc.

### 5. Mode parade

Pin up three to four silhouettes (see Appendix 1) of women with different body weights/shapes over the top of pictures of children/babies.
Divide group participants into pairs. Ask participants to make up a mode 'billboard' on butcher paper with *Inner Critic* statements for approximately five to ten minutes (according to what their *Inner Critic* would tell them if they were that size, e.g. "You're a whale", "Your stomach is disgusting").
Return to pairs and make up a second billboard with messages from the *OC* mode that would be triggered if you were this body weight. Remember that the *OC* mode tries to 'fix' whatever it perceives to be the problem. Its job is to override basic human needs in the interests of productivity, stoicism, achievement, and continually striving to be better/the best. The *OC* mode tries to fix any signs of imperfection – which it views as mess, excessiveness, and self-indulgence.
Each participant is invited to read aloud one *Inner Critic* and one *OC* message as they walk past the pictures holding their billboards.
Tell participants: *"Just notice these messages which come from your modes. These are old modes. The Inner Critic represents the past and is mean. The OC is trying to help, it came along to give you a tangible way of feeling good about*

*yourself. Just notice the messages, without being drawn in, and come back to focus on your breathing."*

Remove the silhouettes, to reveal the pictures of children/babies underneath. Ask the group: *"How does it feel to be passing those Inner Critic messages on to these women [silhouettes]? How does it feel to embody the Inner Critic and OC sides? Notice any discomfort you feel about this. What is making you uncomfortable? Are there any circumstances in which it would be okay to judge anyone this way? What is wrong with that? Although the OC mode is trying to help, what impact do you think it would have on their vulnerable child side underneath?"*

Invite participants to write down sticky note messages for the children [pictures] from their gentle, warm side – the part that cares and feels for others. The part that doesn't judge, but accepts every human as equally deserving of love and compassion.

Participants file past the silhouettes again, reading out their healthy messages, and sticking their notes around the pictures.

Debrief – How did this feel different to the last step? How can we access our compassionate side and direct it toward our own vulnerable side?

Can participants try out different gestures that help them to access the *Compassionate HA* (e.g. hand on heart, hand on cheek, stroking an arm, heart-breathing)?

How can this be generalised to extending compassion to each person's own *VCh* mode? How can we keep the perspective of our vulnerability from our *Compassionate HA* (vs *Inner Critic/OC*) as we go about our everyday business?

Therapists can use self-disclosure to share how they stay connected to their Compassionate *HA* and *VCh* sides in difficult situations.

### 6. Mini-imagery with eating disorder triggers

In this mini-imagery rescripting exercise, participants are helped to recognise their coping modes in action, and to link these to their eating behaviours.

- Identify a situation linked to the ED that is relevant for all participants (e.g. looking in the mirror, trying on clothes).
- All participants are invited to close their eyes and imagine themselves in the trigger situation at some point within the next 24 hours.
- Invite participants to enter the image with all five senses, noticing where they are, what they can see, who else is around, what they can hear, smell, and taste.
- Fast-forward to the most feared, worst part of the image. What is happening, what do you notice? What is the feeling? Where do you notice it in your body?
- What urges do you notice? How do you want to cope?

- Who is giving you that message? Do you notice any of your coping modes there? Perhaps the *OC*? Or a different mode?
- Where is the *OC* (or other coping mode) standing? Just notice – is this mode female or male? Is it to the left or right? What is its expression? What is the tone of its voice? What is it saying to you? What is its message? How is it trying to help you?
- Can you bring your Wise (*HA*) Self into the image [if your *HA* side is not strong enough, bring in the group leaders to help]? Where is your *HA* side standing? What does it look like? What is the tone of its voice? Notice how gentle and soothing it sounds. Listen closely to hear the wise words of the *HA* – she doesn't shout, but she is right there by your side. If it helps, place your hand on your heart to help you access and see your Wise (*HA*) Self even more clearly. Ask your *HA* side for one thing that you need right now to help you to move beyond this situation and closer to the life that is waiting for you.
- Thank the *OC* mode for working so hard to keep you safe, but that its work is done, and the Wise (*HA*) Self will now keep you safe and also help you get your needs met to allow happiness.
- Open eyes and debrief. Reflect on bringing coping modes into conscious awareness so that they don't fly under the radar in the future. Invite participants to notice and *receive* the messages from their *HA* side, both in the context of this and other trigger situations.

### 7. Chairwork with coping modes

In this exercise, participants learn to bypass their own coping modes, keeping in mind that these have helped them to survive, and therefore warrant respect. Rather than fighting with the coping modes, we are trying to befriend them, attain their trust, and negotiate for change to enable the person to get their needs met.

Allocate roles – (1) person who will be the focus of the session; (2) two coping mode helpers; (3) two to four *HA* modes (this can include all remaining group members). Four to five chairs are placed in a circle; place photographs of all group participants as children on *VCh* chair.

- Identify one group member who has an example from the past couple of weeks when ED behaviour or urges were triggered. Participant describes situation that activated the coping mode.
- Ask the client (with one or two helpers) to move to the allocated coping mode chairs and speak from the perspective of the coping mode, explaining how it is trying to help them. For example, for the *OC* mode, elicit functions associated with being the best, or 'on top' of vulnerability (e.g. "If you follow my rules you will be a better person, more likable..."). For the *DetSS*, elicit functions associated with feeling better, relief from anxiety, relaxing, and so on. Draw on the list generated in the pros/cons

exercise. Ask the mode what it is afraid will happen if they show vulnerability, feelings, imperfections?

- Then move participant to the *VCh* chair (sitting beside the photographs); and ask two other group members to move to the *HA* chair (*HA* and *VCh* chairs are close to each other). Ask participant "How does the *VCh* feel when the maladaptive coping side is strong? Explain to the *VCh* that she created this side to keep her safe in the past, when she wasn't getting what she needed. Ask whether she gets what she needs when the coping mode is here? How does it relate to how she feels most of the time? Although its intention is good, is it bringing her the happiness and connection that she needs? What happens when the coping mode is not around...what is she left feeling? Ask the *VCh* to say what she really needs (e.g. to be accepted, loved as she is, to feel safe and protected, to feel seen etc.): "*I know you want to help me, but what I really need is....*"
- Ask all remaining participants to play the role of the *HA*. "*What do you want to say back to the coping mode from the HA perspective?*"
- Remind *HA* participants that the coping mode is trying to be a friend. The trouble is that it is slightly misguided, stuck in old ways of coping that only bring short term relief. Next, the *HA* modes are encouraged to speak to the *VCh*. Remind them that the *VCh* deserves authentic rather than artificial happiness. Encourage *HA* participants to validate needs and reparent the collective *VCh*.
- If the *Inner Critic* pops up at any point, bring in a chair for it, move the client there to briefly voice its message, and then return to the *HA* side to reply and set limits (with the group helping).
- Re-group: How did everyone feel in their role? How has this changed the way you look at your coping mode? Reiterate the importance of recognising the feelings of the *VCh* – if we don't allow ourselves to properly grieve for what happened to us, and what we have missed out on, and feel all the emotions associated with that, then we can't move on and build an authentic *HA* mode.
- For a variation on this exercise, see Devil's Advocate Chairwork in Chapter 7.

## 8. Chairwork – therapist plays the VCh

Identify ED-related coping behaviours amongst group participants over the past week. Choose one person who wants to work on their ED coping mode.

- Allocate a chair to the coping mode. Interview the coping mode: "*How are you helping Little X? How does the exercise/restriction/bingeing help her [in that moment]? (e.g. others won't value you unless you are perfect; no-one will like you as you really are...). What are you afraid will happen if you allow her to talk about her feelings and needs?*"
- Ask client in focus to move in and out of the coping mode chair and answer from that perspective.

- Group leader-one plays the role of the *VCh* (on allocated chair). Verbalise the perspective of 'Little X' – how she feels, what she needs, and the effect of restriction/bingeing/compulsive exercise on her life. E.g. "*I feel so lonely, and invisible. Nobody listens to me. Nobody cares what I need. I'm so hungry. When you binge/restrict, I feel pushed aside, like I don't matter.*"
- The remaining group participants are allocated to play the role of the *HA* (with group leader-two supporting). They are invited to spend 5–10 minutes reflecting on: (1) their new role as carer and protector of the emotional side (*Little X*); (2) the ways in which the coping mode is sabotaging their job; (3) how they can ask the coping mode to step back. Remind participants that the coping mode has good intentions and is trying to be a friend. The trouble is that it is misguided, stuck in the past and old ways of coping that only bring short term gratification. Remind the group that superficial pseudo-happiness blocks the potential for authentic happiness. Explain: "*You need to gently but firmly encourage this side to reduce and convince it that you can look after the VCh – to reassure it that you are going to take care of her.*"
- Invite *HA* mode (group) to respond to 'Little X' ("*Imagine she is just a very little girl, and her feet don't even touch the floor…she is so sad and lonely*").
- Group leader-one can return to the *VCh* chair and describe how frightened she is of letting go of the coping mode – and of learning to trust anyone else (including the *HA*).
- Group participants are coached by leader-two to provide reassurance and promise that as the *HA* side, they won't abandon her, and will prioritise her care.
- If the *Inner Critic* pops up during this exercise, bring in an extra chair, allow it to speak, then leaders coach the group to reply from *HA* side.
- Debrief: How did participants feel in their role? Did this change the way they view their coping modes? Explore the reality that we all have a 'Little X' (*VCh*) mode with feelings and needs. Explore group fears around what will happen when the coping mode has gone…what will they be left feeling? How can they reassure their own *VCh* from the *HA* side and convince her that they will be there for her (so that she no longer needs the coping mode)?
- Set homework: Invite participants to experiment with allowing their *VCh* to express their emotional needs (e.g. to be accepted, unconditionally loved, to feel safe and protected, to be seen/understood etc.). Encourage group members to think about what it means to allow themselves to be vulnerable. Explore *VCh* as a healthy side that facilitates connection, warmth, love, affection, and that in spite of what they may have been taught, it is important to accept and take care of this side of ourselves.

- NB. Advise that participants only express emotional needs/feelings with others who have sufficient emotional intelligence to be capable and trusted to respond in a healthy way – so as to prevent further schema perpetuation. In addition, many participants initially experience a sense of boredom, repulsion of feeling smothered when others are emotionally nurturing – this is a natural reaction to the unfamiliarity of getting needs met. It is important to encourage participants to 'push through' and give healthy relationships/friendships a chance to work.

### 9. Empathic confrontation

Gentle empathic confrontation should also be used to address group behaviours which interfere with participants getting their needs met – such as missing sessions, extreme detachment, overcompensatory or risky behaviours. In addition, this may include more subtle issues such as when group members repeatedly use email instead of the group to raise difficult or emotional subjects. It is important that group leaders reply with a short email which validates participants' willingness to express their feelings and/or needs and to encourage them to raise this with the group. If long emails are sent by group leaders in between sessions, participants will learn to get their needs met by email rather than by connecting with others in person. In general, if group participants do not respect group boundaries then appropriate consequences should be set (e.g. reducing access to email contact).

Farrell and Shaw (2013) describe a six step formula for empathically confronting behaviours in groups: (1) Reinforce your connection with the participant by moving closer and using a soft, gentle voice. Reassure participant that you have no intention of criticising them, but you are raising this issue because of concerns that their emotional needs won't be met in the session. (2) Label the unhelpful behaviour and/or mode: "*I am worried that when you get into analysing situations in a lot of detail, it can feel a bit like we are losing touch with you, and especially with the vulnerable part of you that needs connection.*" (3) Empathise with the fact that this behaviour was developed as a survival mechanism during childhood when other options were not available – but now it stops them getting what they need: "*I understand that in your childhood it just felt confusing – you were always made to feel like you were getting everything wrong, and you had to figure out how to get it 'right' so as to avoid further criticism. The problem is that now we lose connection with you when you get caught up in the details – even though I know it probably feels safer for you to cope that way.*" (4) Offer a correction to allow participant to get needs met in here-and-now: "*I know that in the past there was so much criticism that it would have been too risky to show your vulnerable side – you would have been shamed for that. But we really want to know you and understand you – we want you to tell us a little more about how you are feeling, that would help us to know what you need. This is one of the goals of ST – to learn to be vulnerable with others who are safe."* (5) Decision-making about change – consider the pros and cons of the mode, and possibilities for reducing its strength or frequency: *"Can we think about how this mode affects other relationships, and how easy or hard it is to get what you need? Although it has helped you in the past, could you think about how it might feel to let it go for a short time?";* (6) Offer help with making changes: *"This old way of coping is totally understandable – but we are here for you and want to support you to get what you need from now on."*

Here is an example of empathic confrontation for a client in *Angry Protector/DetPr*: *"I can understand you feel misunderstood and angry, but I also notice that I lose my connection to you when you withdraw, and it feels frustrating to know you are suffering but I can't reach you. It gives others the message that you don't want to connect. The human side of me wants to back off when you do that, but the therapist side of me wants to stay and help, because I understand where that came from. As a child you learned that you would be rejected or shamed for having needs, but this message was unhelpful. We want to hear from you about your feelings of sadness. You're allowed to connect and to ask for what you need."*

Chairwork can also be used to empathically confront each person's coping mode. A chair can be allocated to all of the main coping modes represented in the group, and also one chair to represent the groups' collective child modes.

- Group leaders help participants (in pairs) to identify ways in which their coping modes urge them to avoid, and thereby sabotage, their ability to get their needs met. Each participant is invited to say something to their own coping mode, e.g. *"You helped me in the past, but while you are there I can't connect with and trust other people. I need you to help me learn new healthy ways to trust others and meet the needs of Little X."*
- Therapists should also use this as an opportunity to confront participants' coping modes, identifying ways in which they affect us as therapists, e.g. frustration regarding rejection of help; preventing you from being able to help their *VCh* and give them what they truly deserve. In addition, therapists can explain that if we feel this way in relation to the mode, then this is an indication that others probably feel the same way, e. g. partners and friends may also feel frustrated or rejected/shut out.
- Participants are encouraged to finish by saying one thing to all of the *VCh* modes on the chair from their *HA* side, e.g. *"I am here for you; You do matter; Your feelings are important to me; Others do want to hear what you feel and to connect to you."*

## 10. Historical roleplay

This exercise is aimed at challenging schemas that have developed as a result of selective internalisation or more subtle childhood experiences (e.g. lack of overt affection, overprotectiveness, over-anxious or controlling parenting, unrealistic standards, lack of praise or acknowledgement, dismissive or inva-lidating parenting, excessive emphasis on 'healthy' eating, weight and shape). It can be particularly useful for helping to de-personalise parental behaviour that is driven by their own difficulties or life-stresses, but which is not overtly punitive or abusive. It can also be useful to use this to address memories whereby the parent had their own body image issues – to help the child to draw distinction between the parent's body issues and their own. This exercise can help reveal that our initial assumptions are not necessarily correct and that our assumptions drive our coping behaviours, preventing us from getting our needs met.

- Discuss current situation that a participant is struggling with in which their coping mechanisms are not getting them what they need (e.g. not assertive enough, not able to say 'no', not able to get others' attention, feeling invalidated and invisible, being overly compliant) with a particular person (e.g. their partner, friend, colleague).
- Comment on how this reminds you of how things were in one of their relationships as a child. (e.g. 'your relationship with your mum')
- Ask participant: *"Do you recall a specific situation from the past in which you had a similar experience or felt that the same way?"*
- Identify a situation whereby the child was manifesting the same beha-viour in childhood in response to the way the parent was behaving (e.g. talking incessantly, not asking the child about their feelings, or worrying too much and being overprotective). Avoid using punitive or abusive situations for this exercise.
- Explain to the participant that it might be useful to do a roleplay to better understand the coping behaviour and how they learned it.
- Ask for volunteers from the group to roleplay the parent and ask the client for direction: *"Who will play mum? How did she speak? What did she say? What was her tone? Gestures?"* The focal participant roleplays themselves as a child – help them to get into role by asking questions: *"How old were you? How tall? How did you behave?"*
- *Roleplay ('Take 1')*: Act out the scenario, using tables, chairs, cushions or any other props required. Check to see that it felt authentic for the participant, and if not, repeat with new information.

  - Ask participant: *"How did it feel? What went through your mind?"* On the whiteboard, write down the participant's beliefs/assumptions about themselves and others from this experience (e.g. 'I'm worthless, invisible, I may as well not exist') and rate degree to which they believe this on a scale of 0–100.
  - Check in with the remaining participants to see if any of them share this belief, or have had similar experiences.

- Talk about how that belief and way of coping has stayed with them through their life and now affects other interactions within other relationships.

- *Roleplay ('Take 2'):* Swap roles. Ask participant to really try to get into the mindset of their parent, taking into account everything else they [the parent] was dealing with, their own problems, work pressures, and their own background/childhood. Ask them to really try to be in the shoes of their parent, as authentically as possible. Tell client to notice her thoughts and feelings in the role of other person (e.g. mother) as she plays the role.

  - After role-play, sit down and ask client what she noticed about her mother's thoughts, feelings, motivations? Therapist can interview participant (as mother) to identify what was going on for her under the surface..."*Why are you doing this? Did you hear your daughter?*" etc.)
  - Encourage participant to think about her own responses from the perspective of the parent looking at the child. For example, did she withdraw quickly? Was she submissive? Easily frightened? Such that parent was not confronted with their own maladaptive behaviour? Explain that these were the only options open to her – that she was dependent on the parents and didn't have access to healthy role models.
  - Re-evaluate beliefs: "*What is different now that you have played the role of your mother?*" (e.g. "As mother I am very occupied with myself. My daughter listens and is a good support to me. It's important to me as mother that she is there"). Re-rate original beliefs.

- *Role-play ('Take 3'):* Therapist plays mother. Ask participant: "*What could you think of doing now that you have this extra information to get your mother's attention? How will you get her to notice you?*" – Ask the rest of the group for ideas. Repeat roleplay with new information.

  - After roleplay: Ask participant "*How was it? What was different?*" Write summary on whiteboard: e.g. "As a child I didn't have the information to think of that, as circumstances were too difficult. I have more possibilities available now than when I was a child."
  - Summarise: "*We've clarified the shift from 'I'm invisible, no-one will ever meet my needs to I can be seen and get my needs met' – the other thing we need to add to your summary is 'if others are not listening, I can try another way. I do have possibilities, I can make myself heard'.*"
  - Re-rate belief: "*So, at step 1 you rated yourself as 100% invisible/worthless, after considering a different perspective you re-rated at 60%, what about now after the third role-play? How does this translate to your relationship with your boyfriend?*"

## 11. Visualisations to strengthen Healthy Adult

Visualisation exercises can be utilised to develop and strengthen the *HA* side. The *Healthy Adult Wise Being Worksheet* (see Appendix I) can be used as a starting point for homework, to encourage participants to reflect on the development of their *HA* self. This may be a work in progress, and can take several sessions to flesh out. Participants are encouraged to draw on healthy nurturing images and characters from books, movies and fantasy. Imagery exercises focus on accessing their *HA* side to help them manage difficult situations, and to cultivate self-compassion and empathy. Participants are encouraged to practice being in their *HA* side for parts of each day (even 20 seconds at a time to begin with), and to notice how it feels different in the body to be practicing self-compassion for those moments compared to the embodied felt-sense of coping and child modes. They are also encouraged to find activities and exercises that connect them to their *HA* embodied and creative self, such as dance, tai chi, yoga, pottery, painting or writing.

## 12. Recognising emotional needs

One of the key goals in group ST is to enable participants to learn to recognise their emotional needs and to ask for them to be met within the group. If they struggle with this, we offer to help them: "*Can we help you to figure it out? Could it be that you need…? Can you help me to understand? I want to get it right.*" We also reassure participants that it can take a while to be able to figure out what their needs are. We explain that the best way for humans to learn about our needs and emotions is for our parents to help us to articulate our emotional needs when we are children whilst directly meeting the needs. That way we learn what our needs are and how it feels to have them met. However, when parents have not had their own emotional needs met, they often don't have the skills or understanding to be able to teach this to their children. This is an important skill for participants to gain during the group – to be able to recognise their emotional needs, to ask for their needs to be met (which feels scary if they have been rejected in the past) and to take in the feeling of allowing others to meet their needs, whilst being mindful of potential blocking by coping modes. Whether we are bypassing the coping modes, or confronting the *Inner Critic*, the goal is always to reach the *VCh* mode in order to provide reparenting (attunement, warmth, empathy, validation).

N.B. Remind group members that "it is normal and healthy to 'feel' more as the group progresses, and this can be challenging when avoidant coping has become a habit. This means experiencing more difficult feelings as well as more positive feelings. One of the goals of the group is to learn how to be empathic and attuned to your own vulnerable side, as well as other group members' VCh modes. Even though this might feel alien at first, this is a very important part of the healing process from an ED."

## 13. Attunement/misattunement exercise

This exercise is designed to help participants understand the need for attunement and empathy. As this is an 'invisible' need, it can easily be missed or overlooked.

(1)   Therapists roleplay different forms of invalidating/solution focused messages (that may be linked to their *Inner Critic* and coping modes (Group leader 1 (L1) expresses feelings/needs, vs. Group leader 2 (L2) plays the part of the 'invalidator'). For example:

- L1: *"I'm feeling really worried about the test I have at school tomorrow. I can't sleep. My heart is racing."* L2 replies: *"You'll get over it. You really have to sort yourself out. You've got nothing to worry about. Can't you see I have enough on my plate?"*
- L1: *"I feel sick. I think I ate too much."* L2: *"Well, you should have thought that through beforehand. You really should have more self-control."*
- L1: *"I am feeling anxious about everything. Can you help me plan my eating?"* L2: *"Yes, well we've all had a hard day and you need to learn to manage this stuff."*
- L1: *"I'm feeling really stressed today."* L2: *"You shouldn't feel like that. There is nothing to worry about. You're not being logical. That's a silly thing to worry about – you've got so much to be grateful for."*
- L1: *"I don't want to go out, I feel so bad about my body and my eating."* L2: *"You need to be more sociable/outgoing. You really should have sorted out your eating problems by now."*
- L1: *"I went to my therapy session today."* L2: *"You should do something about that eating disorder, it's taking you far too long to deal with it. It's just selfish to go on like this when plenty of other people have far worse problems."*
- L1: *"I got a high credit for my assignment at uni."* L2: *"That's not a bad grade, but if only you had studied a bit harder, you could have done better."*
- L1: *"I feel so anxious about everything just now."* L2: sigh of exasperation with facial expression of disappointment.
- L1: *"I feel like I can't cope with everything at the moment, it all feels too much."* L2: *"Others seem to manage to cope, what's the matter with you?"*
- L1:*"I'm feeling sad that I've lost so many years to my eating disorder".* L2: *"Look on the bright side, at least you are recovering now and you're luckier than most people."*
- L1: *"I'm so worried about gaining weight. It really stresses me."* L2: *"You don't need to worry about that, you're fine."*

- L1: *"I'm still struggling with my eating. I don't know what else to do to feel better."* L 2: *"We've all done so much for you, I really don't understand why you still have all of these problems. We've been good to you. You're hurting us by doing this."*
- L1: *"I'm feeling really sad."* L2: *"Others seem to manage to cope, I can't understand it, what's the matter with you? The past is in the past...just forget about it and move on."*

(2) Draw an outline of a child on the white board: In pairs, look at the list of L1 comments (printed) and think of a healthier response that would meet the other person's need for compassion, empathy, validation? What does L1 really need? Write it on a sticky note. After five to ten minutes, ask pairs to put their sticky note on top of the relevant L1 message, and read out their 'healthy attuned response' to the rest of the group.

(3) Group discussion. Explore responses to not getting needs met, not having someone available to listen or understand. *'What do you feel when others offer solutions before really taking the time to listen and understand? Most of us end up feeling angry, but don't really understand why. Is this something anyone here in the group experienced? We can feel angry when we are not permitted to feel normal emotions without feeling guilty. It's normal and healthy to feel angry about this, as the anger is a sign that your needs are not being met – it is your body trying to alert you to this. The negative messages that are learned as a result of invalidating experiences, whether overt or subtle and unintentional, can interfere with the child's capacity to have their core needs met both in childhood as well as later in adulthood. Whether the internalised 'voice' in our heads is more punishing or demanding, it's important to keep an eye open for it so that it doesn't get the upper hand. This is a cue for the Healthy Side to kick in and take action.'*

(4) Debrief: Draw distinction between attunement/empathy - and sympathetic reassurance, which can be experienced as invalidating. For example, *"In our busy, fast-paced society, there is minimal space or value placed on attunement. Attunement is the essence of the HA mode. It is tuned-in to one's own and others' vulnerability and needs. If the person we are speaking with is in a coping mode, then it will be difficult for them to be attuned to you or anyone else. In OC mode, that person won't be focused on understanding, but more on being logical and rational."* Explore what the message to the child is if the focus is completely on being rational, logical, and what we 'should' have done/ achieved. *"How much space does it allow a child to be him/herself? How does it make the child feel? In general, these early messages actually teach the child that the normal feelings and needs that every child experiences are unacceptable, a burden, shameful, selfish, immature, and excessive. This can be confusing, especially in the context of a relationship where the child is clearly*

*loved by their parents. It is like an invisible missing ingredient – if the parent hasn't experienced attunement themselves, it is difficult for them to pass it on to the next generation. Absence of attunement can result in the child feeling invisible, undeserving, and inexplicably empty and/or angry. The anger is linked to feeling that you are not allowed to feel normal emotions without being made to feel you are burdening others – however, it is a signal that your needs are not being met. Children need attunement, someone to listen to them, nurture them and love them for who they are (not for how they perform). Having other stuff (e.g. a good school, clothes, possessions etc.) cannot replace true attunement. So, the child ends up feeling ashamed for needing love. Is this something that anyone in the group can relate to? HA is about being available emotionally to the child – it's not about problem solving or fixing or being rational."*

(5) Homework: Notice which people in your life (if any) have strong emotional attunement skills? Notice your internal responses to your own (and others') feelings and difficulties. Is your usual response from the *Inner Critic*, or the *OC* mode that wants to 'fix' the problem, or from the *Compassionate HA* self?

*14. Mini-mindfulness practices (to be included 1–2 times each session, and practiced daily between sessions)*

Body-focused mindfulness exercises focus on tuning in to the body for 20 seconds to a minute at a time, to help participants develop tolerance and curiosity regarding vulnerable feelings contained within the body. For example, an adaptation of the Focusing practice by Gendlin (1978) includes six steps: (1) **Clear a space.** Make yourself comfortable in a quiet space. Close your eyes and kindly ask yourself a question or two to connect to the *VCh* mode, such as *"How am I feeling right now?"* or *"How is my life going"?* (2) **Identify a felt-sense in the body.** Notice what response or sensations come from your body. You might notice a mode clamouring in your mind, trying to get your attention, alongside lots of thoughts – see if you can dip below this until you notice a particular bodily sensation that wants your attention. At this point, the felt-sense may be fuzzy or blurry. However it shows up, turn towards it. (3) **Give the felt-sense a word or 'handle' that captures how it feels in the body.** Silently acknowledge the sensation, for example *"Hello, I know you're there."* Invite a word or image to arise that symbolises the quality of this body knowledge. It might be "jittery", or it might be "tense in my chest". (4) **Resonate.** Slow down the process, and allow your body-mind to gently sway between your descriptive word and your felt-sense, so that you can check out whether your word is the best fit. For example, if your original word was "anxious", it might transform into a more specific felt-sense or image, such as "trapped inside a glass box". Then, just notice that your felt-sense is only one part of you. This is your *VCh* (feeling) part, not your whole being. (5) **Inquire.** As you continue to stay with the felt-sense of your *VCh*, you might inquire

*"What's the hardest part of this for you?"* Then ask, *"What does this felt-sense need?"* Listen for an answer from your body. The felt-sense of *VCh* may formulate a specific problem, or it might just want to hang out with you. When you get a response, notice whether you feel a felt-sense shift – perhaps a sense of feeling less weighed down, or tight muscles loosening, or maybe just a more general sense of aliveness. (6) **Receive the experience.** Welcome whatever has emerged during the session. *"Thank your body and VCh for speaking to you. It's not important whether you believe, agree with, or go with what the felt-sense is saying. You need only receive the message."* Reassure your (*VCh*) felt-sense that you'll be back again if she/he wants to continue the process at a later point. Rather than setting goals, just use this as an opportunity for friendly time with your *VCh* in the body.

Further body-focused mindfulness exercises are included in Appendix 1.

## 15. Reparenting Imagery

(1) Spend time developing an imaginary safe place for the whole group where all participants can allow their *VCh* sides to meet and feel protected. What are the features needed to make it safe and comfortable? Explore ideas until there is consensus. This place is separate from their own individual 'safe/sacred' place, but can be a variation on this. (2) Each participant makes a list of three things that their own *VCh* mode needs to hear (or alternatively three things that all of the *VCh* modes in the group might benefit from) and hands these in to leaders. (3) Invite participants to visualise themselves with all the group participants in their *VCh* mode, in the group safe place, protected by a radiant circle of light. Invite group participants to bring with them their own spiritual being or 'power animal'. This can be anything at all, and ideally whatever first comes to mind. (4) Guide participants to 'thicken' the connection with this 'being/animal' (using all five senses). Invite the group *Vulnerable Children* to listen to the messages the leaders will read out, and allow their 'being/animal' to help them take in the messages in whatever way they need to receive them. (5) Ask them if there are any other message that their 'being/animal' has for them, to listen to these. Remind them that only healthy 'beings/animals' are permitted in this space, and anything else will be blown away by the vortex surrounding this space. (Some of these ideas were adapted from Schwarz, Corrigan, Hull, & Ragu, 2017.)

*Variation*: Group members are guided to visualise their *VCh* side and identify feelings/unmet needs in a current ED-related situation (e.g. looking in the mirror, trying on clothes, choosing a normal yogurt rather than a low-fat version at the supermarket). This is followed by a break in imagery where group members brainstorm specific reparenting messages that will directly meet those needs. Draw distinction between coping mode 'wants' and true emotional needs of the inner child. The group returns (with eyes closed) to the previous image and group leaders read out the compassionate messages for each *VCh*, and sends away the *Inner Critic*. If group members find it difficult to 'take in' the messages, ask them just to notice the messages from the perspective of being a very young child or even a one-day-old baby (to increase connection with their vulnerability).

### Confronting the Inner Critic

The *Punitive/Critical, Guilt-Inducing and Demanding (Inner Critic)* modes (which frequently operate in alliance) set unrealistically high standards and deprive, attack and punish the *VCh*, typically using the body as a target for shame and humiliation (Simpson, 2012). The *Inner Critic* treats emotional needs with disdain, thereby triggering high levels of shame in the *VCh*.

A key function of STE-g is to recognise the origins of this mode (culture, family influences, explicit/implicit messages from parents, caregivers, abusers, media, religion etc.), alongside provision of psychoeducation regarding the emotional needs of children, as a means of starting the process of de-fusion, and reducing the ego-syntonicity of the *Inner Critic*. Group participants are encouraged to recognise that the *Inner Critic* is a memory or 'echo' from the past, which keeps reappearing as an image or voice in the present – but must now be dismantled. This can often be more easily achieved in group settings than in individual work, due to the fact that participants are often able to recognise that the messages coming from other participants' *Inner Critics* are unfair and even outrageous. As participants start to get in touch with their anger and sense of injustice, they are encouraged to fight each other's and their own *Inner Critic*.

Participants are encouraged to develop a pictorial representation of their *Inner Critic* which conveys both explicit and implicit messages. These tend to be associated with the message that their needs and feelings are a burden on others, 'ridiculous', a sign of greed or excessive neediness. The *Inner Critic* and *VCh* modes are often inextricably entwined, so that the experience of shame and powerlessness becomes pervasive. In therapy, we challenge our clients' perspectives so that they become aware of the *Inner Critic* as an 'imposter' that offers nothing and has no useful value or function. In sessions, we begin to differentiate the *Inner Critic* mode from the coping modes, which have a well-intentioned function. We do this by asking group members to find a suitable name for their *Inner Critic* (e.g. the Dictator, the Bully, the Witch) and ask them to draw it and/or find images to represent it. We ask group members to share these images with each other. Showing videos of 'extremely punitive characters that have been portrayed in cartoons/film-clips' can also be useful to magnify the concept of the *Inner Critic* as mean for the sake of being mean, with no redeeming features. It is important here to differentiate the actual parent from the *Inner Critic*, which is often a conglomerate of multiple messages from different sources. Many of the exercises described in this manual are targeted at fighting the generic *Inner Critic*. In particular, we help group members to get in touch with a sense of anger or injustice in order to empower them to fight back against the *Inner Critic*.

The *Inner Critic* frequently appears unannounced during group therapy sessions. It can be triggered by group exercises or discussions, and for many participants it is omnipresent. The term '*Healthy Adult*' can be a trigger for many participants with a strong *Inner Critic*, telling them that they don't deserve to be healthy, or that being healthy will make them 'mediocre/average/ nothing special'. It can be less triggering to use the term 'Good Parent', as this conjures a more of a defined role (Farrell & Shaw, 2012), or 'Wise [Compassionate] Being'. Once the *Inner Critic* message has been identified by a group leader, repeat the words that the client has used (e.g. "*I'm hopeless. I'm undeserving*") and ask the client concerned (and other group members) to notice what emotional and bodily sensations arise for them when they hear those words.

It can be helpful to ask clients to try different postures associated with the *HA* mode (e.g. ensure spine is upright; stand taller; breathe; notice the sensations of the toes and soles of the feet) before speaking to the *Inner Critic*. It can be most effective to have the whole group stand up to the *Inner Critic* (represented by an image or effigy) together as a 'team'. Sometimes it can be more effective to address the *Inner Critic* through a direct body movement or gesture, while the group fights from a *HA* perspective. Many people with EDs have grown up in a very emotionally inhibited environment, where expression of feelings was considered shameful. Therefore, it can be empowering to encourage the expression of emotions by all group participants – you can then remind them that the *Inner Critic* will try to shame them for fighting back after the session, and create a group flashcard (or audio card) to allow them to continue fighting and standing their ground. Flashcards can be used to prepare a *HA* response for frequently occurring situations that trigger maladaptive coping behaviours (see Appendix 1 for a template of a mode flashcard with an example).

N.B. Group leaders should be alert to the fact that what may first appear to be the *Inner Critic* may in fact be the [*Flagellating*] *OC* mode. If you are dealing with the *OC* mode, the chairwork is less about 'fighting' the mode than it is about standing up to an old friend who has become unhelpful (e.g. "Thanks, this helped in the past, but not now…we need to make space for the *HA*, who can guide and nourish us without the dangerous side effects…").

### Exercises to challenge the Inner Critic

#### 16. Group drawing

Draw an effigy of the *Inner Critic* in groups of three to four on large poster-sized paper. The idea is that this should be partly a humorous exercise – participants are encouraged to draw the mode (in colour) in a way that pokes fun at it (e.g. it might have 'crazy' eyes, or a pointy nose, or a self-important expression etc.). For groups that have more of a *Demanding/Guilt-Inducing Inner Critic*, the 'character' of the drawing should reflect this (and for groups that have a mixture, the two different faces of the *Inner Critic* can be depicted on either side of the card). This can then be laid on the floor or removed from the room when it interferes. Alternatively, *Inner Critic* effigies made of fabric can be cut into in the shape of a person (Farrell & Shaw, 2012). Draw/imagine the *Inner Critic* wearing a silly outfit, such as Donald Duck boxer shorts and a lampshade hat (to reduce its 'power') whilst confronting it.

### 17. Confronting the Inner Critic

Participants are encouraged to consider the 'flavour' of their *Inner Critic* mode: is it Guilt-inducing? Punitive? Demanding? Over-anxious? Austere? Consider possible origins of this mode, including explicit and implicit messages from caregivers and teachers, religious leaders, cultural influences, social media, peers, siblings, experiences of abuse, long periods alone, low emotional attunement/empathy, and conditional love. Brainstorm in pairs the typical triggers for the *Inner Critic*, such as being weighed, weight gain, looking in mirror, tight clothing, breaking dietary rules, as well as in group sessions, such as feeling left out.

### 18. Group rescripting imagery

Previous texts (e.g. Farrell & Shaw, 2012) provide detailed instructions on imagery rescripting linked to childhood memories within groups. Imagery rescripting involves the whole group (as opposed to individual therapy within the group), usually with one person as the main focus. Start with a safe place. One person chooses a childhood memory which was upsetting, possibly linked to body/eating/weight/shape and connected to current difficulties. Whole group rescripts ending, and receives messages for their *VCh* mode.

### 19. Visualisations to challenge the Inner Critic

Empowering visualisations based on metaphors, used on a consistent basis, may promote new *HA* neural pathways, and challenge the *Inner Critic*, like a type of 'psycho-physiotherapy'. It is possible that part of the power of visualising the different modes lies in increasing conscious awareness of their presence, making them more tangible, and ego-dystonic.

For example: (1) *"The stronger the Inner Critic becomes, the more successful it is at 'stealing real estate' in the brain. It stops us from functioning in normal ways and increasingly tries to dominate our attention. Your HA can fight back against the Critic 'thief' mode and take back that real estate. Close your eyes and get a visual image of your HA mode returning 'home' to find the Critic has set up camp. The HA's job is to bring in whatever help she needs to remove the Critic from the 'real-estate' of the mind (e.g. using blindingly bright compassionate light that surrounds and overshadows the Inner Critic); or (2) Visualise the HA as white-blood-cell-peace-corps 'soldiers' who are there to protect your health and well-being from potential threat...they are frog-marching the Inner Critic straight to the kidneys to be flushed out of the body."*

### 20. Limit-setting with the Inner Critic

Write a trigger statement on the whiteboard, such as "I really like you and care about you. You are important to the group." Ask group participants to try to take this message in, and then write down any *Inner Critic* messages (on sticky notes) that they notice. Collect and re-distribute the messages to other group members. In pairs, try to think of a message to counter the *Inner Critic*, and to validate the person who wrote this sticky note message. Make it as authentic as possible, based on what you now know of this person. In pairs, stand up and read out the messages with a strong tone of voice, directed at the *Inner Critic* effigy. Group participants are encouraged to use these limit-setting phrases in their daily lives with their own *Inner Critics*. As an aide, they are encouraged to take pictures of these messages and keep them on their smartphones.

### 21. Chairwork exercise – fighting the Inner Critic

- Identify a participant whose *Inner Critic* has been strong this week (e.g. related to eating, weight, shape). Explore details of the trigger and write critical internal messages on the whiteboard. Identify whether this trigger is typical for other group participants, and whether they can identify additional *Inner Critic* messages.
- Group participants spend five to ten minutes in pairs, preparing two to three *HA* responses to the *Inner Critic*. The emphasis is on being firm and not entering into any long discussions or arguments with the *Critic*. The guideline is that we do not 'discuss' with bullies, and responses must be firm.
- Set up three chairs – *VCh* (with photographs of all participants as children), *Inner Critic* (with effigy draped over it), and *HA*. If any other modes appear during the roleplay, label them and then say that we'll deal with that part later (rather than bringing them into the roleplay). Remember to always talk to an empty chair if you are working with the *Inner Critic* or coping modes – only the *VCh* can be addressed directly while the client remains on their chair.
- **Roleplay:** The *Inner Critic* (two participants, including the person who originally identified a strong *Inner Critic*) speaks from behind the *Inner*

*Critic* effigy to the empty *VCh* chair, voicing messages from the whiteboard.

- The focal participant returns to sit in the *VCh* chair and describes their emotional reaction from that side: *"How does it feel to be criticised and put-down in this way?"*
- Participant then moves to sit in the *HA* chair (with all other participants as coaches, standing behind).
- The whole group replies to the *Inner Critic* – coached by group leaders. Prompt the *HA* side by asking: *"What would you think if you saw an adult saying this to a child in the street? Or to your child or niece/nephew? Would that be okay by you?"* Ask them to respond based on how they would feel about any child being treated this way. Encourage participants to focus on affirming and protecting the *VCh* side.
- When participants are responding to the *Inner Critic*, encourage them to use the power of their voice to fight back *"Now say it again, 10% louder...20% louder!"* Remind group members that it is healthy and normal to allow themselves to get *angry* about this message. *"It's never okay to treat someone this way."*
- Check with the client in focus...is the *Inner Critic* saying anything back to them? If so, what?
- Continue dialogue until it comes to a natural end – and *HA* wins, or *Inner Critic* chair is removed.
- Ask participants *"What do you think the VCh needs?"*
- Check in with the participant in focus – what did she feel when we addressed the different sides?
- Debrief – how did it feel to play the different roles? How did the client at the centre of the role-play feel? How did others feel? How much stronger does the *HA* need to be to overcome the *Inner Critic*? What would help (consider voice tone, stance, gestures etc.) to make it stronger?
- If appropriate, repeat last part of the roleplay, taking on board new information. Ask for further feedback from all participants. Explain that the exercise will be regularly repeated in the group to try to fight the *Inner Critic* of all of the group members – to give them the tools to practice ignoring or sending this side away.

## 22. Variation: Chairwork when the Inner Critic is sabotaging progress in therapy

Ask the group if anyone has an example of a time in the past week or so when their *Inner Critic* has been trying to make them feel that they have failed, that the therapy has been all for nothing, and that they are no better off than they were before the group.

- Divide group into two sub-groups to play the *HA* and *Inner Critic* sides. Each side has five to ten minutes to prepare, with therapists coaching.

- The *Inner Critic* side should use the arguments presented by the client, but keep it general, avoiding being too personal. Generally, this would consist of all-or-nothing statements such as: *"The group has been a waste of time. Not one bit of it has helped. No-one in the group understood what you were talking about. None of it applied to you. You didn't get anything out of it at all. Nothing will ever work. You have tried everything and nothing has ever made you better. This will fail, just like everything else in your life. You're so hopeless that you're doomed to misery. You should have put your energy into looking for that magic drug/ solution to your problems."*

- Dialogue starts with the *Inner Critic*, and then the *HA* – alternating until the *HA* 'wins' by sending the *Inner Critic* away.

- The *HA* should be firm and place responsibility for pain and suffering on the *Inner Critic*'s shoulders, for example: *"Look, you are the problem here, not her. We can hear you, but we will not be taking any further notice – you're all doom and gloom, you try to sabotage everything good in her life. In fact, the group has helped her in all sorts of ways, (e.g.) the group is the first step towards a life of health, happiness and self-care."*

- Seek feedback from both sides (+ observer) after roleplay. If necessary, repeat or continue roleplay with extra information gained from feedback.

- If any coping modes arise during this exercise, address them on a separate chair.

- Debrief: *"Because our Inner Critic mode is so convincing and it feels like a fact that is coming from inside our own minds, it feels 100% correct. It is very difficult to fight. Many people say, "yes, but you don't know me...I really am defective!" "The Inner Critic trains us from an early age only to notice information that is consistent with it (e.g. criticism, someone forgetting to call us), and to ignore anything that contradicts it (e.g. encouragement, praise). We therefore need to get used to noticing the Inner Critic and thinking about where it comes from and how it has strengthened over the years. We also need to think about what triggers this mode for us, how it makes us feel (i.e. our vulnerable side) and how it feels in our bodies (e.g. fat, dirty, disgusting, revolting etc.) As we start to notice it more, we can start to fight against it, to protect the vulnerable part within us, thus strengthening our HA side. It can also help start to visualise our own HA side and to imagine the voice of the therapist and other group members when we get stuck, to provide guidance regarding how to respond in different situations."*

### Behavioural pattern breaking:

*23. Invite participants to set specific behavioural goals*

Specific behavioural experiments can be set up to 'break the rules' set by *Inner Critic* and/or coping modes (especially *OC* mode, such as through gradual exposure to feared situations linked to learning to tolerate uncertainty, change, mediocrity, relaxation, non-productivity, mess etc.). Be sure to prepare in advance (e.g. using audio flashcards) for potential attacking messages from the Inner Critic that are triggered by behavioural experiments.

Behavioural change linked to the *OC* mode can start with making a list of all of the *OC* rules (including eating/food/weight related), and generate behavioural goals linked to each of these. These are then addressed using graduated behavioural experiments (from least to most anxiety-provoking).

Behavioural goals should also be set around strengthening the *HA* mode. These may be focused on increasing tolerance for vulnerability and gradually reducing coping modes in and outwith the group, e.g. tell one person what you feel and/or need in a way that they can hear the message; be in your body and feel your body sensations for at least two to three minutes each day (three min. breathing space); change one eating behaviour (e.g. reducing purging) and notice which modes are revealed (have been 'hiding' under the eating behaviours).

### Building and strengthening the Healthy Adult [Wise Self] mode

One of the most important goals of STE-g is to facilitate the development of a strong *HA* within each of the group participants. The preliminary development of a participant's own *HA* side takes place through internalising the *HA* mode, as modelled by group leaders. In both imagery and chairwork, group participants are encouraged to embody the voice of the *HA* mode, both by fighting off parent modes and also nurturing and taking care of the group *VCh* modes. This can be a difficult and slow process. Many participants have experienced very little in the way of empathy, nurturance, warmth and/or attunement in the past. When they start to experience these emotional needs being met in the group by the leaders (and other participants), many participants describe feeling both suspicious and confused at the contrast between this and their previous relationships. Participants are encouraged to consciously internalise this experience, with a view to eventually learning to take care of their own and other group participants' *VCh* modes in an empathic way. In the first half of the program, group leaders provide a significant amount of validation and corrective emotional experiences within the group, through directly challenging the old schema-driven messages, providing psychoeducation and assigning homework linked to the universal needs and rights of a child and, most importantly, through limited reparenting of group participants.

Participants are encouraged to develop their own *HA* mode, as modelled on the therapists and other healthy nurturing role models in their lives. The *HA* mode is strengthened through visualisation exercises, self-disclosure by the therapists, learning to embody a *HA* posture and presence, use of breathing and mindfulness exercises to increase self-awareness, and following the three *HA* steps (as outlined in van der Wijngaart, 2015):

1 Understanding: *"I'm feeling anxious – it's understandable to be feeling this way - because my Inner Critic is telling me that I am unworthy and I don't deserve to eat"*;

2 Reality check:

- Validate needs and identify in what ways are parent/coping modes off track: *"It's not true that eating will make me unlovable/unworthy and out of control. Just like everyone else, my body needs nourishment – that is normal. It's impossible to have 100% control at all times. I can learn to trust my body and listen to what it is telling me."*

- Provide alternative realistic views for trigger event. Offer direction and behavioural choices: *"The Critic has no qualifications in psychology or dietetics! Instead of depriving myself, I could instead defy the Critic and give my body the nourishment it needs by eating this meal. This is part of being healthy, balanced and is the basis for finding true connection with others."*

3 Inspire with Hope: *"Even though I'm feeling scared, I know that I can get through this, as I've been working on this in therapy. I'm learning to stop giving the Inner Critic any airspace. I'm learning that I can help my OC to 'let go', and practice 'being' and taking care of me."*

An effigy of the *HA* [Wise] Self is drawn by participants once they have started to internalise the reparenting messages from group leaders and other group members (Farrell & Shaw, 2012). In addition, participants can experiment with drawing their own individual compassionate *HA* mode, and explore how compassion looks, feels, sounds and smells compared to the 'felt-sense' qualities of the coping and *Inner Critic* modes. 'Flashforward' visualisation exercises can be utilised to practise self-compassion in future trigger events. Chairwork and reparenting imagery are utilised to practise self/other compassion with a focus on 'presence' and attunement to unmet needs. For those who do not yet have a sufficiently strong *HA* side, they can draw any being (e.g. spiritual being or animal) that is able to provide the attunement, warmth and compassion they need (Hodge & Simpson, 2016; Schwarz et al., 2017).

Metaphor for developing a Compassionate HA: *"When you learn to be self-compassionate, you no longer need to rely on eating behaviours to compensate for difficult feelings. Your Compassionate HA is like your new shoes...but to get into them, you have to leave your old shoes behind (coping modes). Moving from the old pair to the new pair of shoes can feel like walking on red hot coals (i.e. experiencing painful emotions)."*

## Guidelines for *Healthy Adult*

In ST, therapists can provide more direct guidance for clients' *Vulnerable Child* side that needs protection, support, nurturance or encouragement. *Healthy Adult* (limited reparenting) messages are designed to directly meet the needs of the inner child. The explicit goal is also for them to internalise these healthy messages. Without this many of our clients have no starting point for learning self-compassion. Some examples include:

- I see you. I care about you for who you are right now, not how you look or what you achieve (*emotional deprivation; approval seeking; unrelenting standards*)
- I'm here to help you find a safe way to connect, I don't have any other agenda. I'm sticking around (*abandonment/mistrust*)
- I always look forward to my sessions with you. I'm so enjoying getting to know you better, and seeing this vulnerable side of you (*defectiveness*)
- When others get to know you, I'm convinced that they will like you too. I especially like your (list specific qualities relevant to the person, e.g. *creativity, sense of humour, warmth, caring nature*). (*defectiveness, social isolation*).
- It's not your job to take care of others' feelings – you are allowed to state your own separate opinions and life goals. You are allowed to be your own person (*enmeshment/subjugation*)
- You can manage more than you realise. I can see you have good intuition, and I trust your judgement. (*dependence, enmeshment/ undeveloped self*)
- You already know what you need – listen to your Vulnerable Side – listen to your body. You can learn to trust yourself, you already have every quality you need to be lovable and happy (*emotional deprivation/ defectiveness/undeveloped self*)
- It's so important for you to have time to play and have fun. Everybody needs time so their mind and body can relax and restore. You're not a machine and you don't have to get everything perfect (*unrelenting standards*)
- I feel closer to you when you tell me about your feelings, and I know that if I feel that way, others will too. Feelings are what connects us to each other (*emotional inhibition*)
- I know that you can control your impulses, even if you don't immediately get the relief you are looking for. I've noticed you have everything it takes to cope with the discomfort, even though it's hard. You have so much determination that can help you with this! (*insufficient self-control*)
- You are allowed to have emotions, to have needs, and to care for yourself. Your happiness doesn't depend on being perfect, or being

accepted by others. It's about seeing that you are already enough, you already have everything you need inside you to heal and be loved (*emotional deprivation, emotional inhibition, approval seeking*)

### Teach the three steps for Healthy Adult *mode*

1. Acknowledge the distress of the *Vulnerable Child* side and start soothing her: E.g. *"I'm feeling scared and that is my Vulnerable side that has been triggered. This is scary and difficult for me because as a child I learned that this situation was unsafe."*
2. Give hope by reminding *Vulnerable Child* that you will take care of her and that the difficult feelings will pass.
3. Help the *Vulnerable Child* to deal with the situation. What does she need? Protection? Support? Encouragement?

### More Healthy Adult *Tips*

- Stand tall. Lengthen your spine, soften your chest and belly. Feel your feet connected to the ground. Breathe.
- Be firm. It's your job to protect the *Vulnerable Child*.
- Make sure that you are stronger than the *Inner Critic*.
- Disagree with what the *Inner Critic* is saying. Don't be drawn into long-winded arguments.
- Clearly state what you are doing right. Affirm your true good intentions and actions. e.g. *"I am trying so hard to get it right. But no matter how hard I try, I hear your relentless criticisms. I've had enough."*
- Stop *Inner Critic* from undermining and sabotaging everything that you are trying to set out to achieve. Then send it away…repeatedly, if necessary.

## 24. Happy Child *exercises*

These are short fun-based activities that can be interspersed at regular intervals throughout the entire group program. These are designed to increase spontaneity and joy through visualisation and body movement in order to help participants to move out of coping modes and return to a more embodied feeling state. Exercises have a particular emphasis on feeling sensations in the body, and establishing rhythm and connection. Participants are encouraged to notice changes in their bodily sensations and emotions as they participate in the exercises. This can include a range of activities, including: (1) Create a 'Funny YouTube videos' listing for the group by asking everyone to take it in turns to bring one along; (2) Create a music listing for the group with songs with uplifting lyrics that help strengthen *HA* and value *VCh* modes (2) *Happy Child* visualisations involving all five senses – e.g.

building a tree-house, playing in the snow, swimming in the sea; (3) Physical exercises such as patting the head whilst rubbing the abdomen; then switching to rubbing the head and patting the abdomen; (5) Blowing up balloons and letting them go; (6) Blowing bubbles. In addition, the following exercises can be used for group bonding and 'playing' with modes: (7) *Happy Child ball game* (Appendix 1); (8) Juggling exercise to increase awareness of modes (Appendix 1).

### Addressing body image disturbance

Many of the exercises described in this chapter can be adapted specifically to work with an *Inner Critic* or coping mode that is linked to body image disturbance. This may involve challenging the *Inner Critic*, as well as bypassing the coping mode that represents the person's current viewpoint. Group participants need to tune in to their bodies to begin to develop a sense of themselves as a separate being. Very often people with EDs can be reluctant to connect with their bodies, due to their fear of dysregulated negative emotions (especially those that are trauma-related). Through very short mindfulness moments throughout the group program, participants are able to move from having very little sense of their bodies to tolerating and noticing their experience of their own body.

In order to begin to externalise body image-related messages, participants are initially encouraged to reflect on a range of possible origins. In pairs, participants are encouraged to list as many *Inner Critic* messages as possible, triggered by looking in the mirror, checking stomach/thighs, standing on scales, trying on a new dress, or eating a meal, feeling distressed, or lonely. They are then asked to identify possible early sources of these messages – e.g. selective internalisation of cultural and media messages, others' (family/peer) actions or words during childhood. These may be a result of direct body-related experiences and/or trauma (such as being teased for being overweight as a child), or more subtle/implicit messages such as others' facial expressions, voice tone or disapproval or rejection.

Alternatively, for some participants the body image distortion may be secondary to 'missing' emotional ingredients (i.e. sufficient warmth, encouragement, approval, praise), which resulted in the person feeling generally 'not good enough' or 'undeserving'. How did family members refer to people who were large or overweight? How were children treated by peers at school if they were not thin (primary and high school)? How has this affected the way participants feel about themselves and what messages did they internalise about themselves? What cultural messages are linked to the *Inner Critic*? How do the body-image-related messages from the *Inner Critic* link to messages regarding vulnerability, feelings and needs?

### 25. Inner Critic body–focused exercise

- Ask group participants to think about a time recently when they experienced negative feelings (e.g. shame, defectiveness) about their bodies or about themselves in general.

- Draw a body shape on the whiteboard, and write down a list of critical messages that have arisen in relation to body/weight/shape triggers.
- Next, in pairs, write down as many healthy/wise-self messages about the body/eating/food as possible on sticky notes (i.e. what would a healthy parent say to their child about their growing body, and about eating?). What would participants tell their own children, nieces, nephews? What are the healthy messages these children need to hear? How would you feel about them being judged in this way? Ask each pair to choose their favourite 8–10 messages.
- Participants are invited to completely cover the generic *Inner Critic* messages with their healthy messages, reading them out loud to the group as they stick them on.
- For a variation of this exercise *Fighting the collective group Inner Critic via Chairwork*, see Appendix 1.

## 26. Internal dialogue between individual and body

- Three-minute breathing space – focusing on sensations in the body.
- Ask participants to focus on their bodies, and to notice what images come to mind.
- Ask participants to draw whatever arises using the coloured pencils or crayons provided. It can just be a shape or they might choose an actual thing or symbol to represent how they see their body. Following this, explore these images in pairs, discussing what led participants to use particular colours, shapes, symbols.
- Share these ideas with the group as a whole and look for common themes.
- What are the main feelings that emerge from these drawings?
- Ask for one group member who would be willing to partake in a dialogue with their body.
- Place the picture that represents the body on one chair and ask the client to sit in the other. Ask the client "*What do you want to say to your body?*" Then ask them to go and be their body and respond with how they feel.
- Identify what modes are present (which mode is in the body? Which mode is attacking the body?)
- Ask the client if they notice that this message is familiar? Do either the body (or individual) fit with a particular mode/schema? How did it feel to be in each chair? What did the group notice about each side? Did any particular modes come up?
- How would the group like to respond to this mode/schema?
- Re-play dialogue using new information. This time there should be a clear healthy side within the dialogue (who is coached by other group members).

- How does this change the way participants see their body? Does their view or perspective of their body appear differently from different chairs (modes)?
- Encourage participants to fight the shaming messages that attack or blame their bodies; and to express compassion toward each other's bodies (and the *VCh* that is locked inside).

### 27. Scientist from Mars: body image exercise

Invite participants to read the following excerpt:

On 21 August 1803 the *Sydney Gazette* informed the public about the first specimens of a new species called the koala at Port Jackson. It read as follows:

> An animal whose species was never before found in the Colony, is in His Excellency's possession. When taken it had two pups, one of which died a few days hence. This creature is somewhat larger than the wombat, and although it might at first appearance be thought much to resemble it, nevertheless differs from that animal. The fore and hind legs are about of an equal length, having five sharp talons at each of the extremities, with which it must have climbed the highest trees with much facility. The fur that covers it is soft and fine, and of a mixed grey colour; the ears are short and open; the graveness of the visage, which differs little in colour from the back, would seem to indicate a more than ordinary portion of animal sagacity; and the teeth resemble those of a rabbit. The surviving pup generally clings to the back of the mother, or is caressed with a ser-enity that appears peculiarly characteristic; it has a false belly like the apposin, and its food consists solely of gum leaves.

- Imagine that you are alien scientists who have just arrived from Mars. You have just spotted your first humans and you are intrigued about the way they look.
- In pairs, spend ten minutes writing a short scientific description of the human being (male and female) from the perspective of an alien.
- Feedback the main ideas to the group and write them on the whiteboard. What do participants notice? What thoughts arise about the human body when they look at that list (funny-looking, strange)? Notice how the *Inner Critic* turns individual characteristics and variations into flaws – why can't it allow bodies to be what they are without making judgements?

### 28. Experiential focusing exercise

This exercise is used to enable participants to explore their visceral felt-sense and emotions associated with interconnectedness/proximity to another person

(Farrell, Shaw, & Reiss, 2014: Chapter 4, p. 8). In pairs, participants walk toward the other person, one step at a time. Following this exercise, explore any modes (especially coping modes) that arise. Also explore whether any *Inner Critic* or coping mode messages arise in relation to the body/self.

### Sessions 22–25

Sessions 22–25 are based on consolidating the work that has been done, pushing for behavioural change, encouraging expression of vulnerability, and strengthening the *HA*. These final sessions are focused on processing schema triggering and loss associated with the ending, drawing on fears and anxieties linked to past endings. Participants are encouraged to create a 'healthy ending', where their *HA* commits to taking care of their *VCh*, and to forever be the internal parent that they really need. They are reminded that grief and sadness are important and healthy signs of healing. It is normal and healthy to feel sad about the parts that have been missing from our lives – our unmet needs from childhood – and to let these feelings take their course without trying to control them. Reassure participants that it is also normal to feel a sense of loss and anger after the group ends. For those with an abandonment schema, this feeling can be even stronger and at a deeper level, and can remind participants of times when they were abandoned in the past. We tell participants that when they experience these feelings, they should try not to just 'react' to the anger or sadness or loss, but remember that a schema has been triggered and that their underlying *VCh* needs extra nurturance, care and warmth. Imagery and chairwork in this part of the group are aimed at consolidation of the work which has already taken place, reinforcing the connection between their healthy self and *VCh*, and pushing for changes in coping patterns that perpetuate their difficulties. Participants are encouraged to increasingly take more of an observational stance of their modes, as they transition from overidentification with coping modes, into an overarching position of an authentic 'I', with the capacity to choose a more expansive awareness. This is an important aspect of developing an autonomous self, which is disidentified with their ED and other problems. In small groups, participants are encouraged to develop mini-flashcards and to dictate these onto their smart phones as audio-flashcards, so that they can access their *HA* on demand.

### Chairwork with modes that sabotage treatment

At this final stage of the group, participants often notice the modes that sabotage their progress and future happiness are starting to rear their heads. Modes may block recovery in many ways.

- *Punishing Inner Critic* believes you don't deserve to recover or be happy. It wants to hurt and punish you for having feelings and needs.

- *Demanding Inner Critic* believes that work and duties are more important than your health and happiness. Rest, nourishment and self-care are perceived as unproductive.
- *Guilt-inducing Inner Critic* believes that you are at fault, and have no right to feel sad or angry about your unmet needs. It believes that self-care is self-indulgence.
- *OC* believes that recovery should be quick and efficient. It believes that needs and feelings are too 'messy' and get in the way of achieving all of your goals and responsibilities. Therefore, this mode may sabotage progress by prioritising work, study, productivity and lists over therapy.
- *DetPr* wants to amble along in the same way as always, and doesn't take responsibility for change. It wants to avoid the difficult feelings associated with working through your problems and attending therapy.
- *CSu* aims to avoid conflict and rejection by pacifying others, and prioritising their needs. It believes that you shouldn't really need help from others, as your job is to take care of others. Meeting others' needs has become a mechanism for earning a sense of being valued by others, at the expense of asserting your own needs and individuality. In this mode, you avoid making decisions or asking for what you want in case it causes disappointment or hurt to others. This mode makes you feel guilty for spending time on yourself or prioritising your health and happiness. It also makes you feel guilty for feeling angry, or for standing up to others. It tells you that your needs are less important, and therefore stops you getting your emotional needs met both in the group and at home.
- *Helpless Surrenderer* (with underlying *Dependent Child/AnCh*) believes that others hold the solution to her problems. She feels helpless to help herself, that nothing works, and wants others to do something to 'fix' her.
- *AnCh* may be angry that recovery is so hard and involves difficult feelings such as sadness, grief, loss and anger. The *AnCh* might also be angry that the old coping strategy is reducing, as it doesn't want to feel the uncertainty and insecurity of coping in new ways.
- *VCh* is scared about the prospect of giving up the coping modes (especially the *OC*). Often, she has viewed the *OC* as a loyal and dependable 'friend' and is fearful of being unable to cope on her own. She is often fearful that without the coping mode, her life will feel too unpredictable. Underneath she feels ashamed, rejected and lonely.
- *Undisciplined Child* doesn't like feeling uncomfortable or facing difficult challenges that will help her to attain her long-term goals. She prefers to use activities that give her short-term relief, such as bingeing, exercise or restricting.

*Chairwork:* Ask participants if they have noticed any of these modes arising over recent weeks. Identify the two strongest modes in the group. Ask group members (two groups of three to four participants) to draw this mode on a large sheet of cardboard, using coloured pens, and to write a list of the main messages it carries, especially those about sabotaging therapy and recovery from the ED.

- Place the finished cardboard pictures on a designated chair and label the mode/chair. A group leader hides behind the cardboard pictures and reads out the list of messages.
- If there is an *Inner Critic* mode, coach participants to stand behind the *HA* chair and set limits and send it away.
- Coach group participants to speak to their own coping mode(s). Remind participants that there is a vulnerable side of them that really needs a true friend who is capable of caring for them, nurturing, seeing and accepting them for who they are. Coach participants to talk to their coping modes, telling them what the *VCh* part really needs, and explaining how the coping mode stops them from getting these needs met, e.g. "*I know you're trying to help, but what I (and every human being) need is....*".
- One group leader moves to the *VCh* chair, playing the role of the collective group *VCh*, and expressing fears about letting go of the coping mode.
- In pairs, participants spend a few minutes brainstorming about what their *VCh* needs to let go of their old 'friend' coping modes. What might they be afraid of happening if they let go? What does their *VCh* need to hear from the *HA* side that will convince them it's safe to start to let go of their old friend the coping mode in little steps? Coach them to meet the *VCh* needs e.g. "*You are already ok just being you; There is so much more to you than your body; It must be so hard to worry that you are only lovable if your body is thin; Nobody deserves to feel that way, you are worth so much more than that.*"
- Encourage group participants to stand behind the *HA* chair and speak to their *VCh* selves, reassuring them that they will stand by them, protect and love them, and meet all of their needs.
- After everyone has had a turn, debrief, and validate the group's emotional needs. Explain that although the coping modes and *Inner Critic modes* will try to sabotage therapy, the reality is that these modes are outdated.
- Remind participants that the only way to be ED-free and happy is to develop their own *HA* to take over from the coping modes, which is more in tune with their own value system and is compassionate toward themselves. "*Although it might still seem alien to you just now, your future happiness lies in your ability to recognise that there is nothing more important that your health and your happiness. And here we are talking about true happiness that is driven by inner contentment rather than based on appearances and productivity.*"

### Relapse prevention and behavioural maintenance

Participants are encouraged to prepare a plan of action in terms of how their *HA* side will respond (to other modes), in the face of future trigger events. Participants are encouraged to use worksheets to re-visit the strategies that have been useful to them in the past, and to plan for future schema activation. The *Managing Modes* and *Responding Wisely in the Schema Zone* handouts (see Appendix 1) can be useful for making concrete plans in moving forward after the group has ended.

### Future-oriented imagery rescripting

In this final part of the group program, imagery rescripting is used to reinforce the strength of each participants' *HA* side in directly meeting their needs. Imagery is focused on preparing for typical trigger situations and bypassing coping mode responses in order to try out new behavioural responses. Participants are encouraged to identify a situation where they have felt connected to their *HA* side, and to anchor the felt-sense of this side in the body (e.g. confident, standing tall, calm). They are then invited to bring up an image of the trigger situation, and using all five senses to get in touch with all of the cues that typically trigger the old coping behaviour, including the visceral feelings in the body. They are then invited to re-connect to their *HA* side to allow them to manage the situation differently – to bypass self-destructive patterns and get the needs of the *VCh* met. We invite the *HA* side to speak to the person or coping mode in the image calmly but assertively, representing the needs of the *VCh*. Participants are instructed to allow this to play out and notice how that feels, then open their eyes and debrief.

## Conclusions

This group program was developed to be used flexibly in accordance with the needs of each group. The overarching goal is for participants to learn to recognise coping modes as survival states which no longer 'fit', and which perpetuate their EDs and other difficulties. Through a range of experiential, cognitive, interpersonal and behavioural strategies, participants learn to challenge their *Inner Critic*, to befriend and bypass their coping modes, and to care for their *VCh*. Throughout the course of the group, participants are actively encouraged to visualise and cultivate their own Compassionate *HA* self. This side learns to attune to their own *Inner VCh*, in order to meet her needs in direct ways rather than throughout circuitous coping mode strategies. Through capitalising on the power of group dynamics, we believe that the techniques described in this manual provide an opportunity for those with EDs to transform self-destructive patterns into healing and a healthier sense of self.

# References

Berk, T. (2005). Leerboek Groepspsychotherapie Utrecht: De Tijdstroom. *Tijdschrift voor Psychotherapie*, 33(1), 37–40.
Broersen, J., & Van Vreeswijk, M. (2012). Schema Therapy in Groups: A short-term schema CBT protocol. In M. F. Van Vreeswijk, J. Broersen, & M. Nadort, *The Wiley-Blackwell Handbook of Schema Therapy: Theory, Research and Practice* (pp. 373–382). Chichester: Wiley.
Burlingame, G. M., MacKenzie, D., & Strauss, B. (2004). Small group treatment: Evidence for effectiveness and mechanisms of change. In M. J. Lambert (Ed.), *Handbook of Psychotherapy and Behavioural Change* (5th edn, pp 647–696). New York: Wiley.
Calvert, F., Smith, E., Brockman, R., & Simpson, S. (2018). Group schema therapy for eating disorders: Study protocol. *Journal of Eating Disorders*, 6, 1.
Fairburn, C. G., Cooper, Z., Doll, H. A., O'Conner, M. E., Bohn, K., Hawker, D. M., ...Palmer, R. L. (2009). Transdiagnostic cognitive-behavioral therapy for patients with eating disorders: A two-site trial with 60-week follow up. *American Journal of Psychiatry*, 166, 311–319.
Farrell, J. M., & Shaw, I. A. (2012). *Group Schema Therapy for Borderline Personality Disorder: A Step-by-step Treatment Manual with Patient Workbook*. Chichester: Wiley.
Farrell, J., & Shaw, I. (2013). Empathic confrontation in group schema therapy. In R. Vogel. *Empathic Confrontation*. Germany: Beltz.
Farrell, J. M., & Shaw, I. A. (2018). *Experiencing Schema Therapy from the Inside Out: A Self-Practice/Self-Reflection Workbook for Therapists: A Self-Practice/Self-Reflection Workbook for Therapists*. New York: Guilford Press.
Farrell, J. M., Shaw, I. A., & Reiss, N. (2014). *The Schema Therapy Clinician's Guide. A Complete Resource for Building and Delivering Individual, Group and Integrated Schema Mode Treatment Programs*. Chichester: Wiley.
Farrell, J. M., Shaw, I. A., & Webber, M. A. (2009). A schema-focused approach to group psychotherapy for outpatients with borderline personality disorder: A randomized controlled trial. *Journal of Behavior Therapy and Experimental Psychiatry*, 40, 317–328.
Gendlin, E. T. (1978). *Focusing* (1st edn). New York: Everest House.
Hodge, L., & Simpson, S. (2016). Speaking the unspeakable: Artistic expression in eating disorder research and schema therapy. *The Arts in Psychotherapy*, 50, 1–8.
Moradi, B., Dirks, D., & Matteson, A. V. (2005). Roles of sexual objectification experiences and internalization of standards of beauty in eating disorder symptomatology: A test and extension of objectification theory. *Journal of Counseling Psychology*, 52(3), 420.
Roberts, T. A., & Gettman, J. Y. (2004). Mere exposure: Gender differences in the negative effects of priming a state of self-objectification. *Sex Roles*, 51(1–2),17–27.
Schwarz, L., Corrigan, F., Hull, A., & Ragu, R. (2017). *Comprehensive Resource Model: Effective Therapeutic Techniques for the Healing of Complex Trauma*. New York: Routledge.
Silver, M. (2013). *Attachment in Common Sense and Doodles: A Practical Guide*. London: Jessica Kingsley Publishers.
Simpson, S. G. (2012). Schema therapy for eating disorders: A case illustration of the mode approach. In M. van Vreeswijk, J. Broersen & M. Nadort (Eds.), *The Wiley-*

*Blackwell Handbook of Schema Therapy: Theory, Research, and Practice* (1ˢᵗ edn, pp. 145–171.). Chichester: John Wiley & Sons.

Simpson, S. G., Morrow, E., van Vreeswijk, M., & Reid, C. (2010). Group schema therapy for eating disorders: A pilot study. *Frontiers in Psychology*, 1, 1–10.

van Vreeswijk, M. F., & Broersen, J. (2013) *Kortdurende Schemagroeps-Therapie: Cognitief Gedragstherapeutische Technieken Deel Handleiding* (Rev. edn). Houten: Bohn Stafleu van Loghum.

van VreeswijkM. F., BroersenJ., & SchurinkG. (2014). *Mindfulness and Schema Therapy: A Practical Guide.* Chichester: John Wiley & Sons.

van der Wijngaart, R. (May, 2015) The Healthy Adult Mode: Ways to strengthen the Healthy Adult of our patients. *The Schema Therapy Bulletin*, pp. 7–10. International Society for Schema Therapy

Part IV

# Challenges when doing schema therapy

# Chapter 11

# Resolving ambivalence and overcoming blocks to change

## A multi-modal and schema informed approach

*Matthew Pugh*

## Abstract

*Ambivalence and impoverished motivation to change are common obstacles in schema therapy for eating disorders (ST-ED). Drawing upon theories of cognition and emotion, this chapter describes a multi-modal approach to conceptualising and resolving ambivalence in schema therapy (ST). The chapter begins by discussing the nature of ambivalence in eating disorders (EDs) and critically evaluates current methods for addressing these issues. Cognitive-affective theories are then used to elaborate a ST compatible framework for generating and enhancing motivation. Based upon this conceptualisation, schema-related and multi-modal methods for resolving ambivalence are described. These include use of the therapeutic relationship, experiential techniques, and behavioural pattern-breaking.*

## Introduction

Low motivation and reluctance to change can be pronounced in the EDs, and may lead to a denial of illness, defence of symptoms, and treatment refusal. Accordingly, schema therapists who practice with the field of EDs often find themselves working with individuals who are difficult to engage, opposed to change, and at risk high risk of dropout (Mahon, 2000; Abbate-Daga et al., 2013).

Ambivalence has multifarious causes in EDs. Valued aspects of EDs are often cited as a primary objection to change (Nordbø et al., 2012). According to schema-focused models of EDs, disordered eating serves to ameliorate distress arising from early maladaptive schemas (EMS) through both avoidant and compensatory coping styles (Waller, Kennerley & Ohanian, 2007). EDs may appear, therefore, to fulfil seemingly adaptive objectives such as stifling distress and installing feelings of control (Vitousek, Watson & Wilson, 1998). Functional avoidance such as escaping intimate relationships may also appear to confer benefits (Cockell, Geller & Linden, 2002). In addition to the valued aspects of disordered eating, fears about change generate ambivalence. Notions of 'recovery' might be perceived as destabilising and threatening to identity in chronic EDs. Pessimism about change can also obstruct motivation: depression, long lengths of illness, and past therapeutic 'failures' engender hopelessness and scepticism about recovery (Vitousek et al., 1998; Nordbø et al., 2012).

Considerable literature highlights the importance of enhancing motivation and self-efficacy in work with EDs. Greater readiness to change is associated with improved treatment response, whilst low motivation has been linked to increased risk of relapse, dropout, and poorer outomes (Vall & Wade, 2015). The transtheoretical model of change (TTM; Prochaska, DiClemente & Norcross, 1992) has identified several phases of change which help contextualise the process of recovery in EDs: precontemplation (opposing change), contemplation (considering change), preparation (planning change), action (implementing change), and maintenance (consolidating change). Movement through these phases is often circular rather than linear, in that individuals may revert to previous stages over the course of recovery. In the context of ST-ED, many individuals will enter treatment in precontemplation or contemplation phases, particularly those with anorexia nervosa (AN) (Blake, Turnbull & Treasure, 1997). Furthermore, clients' readiness to change will likely be in accordance with the particular schema modes or ED behaviours in question (e.g. a willingness to reduce purging but not dietary restriction) (Waller et al., 2007). Therapists will, therefore, need to adapt both their stance and technique depending upon clients' stage of change.

### Current approaches to resolving ambivalence in schema therapy

ST was designed to treat complex difficulties in which ambivalence and low self-efficacy are often pronounced. Motivational interviewing (MI) (Miller & Rollnick, 2002), can be provided either as a pre-treatment intervention or augmentation, however, findings to date indicate it has been of limited value in enhancing outcomes for EDs (e.g. Romano and Peters, 2015). A second approach has been to conceptualise ambivalence in terms of the schema modes which block progress (Bernstein et al., 2012) (see Table 11.1). This approach has the advantage of both maintaining a schema-focused framework and enables therapists to utilise the full-range of ST techniques to bolster motivation. However, high risk EDs may require more explicit input around motivation to support urgent behavioural change.

### Conceptualising ambivalence: A schema-informed perspective

Schema-focused models of eating pathology suggest that disordered eating functions to prevent and relieve distress associated with EMS. Given this functionality, ambivalence about behavioural change is comprehensible. Ambivalence in EDs can be linked to three key forms of motivation-related appraisal: negative appraisals about behaviour change ('fears about change'),

*Table 11.1* Dysfunctional schema modes associated with ambivalence and change resistance

| Mode category | Exemplar statements |
|---|---|
| **Dysfunctional child modes** | |
| Vulnerable child | "I'm scared about getting better" |
| Abandoned child | "People might forget about me if I recover" |
| Dependent child | "It's too hard to get better on my own" |
| Angry child | "I don't want others to feel relieved about my recovery" |
| Impulsive child | "I'll feel terrible if I don't binge anymore" |
| Undisciplined child | "It's too hard to resist the urge to binge-eat" |
| **Dysfunctional coping modes** | |
| **Avoidance** | |
| Detached protector | "Not eating cuts me off from my feelings" |
| Avoidant protector | "I don't have to make decisions when I'm this unwell" |
| Detached self-soother | "I don't think when I'm exercising/binge-eating" |
| Angry protector | "Just stop bothering me about getting better" |
| **Overcompensation** | |
| Perfectionistic overcontroller | "I need to lose a little more weight before I'm ready" |
| Paranoid overcontroller | "I'll start being noticed by others if I get better" |
| Self-aggrandiser | "Being underweight makes me special" |
| Attention-seeker | "I get care as long as I'm this unwell" |
| **Surrender** | |
| Compliant-surrender | "My partner prefers the way I look at this weight" |
| **Dysfunctional parent modes** | |
| Punitive parent | "I don't deserve a better life" |
| Demanding parent | "I'm not allowed to eat any more than this" |
| Guilt-inducing parent | "Other people need your support more than I do" |

positive appraisals about the status quo ('pro-illness beliefs'), and dubitable appraisals about one's ability to change ('low self-efficacy'). These change-obstructive appraisals map neatly on to the dysfunctional schema modes observed in ST (Table 11.1). For example, maladaptive coping modes may reinforce positive beliefs about illness via distress reduction (e.g. "restricting numbs my feelings"; detached protector mode), whilst parent modes undermine self-efficacy via self-reproach ("I don't deserve to recover"; [punitive parent] mode).

## A multi-modal approach to resolving ambivalence

ST was born out of the limitations observed when cognitive therapy was applied to complex psychological difficulties. To treat these presentations more effectively, cognitive-behavioural interventions were combined with experiential techniques to modify entrenched EMS. These same principles apply to motivational enhancement: in order to resolve ambivalence and modify the appraisals which obstruct motivation to change, ST utilises multi-modal techniques such as the therapeutic relationship, cognitive interventions, experiential techniques, and behaviour pattern-breaking. These multifarious methods for enhancing motivation in ST-ED are now outlined.

## The therapeutic relationship

The effectiveness of both ST and motivational interventions are inextricably linked to the therapeutic relationship (Geller, Williams & Srikameswaran, 2001). Schema therapists emulate Rogers' (1951) core conditions of warmth, genuineness and positive regard, but extend these through limited reparenting and empathic confrontation (Young, Klosko & Weishaar, 2003). In ST-ED, therapists aim to meet the ambivalent client's needs whilst simultaneously using therapeutic confrontation to counteract reluctance to change.

### Limited reparenting

Limited reparenting describes how schema therapists fulfil clients' basic emotional needs within the therapeutic relationship (Young, Klosko & Weishaar, 2003). How these needs can be fulfilled with ambivalent clients is summarised in Table 11.2. Three core needs require particular attention. Firstly, if the client is to give up the security conferred by their ED, their need for *safety* must be satisfied within the therapeutic relationship. To achieve this, therapists express empathy for their ambivalence, insofar as concerns about change are viewed as fully comprehensible (Vitousek, Watson & Wilson, 1998). Validation is also needed; therapists acknowledge the functionality of ED symptoms and convey an understanding that these symptoms perform important roles. Curiosity, rather than persuasion, also establishes safety: therapists seek to understand clients' experiences of, and attachment to, disordered eating to stimulate the client's own curiosity and self-empathy (Geller et al., 2001). Finally, therapists are responsive to the difficult emotions which accompany decisions to change and appreciate the courage this requires (Vitousek, Watson & Wilson, 1998).

Secure attachment begets respect for clients' *autonomy*. Individuals with EDs are acutely sensitive to issues around control, and unilateral attempts to change eating will be experienced as both threatening and invalidating. Collaboration and supporting autonomy are key to minimising such ruptures. As far as possible, and within the limits of safety, collaborative decision making is

Table 11.2 Core emotional needs and their fulfilment with ambivalent clients

| Core emotional needs | Description | Requirements in work with ambivalence and resistance |
|---|---|---|
| Secure attachment | Stable attachments to others<br>Acceptance<br>Nurturance<br>Warmth<br>Social contact | • Accepting ambivalence and blocks to change<br>• Validating the functions of disordered eating<br>• Honesty and transparency<br>• Patience<br>• Expressing care, concern and hope about change and recovery<br>• Encouraging social activity |
| Autonomy | Competence<br>Stable identity<br>Healthy self-reliance<br>Help-seeking when needed | • Collaborative working<br>• Emphasising client choice<br>• Supporting the client in feeling 'in control' of change<br>• Shared decision-making and treatment planning<br>• Offering guidance (when needed) |
| Emotional expression | Free expression of needs<br>Sharing emotions and desires Openness to compromise | • Validating conflictual feelings about change<br>• Encouraging emotional disclosure<br>• Supporting the expression of hopes and fears related to change<br>• Soliciting honest feedback |
| Spontaneity and play | Emotional openness<br>Spontaneity<br>Playfulness<br>Flexibility | • Adapting stance and interventions according to clients' stage of change<br>• Exercising creativity<br>• Encourage client flexibility, playfulness and 'letting go'<br>• Humour |
| Realistic limits | Setting adequate limits<br>Exercising self-control<br>Appropriate self-discipline | • Setting clear limits in therapy<br>• Establishing non-negotiables<br>• Gently naming avoidance or subversion<br>• Managing expectations and accepting limited change for some individuals |

Young, Klosko & Weishaar, 2003

maximised for clients. Encouraging honest feedback about the therapist's support, coupled with an appreciation for the client's preferences, also supports autonomy. When discussing behaviour change, guidance is initially offered by the therapist and (as trust develops) eventually solicited from the client. Most importantly, therapists communicate that responsibility for change rests with the client. Whilst insight and schema modification encourage behaviour change, it is ultimately the client's decision in regards to what they want to do about their eating (Geller et al., 2001).

Lastly, *limit setting* is needed in ST-ED, particularly with high-risk clients. Clients need to experience their therapist both holding and handling their destructive behaviours (Abbate-Daga et al., 2013) and this necessitates the inclusion of 'non-negotiables' in therapy (e.g. in-session weight monitoring, health tests, and conditions under which hospitalisation may be required).

### Empathic confrontation

Work with ambivalence necessitates some degree of empathic confrontation. Indeed, generating motivation to change is usually contingent upon the client fully acknowledging the consequences of their disorder. Confrontation allows therapists to function as a source of trustworthy and reality-based feedback. Limited reparenting also requires transparency when the therapist's opinion does not match that of the client, particularly regarding safety and fulfilment of core needs. As Vitousek and colleagues state, "clinicians should be candid in acknowledging their belief that the eating disorders are a poor solution to real problems, and clear in characterising the purpose of treatment as a search for better alternatives" (Vitousek, Watson & Wilson, 1998: 403).

## Cognitive techniques

### Psychoeducation

Psychoeducation raises awareness about ED associated risks, corrects mis-information, and highlights the benefits of change. Important topics for discussion include the biopsychosocial effects of starvation, health risks associated with EDs, basic nutritional information, and the positive effects of normalised eating (see Waller et al., 2007). In the spirit of autonomy and collaboration, psychoeducation is offered to the client rather than being imposed (*"Would you like to know more about…?"*).

> **Therapist tip**: It is helpful to supplement psychoeducation with written handouts. Not only does this aid information processing, but written materials are often seen as more credible than 'therapist opinion' (Vitousek, Watson & Wilson, 1998).

### Decisional balancing

The decisional balance is a popular way to explore attitudes towards change. This exercise involves making a list of the Pros and Cons of living with one's ED or coping modes associated with disordered eating (e.g. the 'overcontroller mode'). With highly ambivalent individuals, it is best to explore what is valued about the mode or the ED first. Rating each item on a 0–10 scale can help establish which aspects are most valued or compelling. Completed lists can later be divided into short and long-term consequences to demonstrate that whilst EDs confer short-term benefits, the advantages of change are more pervasive and enduring (Waller et al., 2007).

### Life planning

Disordered eating can encourage preoccupation with short-term behaviour at the expense of longer-term goals. To address this, the client can be asked to formulate a 'life plan' outlining their aspirations in important domains of living (e.g. relationships, health, career, etc.) over various time points (e.g. in one, five and ten years' time). This plan is then compared against how the client predicts each life domain will be if the ED were to continue or a mode were to continue to dominate. Most clients will recognise that some, if not all, life goals would be frustrated without change.

*Therapist tip:* Asking the client to transform their life plan into a 'picture board' (e. g. a photo collage capturing key life ambitions) can further reinforce the benefits of change and recovery.

### Point-counterpoint (or 'cognitive restructuring')

This exercise involves making a list of the client's fears about change and elaborating an alternative, 'healthy adult' perspective for each. Socratic questions for generating alternative perspectives include: *"What would you say to a friend who had this fear?"*, *"How did you think about this issue before you became unwell?"*, and *"What would the psychoeducation suggest about this issue?"*

### Values

Identifying clients' core values, and exploring whether maladaptive schema modes support or compromise these, encourages change. Alternatively, clients can compare how their personal values match those held by problematic coping modes. Research suggests that interpersonal values (e.g. establishing close relationships) are most compromised by EDs and so provide valuable leverage for change (Mulkerrin, Bamford & Serpell, 2016).

*Therapist tip:* Values can be an abstract concept and are easily confused with personal goals. Value lists and questionnaires can help clients concretise and identify core values.

## Experiential interventions

### Expressive writing

Expressive writing is a popular method for resolving ambivalence in EDs. In the context of ST-ED, writing helps clients better connect with healthy adult and child modes. Other benefits include aiding the expression of thoughts and feelings which might usually be avoided, facilitating healthy perspective-taking, and enhancing self-reflection (Campbell & Pennebaker, 2003; East et al., 2010). Clients with EDs may also find writing more comfortable than discussion, insofar as they can control what, and how much, is shared (Schmidt et al., 2002).

### Friend and foe letters

Clients often describe EDs in personified ways. Friend and foe letters capitalise on this and are an evocative means to explore attitudes towards one's illness (Serpell et al., 1999). In ST-ED, clients are asked to write two letters to their ED or a key coping mode(s) associated with disordered eating: the first addressing the mode as a friend, and the second addressing it as a foe. This allows clients to explore valued functions of problematic modes whilst also raising awareness of the troubles they cause.

> **Therapist tip**: It can also be helpful to explore the advantages and disadvantages of viewing problematic modes as either a friend or foe. This helps establish a metacognitive stance towards problematic coping modes and how one choses to relate to them.

### Writing to and from schema modes

Connecting with the vulnerable child and healthy adult modes through writing can be a powerful means to highlight the distress caused by EDs. For example, clients might be asked to write a motivating letter from the viewpoint of a trusted and caring individual (i.e. an embodiment of the healthy adult mode) regarding the clients' current opportunity to change and recover. Alternatively, clients can be asked to write to, or from, their vulnerable child mode regarding the suffering brought about by disordered eating. This can help illuminate how EDs compromise one's basic emotional needs.

> **Therapist tip**: Individuals with EDs will often hide or suppress their child modes. Accordingly, writing from the perspective of the vulnerable child mode can be

reframed as writing about the 'hidden parts of me' (i.e. aspects of the self which others do not usually hear, see, or notice) (Johnston et al., 2010).

### Letters from the future

Letters from the future are an evocative means to elucidate the short- and long-term consequences of ED. This exercise involves writing two letters addressed to a loved one from two perspectives: letter one describes life in ten years' time 'as if' the client was still living with an ED or in accordance with a maladaptive mode, whilst letter two describes life in ten years' time 'as if' they were living in accordance with the healthy adult mode (or recovery). In both letters, clients explore how life is progressing in various domains (e.g. at work, in close relationships, etc.).

**Therapist tip**: This exercise tends to be most motivating if the letter from the healthy adult/recovered future perspective is read last (i.e. ending the exercise on a positive note).

## Chairwork

Research indicates that chairwork is an effective method for resolving indecision (Clarke & Greenberg, 1986). These techniques provide a natural progression from expressive writing and often generate important insights which are experienced at a deeper level. As one client reported, *"the immediacy of [chairwork] meant I couldn't hide or deny the issues I have with getting better…I am now much more connected with the recovering me"* (Pugh & Salter, 2018).

### Chairwork for assessment

The chair-based representation of illness (CRIB) is inspired by the pictorial representation of illness and self measure (PRISM) (Büchi & Sensky, 1999) and creates a concrete working space for exploring clients' attitudes towards change. The client is first asked to imagine that the therapy room represents their life. They are then asked to place a chair, symbolising their ED or a problematic mode, somewhere in the room representing its current significance: the closer the mode's chair is to the client's chair, the more important and dominating it is. The exercise can then be taken in different directions. This might include exploring the costs and benefits of the mode's current importance (*"What are the good and bad sides of having the* 'overcontroller' so close to your self?"); reflecting on what life might be like if a mode were less significant ("*Where would you prefer the mode's chair to be and what benefits would come from that?*"); and using extra chairs to represent life goals or personal values ("*If this chair represented your hope to have a family, where would you place it to represent how near or far you are from achieving that because of this mode?*").

> **Therapist tip**: CRIB exercises can be summarised diagrammatically to aid reflection and emotional processing. An example diagram is provided in Figure 11.1.

### Mode dialogues

Exploring attitudes towards change from the perspective of relevant modes can clarify which modes obstruct or encourage change. In short, the client is

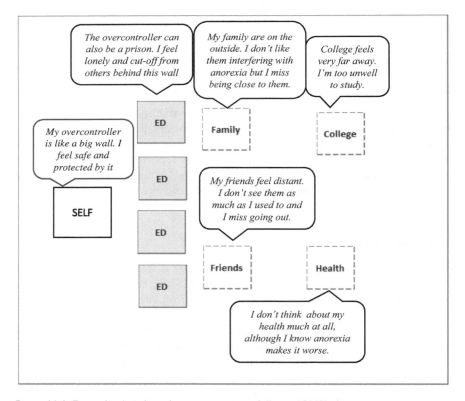

*Figure 11.1* Example chair-based representation of illness (CRIB) diagram

asked to speak about recovery from different chairs representing particular modes ("*How does your vulnerable child feel about recovery? And now your detached protector?*"). This technique can be used as both a stand-alone intervention or in conjunction with other exercises ("*What do your modes think about your pros and cons list? Which side is your 'overcontroller' mode on – the recovery side or ED side?*").

> **Therapist tip**: If a client's modes have not yet been identified, clients can be invited to speak from chairs representing their primary emotions (i.e. the client's 'emotional selves'; Kolts, 2016). For example, the client can outline their attitudes towards change from the perspective of their sad, anxious, angry, and healthy self-parts. Links between these emotional selves and schema modes can then be made.

### Two-chair decisional balance

Two-chair decisional balancing explores attitudes towards change in a more evocative and experiential manner than pros–cons listing. Starting with whichever side feels strongest, the client outlines the perceived advantages (chair one) and disadvantages (chair two) of their ED or mode. Once each side has been fully expressed, the client can be invited to stand and explore their reactions towards each perspective from an observing, healthy-adult viewpoint. This also provides an opportunity to establish links between schema modes and particular attitudes towards change ("*Which of your modes sides with the 'I don't-want-to-get-better' chair?*").

> **Therapist tip:** Therapists are encouraged to also switch seats as the client moves between the 'advantages' and 'disadvantages' chairs: remaining by the client's side throughout this exercise models the 'shoulder-to-shoulder' reparenting relationship and aids facilitation.

### Future selves dialogue

This dialogue provides clients with an experience of their possible future lives with and without an ED (Pugh & Salter, 2017). First, the client is asked to imagine their future self with the ED in an empty chair ("*What would that version of yourself look like in ten years' time?*"). The client then changes seats and enacts this 'future and non-recovered self' whilst the therapist poses questions about what life is like in various domains ("*How is your health these days? And your relationships?*"). An empty chair representing the 'current ambivalent self' is later introduced into the dialogue so that the client can impart any final words of advice (*"Imagine this empty chair holds the 'you' who was unsure about recovery when we first met...If you could go back in time, what advice would you give that version of yourself?"*). The exercise is then repeated once more with the client now embodying their 'future recovered self'.

> **Therapist tip**: Embodying the 'future recovered self' (essentially, the healthy adult mode) is often a powerful experience and provides therapists with a valuable resource to draw upon later in therapy (*"I wonder what your 'recovered self' would think about the idea of reaching a healthy weight – can you change seats and speak from that perspective?"*).

### Diagnostic interviewing or intrapersonal role-play

Insight into the functions of disordered eating can help resolve ambivalence (Cockell, Geller & Linden, 2003). To this end, diagnostic interviews (Kellogg, 2015) allow the therapist and client to clarify the intents and motivations of schema modes underlying ambivalence. This exercise involves the client changing seats and assuming the voice of a change-obstructive coping mode. Therapists can then put informative questions to the mode such as:

- What role do you play in this individual's eating disorder?
- How do you feel about this individual getting better?
- What are your concerns about recovery?
- How do you stop or prevent this individual from changing?
- How do you feel towards the parts of this individual that do want to get better?

At the end of the dialogue, clients can be invited to respond to the change-obstructive mode (*"Is there anything you want to say to that side?"*), express their needs (*"What do you need from that side?"*) or, if appropriate, begin challenging its sentiments (*"Tell that side how your relationship with one another is going to change"*).

> **Therapist tip**: The process of 'stepping-in' and 'stepping-out' of roles is important during intrapersonal role-plays. For example, therapists might end the dialogue by saying: *"Come back to your original chair and leave the mode/ED in the other chair... Take a moment to connect with your self and separate from that side"*. Slowing down the process of separating helps create psychological distance from both problematic modes and the ED mindset.

### Vector dialogues

Vector dialogues (Kellogg, 2017) are a useful means to explore ambivalent attachments with disordered eating or particular modes. A triangular chair formation is used here. First, the client is asked to imagine a mode or their ED in an empty chair; personification can help at this point (*"How do you imagine your ED/mode would look if it were a person?"*). The client is then encouraged to express their positive attitudes towards the ED mode in chair one, followed by negative attitudes in chair two. Therapists will tend to purposefully deepen the emotions expressed from chair two to stimulate motivation (*"Tell the ED more about the anger/sadness it causes you"*).

> **Therapist tip**: Vector dialogues can be challenging for emotionally inhibited clients. Asking the client to read their 'friend' (chair one) and 'foe' (chair two) letters aloud can be a helpful way to open this exercise and scaffold emotional expression.

### Devil's advocate

The devil's advocate is a useful method for reinforcing motivation to change. This technique involves the therapist presenting reasons not to change (chair one) whilst the client responds with compelling counter-arguments which support change (chair two). Reframed in the terms of schema modes, this intervention essentially constitutes a dialogue between a maladaptive coping mode (enacted by the therapist) and the healthy adult mode (enacted by the client).

> **Therapist tip:** The devil's advocate technique is used to reinforce motivation rather than to resolve ambivalence (e.g. for clients in the 'action' stage of change). If the client finds it difficult to respond to arguments in favour of not changing, this would suggest that ambivalence has not yet been resolved. Techniques for the contemplative and pre-contemplative stages of change are indicated in such circumstances (e.g. decisional balancing and/or friend-foe techniques).

## Imagery

Schema therapists often use imagery to identify and modify EMS. Similarly, imagery can identify and overcome blocks to change, as well as concretising abstract concepts such as ambivalence.

### Imagery for assessment

Like the imagery for the assessment of EMS (Young, Klosko & Weishaar, 2003), imagery can identify EMS and associated modes which obstruct change. Imagery for assessment involves the client describing spontaneously occurring images or memories which are linked to the idea of 'change' or 'life without an ED' (Therapist: "*When you imagine recovery, what memories or images comes to mind?*"). To illustrate, one client associated her fears about recovering from AN with a memory of being ignored and eating alone at a party. This memory carried the meaning, "*people won't care about me if I get better*".

> **Therapist tip**: Imagery for the assessment of ambivalence can be extended by using the 'affective-bridge' (Young, Klosko & Weishaar, 2003). For example, the client described above traced this image back to a childhood memory of eating alone in her school canteen. Links were subsequently made between her fear of recovery and a social isolation EMS.

### Negative imagery

Negative memories associated with ambivalence can be modified using imagery rescripting and other transformative techniques (see Young, Klosko & Weishaar, 2003; Hackmann, Bennett-Levy & Holmes, 2011). For example, the client described earlier linked her fears about recovery to a childhood memory of social isolation. The therapist entered this image and supported her vulnerable child in expressing anger towards the peers that isolated her. Following this intervention, the client reported greater readiness to change.

> **Therapist tip:** Working with negative imagery in the context of ambivalence often takes place in the early stages of therapy. For this reason, therapists will usually need to enter and transform these images on behalf of the client.

### Positive imagery

In line with the principles of retrieval competition (Brewin, 2006), constructing positive representations of recovery can bolster motivation to change. For example, clients can be guided in generating a positive image of 'a day in the life of recovery': "*Imagine that you are waking up in two years' time and your ED is no longer in your life…Describe how your day starts and unfolds…Now imagine telling me how you achieved this…*". Some clients struggle to construct positive, recovery-related imagery, in which case other sources of inspiration can be used (e.g. the client's 'letter from the future' or use of the 'miracle question' [see de Shazer & Dolan, 2007]). Therapists should note, however, that positive imagery can sometimes trigger parent or coping modes ("*My recovery must be quick and perfect*").

> *Therapist tip*: Positive imagery is most powerful when a field perspective is adopted (first-person) rather than an observer perspective (third-person) (Holmes, Coughtrey & Connor, 2008). For example, therapists may say, "*Imagine you are looking out of the eyes of your recovered self. What do you see and what are you doing?*"

### Metaphorical imagery

Descriptions of ambivalence are often imbued with metaphorical imagery. Much like coping modes, precontemplative individuals may describe their ED as like a "guardian" or "protector". Contemplative individuals may experience ambivalence as being "stuck" between their healthy adult mode and a coping mode. Transforming metaphorical images so that more realistic, empowering or constructive perspectives are established can help build motivation (Hackmann et al., 2011).

> *Therapist tip*: Work with metaphorical images can be consolidated through the use of drawings (Hackmann et al., 2011). For example, clients can be asked to depict 'how things currently are' with their ED followed by drawing 'how I would like things to be' in relation to a problematic mode.

### Stories and analogies

Whilst stories and analogies have been linked to better treatment outcomes in psychotherapy (Martin, Cummings & Hallberg, 1992), little has been written about these interventions in ST. This is surprising given the importance of connecting with child modes through child-appropriate communication. When working with ambivalence, analogies tend to elicit less opposition than advice giving and allow therapists to discuss sensitive issues from a 'safer distance' (Burns, 2007). Useful analogies related to ambivalence are presented in Box 11.1. Therapists are always encouraged to work with the client's own stories and analogies as these are often more meaningful.

## Box 11.1 Stories and analogies for resolving ambivalence

'Itchy jumper' or 'uncomfortable armour' analogy (adapted from Waller et al., 2007)

Eating disorders (or coping modes) are like an itchy jumper. Initially this jumper helps keep out the cold, but over time it feels itchy and irritating. Although the jumper still keeps you fairly warm, you may be wondering if there are more comfortable ways to stay protected. If you decide to change this jumper, it is likely you will feel cold for a while whilst you try out new ways of staying safe and warm. In the longer-term, this will help you stay protected in an itch-free way. My hope is that therapy will be a camp-fire during this process: a safe place where you feel protected whilst you try out better and more helpful outfits. However, an important question is how itchy you find your current jumper and whether you feel ready to swap it for a different one?

**Domestic violence analogy**

Individuals sometimes describe life with an eating disorder as like being in an abusive relationship. Perpetrators of domestic violence (like eating disorders) can seem helpful and supportive, particularly at the start of the relationship. However, these partners often become controlling and harmful over time. Repeated attacks may also cause the victim to lose confidence in their ability to change the situation or wonder how they would survive without their partner. They may even come to believe they don't deserve any better or go to increasingly extreme lengths to 'keep the peace' in the relationship. To make matters worse, perpetrators will usually become most abusive if the victim considers changing or leaving the relationship. Can you relate to these experiences? What advice would you give a loved one if they were in a relationship like this?

**Two islands analogy (Ulrike Schmidt, personal communication)**

Having an eating disorder can feel like living on desert island. Perhaps you found yourself caught in a bad storm in life and washed up in this new place. There are probably parts of this island that seem nice, but also some uncomfortable and dangerous regions too. Now, over the sea, there is an island everyone keeps telling you about: 'Recovery Island'. Perhaps your friends and family are standing on the beach, encouraging you to join them. However, the water between these islands might seem choppy and unpleasant from where you are. Maybe you aren't sure if this other island is as great as everyone says. Perhaps you quite like your current island, despite its dangers. I'd like to help you think through the journey you are considering. If you do decide to embark, I will be there to help you build a raft and stand by you as you journey across the sea.

### Behaviour change and pattern-breaking

Behaviour change plays a vital role in resolving ambivalence. Developing motivation to change is often best enhanced through direct experience rather than through discussion alone (Vitousek, Watson & Wilson, 1998). Furthermore, experiential interventions tend to prove most effective when they are followed by planned behavioural changes (Johnston et al., 2010). Finally, the case for early behavioural change in ST-ED is also empirical: research indicates that early symptom reduction improves both therapeutic outcomes and the quality of the therapeutic relationship in treatments for EDs (Brown, Mountford & Waller, 2013). Accordingly, any decisions to change eating should be "immediately and repeatedly put into practice" by the client (Vitousek, Watson & Wilson, 1998, 414).

### Further considerations

#### 'Non-specific resistance'

- Many individuals struggle to articulate specific reasons for their ambivalence (e.g. *"I don't know what is holding me back"*). This is consistent with theories of cognition, which recognise that internal representations can be based on emotions, somatic sensations, or operate outside of conscious awareness, and so may be difficult to convey in words (Teasdale, 1999).
- Experiential techniques can help resolve instances of 'non-specific resistance'. For example, the client can be asked to embody the block through chairwork (*"Change seats and be the part of yourself that gets in the way of eating...What does this part think about recovery?"*), or to personify the barrier in the empty chair (*"What would this obstacle look like? What would it be saying to you right now?"*). Therapists can then speak to the block or invite the client to respond from the perspective of modes which encourage change.

### Consolidating motivation

In line with retrieval completion, consolidation plays an important role in work with motivation. Clients can be reminded of the benefits of recovery, their reasons for change, and healthy adult responses to feelings of anxiety in many ways, including:

- Written and audio flashcards (*"Right now I am feeling scared about recovery...What I need to remember is..."*).
- Transitional objects (e.g. items which remind the client about the advantages of change and healthy attachments).
- Anchors (e.g. songs or pictures embodying the client's reasons for recovery).
- Picture boards (e.g. photographs which capture recovery-related aspirations).

## Mode reactions

- Schema modes will cause clients to respond to motivational interventions in different ways. For example, parent modes may attack the client for a lack of progress, whilst coping modes may discount or minimise conversations regarding recovery.
- Therapists must be poised to respond appropriately depending upon which modes become activated by this type of work.

## Clinical supervision

- Clinicians should anticipate strong reactions to ambivalent clients including frustration, worry, boredom, pity, and a desire to escape.
- Supervision creates space for managing therapist EMS and schema modes which are activated by ambivalent clients. Therapist reactions can also provide insights into how others tend to respond to the client's indecision.
- Other important topics for consideration in supervision include the client's stage of change, which motivation-focused interventions are appropriate, and how ambivalence-associated modes inform the schema conceptualisation.

## Conclusion

Working with ambivalence poses unique challenges and can be uniquely rewarding in ST-ED. Informed by theories of emotion and cognition, and in line with the principles of ST, a multi-modal approach to ambivalence has been presented, which allows schema therapists to draw upon a variety of multi-modal techniques to resolve ambivalence and generate motivation. The application of analytical and emotion-focused techniques, alongside behavioural pattern breaking and limited reparenting, ensure that motivation is bolstered across both cognitive-affective domains and multiple levels of information-processing, thus ensuring that change-obstructive modes are fully addressed in therapy.

## References

Abbate-Daga, G., Amianto, F., Delsedime, N., De-Bacco, C., & Fassino, S. (2013). Resistance to treatment and change in anorexia nervosa: a clinical overview. *BMC Psychiatry*, 13(1), 294.

Bernstein, D. P., de Vos, M. K., Jonkers, P., de Jonge, E., & Arntz, A. (2012). Schema therapy in forensic settings. In M. van Vreeswijk, J. Broersen & M. Nadort (Eds.). *The Wiley-Blackwell Handbook of Schema Therapy: Theory, Research, and Practice* (pp. 425–438). West Sussex: John Wiley and Sons.

Blake, W., Turnbull, S., & Treasure, J. (1997). Stages and processes of change in eating disorders: Implications for therapy. *Clinical Psychology & Psychotherapy: An International Journal of Theory and Practice*, 4(3), 186–191.

Brewin, C. R. (2006). Understanding cognitive behaviour therapy: A retrieval competition account. *Behaviour Research and Therapy*, 44(6), 765–784.

Brown, A., Mountford, V., & Waller, G. (2013). Therapeutic alliance and weight gain during cognitive behavioural therapy for anorexia nervosa. *Behaviour Research and Therapy*, 51(4–5), 216–220.

Büchi, S., & Sensky, T. (1999). PRISM: Pictorial Representation of Illness and Self Measure: A brief nonverbal measure of illness impact and therapeutic aid in psychosomatic medicine. *Psychosomatics*, 40(4), 314–320.

Burns, G. W. (2007). Metaphor and therapy: Clarifying some confusing concepts. In G. W. Burns (Ed.). *Healing with Stories: Your Casebook Collection for Using Therapeutic Metaphors*. John Wiley & Sons.

Campbell, R. S., & Pennebaker, J. W. (2003). The secret life of pronouns: Flexibility in writing style and physical health. *Psychological Science*, 14(1), 60–65.

Clarke, K. M., & Greenberg, L. S. (1986). Differential effects of the Gestalt two-chair intervention and problem solving in resolving decisional conflict. *Journal of Counseling Psychology*, 33(1), 11–15.

Cockell, S. J., Geller, J., & Linden, W. (2003). Decisional balance in anorexia nervosa: Capitalizing on ambivalence. *European Eating Disorders Review: The Professional Journal of the Eating Disorders Association*, 11(2), 75–89.

East, P., Startup, H., Roberts, C., & Schmidt, U. (2010). Expressive writing and eating disorder features: A preliminary trial in a student sample of the impact of three writing tasks on eating disorder symptoms and associated cognitive, affective and interpersonal factors. *European Eating Disorders Review: The Professional Journal of the Eating Disorders Association*, 18(3), 180–196.

Geller, J., Williams, K. D., & Srikameswaran, S. (2001). Clinician stance in the treatment of chronic eating disorders. *European Eating Disorders Review: The Professional Journal of the Eating Disorders Association*, 9(6), 365–373.

Hackmann, A., Bennett-Levy, J., & Holmes, E. A. (2011). *Oxford Guide to Imagery in Cognitive Therapy*. Oxford University Press.

Holmes, E. A., Coughtrey, A. E., & Connor, A. (2008). Looking at or through rose-tinted glasses? Imagery perspective and positive mood. *Emotion*, 8(6), 875.

Johnston, O., Startup, H., Lavender, A., Godfrey, E., & Schmidt, U. (2010). Therapeutic writing as an intervention for symptoms of bulimia nervosa: Effects and mechanism of change. *International Journal of Eating Disorders*, 43(5), 405–419.

Kellogg, S. (2014). *Transformational Chairwork: Using Psychotherapeutic Dialogues in Clinical Practice*. Rowman & Littlefield.

Kellogg, S. (2017). Transformational chairwork: Complex emotions, trauma and the inner critic. One-day workshop, London, October.

Kolts, R. L. (2016). *CFT Made Simple: A Clinician's Guide to Practicing Compassion-focused Therapy*. New Harbinger Publications.

Mahon, J. (2000). Dropping out from psychological treatment for eating disorders: What are the issues? *European Eating Disorders Review: The Professional Journal of the Eating Disorders Association*, 8(3), 198–216.

Martin, J., Cummings, A. L., & Hallberg, E. T. (1992). Therapists' intentional use of metaphor: Memorability, clinical impact, and possible epistemic/motivational functions. *Journal of Consulting and Clinical Psychology*, 60(1), 143.

Miller, W. R., & Rollnick, S. (2012). *Motivational Interviewing: Helping People Change*. Guilford Press.

Mulkerrin, Ú., Bamford, B., & Serpell, L. (2016). How well does Anorexia Nervosa fit with personal values? An exploratory study. *Journal of Eating Disorders*, 4(1), 20.

Nordbø, R. H., Espeset, E. M., Gulliksen, K. S., Skårderud, F., Geller, J., & Holte, A. (2012). Reluctance to recover in anorexia nervosa. *European Eating Disorders Review*, 20(1), 60–67.

Prochaska, J. O., DiClemente, C. C., & Norcross, J. C. (1992). In search of how people change: Applications to addictive behaviors. *American Psychologist*, 47(9), 1102.

Pugh, M., & Salter, C. (2017). Motivational chairwork: A novel method for enhancing motivation and resolving ambivalence in eating disorders. Workshop presented at the London Eating Disorders Conference, London, March.

Pugh, M., & Salter, C. (2018) Motivational chairwork: An experiential approach to resolving ambivalence. *European Journal of Counselling Theory, Research and Practise*, 2(7), 1–15.

Romano, M., & Peters, L. (2015). Evaluating the mechanisms of change in motivational interviewing in the treatment of mental health problems: A review and meta-analysis. *Clinical Psychology Review*, 38, 1–12.

Schmidt, U., Bone, G., Hems, S., Lessem, J., & Treasure, J. (2002). Structured therapeutic writing tasks as an adjunct to treatment in eating disorders. *European Eating Disorders Review: The Professional Journal of the Eating Disorders Association*, 10(5), 299–315.

Serpell, L., Treasure, J., Teasdale, J., & Sullivan, V. (1999). Anorexia nervosa: Friend or foe? *International Journal of Eating Disorders*, 25(2), 177–186.

De Shazer, S., & Dolan, Y. (2007). *More than Miracles: The State of the Art of Solution-Focused Brief Therapy*. New York: Routledge.

Teasdale, J. D. (1999). Emotional processing, three modes of mind and the prevention of relapse in depression. *Behaviour Research and Therapy*, 37(Suppl. 1), 53–77.

Vall, E., & Wade, T. D. (2015). Predictors of treatment outcome in individuals with eating disorders: A systematic review and meta-analysis. *International Journal of Eating Disorders*, 48(7), 946–971.

Vitousek, K., Watson, S., & Wilson, G. T. (1998). Enhancing motivation for change in treatment-resistant eating disorders. *Clinical Psychology Review*, 18(4), 391–420.

Waller, G., Cordery, H., Corstorphine, E., Hinrichsen, H., Lawson, R., Mountford, V., & Russell, K. (2007). *Cognitive Behavioral Therapy for Eating Disorders: A Comprehensive Treatment Guide*. Cambridge University Press.

Waller, G., Kennerley, H. & Ohanian, V. (2007). Schema-focused cognitive-behavioural therapy for eating disorders. In L. P. Riso, P. L. du Toit, D. J. Stein & J. E. Young, (Eds.), *Cognitive Schemas and Core Beliefs in Psychological Problems: A Scientist-Practitioner Guide* (pp. 139–175). Washington: APA.

Young, J. E., Klosko, J. S., & Weishaar, M. E. (2003). *Schema Therapy: A Practitioner's Guide*. Guilford Press.

# Chapter 12

# Overcoming challenges and stuck points in the treatment of eating disorders

*Sally Skewes, Michiel van Vreeswijk and Wendelien Merens*

## Abstract

*Eating disorders (EDs) are amongst the most complex and challenging conditions to treat. In this chapter three case examples are presented from the viewpoint of the therapist providing individual, group and inpatient schema therapy for eating disorders, respectively. Case examples are used to illustrate how to cope with potential problems in treatment. The potential obstacles and factors that impact treatment, together with solutions to overcome obstacles in schema therapy (ST) for EDs are presented. The implications for overcoming obstacles and the learning points drawn from the case examples are discussed, and may be helpful for therapists working with ED populations in various treatment settings.*

Stuck points in the treatment of EDs are defined as the common struggles that many therapists face. In this chapter, we will highlight the stuck points linked to the complexity of treating EDs. For each case example we generate solutions and explore how to help therapists and patients address these issues. At the end of each case example we reflect on therapeutic pitfalls and mistakes with the intention of acknowledging therapists' vulnerabilities and reinforcing the importance of self-reflection. We find it highly important that therapists maintain awareness of stuck points and reflect on therapeutic pitfalls and mistakes through supervision led by an external person, peer supervision and directly with their clients (when appropriate). The examples given here are only a small sample of the exhaustive list of potential problems that can arise when working with complex clinical issues, but are designed to give a flavour of potential ways of working with stuck points. Although the patients presented in this chapter are all fictional, they illustrate struggles that are common to many patients in the treatment of EDs.

ST interventions aim to connect and circumvent the resistance of dysfunctional coping styles, including bypassing avoidant or overcompensatory coping modes, fighting self-punitive thinking (*Punitive Parent Mode: PP*) and self-critical thinking (*Demanding Parent Mode: DemP*) (Young, Klosko & Weishaar, 2003). Experiential interventions, such as imagery rescripting and mode role plays are used to introduce the *Vulnerable Child Mode (VCh)* and establish trust in the process of attachment and limited reparenting (Young, Klosko & Weishaar, 2003). The focus on core emotional needs is highlighted, which is increasingly recognised as an important focus for treatment of clients with EDs (Lockwood & Perris, 2012). The possible conditions necessary for change and the processes involved in preventing or leading to change, including addressing engagement and retention are explored.

## Case example one: Individual ST for EDs in an outpatient setting

### Part I: Presenting issues

Elizabeth was a 28-year old woman living with her husband and three children. She was 26 when she presented for ST and was diagnosed with bulimia nervosa (BN), obsessive compulsive disorder (OCD), dysthymia, borderline personality disorder (BPD) and avoidant personality disorder (AvPD). In the past, Elizabeth had been successfully treated for alcohol abuse and she had not consumed alcohol for two years. Treatment for OCD and dysthymia had limited success. Elizabeth sought help for her ED as her eating patterns had become so disturbed that she was afraid of not being a good role model for her children. Her husband mentioned that she was 'getting fat'. This brought Elizabeth back to childhood memories in which her grandfather looked at her in a 'funny' way and made sexual remarks she did not feel comfortable with. Elizabeth's father committed suicide shortly after being informed of his father's (i.e. Elizabeth's grandfather's) sexual behaviour toward his daughter. At that point in time, Elizabeth's father and mother had been divorced for six months, having had a conflictual marriage for the last ten years. Elizabeth was 14 years old when her parents were divorced. Elizabeth perceived her mother as a cold, absent woman who only focused on her appearance and flirted with every (mostly younger) man she met. Talking about emotions and needs was unheard of in Elizabeth's family.

A comprehensive assessment consisting of a full developmental history of Elizabeth's ED and exploration of her background, data from her YSQ, SMI and diagnostic imagery revealed the case conceptualisation as presented in Figure 12.1. In contrast to what is regularly conducted in schema therapy, no arrows were drawn between the background, situation in the here and now, the schemas, modes, emotions and schema-related behaviour. When using arrows, this can suggest a premature assumption by the therapist that there is only one particular way in terms of how schemas and modes developed and are triggered. The case conceptualisation is a theoretical working model which cannot fully epitomise the complexity of real life. It serves its purpose for psychoeducation and is for that reason an overly simplified representation of reality. Although therapists might realise that this is what the case conceptualisation stands for, the patient might experience it differently and accept it as the 'truth'. To stimulate patients to constantly explore and adapt their view of the world, we believe that it is best to avoid using arrows within mode maps and case conceptualisations. Future research

**Background**
Elizabeth was shy and timid as a child
Grandfather made remarks about being sexually attracted to Elizabeth
Divorce of parents when Elizabeth was 14
Father committed suicide when Elizabeth was 14
Mother was emotionally unavailable

*Family rules*:
The only thing that counts in life is how you present yourself and what you achieve
Experiencing and showing emotions is a sign of weakness
You have to be strong at all times

| **Situation in the here and now** | **Schemas** | **Modes** |
| --- | --- | --- |
| Husband mentioned that Elizabeth was getting fat | Abandonment/ Instability Self-Sacrifice Emotional Inhibition Defectiveness/ Shame | Demanding Parent Healthy Adult Impulsive Child Detached Protector Angry Child |

**Emotions**
Anxious
Angry

**Schema behaviour**
Impulsive eating
Extreme fitness
Cleaning the house obsessively

*Figure 12.1* Case conceptualisation

could investigate whether or not the use of arrows within mode maps has an effect on treatment outcomes.

### Part 2: Stuck points and solutions

(1) During the process of ST with Elizabeth, several stuck points appeared. In the beginning of treatment, Elizabeth expected quick results. She read all of the ST material she received from her therapist and homework was quickly completed. She looked for more ST material on the internet, read articles and books on ST and wrote lengthy summaries which she e-mailed to the therapist to read, in the hope that he could speed up the process. It was difficult for the therapist to discuss with Elizabeth that her *DemP* was pushing him to use the best techniques and to hurry up, let alone to discuss that her own *VCh* was being excluded by the *DemP*. The use of multiple chair techniques was refused as Elizabeth found it 'nonsense' to talk to empty chairs. She stated that it was her *Healthy Adult* (*HA*) which worked so hard in ST.

*Solution*: At the beginning of therapy there was a strong focus on educating Elizabeth about the negative consequences of avoiding feelings and not connecting with other people. The therapeutic relationship was used to illustrate the lack of growth in the connection between Elizabeth and her therapist by using empathic confrontation when Elizabeth was detached or demanding. The therapist also modelled showing vulnerability in verbal and non-verbal communication. The therapist also made clear to Elizabeth via empathic confrontation that he did want to reach out to her, but needed her *VCh* to be involved in this process as well. Chair techniques were used for sending away the *DemP* and making contact with Elizabeth's *VCh*. In imagery a safe place was created where Elizabeth and the therapist could do playful things like blow bubbles, play tag, hide and seek to stimulate the *Happy Child Mode (HCh)* and *VCh* to be together with the therapist. Elizabeth was also asked to explore how inhibition of her affect might be experienced by significant others in her life, like her husband. Elizabeth learned to let her husband know when her *emotional inhibition* schema had been triggered and the couple found ways to overcome this obstacle (e.g. sharing the triggering of schemas and modes in the relationship helped them to connect with each other).

(2) Following a break whereby the therapist missed a session through being in hospital, Elizabeth did not arrive for the next two sessions as she 'forgot' that she had an appointment. This pattern occurred repeatedly (e.g. when the therapist went on holiday or Elizabeth went on holiday). In these periods Elizabeth 'forgot' her homework and she reported more frequent episodes of binge eating or restricting her diet.

*Solution*: One of the main lessons Elizabeth learned in ST was that it was okay to be vulnerable. The therapist explained that being authentic comes not from detachment, but from a healthy balance between the *HA, HAC* and *VCh*. Elizabeth learned about showing emotions, comforting her *VCh* from the *HA* perspective and having fun, experiencing feelings of safety and freedom from the *HAC* perspective (countering the *emotional inhibition* schema). Chair work was helpful in creating a mode dialogue between the *HA, HAC* and *VCh*. Imagery rescripting was used with regard to the schemas: *abandonment/ instability, defectiveness/shame*. Painful memories from the past were rescripted.

The therapist offered Elizabeth his phone number and work email, which she was encouraged to use in between sessions to call or to send a text message. This availability of the therapist was an antidote for the perceived coldness and absence of her mother. The therapist and Elizabeth agreed upon the response time of the therapist in office hours and outside hours. Elizabeth rarely made use of the option to call her therapist. At times when she felt abandoned by someone, she sent a text message. A message from her therapist calmed her down and she gradually felt like she was becoming stronger and needed less and less out of session contact.

(3) Elizabeth complained that her husband was not happy with how she maintained the house. He thought she was not doing anything in the house or for the children and that he had to take care of everything. For a long time, Elizabeth refused to allow her husband to attend therapy sessions to allow

joint discussion of these subjects. When she finally allowed him to come for a couple of sessions, she responded to him either from the *DemP*, the *Impulsive Child Mode (ICh)*, *the Angry Child Mode (AnCh)* or the *Detached Protector Mode (DetPr)*, every time he expressed his perspective on the situation.

*Solution*: Elizabeth asked her husband to come to a couple of joint sessions with her and the therapist. In the therapy sessions it became clear that it was difficult for Elizabeth's husband to discuss what his perspective was with regard to his wife, as Elizabeth labelled all of his views as attacks on her. Both Elizabeth's husband and Elizabeth were asked to sit in front of each other and to speak from the *VCh* perspective regarding how they felt, what they needed and what they were missing. This opened a pathway for Elizabeth to realise that her husband also had a *VCh* who needed not only the help of her *HA* and *HAC*, but more importantly needed to feel the connection with her *VCh*. Both were able to express emotions and needs and listen openly to each other. Elizabeth and her husband were able to talk about schema triggering in a healthy way and even make fun of their modes.

(4) Before treatment review sessions, Elizabeth's eating difficulties increased and although this became less of an issue over time, the eating problems returned slightly at the end of treatment when Elizabeth knew that the moment of saying goodbye to her therapist was approaching.

*Solution*: The therapist prepared Elizabeth for the end of therapy by having her write down what she had learned in ST, what was helpful and what to do when a schema or mode was triggered. To prepare her for the ending of their therapeutic relationship they had two sessions using flash forward imagery, one in which they said goodbye to each other and one where she lived a happy life with her husband, without the therapist. In the last ST session the therapist gave Elizabeth a post card as a transitional object, on which he had written a memory of a session with her and how she had grown in ST. By doing so Elizabeth was helped to remember what she had learned on a practical level and emotional level. Reading the post card once in a while after therapy gave Elizabeth the feeling of still being connected with her [former] therapist with whom she had been able to build a therapeutic relationship, which was a helpful template for developing healthier relationships with her husband and friends.

### Part 3: Therapeutic pitfalls and mistakes

(1)  It was the 15th of November, 2014 that the therapist came home early from work with the flu. Three hours later when he had gone to bed he received a text message from Elizabeth mentioning that she was not feeling well. The therapist read the text message but as he was not feeling well himself, decided to leave the message for the moment and to respond the following morning. The following morning, he responded and received an angry text message back asking why he had not

responded within the timeframe they had agreed on. He hypothesised that this event had triggered her *abandonment/instability* schema. He texted back that he had not been feeling well and that he could imagine that she might be feeling abandoned. The therapist invited her to text back on what her thoughts and feelings were on this. Elizabeth texted back that she had not thought of the idea that her therapist might have had a good reason for not texting back in the agreed time frame as her *abandonment/ instability* schema was so intensely triggered. In the next session that Elizabeth met with her therapist she acknowledged that it was understandable that he was unable to reply immediately due to his illness and that she had appreciated the fact that he texted her later to let her know.

(2)    There were five months in therapy where Elizabeth started each session in the *DemP*, from which she did not shift despite all of the ST techniques which were used. At times when Elizabeth connected with her *VCh* for parts of the session, she did not attend the following session and sent an e-mail stating that she or her children were ill, that she had forgotten about the appointment or that her boss had changed her work schedule and that she had to go to work. The therapist started to empathically confront this maladaptive behaviour. More importantly the therapist recognised later in therapy it would have been therapeutically beneficial if he had explored this behaviour in the context of past relationships (the transference of the cold and absent mother figure onto the therapist).

(3)    After what felt like the ten thousandth time that Elizabeth became angry when the therapist asked her about her ED and Elizabeth replied that he should leave her alone and direct his energy and attention toward other patients, the frustrated therapist answered "Okay, you have won the fight, let us talk about ending therapy." A smile of victory, almost devious, appeared on Elizabeth's face and the therapist immediately realised that a maladaptive mode had won the battle at that moment. The therapist then confronted Elizabeth with his feelings of becoming emotionally exhausted by her fighting him, wondering if she did this with other people as well. The therapist invited Elizabeth to explore with him how they could make contact with her *VCh* in a healthy way and how they could reduce the amount of having to battle over this.

## Case example two: Group ST for EDs in an outpatient setting

### Part 1: Presenting issues

The group case conceptualisation presented in Figure 12.2 illustrates the schemas and maladaptive modes that had a strong presence in the group for each group member. There was comorbidity in terms of personality disorders for 5 of 8 group members; Jackie, Jo and Nadia were diagnosed with AvPD and Lisa and Sarah were diagnosed with BPD.

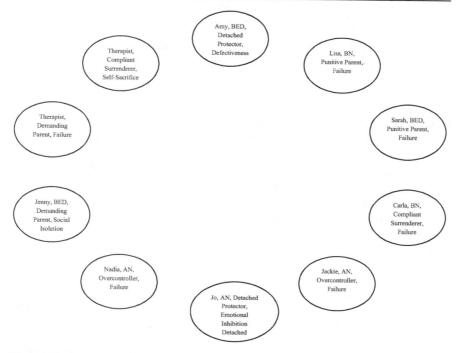

*Figure 12.2* Group case conceptualisation

## Part 2: Stuck points and solutions

(1) The mixed composition of the group was a challenge [stuck point] as group members were diagnosed with different types of EDs, although all were experiencing distress and using their eating behaviours to cope. Group members reflected on seeing the deprivation and excess before their eyes. In the beginning of the group, group members were wondering why they were all receiving the same treatment. Lisa and Carla (BN) saw themselves as failures compared to Nadia, Jackie and Jo (AN), as a result of a strong *DemP* and triggering of the Failure schema. Nadia, Jackie and Jo expressed being confronted with their 'feared self' – the person they thought they would become if they loosened any of their ways of controlling themselves through the *Overcontroller Mode* (*OC*) or hiding their thoughts and feelings from others (*DPr*).

*Solution*: At the beginning of the group the therapists focused on bringing the group members together by exploring shared schemas and modes, rather than speaking about specific ED diagnoses. The first challenge the therapists faced was how to openly discuss the composition of the group. The therapists modelled openness from the *HA* by saying: "We talk about all types of EDs. You might wonder why we're all together? It's because these are ways of coping which are harming you. If we look at what's driving it, it's similar."

The therapists placed an emphasis on conceptualising the group as one individual with different sides that they needed to contain in order to keep the focus on working with the group (as opposed to individual therapy in a group). To promote bonding and cohesiveness, the therapists focused on the modes that were currently present for each group member. This was very important, as bonding and cohesiveness provided safety, hope and commitment for treatment. The therapists also discussed the origins of EDs in terms of unmet childhood needs and experiences of trauma, allowing group members to bond around similarities in their childhood experiences. There was a strong focus on developing trust and strengthening a connection between group members and therapists in the assessment phase. A comprehensive pre-group assessment and history-taking was invaluable in enabling therapists to attune to individuals within the group, thereby increasing connection, trust and potentially reducing drop out. Therapists learned to facilitate the group in a way that enabled a transition from functioning as a 'family' of separate individuals to a 'family' of healthily emotionally connected members.

(2) After a couple of weeks, a fear of failing at their attempts to recover emerged in the group. This fear was related to a strong *DemP*, linked to triggering of the Failure schema, with some group members too scared to try, falling back on their natural inclination to use their eating behaviours as a means of coping.

An example of the fear of failing at their attempts to recover was shown in the review of homework in the early stage of group therapy. Jenny started sharing her homework assignment with the group, in which she had drawn her *VCh* mode surrounded by *HA* messages that she had found on the internet when looking for ST material. Although the therapists had explained that the exercise focused on connecting with the *VCh*, Jenny expressed it was quicker to do research on the internet and she wanted quicker results because this was her last chance of recovering, so she had to work harder. Jenny's *VCh* was being excluded by the *DemP*. When the time came for Jackie to share her homework assignment, she expressed that her *DemP* had been strong during the week and she did not attempt the homework exercise out of fear of failure at her attempt to recover. She had fallen back on the *OC* and restricted her diet, losing two kilograms.

*Solution*: The stuck point of the fear of failing at their attempts to recover was addressed through chair work to better understand the feelings of the *VCh* and influence of the *DemP*. The therapists expressed that they wanted to reach out to the *VCh*. The group members each spoke from the *VCh* and were able to express emotions and needs and listen openly to each other. This led to an open discussion amongst all group members about their childhood experiences and origin of the *DemP* in their lives. The group therapists also stimulated the group members to explore their personal changes in treatment over time.

(3) In the review of homework Jenny expressed concern that by Jackie not attempting the homework exercise her healing process may have been affected: "If a homework exercise is set, I think we should complete it otherwise it takes up too much time in session and I am afraid that it will interfere with my recovery." Jackie's Failure schema was triggered. The group therapists were concerned that Jenny's *DemP* was active, perhaps trying to get results too quickly which was excluding her *VCh* and contributing to division in the group. Jackie's Social Isolation/Alienation schema was activated, leading her to withdraw from Jenny as a consequence of feeling that she [Jenny] had ignored her feelings when she was struggling with the homework assignment.

*Solution*: A chair work exercise was used to help Jenny to feel the connection with her *VCh*. This opened a pathway for Jackie to realise that Jenny also had a *VCh* who expressed fear of failing at her attempts to recover. Jenny realised that her *VCh* needed to feel a sense of belonging and the connection with the *VCh* of others in the group.

(4) A stuck point emerged between the group therapists whereby the therapist with a Self-Sacrifice schema struggled to set limits and respond in the time frame agreed with her co-therapist. Due to the Self-Sacrifice schema being triggered the therapist felt she had to always be available to help the group members. The therapist's *DemP* and Failure schema were triggered, expecting more and more of herself around giving to others.

*Solution*: In the context of supervision led by an external person the therapists explored their own schemas and modes. Through chair work the therapists were able to connect to their *HA* and gain a different perspective on balancing their needs with those of the group members.

### Part 3: Therapeutic pitfalls and mistakes

(1) One of the individuals included in the group presented to therapy with severe depression and suicidality. Over the course of therapy the therapists observed that the group member's extreme depression and suicidality triggered fears and anxieties within the group, leading to a higher prevalence of maladaptive coping modes. This pitfall highlighted the importance of identifying individuals who are not are suitable or ready for group therapy.

(2) During the group it was difficult to stimulate the expression of anger because all group members were emotionally inhibited in some way. While shared avoidant coping modes allowed the group members to feel there was commonality between them (especially given the disparity between diagnostic groups) it also led to pervasive inhibition. Perhaps in future therapists could consider limiting the number of AvPD patients in each group. If the therapists had ensured the balance was met between schemas and modes and prevented the group from being too avoidant, it may have been more helpful for treatment. Due to high levels of avoidance in the group, the therapists observed that group members felt irritated at times but it was difficult for them to express anger.

(3) During treatment the therapists were not always on the same page. The therapists felt that the group members may not have felt safe at times when they were not connected and inconsistent (e.g. not following what had been agreed on regarding out of session content). This pitfall highlighted the importance of managing the therapists' relationship in ongoing supervision. Particular tips for setting this up include discussing expectations relating to the importance of self-reflection meetings at the outset and scheduling supervision sessions led by an external person which focus on therapists' schemas and modes. Qualities of an external person should include an ability to acknowledge therapists' vulnerabilities (to help the therapists feel safe and accepted) and see patterns and problems the therapists may not be aware of. A comprehensive assessment before the group led by an external person could help the therapists be aware of potential schema and mode interactions in the relationship prior to the triggering of schemas and modes in the group.

## Case example three: Inpatient ST for EDs

### Part 1: Presenting issues

Kate was a 25-year old primary school teacher, who lived with her husband, Mark. Kate was the oldest of 11 brothers and sisters in a strictly religious and conservative family. Kate met Mark at her first job at a Christian school. Soon after they met, they told their parents and were allowed to officially start dating, which meant that they could visit each other at their parents' houses. After less than a year they were engaged, Kate was 23 years old and Mark 22 years. After their engagement, Kate became increasingly anxious by the thought of sexual intercourse following marriage. She had had no interest in sex and was very shy about her body. She had never seen a naked body before, since her parents had very strict rules about nudity. She started to eat less and less, lost weight, became increasingly active around the house, with difficulties sitting still and reading a book, which she had previously enjoyed. By the time she was married, she had lost 18 kilograms and was feeling tired and cold constantly. She claimed she was not feeling well on the wedding night, so Mark left her alone. After that, her weight loss declined rapidly, losing one kilogram per week which left Kate with a BMI of 11 within a few months. Kate was weak and numb and was admitted to an inpatient mental health clinic for patients with anorexia nervosa.

Kate was admitted to the high care unit where the primary goals were to receive medical care, start a regular eating pattern and gain weight. After gaining weight to a BMI of 17.5, she was admitted to the psychotherapeutic program at the inpatient unit. She was treated individually by a clinical psychologist and a psychiatrist and received group psychotherapy. Meals and snack times were supported by nurses. There was also psycho-motor therapy and family therapy at the unit. Kate was diagnosed with AN, restrictive type, OCD (cleaning) and with a personality disorder with dependent and obsessive compulsive personality traits.

**Background**
Conservative, religious family
Oldest of 11 brothers and sisters
God's will is paramount, own feelings and thoughts treated as unimportant
Individual needs were irrelevant
Marriage is arranged by parents of similar churches

**Situation in the here and now**
Recently married and moved out of parents house

**Schemas**
Self-sacrifice
Defectiveness/Shame
Emotional Inhibition
Dependence/Incompetence

**Modes**
Compliant-Surrenderer
Punitive Parent
Demanding Parent
Overcontroller

**Emotions**
Anxiety
Shame
Fear (of her body and having sex)

**Schema behaviour**
Restrictive eating
Excessive exercising
Obsessive cleaning
Avoiding physical contact with husband

*Figure 12.3* Case conceptualisation 2

## Part 2: Stuck points and solutions

(1) After admission, Kate started to eat and initially gained weight relatively easily. Underlying the anorexia however, Kate suffered from severe identity problems. She behaved as an overly adapted, friendly, dependent, forthcoming patient (*Compliant Surrenderer: CSu*). She was quiet, shy and anxious, desperately trying to avoid feelings of shame or failure, or any feelings at all (*OC*). The anorexia had quickly become a new identity and served a major role in avoiding adult life and corresponding responsibilities. The clinic served as a safe 'hideaway' from real life.

Contact with family: Kate had a few meetings with her mother (her father never came to the clinic) and the family therapist. In these, she was mostly in the *CSu*, not saying much, agreeing with everything her mother said. Her feelings of shame and anxiety interfered with her capacity to stand up to her parents. Contact with parents repeatedly triggered her internal *PP*, telling her that it was all her fault and that she was a burden on her parents. Because of her submissive behaviour, the family therapist decided to switch to sessions with Kate and her husband only. Again it was difficult for Kate to open up. Her husband was very calm, open and supportive, which finally enabled Kate to switch to *HA* and open up about some of her anxieties. She told him that being married, having to engage in sex and getting pregnant scared her. However, it was not possible for her to allow him to see her *VCh* (e.g. by telling him she felt her body was disgusting), which made progress difficult.

*Solution*: When Kate's parents were present, Kate did not succeed in coming out of the *CSu*. Therefore, sessions soon shifted to include Mark. However, in retrospect, in order to help her overcome her stagnation in the *CSu*, it could have been fruitful to have continued working with mother and daughter to help mum give Kate permission to start her own life. Chair work with Mark and Kate together helped them both to step out of *CSu* into *HA*.

(2) Contact with clinical psychologist: In the individual sessions with her female therapist Kate started in the *OC*. She was unable to overcome her shame and anxiety to show her real feelings and thoughts. Eventually this improved and the *VCh* sometimes appeared, in which Kate could talk about her fears of her own sexuality, the disgust she felt when thinking about having sex with her husband and the conflict she had regarding the demands of her upbringing (marry and have many children) and her own feelings about her future. She desperately needed approval when opening up, to be reassured that she was allowed to have her own thoughts and feelings and choose her own way in life. This was however very difficult for Kate and many sessions were ended with her remaining in the *OC* mode and sometimes *PP*.

*Solution*: In individual therapy, Kate continued to hide her feelings (Emotional Inhibition schema). Her anxiety about showing her feelings and allowing her *VCh* to speak remained strong. When Kate had reached a BMI of 17.5, her weight gain stagnated. Chair work was used to learn to set aside her *PP* and *CSu*, to increase contact with her *VCh*. She became increasingly able to show her *VCh* and speak more openly about her need to feel safe and accepted. Also, imagery rescripting was used to rescript some of the negative childhood experiences, which were connected with the onset of her Emotional Inhibition schema. Subsequently, the *OC* became less actively present and Kate's own feelings and needs began to surface. One thing that appeared to make the therapeutic connection stronger was the use of humour. Kate appeared to have a funny, playful side that, at BMI 17.5 to 18, emerged. By making small jokes about her modes (e.g. Kate labelled her *CSu* 'Blondie') the therapeutic alliance was strengthened and also made it possible for Kate to loosen up a little.

(3) Contact with and within multidisciplinary team: Staff meetings in which Kate's treatment was evaluated, revealed conflicts with the psychiatrist and

the psychiatric nurses (*PP*), the clinical psychologist (trying to offer limited reparenting to Kate by being the opposite; warm, non-judgemental) and the family therapist (who switched to *DPr* after working so hard and making limited progress). Kate moved into the *OC* and briefly started to lose weight again when she noticed that the treatment team were thinking about releasing her from hospital care once her medical condition had improved. This triggered Kate's fear of independence and her fear of losing the safe environment which the clinic had become for her *VCh*.

*Solution*: When Kate reached BMI 17.5, staff members gradually started to remind Kate that the inpatient treatment was only temporary and that the staff wanted to help her move into *HA*, expressing confidence that she could function on her own if she kept eating healthily. This made it possible for Kate to limit her time at the clinic, start to spend the weekends at home and step by step, build up her life outside the clinic, while keeping contact with her therapists. Only when she was stable at BMI 18.5, was she was discharged from the clinic.

### Part 3: Therapeutic pitfalls and mistakes

(1) In individual sessions Kate mostly avoided emotional subjects. Kate could only show her *VCh* and express her multiple anxieties about regaining a womanly figure, being seen as a responsible Christian woman and married wife when tension grew high enough. The clinical psychologist found it hard to constantly push her to open up. Doing this made the psychologist feel like the *PP*.

(2) Trouble-shooting: One possible way of addressing this could have involved addressing this interaction earlier in treatment. By not doing so, some of the therapy sessions were not effective, keeping Kate and her therapist stuck. Also, more disclosure of Kate's therapists own thoughts and feelings could have helped to set an example for Kate, since her parents and her husband were all emotionally inhibited and could not serve as role models for her in this respect. Staff supervision sessions, discussing limited reparenting in the different contexts of the clinic, could have helped staff members to bring this into practice more fully.

(3) During treatment, therapy goals often seemed to be in conflict with the Christian values that were so important to Kate. The identity issues Kate suffered with were difficult to talk about, since within her family, being obedient and compliant was the norm. Identity development was therefore an issue that could not be treated separately from Kate's religious background. This was one of the reasons that after discharge from the clinic (after in total six months), Kate was referred to a Christian psychiatric facility, where she could receive ambulatory care; individual and couples therapy on Christian grounds.

## Implications for overcoming obstacles in the treatment of EDs

As illustrated by the case examples, through a process of working with schemas and modes, patients are encouraged to focus on emotional work in order to get their core emotional needs met and produce lasting change in their lives. One of the guiding strategies illustrated in all three case examples is the benefit of using the schema mode model to develop a formulation and treatment plan that addresses the underlying function of eating behaviours. This has been highlighted in previous literature as essential to effective treatment with ED populations (Vitousek, Watson & Wilson, 1998; Wildes, Ringham & Marcus, 2010; Simpson, 2012).

## Learning points drawn from the case studies

- The importance of involving patients' family systems. Alternatively, if patients are not willing to work with family members, missing family members can be addressed through 'empty' chair work.
- The importance of team members/therapists being on the same page and highlighting the importance of regular supervision led by an external person and self-reflection meetings focused on schemas and modes.
- To be aware that the *DemP* or *DPr* are likely to avoid affect and to actively work on these modes as well as explaining the healthy function of actually experiencing and expressing emotions.
- To focus on helping clients to learn healthy ways of connecting with others and not detaching when others connect with them.
- To take the client's value system into account when working to strengthen their *HA*.

## References

Lockwood, G. and Perris, P. (2012) A new look at core emotional needs. In M. van Vreeswijk, J. Broersen and M. Nadort (Eds.), *The Wiley-Blackwell Handbook of Schema Therapy: Theory, Research, and Practice*. Chichester: Wiley, pp. 41–66.

Simpson, S. (2012) Schema therapy for eating disorders: A Case study illustration of the mode approach. In M. van Vreeswijk, J. Broersen and M. Nadort (Eds.), *The Wiley-Blackwell Handbook of Schema Therapy: Theory, Research, and Practice*. Chichester: Wiley, pp. 145–171.

Vitousek, K. M., Watson, S. and Wilson, G. T. (1998). Enhancing motivation for change in treatment-resistant eating disorders. *Clinical Psychology Review*, 18(4), 391–420.

Wildes, J. E., Ringham, R. M. and Marcus, M. D. (2010). Emotion avoidance in patients with anorexia nervosa: Initial test of a functional model. *International Journal of Eating Disorders*, 43(5), 398–404.

Young, J. E., Klosko, J. and Weishaar, M. E. (2003). *Schema Therapy: A Practitioner's Guide*. New York: Guilford Press.

# Chapter 13

# Transference and therapist–client schema chemistry in the treatment of eating disorders

*Eckhard Roediger and Christina Archonti*

## Abstract

*Working with clients with eating disorders (EDs) presents therapists with some of the most challenging modes. These modes trigger therapists' schemas and tend to exacerbate fruitless battles that therapists rarely "win". To avert these pitfalls, a good deal of self-reflection and mode-management is needed from the therapist's side. Beginning with some introductory remarks regarding how to balance the therapeutic relationship in general, this chapter goes on to explore the most prevailing therapist schemas. It provides recommendations about how to use self-disclosure using advanced chairwork techniques, in order to bypass clients' most powerful coping modes and form a stronger emotional connection with them. The specific techniques we present are centred around the idea of weakening clients' automatic coping modes by changing body positions in strategic ways.*

## The impact of the therapy relationship

The therapeutic relationship is the most influential factor across all interventions to impact on positive outcomes (Lambert, 2013). But what is a relationship based on? A relationship between two people results from mutual perception, appraisal and action. In a nutshell, two individuals with different internal working models (Bowlby, 1969) encounter each other in order to bridge the gap between them and interact in some way.

If things go well, this happens mostly unconsciously in something we call resonance (Siegel, 1999). When the going gets tough (as can sometimes be the case in therapy), we have to slow down, eventually stop, separate the ongoing process into its sequential pieces and make sense of them in the context of an overarching case conceptualisation. The case conceptualisation facilitates the development of a joint perspective with the client (Siegel, 1999), by providing a common reference point to reconnect and fine-tune the relationship. To fully understand any given interaction in the therapy room we have to analyse both sides: the client's perspective as well as the therapist's. This chapter is about the therapist's side. However, we do not use the term transference, because it is rooted in psychodynamic concepts. We talk about *client–therapist chemistry* instead. But – in essence – we are referring to more or less the same thing.

## Therapist schemas and how to deal with them

Given the universality of schemas, the process of schema activation is relevant to both therapists and clients. Therapists are just one step ahead of their clients when it comes to identifying, understanding and dealing with schema activation. Through revealing their own emotional reactions, the therapist serves as a healthy role model.

Let us first explore schema dynamics from the therapist's side. We do not differ much from our clients in terms of schema loading. It appears that therapists frequently have schemas from the disconnection and rejection domain (Bamber & McMahon, 2008; Simpson et al., 2018). Furthermore, therapists tend to score high on the conditional (or coping) schemas *unrelenting standards* and *self-sacrifice* (Kaeding et al., 2017; Simpson et al., 2018). If we dig deeper to identify those schemas that are underneath the coping schemas, we are likely to reveal primary schemas such as *failure to achieve* or *vulnerability to harm*.

Many of us are "parentified children" (Gardner, Sauber & Lorandos, 2006, p. 200) who learned early in life to care for other people. We just turned "lemons into lemonade" by learning to use our early skills in a professional way. To cut a long story short: the difference between therapists and their clients is that we are coping with our schemas more successfully than our clients. Learning to deal with our own vulnerabilities provides a great opportunity to become a better therapist. Being in touch with loneliness, hopelessness, helpless anger or humiliation can increase our capacity to resonate with what our clients feel and give them a sense of being really understood (or "feeling felt"; Siegel 1999). A good starting point to develop the capacity to be centered and compassionate is working through the eight-week program in the book *Mindfulness for Therapists* (Zarbock, Lynch, Ammann & Ringer, 2015).

## Working with the therapy relationship

Before we go deeper into the details of how to guide the therapy relationship and make use of your own schema activation, we would like to introduce some basic concepts on how to work within the therapy relationship. You can find a broader description of this approach in the book *Contextual Schema Therapy* (Roediger, Stevens & Brockman, 2018). The therapeutic relationship evolves in a field that can be conceptualised along two dimensions, both of them between two poles (see Figure 13.1). On the vertical axis we guide the client's self-experiencing between diving into the process of emotional activation (the pole of self-actualization; Millon, 1990) and emotionally distancing

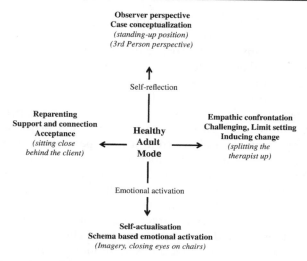

Figure 13.1 Dimensions of the therapy relationship

by shifting into an internal observer level (the pole of self-reflection). The horizontal axis describes our relationship to them, the pole on the left is the reparenting one. We feel emotionally connected and supportive towards our clients. Lockwood and Perris (2012) called this the "maternal mode". This is the starting point of therapy. To support the client's autonomy over the course of therapy we need to challenge them by moving to the pole on the right using empathic confrontation and limit setting. Lockwood and Perris (2012) called this the "paternal mode". The whole process of therapy evolves between these poles: change requires sufficient emotional activation (bottom pole). But the experienced emotions need reappraisal to make new meaning (top pole; Boston Change Process Study Group, 2008). Clients in a *Vulnerable Child* (*VCh*) mode need our support and guidance (pole on the left). Passive-aggressive as well as impulsive or undisciplined child or coping modes need empathic confrontation (pole on the right). Thus, this figure provides us with a road map, giving us direction in terms of how to guide the client to move towards self-awareness, integration, flexibility and functional behaviour. *Healthy Adult* (*HA*) mode behaviour on the therapist's and client's side is represented by flexibly balancing between these poles. We will now go into the details regarding how to move between these poles.

### Balancing the level of emotional activation

When we try to induce a deeper level of emotional activation, we ask clients to close their eyes, focus on their basic emotions and body sensations and eventually ask them to float back in time into their youth or childhood days, e.g. in imagery work. This means guiding them towards the lower end on the vertical axis in Figure 13.1, towards emotional activation. In contrast, if we want to support them to step out of schema activation, we ask them to stand together with us side by side, look down on the process of chairwork from an observer perspective, and talk about the modes on the chairs in third person language. This results in a movement to the upper pole of the vertical axis, towards self-reflection. The combination of physically standing up, looking down from above from a joint perspective with the therapist, and talking as if it was another person, cools the emotions and reinforces the working alliance with the therapist. This allows us to step out of a concrete situation in which the client might feel trapped, and connect the situation with the overarching case conceptualisation based on the mode model. Thus, we can extract underlying, repetitive behavioural patterns. Detecting the underlying patterns gives clients a greater sense of perspective, coherence and manageability (Antonovsky, 1987).

### The emotional window of tolerance

Fine-tuning the level of emotional activation is meaningful for both clients and therapists. On the client's side we have to be aware to keep them in their window of emotional tolerance (see Figure 13.2). Our capacity to learn something new depends very much on our level of emotional activation. The learning curve follows an inverted U shape (Yerkes & Dodson, 1908). If the level of activation is too low (for example, due to detachment or a lack of motivation), no learning happens. The information processing remains stable and unchanged. If the level of activation rises too high, the alarm system gets activated, shuts the processing down at a level of emotion-driven, automatic processing, and new information is blocked (this is called emotional hijacking; Goleman, 1995). No change occurs in this state either. Only when the level of activation stays within the so-called *emotional tolerance window* is new information processed, inducing changes in information storage on a deeper level guided by the *HA* mode (this is called cortical override; Siegel, 1999).

With this in mind, clients with impulsive behaviour driven by intensive emotions (like binge eating) find themselves in a state of hyper-arousal and need support to step out and change into a more self-reflective state. In contrast, emotionally withdrawn or detached clients (e.g. like most clients with anorexia nervosa (AN)) need the "warmth" (or maybe sometimes the "heat") of "heating up" emotions to bring them in touch with their underlying blocked needs.

But moderating emotional activation is also relevant for therapists. Some clients can easily "turn the table on us" and put us under emotional pressure. When in a hyper-aroused state, our cognitive performance is compromised

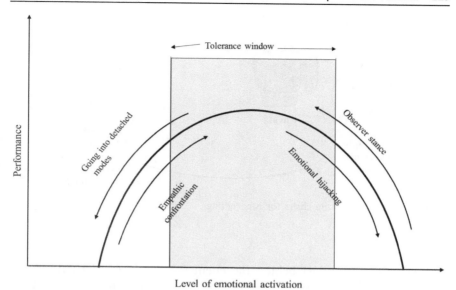

*Figure 13.2* The emotional window of tolerance

too, and we tend to react in a schema driven way. Some clients are actually masters at detecting and pushing our "buttons". To avoid acting out our own patterns it helps to pull the "emergency break", interrupt the ongoing process and change into a conjoint observer perspective with words like: "I am sorry to interrupt you here. I realise this might seem a bit abrupt, but I am getting a bit lost in the present process. There are a lot of important things going on, but I don't fully understand them. So, would you mind if we stood up together so we can try to gain an overview?" If the client remains reluctant, you can say something like: "Ok, this is primarily not for you. It is meant to help me to better understand you. As you have come along to the session anyway, could you just give me five minutes to give it a try, please? Then you can just think of it as one of the craziest things you ever did, ok?" (for more details see Roediger, 2016).

### The reparenting pole

On the horizontal axis (see Figure 13.1) we move between the poles of accepting, supporting, validating, modeling and directly soothing clients (reparenting, see Chapter 10), and at the other end, confronting them with [constructive] critical information, challenging them to become more responsible and autonomous, supporting behavioural experiments and eventually setting limits. To increase the effect of reparenting, we recommend leaving the conventional face-to-face sitting position and moving

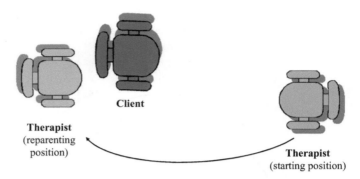

Client

Therapist
(reparenting
position)

Therapist
(starting position)

*Figure 13.3* Positions of the chairs for reparenting

your chair close by, just behind the client (as shown on the left side of Figure 13.3). This enables the therapist to directly address the client's child mode in a very low and warm voice, using child-like language. Asking the client to close their eyes and focus on their basic emotions and bodily sensations, facilitates activation of the child mode. Leaving the face-to-face position is especially challenging for clients with AN who constantly try to control us. Through physically bypassing their control-ling coping mode, we offer them accepting contact with their child mode, instead of getting caught up in talking things through with their pro-tector modes. Eventually, with permission, you might support this inter-nal "float-back" with some physical connection such as a supportive touch on the client's back with one hand (with permission). In ST, phy-sical connection can provide a critical bond between clients and therapists.

In the situation described above, the client can no longer see the thera-pist but can feel their support. The client is in a child mode state, deeply in touch with their emotions in their inner world. In this state, the client no longer perceives the therapist acting as an every-day person, but as a supporting depersonalised healthy "force" in their head. Zindel (2009) called this a "transference free space". Looking at such an interaction from an observer stance gives the wrong impression. We frequently experience this when showing videos of this kind of work (or a compar-able imagery session) in workshops or lectures. The participants looking at the scene from outside often perceive the therapists as too dominant or manipulative. Interestingly this is in stark contrast with what the clients (or therapists in self-therapy) experience: they describe feeling safe, well-guided and fully understood.

### Empathic confrontation

Now we move to the right end of the poles on the horizontal axis of Figure 13.1: Empathic confrontation. Due to their *self-sacrifice* schema, many therapists prefer reparenting much more than empathic confrontation. But if we regard ST as an opportunity to facilitate maturation of clients' capacity to connect and interact with others, then it is essential for therapists to elicit opportunities for them to learn how to take responsibility for their own behaviour. The setting of internal limits is essential in order to develop a healthy balance between autonomy and pro-social behaviour. Empathic confrontation is best delivered in the context of chair-dialogue work. The therapist is split into two parts, which are literally "placed" on two separate chairs. This makes empathic confrontation much easier compared with a face-to-face position, and is similar to the "good cop–bad cop" concept referred to in the movies (see Figure 13.4). Let us look at how to proceed with a passive-aggressive client who is not complying with homework assignments. To introduce empathic confrontation, the therapist takes the lead: "If you agree, I would like to add something from my side to the table today". If the client agrees and there is no other more urgent issue on the agenda, the therapist continues: "Well, there are some more challenging things I want to say. To make this safer for both of us I am moving to this additional chair here." The therapists moves over to the "bad therapist" chair before continuing: "Talking from this part I must admit that I am not satisfied with your contribution in the past few sessions. I gained the impression that you are expecting me to rescue you, and you have relied on me to do too much of the work. I am not willing to go on this way anymore." While gradually increasing the emotional pressure on the client sentence by sentence, we carefully look for physical signs of emotional activation, such as the client looking away, moving their legs or hands, leaning back, or frowning. Once a slight change in the body

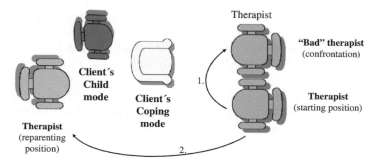

*Figure 13.4* Positions of the chairs for empathic confrontation

language appears, we immediately stop, take the "good therapist"-chair and place it behind the client's chair in the reparenting position described above: "Here I am again to support you. Look at this chair in front of you. How does it make you feel when this impatient therapist says things like...". By looking at the "afterglow" of the "bad therapist" and repeating the [bad-cop] therapist's self-disclosure, we try to release any kind of basic emotional activation within the client, as described in the section above. It can be useful to draw clients' attention away from cognitive processing, toward bodily entrenched basic emotions and their attendant physiological felt-sense. In one of the following sections we will describe how to deal with the basic emotional activations that have been revealed.

## Typical challenges to the therapeutic relationship in treating EDs

We now invite you to take a closer look at the most prevalent EDs. EDs manifest a wide range of symptoms, some of which can seem almost contradictory. Thus, we will look at the syndromes and resulting interactional pitfalls by relating them to the mode model in a very cursory manner, since you will find more details in other chapters of this book.

### How to deal with impulsivity such as overeating or binge eating

In terms of coping modes, we regard overeating in the context of the *Detached Self-Soother*, driven by an *Impulsive Child* mode. On a personal level, we prefer not to use the term "undisciplined child mode", because it appears too judgmental to us (maybe driven by the therapist's own *unrelenting standards* schema). Or in other words, if the client shows impulsive behaviour, this indicates that they are lacking sufficient self-regulation skills from their *HA* mode side. Nevertheless, they are likely to have very strong self-directed *Inner Critic* mode voices beating themselves up for their "undisciplined" behavioural excesses. Thus, the key internal dynamic of a person with impulsive binge eating is finding themselves in a vice between the impulsive and needy child mode and a harshly criticising internal voice. Often this replays the client's childhood patterns, an overload of expectations but with no help to fulfill them. The lonely and needy child inside remains unseen and abandoned.

Remember that most therapists are good overcompensators of their own schemas. It takes a lot of discipline to achieve good grades, pass university successfully and undergo a long training to become a licensed therapist. In addition, looking at the participants of our trainings, relatively few of them are overweight. We actually learned to control our *Impulsive Child* mode by a more or less functional *Demanding Inner Critic* mode voice. If we now meet a client who describes the behaviour we had (or are still striving) to defeat within us, this is likely to activate our own *Demanding Critic* mode. This, in turn, leads us to perceive our clients through their own [*Inner Critic*] eyes, eventually fueling feelings of annoyance, disgust or even contempt.

If their (self-directed) *Demanding [Inner] Critic* mode allies with the therapist's (client directed) critical mode, then history repeats itself and the client finds themselves in the old trap once again. But shifting into an *Inner Critic* mode that blames us for having these feelings misses the point. Our own schemas induce these feelings within us. Going into a *Detached Protector (DetPr)* mode ignores these feelings. Putting them aside will not make them disappear. Self-disclosure and at least partially revealing our own struggles in order to model healthy vulnerability seems to be a more compassionate and promising road to take. We need to learn to practice what we preach. We need to acknowledge the existence of these feelings, accept them, connect them with our schemas, reappraise them as dysfunctional, distance ourselves from them and let them go.

Another way of managing these schemas is by disclosing the critical mode voice by placing it on an extra chair (together with the client's *Inner Critic* mode), then stand up together with the client to physically take an observer stance, and reconnect with them as a "consultation team" (Anderson, 1987; see Figure 13.5). Connecting the collaborating *Critic* modes' voices with the case conceptualisation, allows reappraisal of the situation in the light of a mindful and accepting observer stance (or a "good parent" perspective). Some of the *Critic* mode beliefs might actually be true, e.g. "If you eat too much this way you will get fat like a beached whale!" Looking at the effects of the *Critic* mode voices on the *Child* mode quickly reveals how dysfunctional or "toxic" they are – much more effectively than simply looking at their content. Looking at the toxic effects of the *Critic* paves the way to impeach the *Critic* mode voices together, while standing side-by-side. This conjoint action gives the client a feeling of deep support. Now the stage is set to look at the needs of the child mode, connecting with realistic values, and seeking functional ways of dealing with the situation. The upper part of Figure 13.5 gives an impression of how this arrangement might look.

A personal note: Like Joan Farrell and Ida Shaw (2017) we no longer use the term "parent mode" because it doesn't resonate well with all clients. The term "*Inner Critic* mode" already introduced by Les Greenberg (2015) better describes the internalised beliefs and appraisals taken from the child's environment in multiple ways.

### How to deal with emotional instability and mode flipping caused by ambivalent child modes

For a client with bulimia nervosa, both child mode poles are subsequently activated: flipping into self-soothing binging, the *Impulsive Child* prevails and

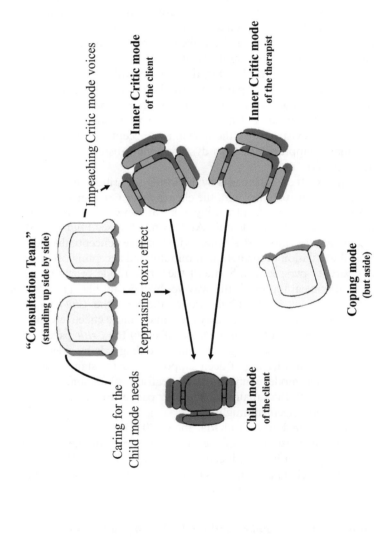

"Consultation Team"
(standing up side by side)

Impeaching Critic mode voices

Inner Critic mode
of the client

Inner Critic mode
of the therapist

Repraising toxic effect

Caring for the
Child mode needs

Coping mode
(but aside)

Child mode
of the client

Figure 13.5 Positions of the chairs when impeaching Critic mode voices

the *Inner Critic* mode steps back for a moment. After the bingeing and acting out the impulsivity, the power is gone, feelings of vulnerability pop up again and the *Inner Critic* mode is resurrected, with increased strength, beating up the client and inducing feelings of incompetence and shame, pushing him or her back into the *VCh* mode. Over time the loneliness might turn into neediness and the clients may shift into the *Impulsive* (or sometimes *Angry (AnCh)*) *Child* mode pole again, inducing self-soothing behaviour once more. This history repeats itself in a never-ending emotional see-saw. We already described the way out: interrupt the cycle, label the modes, connect them with the model, take a "good parent stance" as the *HA* team, reappraise the situation and treat both child mode poles as good parents would. When trying to take care of the child modes we have to be aware that the two poles of the child mode spectrum have needs that point in different directions.

- In the *VCh mode*, clients primarily feel fear or sadness, because their needs for attachment, connection and unconditional love are not met. Thus, the question to connect with this need is: "What do you need now, what do you really desire?"
- In an *AnCh* or *Impulsive Child mode*, clients primarily feel annoyed or angry, because their more self-centred needs for autonomy, assertiveness, satisfaction, approval or control are not met. Thus, the question accessing this pole of the need spectrum is *"what are you dreaming of, what would you like to be doing if anything was possible?"* These questions try to open the door for blocked goals or visions, in order to encourage clients to become more active in their real life, and to overcome stuck states caused by prior frustrations of their intentions and goals in childhood.

*Future directed imagery* is another helpful technique to activate clients on an energetic level beyond cognitive operations. After inviting clients to close their eyes, ask them to imagine themselves 10 feet tall, full of power, able to do everything they want to do, like in a science fiction movie. Identify any self-limiting thoughts and put them aside. Ask them to day-dream just like they do every night. Push them gently in a creative, playful mood. In mode terms, you are both diving into a playful child mode. This is a variation of the "crystal ball technique" (de Shazer, 1985). Once they have generated some ideas, extract the expressed need and name it. Then stand up together shifting into the "consultation team" to look for the first tiny steps the client might take to approach the named goal just a little bit. For example: If the client dreams of travelling to a foreign country or going to a party, in the standing-up position you might ask them as a first step to think of a place nearby where they would like to go, or an (already familiar) person they would like to meet up with. The idea is to create an "energetic wave" inside the client first, and then "ride it" as well as they can towards the "shores of reality".

For details about the model and further instructions how to use the described techniques see Roediger, Stevens and Brockman (2018).

Accessing the underlying basic emotions of a child mode works best when the therapist moves into the reparenting position we described above. When we work with the *AnCh* or *Impulsive Child* pole in order to increase assertiveness and motivate clients to take action, it helps to place an empty chair in front of them representing either a discouraging person, a critical thought or another obstacle paralyzing the client's power. This helps the client to address their anger to a symbolic representation of an external figure, whilst drawing on the encouragement from the therapist behind them. The left side of Figure 13.6 shows the positions of the chairs during this exercise.

In a nutshell: To guide this process we first activate the child mode emotions on the chair level sitting close to the client in the "reparenting position" as already described. Once they are activated, we change into the *"Healthy Adult"*-level in the standing-up position to broaden the mind of the clients, enabling them to find a workable solution to deal with the obstacles and guide the child modes.

### Dealing with hostility and overcompensatory coping modes

Very ego-syntonic overcompensatory coping modes driven by remorseless *Critic* mode voices (frequently prevailing among clients with AN) can be a real challenge. There is little motivation to distance from the deeply entrenched beliefs and automatic behaviours because to the clients these beliefs just "feel right". Naturally, by addressing the coping modes there is a great risk that the therapist will become one of the client's "enemies", with clients reacting in resentful and hostile ways. In return this can lead to intense activation of therapist schemas, triggering negative emotions eventually leading to reactive compensatory aggressive or coercive behaviour, e.g. restrictions or forced re-feeding. The detached or hostile behaviour of, for example clients with AN, violates the therapist's underlying need for attachment and emotional connection that is part of their professional motivation. It is important to remember that therapists also have schemas, such as *emotional deprivation* or *abandonment*. Working as a therapist can provide an emotionally connected and soothing environment that to some extent meets our own needs for attachment (within professional boundaries). Passive-aggressive clients frequently violate these underlying therapist needs and trigger the related schemas. In reaction, the therapist might shift into a compensatory withdrawal and secondary angry and dominant behaviour (see Edward Tronick's "still-face"-experiment you-tube video for an illustration of how this cycle operates in early childhood when attempts to connect are frustrated).

In terms of modes, there is a risk of a *Detached–Overcompensation* mode cycle between client and therapist with a propensity to escalate: the more the client closes up or shows passive-aggressive behaviour, the more the therapist

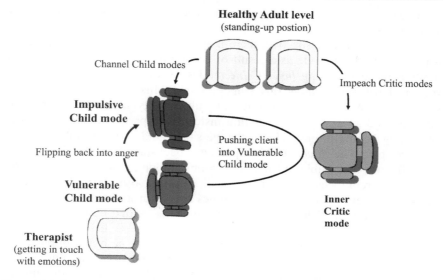

*Figure 13.6* Positions of the chairs when exploring the child mode needs and looking for a functional solution

tends to become angry and coercive – in a similar way to dysfunctional couples (for details see Roediger & Laireiter, 2013). In treatment units this might affect the whole team, even leading to a split into two parties: one sympathising with the underlying *VCh* mode behind the client's dysfunctional coping modes, the other taking the *Punitive* or *Demanding Critic* mode stance struggling with the client's maladaptive coping modes. To deal with these team dynamics, supervision by a third party should be a mandatory part of the therapy concept.

Dealing with *Inner Critic* mode activation brings a dual challenge: we need to deal with our own inner critics as well as with those of our clients. Because this is really essential when working with clients with AN, we will describe this in detail here. Like the underlying *punitiveness* and *unrelenting standards* schemas, the critical modes can be directed both toward the self and others (Young, Klosko & Weishaar, 2003: 264). We tend to feel deflated when our attempts to help our clients fail, subsequently leading to an increased urge to be even more supportive, forgiving and "nice". However, this can result in the therapist becoming excessively submissive and subsequently easily abused by clients' manipulative coping modes. Alternatively, we might respond by getting angry and sliding into overcompensating behaviour, which designates the client as the "guilty party". A third maladaptive option may be to step back, detach emotionally and let time pass and things go their own way. It is important for therapists to recognise and reflect on these tendencies before we act them out.

From the client's perspective, there may be a strong sense of failure deep inside in their *VCh* mode as a result of constantly being put down by their punitive and devaluating *Inner Critic* modes. However, they are desperately working hard not to show this vulnerable side. Instead they have learned to overcompensate for the feelings of vulnerability associated with their schemas (and *Inner Critic*), switching instead into perfectionistic and over-controlling coping modes. They "change sides" and start to look down on other people: The *Inner Critic* operates "backstage" inside the client's mind, fueling the visible "frontstage" coping modes, leading to outwardly focused, overcompensatory behaviour like putting other people down or acting out of entitlement. This sometimes results in a climate that is a bit like being in a battlefield: every move we make is treated by the client with suspicion. In return, we constantly doubt if they are being truthful or trying to deceive us. Mistrust is everywhere. This is exactly the opposite of what it takes to heal the wounds of the deeply hidden *VCh*. Putting all these obstacles out of the way is a real therapeutic challenge. But unfortunately, this is not the only one!

The other challenge lies in revealing the concealed, but nevertheless deeply rooted *AnCh* mode. Superficially, the *AnCh* mode is not visible nor accessible. All we see is an instrumentalised and "cold anger" in terms of manipulative or passive-aggressive coping modes. However, there are two ways that these kind of clients induce anger within the therapist.

- First, they subtly communicate the hidden anger through implicit, non-verbal channels. Therapists are usually quite sensitive to these signals, even if they cannot fully mentalise them on a conscious or explicit level. Via these channels therapists can get "infected" emotionally by what Hatfield, Cacioppo, and Rapson (1994) called "emotional contagion".
- Second, the constant frustration of our natural need to connect with the client, which is part of our professional motivation, over time can induce anger. The clients violate our striving for resonant relationships. From both sources a strange brew of antipathy can emerge toward the client.

Caught in the crossfire of critic modes and *AnCh* mode, on both sides we find ourselves caught between a rock and a hard place. So, what can we do to cope with this multitude of challenges?

*First of all:* Avoid any kind of acting-out, but remain centred and in a self-reflective stance. Be aware when you are emotionally triggered as a sign of your own schema activations. Step back, stop the evolving interactional mode cycle, take a break standing up together in order to shift into your *HA* observer mode again (see Figure 13.6 above). Connect your own mode activations with the mode model. As already described we strongly recommend the use of self-disclosure to build a bridge with the client's *HA* mode. From a joint perspective in the standing position it is much easier to initiate some self-reflection within the client by identifying and labeling the behaviour and underlying emotions on their side, and connect these with the mode model. It feels a bit like *"talking about other people while they are in the room"*.

Building trust and bypassing the sceptical and hostile protector modes actually works best if we reveal our own modes first. This serves as a powerful way of demonstrating that it is possible to show "soft" feelings without turning into a "wimp". Our clients over-identified with the internalised beliefs of their *Inner Critic*, and learned to treat the *VCh* mode (and emotions) in an abusive and toxic way. The body became the symbolic representation of the feelings of weakness and perceived "lack of discipline" associated with the *VCh*. The resulting parallels are terrible: Many clients with AN refer to their *Inner Critic* mode as a "dictator" that "imprisons" them within their body and sentences them to death.

There is no cognitive access to this inner world dichotomy. The *Inner Critic* is usually very clever and hyper-aware of our intentions. The best way to deal with this is persistent honesty and modesty. Looking at the modes from the "outside" helps client and therapist to cool down the underlying emotions, soften the coping modes and makes it easier to create distance from maladaptive mode cycles that clients unconsciously try to drag us into. The mode model provides us with a neutral and overarching framework. Combining stepping out with using third-person language as described above clears the air even more. It aims to answer *"How can we both do better now?"* Once the client is somehow emotionally connected with the therapist on the observer stance level, the therapist can express honest empathy for the starving child behind the *Overcontroller* coping mode as a preliminary means of helping them to develop some self-compassion with their own blocked of *VCh* mode: *"It really hurts me to see this child there at the back. I can feel a bit of its loneliness and desperation and I have to tell you, seeing this makes me sad. I think this child is not bad and deserves something better than starvation"*.

If the client starts slipping into the coping mode again, stop them gently, asking them to identify what kind of mode they just shifted into, label the mode, validate them as a "good old friend", put the mode on the coping mode chair and ask for the feelings of the child mode behind. Focus here gently but persistently. Don't allow them to distract you with any cognitive detours. Stay with the here-and-now interaction between you. This is what we can control best and what provides us with the strongest impact on clients by constantly labelling the modes, separating them, putting them on the chairs and relentlessly addressing the underlying child mode feelings while remaining connected. It might be helpful to use the "substitution technique" (see next section) and picture a real child on the child mode chair being treated the same way by the *Inner Critic* mode. This usually activates our innate "caretaking system" (Panksepp, 2011) and thus a bit more compassion. Once you manage to access some emotions you can change back to the chair level, ask the client to sit down on the child mode chair, with you sitting behind in the reparenting position, thereby diving deeper into the client's inner world by asking them to connect more deeply with this side and the related body feelings. Once they get there, let them stay in touch with them for a while to induce some acceptance: "*Yes, great! You feel under pressure. As if a rock is pressing on your head. And your chest feels tight. You can hardly breathe. Like in a dungeon of despair. This is your VCh mode. This is the sad part inside of you. It was waiting there for years in the dark. But we finally reached him (or her) and can bring some light of day into this darkness. Stay with these feelings for a moment. I am on your side.*" However, we have to admit: There are few things in therapy that are harder to do! So, let us go into some more detail in the final section of this chapter.

## Special techniques to bypass the *Detached Protector* and access hidden *Child* modes

Putting the example in the previous section into a more general frame, we as therapists need to respond to the "frozen" emotional states of the client with our own warmth and compassion. This requires that we create a warm and caring atmosphere and model how we deal with our own schema activations and resulting modes. There is a saying about raising children: "No matter what you tell a child, they will do as you do anyway." The same is true in the very difficult reparenting therapy phase especially with clients with AN: cognitive discussions won't help. It is important for the therapist to address the client's *VCh* (and later, *AnCh*) mode as they would address a child that they really love and care about. This is the most promising way to create a healing atmosphere that is able to melt the frozen *DetPr* walls. In the following we introduce some techniques that may assist with reaching this goal.

### a) Therapist self-disclosure of feelings towards the "Inner [Critic] dictator"

You can use this technique relatively early in therapy because it is comparatively safe if you apply it in the standing position. After putting the client's coping mode, the child mode, and the critic mode on their respective chairs, the therapist starts: "*Ok, we already know that behind the front-stage coping modes there are active beliefs and emotions, even though we might not have directly worked with them yet. It is exactly the job of the protecting coping modes to hide this inner world from other people, including me. But as a therapist I know that behind every person's frontstage, there is also a backstage. If you agree, I would like to share my hypotheses with you about what is going on down there inside [client's name, let's say 'Mary']".* If the client agrees, the therapist continues: *"I feel there is a very powerful and smart Demanding Critic mode voice inside of Mary. It has really achieved a lot in the past and I understand that it has a very strong position inside her head. I don't want to judge if its intentions are good or bad. I just want to look at the effects. It seems to me that in the past this mode might have done too much of a good thing. Like leaders that become dictators, they tend to lose contact with the needs of the people they are responsible for. Then the people start to suffer and have to pay the price for the overly ambitious goals of the dictators. But the dictators don't want to acknowledge that and keep on pushing. It seems to me as if Mary is in a situation like that because things have become a bit out of balance. Does that make sense to you?"* Once the client basically buys into that picture, you can try to propose an alternative goal: *"When a person begins to suffer [name some symptoms here] and the dictator refuses to take this into account, we might look for a better government. What do you think if the two of us try to revise the dictator's agenda and look for a sustainable solution for the person down there [pointing at the child mode chair] instead of slowly driving her to death? I want you to be the head of this new government and I will consult you with all I know. How does that sound?"*

### b) Inducing perspective change by using substitution technique

Interestingly many clients care much better for other people than for themselves. Instead of discussing this phenomenon on a cognitive level we can use a technique on the process level we called "substitution technique" (Roediger, Stevens & Brockman, 2018). When standing up together you "replace" the client's child mode with a real person taken from the client's life, e.g. a true child or another person the client likes very much. Then ask the client how it makes them feel seeing the critic mode (or "dictator") treating this person the way it treats the child modes. Usually this creates some irritation within the client because they will never treat anybody else this way. Now you can dig deeper asking questions like: *"How does it make you feel seeing [the other person's name] in this situation? Can you imagine doing this to her in real life? What would it mean if you were to do it in real life? How would people react seeing you treating [other person's name] this way? Do you think they are right? Looking from the outside now: What is different between your child mode and the other person?"* Once you have induced some ambiguity within the client, you can start looking for an alternative agenda as described at the end of the previous section, heading towards some kind of behavioural experiment.

It is important to leave as much control as possible in the client's hands and limit behavioural experiments (like eating plans). Although schema therapists prefer being the "nice guy", especially with rigid clients we have to balance support with good skills in empathic confrontation and sometimes limit setting too. Thus, client and therapist have to agree on some "objectives" (in terms of measurable) thresholds (e.g. a weight gain) as a kind of "reality check". If the goal is not reached, this makes it easier for the therapist to move to the next step of a pre-agreed treatment plan (e.g. stricter management). After a failed experiment this next step is less a punishment than a consequence that the client agreed to beforehand. Progress in terms of weight gain is slower than in conventional feeding programs, but there is greater potential for lasting change. This approach is less confrontational than fighting the critic modes directly through chairwork. However, it is possible to proceed with doing so later, once the client buys into the therapy more.

### c) Addressing the "hidden" child sitting behind the Detached Protector

Some clients may block you out and prevent you from accessing their child modes. Therefore, we describe an additional technique that is about addressing the limitations of therapy which may ultimately lead to ending it, or changing the setting (e.g. into a conventional feeding program). The therapist remains in the face-to-face position, but adds an additional chair for the hidden child mode behind the client, who sits in the *DetPr* chair. The therapist addresses the hidden child mode, whilst leaning slightly to the side, as if they were talking to a real person sitting on the empty chair behind the *DetPr* chair (see Figure 13.7).

The therapist starts in a very soft voice, while moving a little closer to the client in the *DetPr* chair: "*Mary, I want to tell you that I know you are there, even if the Protector constantly tells me there is nobody there. I am trying to show you that I understand a little about your feelings of loneliness and desperation, and I would really like to work with you. But I can't blow the Protector wall away. If you have any ideas about how to get in touch with me, I would really appreciate that. Maybe you can draw me a picture, send an email at night or drop a message in any other way you can think of. You should know that I am waiting here for you.*"

If the client shows an interest, the therapist can ask the client to sit on the child mode chair and then move in beside the client, sitting in an additional chair in the reparenting position, asking how it feels when the therapist over there talks this way (pointing at the empty therapist chair on the other side). We constantly change positions in order to destabilise the client's *Protector* modes. If all of this doesn't work, we suggest that the

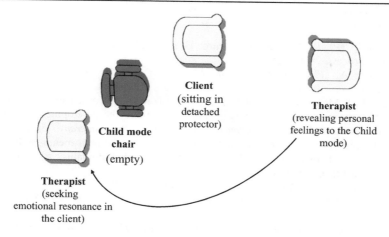

*Figure 13.7* Chair position for therapist self-disclosure

therapist can express their deep sadness, whilst informing the client that we cannot continue in this way – that we will need to change the therapeutic setting (e.g. to a day- or in-patient unit) unless they can learn to start to trust us and collaborate. Colluding with a dysfunctional system by going along with it, may only serve to reinforce these self-destructive patterns. Nevertheless, we can "leave a foot in the door", and continue to reach out and offer a hand to both the *HA* and the *VCh* whenever they do make an appearance.

### Conclusions

This chapter aimed to increase therapists' understanding as to why clients with EDs are so challenging and can deeply trigger our own schemas. We tried to shed some light on our side of the process and how we are at risk of further increasing the likelihood of therapy failing. Stepping out requires a good deal of self-reflection and self-disclosure. Not every therapist is willing to do this, but we believe that without this they will struggle to bypass the client's well organised coping and *Inner Critic* modes and to connect with their child modes on a deep emotional level. We have also provided some strategies for dealing with the specific challenges of working with eating difficulties. This included a general roadmap of how to guide the process, and a tool-box with specific techniques that can be tailored to particular behaviours, and guide the next steps you can take. We hope these suggestions contribute to future successful therapeutic endeavours.

## References

Anderson, T. (1987). The reflecting team: Dialog and meta-dialog in clinical work. *Family Process*, 26(4), 415–428.

Antonovsky, A. (1987). *Unraveling the Mystery of Health – How People Manage Stress and Stay Well*. San Francisco: Jossey-Bass Publishers.

Bamber, M., & McMahon, R. (2008). Danger—early maladaptive schemas at work! The role of early maladaptive schemas in career choice and the development of occupational stress in health workers. *Clinical Psychology and Psychotherapy*, 15(2), 96–112.

Boston Change Process Study Group (2008). Forms of relational meaning: Issues in the relations between the implicit and reflective-verbal domains. *Psychoanalytic Dialogues*, 18(2), 125–148.

Bowlby, J. (1969). *Attachment and Loss*. New York: Basic Books.

De Shazer, S. (1985). *Keys to Solution in Brief Therapy*. New York, NY: WW Norton & Co.

Farrell, J. M., & Shaw, I. A. (2017). *Experiencing Schema Therapy from the Inside Out: A Self-Practice/Self-reflection Workbook for Therapists*. New York: Guilford Press

Gardner, R. A., Sauber, S. R. & Lorandos, D. (2006). *The International Handbook of Parental Alienation Syndrome: Conceptual, Clinical and Legal Considerations*. Springfield, IL: Charles C Thomas Publisher.

Goleman, D. (1995). *Emotional Intelligence*. New York: Bantam.

Greenberg, L. S. (2015). *Emotion Focused Therapy: Coaching Clients to Work through their Feelings*, 2nd edn. Washington, DC: American Psychological Association.

Hatfield, E., Cacioppo, J. T., Rapson, R. L. (1994). *Emotional Contagion*. Cambridge: Cambridge University Press.

Kaeding, A., Sougleris, C., Reid, C., van Vreeswijk, M. F., Hayes, C., Dorrian, J., & Simpson, S. (2017). Professional burnout, early maladaptive schemas, and physical health in clinical and counselling psychology trainees. *Journal of Clinical Psychology*, 73(12), 1782–1796.

Lambert, M. J. (ed.) (2013). The efficacy and effectiveness of psychotherapy. In *Bergin and Garfield's Handbook of Psychotherapy and Behavior Change* (pp. 169–218), 6th edn. Hoboken: Wiley.

Lockwood, G., & Perris, P. (2012). A new look at core emotional needs. In M. van Vreeswijk, J. Broersen, & M. Nadort (Eds.), *The Wiley-Blackwell Handbook of Schema Therapy: Theory, Research, and Practice* (pp. 41–66). Chichester, UK: Wiley-Blackwell.

Millon, T. H. (1990). *Towards a New Personology: An Evolutionary Model*. New York: Wiley.

Panksepp, J. (2011). Cross-species affective neuroscience decoding of the primal affective experiences of humans and related animals. *PLoS One*, 6(9): e21236. doi:10.1371

Roediger, E. (2016). Resource activation through perspective changes: Why don't you just stand up? *Verhaltenstherapie*, 26, 117–123.

Roediger, E., & Laireiter, A.-R. (2013). The schema therapeutic mode cycle in behavior therapy supervision. *Verhaltenstherapie*, 23, 91–99.

Roediger, E., Stevens, B.,& Brockman, R. (2018). *Contextual Schema Therapy: An Integrative Approach to Personality Disorders, Emotional Dysregulation, and Interpersonal Functioning*. Oakland, CA: New Harbinger.

Siegel, D. J. (1999). *The Developing Mind: How Relationships and the Brain Interact to Shape Who We Are*. New York: Guilford Press.

Simpson, S., Simionato, G., Smout, M., van Vreeswijk, M. F., Hayes, C., Sougleris, C., & Reid, C. (2018). Burnout amongst clinical and counselling psychologist: The role of early maladaptive schemas and coping modes as vulnerability factors. *Clinical Psychology & Psychotherapy*.

Yerkes, R. M., & Dodson, J. D. (1908). The relation of strength of stimulus to rapidity of habit-formation. *Journal of Comparative Neurology and Psychology*, 18, 459–482.

Young, J. E., Klosko, J. S., & Weishaar, M. E. (2003). *Schema Therapy: A Practitioner's Guide*. New York: Guilford Press.

Zarbock, G., Lynch, S., Ammann, A., & Ringer, S. (2015). Mindfulness for therapists: Understanding mindfulness for professional effectiveness and personal well-being. London: Wiley-Blackwell.

Zindel, J. P. (2009). Hypnose – eine ganz besondere Beziehung. *Hypnose-ZHH*, 4(1–2), 107–125.

# Chapter 14

# Schema therapy for eating disorders

## Therapist self-care

*Michiel. F. van Vreeswijk and Aglaia Zedlitz*

### Abstract

*The current chapter deals with how to take care of yourself as a therapist for clients with eating disorders (EDs). Due to the challenges of working with this population, which is often characterised by significant suffering and distress in the face of complex and entrenched psychopathology, clinicians may be particularly at risk of suffering from reduced compassion satisfaction, alongside increased compassion fatigue and ultimately burnout. These risks are discussed along with possible solutions, with a focus on personalising options, depending on therapists' own schemas. Two case studies illustrate the dynamics and possible pitfalls and solutions. Knowledge and understanding of our own schemas and modes may thus be helpful in guiding our 'Healthy Adult self' in taking appropriate actions to fulfil our own needs and build resilience and compassion satisfaction.*

## Introduction

Treating clients may bring satisfaction, personal growth and joy but also worries, frustration, social isolation and fatigue. The positive feelings health care professionals experience when helping clients are generally referred to as compassion satisfaction (Stamm, 2005). With compassion satisfaction health care providers benefit vicariously from their clients' therapeutic gains, as they share the positive outcomes and feelings of empowerment (Wagaman, Geiger, Shockley & Segal, 2015). As such, compassion satisfaction is antithetical to compassion fatigue where hopelessness and exhaustion take over. Compassion fatigue may ultimately lead to burnout, in which a person no longer feels that their work efforts matter (Stamm, 2005; Craig & Sprang, 2010). Burnout, compassion fatigue and a reduction of compassion satisfaction are all likely risk factors for therapists who do not take adequate care of themselves. Furthermore, characteristics of the work setting (e.g. difficult client populations including those with EDs, high job demands, reduced autonomy) and personal life stressors (e.g. illness, responsibility for ill family members, financial worries) are additional burdens. In the UK, the Health and Safety Executive (2018) reported that the highest proportion of work related stress, anxiety and depression was found in individuals who work in the human health and social work services. About 2.2% of these professionals reported these psychological problems – almost twice as much as in other industries (HSE, 2018).

Several factors have been found to be associated with increased burnout, compassion fatigue and reduced compassion satisfaction. These risks can be broadly divided into work and personal factors. Norcross and Guy (2007) cluster work and personal risk factors into seven main categories: Client behaviours (e.g. hostility, detachment and severe illness), work-setting (e.g. workload and high expectations), emotional drain (e.g. compassion fatigue), psychological isolation (e.g. lack of opportunity to share, having to set aside your own emotions and needs), therapeutic relationships (e.g. counter-transference, loss of authenticity in working with clients), personal circum-stances (e.g. personal losses and illness) and other stressors (e.g. unrelenting standards, doubts about efficacy of treatment). In the domain of work factors, the use of evidence-based practice seems to decrease the likelihood of burnout and compassion fatigue and increases compassion satisfaction (Craig & Sprang, 2010). Furthermore, less work experience (Craig & Sprang, 2010), working more hours (e.g. more than 40 hours and overtime) and a larger caseload increase the risk of burnout (Warren et al., 2013). Further, there tends to be a higher rate of burnout amongst health care workers treating more severe clients (Warren et al., 2013), which is often the case when work-ing with EDs. The risk of burnout further increases when the work environ-ment is perceived as exceeding one's abilities, when work demands are experienced as uncontrollable and when acknowledgement for positive out-comes is scarce (Warren et al., 2013). In the personal domain, having experi-enced a negative life event in the previous year (Rossi et al., 2012) and absence of a supportive partner (Warren et al., 2013) have both been found to be risk factors for burnout. Interestingly, Warren et al. (2013) found that overcoming an ED yourself may be a protective factor against burnout when working with clients with EDs. Furthermore, higher self-reported emotional intelligence and actively coping with one's own emotions are negatively cor-related with compassion fatigue (Zeidner, Hadar, Matthews & Roberts, 2013).

It is hypothesised that people may be (unconsciously) drawn to occupations and working environments that fit with their maladaptive schemas and maladaptive coping styles (Bamber, 2006; Bamber & Price, 2006). Working in these schema-toxic environments can lead to self-destructive re-enactments for those with severe and rigid schemas. This can then further contribute to the risk of burn-out. In a study of 249 mental health professionals, IT-staff and managers working in NHS-England, almost all schemas were significantly positively related to burn-out. Specifically, *emotional deprivation, subjugation, entitlement* and *emotional inhibition* uniquely contributed to explaining variance in scores in burnout. In a study based on a sample of 1,297 trainee psychologists, burnout was found to be significantly positively correlated with almost all schemas, and significantly predicted by the *unrelenting standards* schema (Kaeding, et al., 2017). Lastly Simpson et al. (2018) found 48% of their sample of 443 psychologists rated moderate to high levels of burnout. The two most common schemas in this sample were *unrelenting standards* and *self-sacrifice* while the two most common maladaptive modes were *Detached Protector* and *Detached Self-soother*. Schemas from the disconnection and rejection domain (*abandonment, mistrust/abuse, emotional deprivation, social isolation and defectiveness/shame*) and the maladaptive mode *Detached Protector* had the highest correlation with burn-out (Simpson, et al., 2018).

The question now is whether there are ways to increase compassion satisfaction, and decrease its counterpart fatigue and the ultimate consequence - burnout. A recent Cochrane review concluded that preliminary studies suggest that cognitive behavioural therapy (CBT) and mental and physical relaxation are both moderately effective interventions on the personal domain (Ruotsalainen, Verbeek, Mariné & Serra, 2015). Moreover, self-compassion and mindfulness have been found to be related to happiness and also to sleep and resilience (Benzo, Kirsch & Nelson, 2017). Self-compassion is the ability to respond to one's failures, shortcomings, and difficulties with kindness and openness rather than criticism. In that regard, self-compassion might be viewed as the *Healthy Adult* mode. Thus, engaging in healthy-adult mindfulness exercises, good self-care and/or physical relaxation might help to increase well-being and resilience. With regard to the work domain, only interventions that focus on changes in work schedules were shown to reduce stress, whereas other organizational interventions did not show such clear effects (Ruotsalainen et al., 2015). In the face of uncontrollable increasing job demands and low rewards, we suggest that a mindful acknowledgement of the situation from the *Healthy Adult* stance, alongside the consideration of taking action (if possible) might be beneficial. Being able to vent your frustrations and build connections with others to adequately view the (im)possibilities of the situation might be achieved by safe peer-supervision sessions. However, these hypotheses come from clinical judgment, and remain to be studied and elucidated.

A schema therapy (ST) approach to self-care emphasises the importance of focusing on identifying and meeting specific needs in accordance with one's own schemas (Lockwood, & Perris, 2012). For those with schemas in the disconnection and rejection domain, it is of paramount importance to address needs for connection and acceptance, by seeking out or creating work environments where co-workers work collaboratively in teams with a safe and healthy team climate. For example, co-workers may invite each other to join in team building activities such as having a lunch or a walk together, whilst ensuring that nobody is left out, even those who are less inclined to join in. In the impaired autonomy and performance domain (schemas: *vulnerability to harm and illness, dependence/incompetence, enmeshment/undeveloped self, failure*) the needs associated with increasing autonomy and performance take a central place. Therapists scoring high on schemas in this domain can benefit from (peer) supervision with a healthy attitude that enables them to stimulate each other to come out of their comfort zone, and give praise for initiative. This setting also provides reassurance regarding the importance of being able to share mistakes without judgement or disapproval. In the other-directedness and overvigilance domains (schemas: *self-sacrifice, subjugation* and *unrelenting standards*) a greater balance between one's own and others' needs should be sought. In personal therapy or coaching, therapists scoring high on these schemas can learn to send away their demanding side and to increase playful activities (enact more from the *Happy Child* mode) in order to find a healthier balance between work and private life. Lastly, in the impaired limits domain (schemas: *entitlement* and *insufficient self-control*) adequate limits should be set, with empathic consideration for others and healthy self-discipline. Therapists scoring high in this domain quite often find it difficult to be challenged by co-workers, bosses, supervisors and coaches and they can be resistant to making changes because they experience learning as boring and feel exposed whenever they express any vulnerability. It can be helpful to gently tease them a little bit by giving them the challenge of trying to be more vulnerable whilst explaining and modelling that it is a sign of inner strength to be able to accept and show your own vulnerability and needs. When they receive regular praise for every (small) step of change, this can gradually help to coax them to move out of their comfort zone.

## Ideas for self-care and personal therapy

In this chapter we present two case-examples to illustrate the risk factors for psychotherapists and how focusing on healthy needs can operate as a guide in self-care and personal therapy.

### Case one: Ann

*Ann is a 32-year-old psychotherapist who has overcome AN in the past herself. Ann's schemas are: emotional deprivation, self-sacrifice and unrelenting standards. Her dominant modes are Perfectionistic Overcontroller, Punitive Parent and Healthy Adult. Being beautiful and well-dressed has always been very important to Ann. She also likes to be in control and complete every task to perfection. After Ann lashes out at a male client with AN who has been in treatment for two years without much progress, her supervisor advises her to seek personal therapy. Reluctantly she starts personal therapy with Catherine, a 40 year old attractive female schema therapist.*

## Case two: Frank

*Frank is a 52 year old clinical psychologist who had a very dominant, authoritarian father, and a passive aggressive mother. Frank was bullied throughout kindergarten and school, right through to studying psychology at the University of Oxford. His schemas are: defectiveness/shame, social isolation and failure and his dominant modes are: Self-Aggrandiser, Healthy Adult and Demanding Parent. Frank has never had a long-term relationship with a woman. He avoids showing his emotions (Vulnerable Child) and talks a lot about how clients like him as a therapist (Self-Aggrandiser). Frank finds himself feeling "stuck" when a 24-year-old female with an ED, after a long period of dependency on him, becomes angry at him for not helping her out of her misery. Frank doesn't know what to do and starts to believe that he is a "loser" as a therapist, who should take early retirement. Frank has trouble telling his friends that he is becoming depressed. He does not want to appear a failure, and thus he withdraws from them. One of his few old college friends notices this, and recommends ST with Marc, a 67-year-old schema-therapist.*

Ann and Frank started treatment, and their cases are described below.

## Case one: Ann

*At the start of Ann's personal ST, her therapist gets the feeling that she is walking on eggshells during sessions; that she is not allowed to approach any closer or to empathetically confront Ann. It takes ten sessions to make a case conceptualisation and carry out diagnostic imagery around schemas, modes and unmet needs (Disconnection and Rejection, and Other Directedness). Following a chair-work technique in which Ann's Demanding/Punitive Parent mode expresses self-criticism from an empty chair, Ann breaks down a little and reveals her Vulnerable Child. It becomes clear that Ann isolates herself from her colleagues as a result of feeling competitive towards them. It becomes clear that this also happens in her relationship with her personal schema therapist. She does not want to feel vulnerable, as her Demanding Parent mode tells her that she has to strive to be better than her therapist; both in her work as in her appearance.*

*In the relationship with her male client, she could not stand it that he did not compliment her for all her hard work and she was utterly frustrated that she could not bypass his Detached Protector sufficiently. She felt that she deserved to be complimented by him for all her hard work trying to connect with him (Ann's emotional deprivation was triggered, and as a result her Demanding Parent mode was activated in this relationship).*

In Ann's personal therapy, her schema therapist (Catherine) chose to raise the issue of the relevance of her own *personal problems* (past ED) in order to explore how her own health-beliefs might be influencing her work. After some initial reluctance and hostility, Ann acknowledged that although her ED was in the past, it may at times increase her vulnerability when treating clients with similar problems. She realised that her feelings of competitiveness with her colleagues and her therapist might actually be linked to her own schemas. Catherine and Ann utilised imagery rescripting in relation to situations in which she felt emotionally invisible. Ann was encouraged to carry out behavioural experiments in which she practiced showing vulnerability to her co-workers, and asking for help. In doing so, her *psychological isolation* subdued and she developed more feelings of connection and self-acceptance. Historical roleplay was used to enable Ann to become aware that her mother had not intentionally neglected her, but was unable to fulfil Ann's childhood needs due to her own mental illness. This was helpful in relation to the discussion around Ann's *therapeutic relationship* with her male client. She became more aware that her client was unable to meet her expectations due to his mental health-difficulties, and that her own dismissive reactions led to further therapeutic detachment. Ann's schema therapist modelled the importance of being authentic in the therapeutic relationship, and also empathetically confronted her to develop greater balance between helping her clients whilst maintaining an awareness of her own boundaries and needs.

### Case two: Frank

*Frank's schema therapist (Marc) collaboratively developed a case conceptualisation in which it became clear that Frank had unmet needs in the domains of disconnection and rejection, and impaired autonomy and performance. They discussed the way in which the "narcissistic triad' of Self-Aggrandizer, Healthy Adult and Demanding Parent was a way in which Frank protected himself against the pain of not feeling accepted, feeling disconnected from others, and lacking a sense of autonomy and success as a therapist. By overcompensating and behaving as though he was better than others and not needing help, pretending that he was mentally and physically super-healthy, he created a self-fulfilling prophecy of shame, isolation and failure.*

Marc discussed the importance of developing a closer therapeutic relationship (*connection and acceptance*) with Frank, whilst anticipating that he might revert to his coping mode "mask" when the therapist tried to reach out for his vulnerability. Frank noted that colleagues referred to this as his excessively cognitive side, characterised by the message: "I am so healthy, I do not need help – you can learn from me as I have all the experience". Marc also predicted that when triggered, Frank might experience him [his therapist] as an authoritarian figure like his father who always told him that he was a failure, and he therefore openly discussed ways of overcoming these potential problems. Marc explicitly reassured Frank that he wanted to connect with little Frank, that he accepted him just the way he was, and that there was no need for him to try to seek approval and prove his worth. Marc asked Frank to help him to look for ways in which they could connect with each other. This was an explicit shared decision, in which Frank was encouraged to take the lead (to address his schemas in the *impaired autonomy and performance domain*). Frank suggested starting treatment with imagery rescripting based on situations with his father and later with regard to his mother. Toward the end of the therapy they also carried out flash-forward imagery rescripting focused on the point in time when Frank planned to retire (i.e. as a potential risk event associated with the fact that Frank's identity was so closely tied up with his role as a therapist). In roleplay, they practiced ways in which his *Healthy Adult* could take care of his own needs in the context of managing relationships with his clients (associated with the *risks of being triggered by specific client behaviours; for example, clients who are demanding, emotionally deprived and make excessive demands on him*). It was essential for Frank to learn that he needed to be in tune with the needs of his own *Vulnerable Child* mode. In behavioural experiments he started asking friends to empathically confront him when he was wearing his narcissistic mask or was withdrawing into himself. He shared details regarding his upbringing with a good friend who responded warmly by also showing his own vulnerability, through telling some of his own life stories.

## Pitfalls and solutions

### Case one: Ann

*The atmosphere at the mental health care institute where Ann worked changed when a new leadership board took over. Therapists were expected to be more flexible with working hours and also to work in the evenings. They were required to see more clients each day by reducing therapy sessions from 50 minutes to 30 minutes. Ann attempted to continue to see all of her clients for 50 minute-sessions, whilst fitting in more new clients by extending her working day to 10 hours per day.*

In personal ST Ann discussed her *work environment* and the danger of *emotional exhaustion* associated with continuing this pattern. These were discussed in relation to her schema activation (*unrelenting standards, self-sacrifice*). The chair technique was used to send away the *Demanding Parent* mode. Ann chose to change jobs and to start working at an institute where she felt more emotional connection with her co-workers and a less demanding attitude (and trigger for her own *Demanding Parent*) from the institute. This was not an easy task due to feelings of concern regarding abandoning her clients, but Catherine encouraged her to take care of herself and to focus on a work life balance in which her needs were met in a healthy way, with more *connection and acceptance* and *balance between her own needs and others.*

### Case two: Frank

*Frank's father became ill and his mother mentioned in a passive-aggressive manner that Frank had never been of use to them. Frank then started to make daily visits to his parents' house.*

While Frank initially coped by reverting to his narcissistic mask (increasing *risk of emotional exhaustion*) by insisting that he could continue to both do the fulltime job at the ED institute whilst taking care of his dying father without any help, he was encouraged by his schema therapist to explore the possibility of part-time work for a couple of months. Frank's boss agreed, bringing a huge sense of relief. He recognised his vulnerability and realised that he wanted to cope differently. He started to share more with friends and by the end of his therapy he had maintained a connected and intimate relationship with a girlfriend for over six months.

### Conclusions

This chapter demonstrates some examples of the way in which self-care can be promoted in the context of personal ST. However, one does not need to attend personal therapy in order to develop self-care. Being aware of schemas and modes associated with underlying unmet needs and being able to access one's *Healthy Adult* mode to assess the risks at work and private life might be sufficient to clear the path for self-care (Lockwood & Perris, 2012; , Lynch, Ammann & Ringer, 2015; Farrell & Shaw, 2017). Supervision and/or peer supervision in which the interactions of schemas and modes between client–therapist and/ or between colleagues can be openly discussed, is another important aspect of self-care. This can also help the growth of a healthy intrapsychic collaboration within the therapist – between the *Healthy Adult, Vulnerable Child, and Happy Child* modes. It is important that we as therapists keep in mind that it is normal and healthy to experience vulnerability, to share our thoughts and emotions with others and that it is healthy to be aware of our own needs even in the context of helping our clients. To be aware that we cannot save all our clients, and that not saving them is not a personal failure, even though we recognise the pain and suffering of those who cannot be cured. It is important to remember that the job of being a therapist is not only a fulfilling one, but also emotionally exhausting and with a high risk of secondary traumatisation. It is therefore important that we practice what we preach: we should first take care of ourselves in a healthy way before taking care of others.

# References

Bamber, M. R. (2006). *CBT for Occupational Stress in Health Professionals: Introducing a Schema-Focused Approach.* London and New York: Routledge.

Bamber, M., & Price, J. (2006). A schema focused model of occupational stress. Chapter 12. In M. R. Bamber (Ed.), *CBT for Occupational Stress in Health Professionals: Introducing a Schema-Focused Approach* (pp. 149–161). London and New York: Routledge.

Benzo, R. P., Kirsch, J. L., & Nelson, C. (2017). Compassion, mindfulness and the happiness of health care workers. *Explore,* 13(3), 201–206.

Craig, C., & Sprang, G. (2010). Compassion satisfaction, compassion fatigue, and burnout in a national sample of trauma treatment therapists. *Anxiety, Stress & Coping,* 23(3), 319–339.

Farrell, J. M., & Shaw, I. A. (2017). *Experiencing Schema Therapy from the Inside Out. A Self-Practice/Self-Reflection Workbook for Therapists.* New York: Guilford Press.

HSE (2018). Work-related stress, depression or anxiety. Retrieved May 2, 2018 from http://www.hse.gov.uk/statistics/causdis/stress/stress.pdf

Lockwood, G., & Perris, P. (2012) A new look at core emotional needs. In M. Van Vreeswijk, J. Broersen & M. Nadort (Eds.) *The Wiley-Blackwell Handbook of Schema-Therapy: Theory, Research and Practice* (pp. 41–66). Chichester: Wiley-Blackwell.

Kaeding, A., Sougleris, C., Reid, C., Vreeswijk, M., Hayes, C., Dorrian, J., & Simpson, S. (2017). Professional burnout, early maladaptive schemas, and physical health in clinical and counselling psychology trainees. *Journal of Clinical Psychology,* 73(12), 1782–1796.

Norcross, J., & Guy, J. (2007). *Leaving it at the Office: A Guide to Psychotherapist Self-care.* New York and London: Guilford Press.

Rossi, A., Cetrano, G., Pertile, R., Rabbi, L., Donisi, V., Grigoletti, L. … Amaddeo, F. (2012). Burnout, compassion fatigue, and compassion satisfaction among staff in community-based mental health services. *Psychiatry Research,* 200(2–3), 933–938.

Ruotsalainen, J. H., Verbeek, J. H., Mariné, A., & Serra, C. (2015). Preventing occupational stress in healthcare workers. *Cochrane Database of Systematic Reviews,* 4, Art. No.: CD002892.

Simpson, S., Simionato, G., Smout, M., van Vreeswijk, M. F., Hayes, C., & Reid, C. (2018). Burnout amongst clinical and counselling psychologists: The role of early maladaptive schemas and coping modes as vulnerability factors. *Clinical Psychology and Psychotherapy,* 26(1), 35-46.

Stamm, B. (2005). The professional quality of life scale: Compassion satisfaction, burnout & compassion fatigue/secondary trauma scales. Retrieved January 15, 2006, from Idaho State University, Institute of Rural Health Web Site: http://www.isu.edu/_bhstamm.

Wagaman, M., Geiger, J., Shockley, C., & Segal, E. (2015). The role of empathy in burnout, compassion satisfaction, and secondary traumatic stress among social workers. *Social Work,* 60(3), 201–209.

Warren, C., Schafer, K., Crowley, M., Olivardia, R., & Hilsenroth, M. J. (2013). Demographic and work-related correlates of job burnout in professional eating disorder treatment providers. *Psychotherapy,* 50(4), 553–564.

Zarbock, G., Lynch, S., Ammann, A., & Ringer, S. (2015). *Mindfulness for Therapists – Understanding Mindfulness for Professional Effectiveness and Personal Wellbeing*. West-Sussex: Wiley-Blackwell.

Zeidner, M., Hadar, D., Matthews, G., & Roberts, R. (2013). Personal factors related to compassion fatigue in health professionals. *Anxiety, Stress & Coping*, 26(6), 595–609.

# Chapter 15

# Schema therapy for eating disorders

## Therapist reflections from implementation of a multisite trial

*Evelyn Smith, Robert Brockman and Claudia Mendez*

## Abstract

*Implementing a psychotherapy trial presents difficulties to even the most seasoned clinical researchers. Implementing a psychotherapy trial in the context of eating disorder (ED) patients presents inherent additional challenges, particularly in a group context. In this chapter, we reflect on and share key lessons learned from implementing a multisite trial of group schema therapy (ST) for EDs. We believe these lessons will have clear implications for those seeking to implement similar schema group programs, and include coverage of some key issues that arose from the assessment phase, through to therapy implementation and follow-up.*

## Background

We conducted six groups of ST for individuals with EDs, promoting a secure space to communicate about their condition, and to attempt some recovery. Each group consisted of five to eight individuals with a diagnosed ED: anorexia nervosa (AN), atypical AN, bulimia nervosa (BN) or binge eating disorder (BED). This was a group of people who experienced high levels of isolation, shame and who had been generally struggling with ED symptoms for many years. Most had reported engaging in psychological treatment in the past, most commonly enhanced cognitive behavioural therapy for EDs (CBT-E), with little improvement in their symptoms. In fact, the study was originally set up as a randomised controlled trial to compare cognitive behavioural therapy (CBT) to ST, but the CBT arm had to be closed early in the process due to the fact that the majority of participants refused to partake in a therapeutic approach which they had already tried. This is likely to be an indication of the level of chronicity, comorbidity, and treatment-resistance in this population.

In the assessment phase, we conducted a diagnostic interview, measured schemas and modes, and followed the clinical protocol (for protocol see Calvert et al., 2018). In the early phase of group therapy, we ensured participants identified their own early maladaptive schemas and coping modes, and understood their function, before intervening by disempowering maladaptive modes and building the *Healthy Adult (HA)* mode. Participants in the groups supported each other in learning how to get their emotional and physical needs met (e.g. connect with *Vulnerable Child (VCh)* and *Angry Child (AnCh)*, fight the *Inner Critic* mode, strengthen the *HA*. We also conducted chairwork and other experiential group exercises that facilitated change. The manual used is summarised in Chapter 10.

## Reflections

### Screening

The selection for group participants ideally should take into account the need for some homogeneity across EMS and eating patterns, whilst balancing this with some heterogeneity in personality style. Clinical experience suggests that groups generally benefit from a mix of interpersonal coping styles. A balance of over-compensatory, surrendering and avoidant coping modes within the group can provide ample openings for interpersonal learning. However, a group composed entirely of participants with avoidant and/or obsessive-compulsive personality traits can lead to high levels of detachment and avoidance, with fewer opportunities for emotional challenging and learning. In our experience, a group that includes a mix of participants who have traits of borderline personality disorder, alongside participants with traits of avoidant and/or obsessive-compulsive personality disorder, can provide more dynamism and group cohesion than a group that is purely in the latter diagnostic grouping. Whilst it can be helpful to include participants with both restrictive and bulimic pathology, it is important that each participant has EMS and eating behaviours that are in common with other group participants. This helps to minimise the chance that any one person will feel significantly 'different' from others in the group, thereby reinforcing any underlying social isolation EMS.

The group should operate as a 'family', whereby differences are valued and have the potential to become opportunities for connection and development of insight. Ideally, the group should also have a similar level of *HA*, as shown by their (in)ability to make healthy choices in order to get their needs met, to regulate difficult emotions and to tolerate discomfort and stress.

Group therapy is particularly useful for client groups who experience significant difficulties associated with interpersonal relationships and disrupted attachment. The group process can be stimulating and challenging for those who may be initially lacking in self-awareness, and those who tend to be emotionally avoidant (Bellak, 1980; Rutan & Alonso 1982). In particular, those whose difficulties are largely egosyntonic may benefit from group work due to the dynamic nature of group interactions, and vicarious learning of new perspectives through observation of and interaction with other group participants. Generally speaking, clients with narcissistic or anti-social personality types should be excluded from groups of this nature. Domineering or dismissive group behaviour can have a destructive influence on the rest of the group, interfering with the potential for other group members to trust and openly work on their own issues, especially if they are not balanced by a strong component of group members who are able to actively engage in the group processes and to take interpersonal risks (AGPA, 2007). Potential group members should be screened to ensure that they possess some potential to engage in the key group processes, including the development of self-awareness, insight, interpersonal connection and learning (Yalom & Leszcz, 2005).

### Assessment

The assessment phase in ST is of key importance in developing both the therapeutic relationship and identifying and understanding schema mode formulation. For the purpose of the research trial, a pre-treatment assessment was conducted by a clinical psychologist or one of the group facilitators (also a clinical psychologist). At treatment onset, this meant that some participants had commenced forming a therapeutic relationship with a facilitator and others had no connection with either facilitator. The importance of having both facilitators involved in the assessment process became clear throughout the process. The therapist not involved in the assessment process lacked the therapeutic relationship and context about each client's schemas. This lack of familiarity led to caution on the part of the therapist in empathic confrontation and limit setting.

### Participants

After the first group, we found that it was important for each group to include a cross-section of ED diagnostic groups. Individuals with AN present with strong *Detached Protector* or *Overcontroller* mode which can be difficult to bypass. A group comprised solely of individuals with a rigid coping mode that is fused to their identity can introduce significant barriers to building connection with participants.

One of the benefits of ST groups lies in the transdiagnostic utility of the model. Connections are built though the exploration of core schema and awareness of emotional triggers. Differences in reactions to schemas are understood through coping modes. Participants' varying ability to demonstrate vulnerability in the group creates opportunities for connections with other participants. Consequently, it was beneficial to include a diversity of diagnoses, schemas and modes within the group. Participants were still able to relate to similar ways of looking at their schemas but different ways of reacting to them (through diversity in coping modes). Participants were mostly very engaged in the ST groups and reported feeling highly validated by the mode model. In evidence of this, only four participants out of 30 dropped out and usually due to changes in work or timing clashes with classes. This is of course a lot lower than group CBT, which can reach up to 50% drop-out (Hay, 2013).

Participants had high levels of comorbidity, including personality disorders, anxiety and mood disorders. Some also struggled with addiction and self-harm and required risk management between sessions.

### Therapists

We found that two therapists were essential to manage the group well. While the use of two therapists is not uncommon in group work, it seems crucial for ST groups. The emotional intensity and sensitivity required throughout the group can leave a solo therapist fatigued. This is especially the case where comorbidity is high, leading to greater complexity and emotional fragility within the group. The varying needs of group participants are difficult to meet by a sole therapist and can lead to missing key opportunities to provide reparenting. Farrell and Shaw (2012), describe the role of a co-therapist team as one that balances individual needs, maintains connection and focuses on the group. Balancing these tasks would be difficult for a sole therapist. Results from a pilot study found effect size in a single therapist group differed to a cotherapist group (Reiss et al., 2014). With this in mind, if two therapists are not available to facilitate a group, one option is to postpone the group for the week. However, a balance needs to be struck between maintaining group continuity, and avoiding triggering of group participants' *abandonment/emotional deprivation* schemas through inconsistencies. Additionally, it must be ensured that both group participants and therapists are not negatively affected by the prolonged (> two sessions) absence of one of the therapists. The first three groups were completely unfunded, and therapists ran the groups pro bono outside their usual work hours. We noticed significant effects in terms of therapist burnout and sickness, leading to disruptions caused by absences and changes in therapists midway through the program. This led to us generating sufficient funding to ensure that subsequent groups were run by therapists who were adequately remunerated for their time. This led to significant improvements in supporting therapists to consistently run groups in a sustainable way.

The therapists work together to keep the focus on the entire group. The group facilitators take the 'parental' role and model interpersonal communication and gentle confrontation. One leads the experiential exercises, the other one observes the group for changes in modes and addresses them as a group, or individually if needed. For example, when one therapist is leading experiential work with a patient, there is always potential for other participants to become vulnerable or detached. The co-therapist plays a key role in aiding the individual patient and/or highlight this to the group, to provide care and attempt to reengage all patients. Whilst at times this may be done individually, it is best done as a group to encourage and strengthen the group bond.

The role of a schema therapist within individual therapy relies on a therapist's ability to provide limited reparenting as an antidote to gaps in early emotional learning. The relationship mirrors that of a parent–child relationship. Through this process, the path towards autonomy is initiated and requires the participant to pursue change outside of the therapy session. This can be a daunting task for patients with a high level of social isolation. This is where group ST provides a unique opportunity for patients to begin to experiment with connection, autonomy and belonging, within a safe environment. Within the group, participants have the opportunity to access learning experiences that go beyond relationships with an individual therapist "parent", to include the peer group. This participant's comment was frequently reiterated by others across the pilot trial: "you're my therapist and to some extent I know you are paid to be kind to me…but when the message comes from other people in the group, in some ways it seems to affect me even more deeply."

This highlights the important role the therapist plays in order to create and maintain safety for participants, and balance the needs of the group. If individual ST is about attachment needs and the therapist meeting these needs through limited reparenting, the focus becomes how to optimally meet the needs of children in early development. The group assists with the next stages of healthy development, that of late childhood, adolescence and adulthood. Here there is a stronger focus on children's need for individualisation, identity formation, healthy autonomy and more equal relationships. The group can provide learning experiences that go beyond relationships with an individual therapist "parent", to include "siblings" and a peer group.

## Manual

Therapists were provided with a comprehensive manual with weekly session plans (Chapter 10). Thoroughness of the manual ensured therapists were put at ease when both preparing for, and facilitating the group. One of the challenges when facilitating the group was the balance between delivering all content outlined and activities outlined versus addressing modes in the room. It was recognised that attempting to cover all of the content could trigger a therapist's own demanding mode, detracting from the session and connection. A key feature of ST lies in the therapist's ability to identify modes and match intervention to the client's mode. This requires a great deal of flexibility from a therapist and knowledge of the various intervention options. The manual is a great resource for therapists as it provides a variety of interventions, but within the group it is best to remain attuned to the patients and weave the activities in as required. This requires the therapist to sit with a level of uncertainty about the sessions, and to choose the content of each session (from the manual) based on the needs of the group rather than a rigidly set order or structure. The therapists and supervisors were required to draw on their own healthy adult side, to find a balance between structure, whilst covering a range of cognitive, experiential, interpersonal and behavioural interventions and most importantly, meeting the needs of the group in an attuned and attentive manner.

### Treatment

The Schema Therapy for EDs Group (STE-g) focused on developing a formulation that addressed the function of ED behaviour. In the group the primary focus was not on the links between eating behaviour, thoughts and feelings in the here and now. By keeping the focus on unmet emotional needs, we addressed ED behaviour without always focusing directly on ED behaviour. However, we did link the eating behaviour to one or more of their modes and set behavioural targets that were linked to reducing eating behaviours linked to coping modes, whilst increasing healthy behaviours that successfully enabled them to get their needs met. For example, if the client was severely restricting, we addressed that as the *Perfectionistic Overcontroller*, and evaluated the role of this mode by providing protection, mastery and a sense of inner coherence for the participant (e.g. usually a participant would feel vulnerable if their controlling mode was not active). The client understood the ED behaviour helped them cope with the deeper schema. This approach bridges separation that a mixed diagnostic group could create. The concept of vulnerability is one that everyone can relate to, but also fear. How patients cope with vulnerability differs. In the group setting both differences and commonalities in coping were proactively highlighted. The group allowed participants to express and develop deeper understanding of their vulnerabilities, with an opportunity to reflect on these.

The egosyntonic nature of the maladaptive schemas and modes were addressed within the group relationship. In the group, there were times when participants with the same schema mirrored beliefs e.g. defectiveness schema in which two people voiced a belief that "other participants deserve compassion". These opportunities added to the corrective experience as it allowed for defusion from the schema. In this situation, therapists allowed participants to make these comments back and forth, and finally brought attention to "how it could be that both participants believe the same thing about themselves and yet can see each other as deserving?" This allows for defusion and reality testing that comes directly from the group process rather than from therapists.

## Sessions

Each group session ran for one and a half to two hours. Each session commenced with review of the past week and a check in on how they were doing. Participants with strong *Detached* and *Avoidant Protector* modes tended to avoid and be unwilling to share. In this case, the time was spent identifying the coping mode and using empathic confrontation to encourage engagement. Each participant was encouraged to share something challenging over the week.

At times a participant would detach during the course of an activity. *Detached Protector/Overcontroller* modes prevented emotional processing from taking place, highlighting that participants were at times avoiding painful emotions. The therapists aimed to re-connect detached participants with the underlying emotion. Their goal was to remain emotion focused in order to promote connection with *vulnerable child* mode. At these junctures, the aim was not to present cognitive information that would reinforce avoidant coping by pulling participants further away from their emotional state and into reasoning/analysing. When a participant shifted into *Vulnerable Child* mode, the therapists aimed to keep them there, through attunement to their current emotional state, and providing reparenting sentiments linked to their unmet needs and schemas.

Scarfs were placed around the room. When participants were observed to be in *Detached Protector* mode the scarf could be used as a reminder to connect with their vulnerable side in order to bring them back to connect with the group. When participants shifted into their *vulnerable child* mode mode, others used scarfs to connect with that group member and remind them that the group cared about them. The group as a whole took responsibility for the scarfs. Across all groups, therapists made consistent efforts to remind participants how important they were to the group and to each person's recovery. For example, when a participant's aunt passed away and she missed some sessions, the group members used their cameras to send messages of support. When participants were in hospital or interstate, we used Skype to ensure they could be included in the session. Features of the group augment ST techniques by allowing participants to experience validation/support and a safe place to experiment with emotional expression and new behaviours with peers. The program included psychodrama, chair work and imagery rescripting activities modified to incorporate the whole group. The aim of all of these techniques was to connect with participants' *Vulnerable Child* modes, and also to help them to begin to internalise their own *HA* self. Imagery related activities were the most difficult to implement in the group setting as participants were more likely to revert to their coping modes and detach, so this was also prioritised in individual sessions. The chair work activities, which allowed group participation was active and engaging.

*Happy Child* activities were essential to bond the group and provided positive memories of an experience shared with peers. This functioned as an antidote for unmet needs for joy and spontaneity, and a non-threatening way of "loosening-up" rigid coping modes – especially the *Perfectionstic Overcontroller*. These activities happened mostly at the beginning of sessions, and they allowed participants to see the therapists as genuine. Although it was considered important to work with pain and suffering during sessions, it was important to strike a balance with engaging in joy and play as an important way to connect to child modes. The value of happy child activities cannot be overlooked. It is easy to become focused on the "heavier" change work. It was important for the therapist to balance the emotional work with activities that create joy in order to provide corrective emotional experiences and memories that participants could internalise, as part of their own emotional development and growth. The *happy child* activities at the conclusion of the group helped participants cope with the anxiety and fear that comes with ending a therapeutic group. This assisted participants to create a positive end to the group and encouraged celebration of the emotional risks they had taken and bonds formed, leaving with some corrective experiences.

The group program allowed for four opportunities for individual sessions. We had some questions we reflected on in the next section: Is there an optimal combination of group and individual sessions? What services were appropriate at follow up? Participants in the group were not financially able to afford ongoing treatment, but not deemed suitable for public health services. For those who required further follow-up due to the need for trauma processing (i.e. regarding childhood sexual abuse), there was a distinct lack of treatment services equipped for working with significant comorbidity and trauma alongside EDs. Many participants were encouraged to attend follow up sessions through GP mental health care plans. Participants were provided with a list of schema therapists who operated locally, so that they could pursue further therapy if required.

### Dosage matters

We believe that the dosage of ST for many of the study participants was likely too small. While we observed positive changes in many, we suspect that for around half of our participants, 25 sessions of group therapy and four individual sessions was insufficient to adequately challenge and fight the schemas at the root of the eating symptoms. We suspect that some participants, perhaps those with the most chronic EDs (alongside other comorbidities), which was the predominant type of client recruited to this study, would have benefited more if 25 sessions of both individual and group were incorporated into the treatment. Some participants appeared to benefit greatly from the individual sessions as a safe space to reflect on their own issues, which they could not initially disclose within the group, and some only started to feel comfortable disclosing in the last sessions. This is a testament to the strength and rigidity of the coping modes characteristic of this population, in particular the *Perfectionistic Overcontroller* and *Detached Protector* modes. These modes are often fused with identity, and become reinforced by family and wider systems. Similar findings from other studies suggest that perfectionism is a trait that appears to be resistant to short-term therapies in general (Aguera et al., 2012; Cassin & von Ranson, 2005; Segura-Garcia et al., 2013). The strength of these coping modes is also likely to play a role in the poor outcomes in general for AN across a range of treatment models, and the relatively high levels of relapse with bulimic/binge eating populations (Agras et al., 2000; Khalsa et al., 2017; Zerwas et al., 2013).

### Know your own stuff

It is our perception that running these groups is both very rewarding but also challenging. On reflection and in supervision, we observed that due to the complexity of this population, and the strong emotional focus, these groups could be triggering for group facilitators, and that at these times it can be very helpful for the second facilitator to be ready to step in and continue with the group. In this way, the therapist dynamic can be a great strength for the group, but can also be detrimental. We observed on a few occasions, problematic dynamics between therapists that would be likely to lead to suboptimal outcomes (e.g. two therapists fusing with a demanding mode; different styles of facilitation; and therapists' overcontroller modes leading to competitiveness). For these reasons, we think supervision is of prime importance, to facilitate awareness of therapists' own schemas and coping styles, and the interaction and dynamics that emerge between therapists. Optimally, this dynamic should be harnessed to model *HA* modes, and promote corrective experiences for the group. We believe that given the demanding nature of these emotion-focused groups, and the importance of moment-to-moment awareness of both group-participants' and therapists' own responses, some form of self-therapy is likely to be beneficial in order to promote therapist self-reflection and to facilitate connection to their own *HA* self throughout the group program (Bennett-Levy, 2018).

### References

AGPA (American Group Psychotherapy Association) (2007). Practice guidelines for group psychotherapy: The American group psychotherapy association science to service task force. Available from: https://www.agpa.org/home/practice-resources/practice-guidelines-for-group-psychotherapy

Agras, W. S., Walsh, B. T., Fairburn, C. G., Wilson, G. T., & Kraemer, H. C. (2000). A multicenter comparison of cognitive-behavioral therapy and interpersonal psychotherapy for bulimia nervosa. *Archives of General Psychiatry*, 57(5), 459–466.

Aguera, Z., Krug, I., Sanchez, I., Granero, R., Penelo, E., Penas-Lledo, E., ... Fernandez-Aranda, F. (2012). Personality changes in bulimia nervosa after a cognitive behaviour therapy. *European Eating Disorders Review*, 20, 379–385.

Bellak, L. (1980). On some limitations of dyadic psychotherapy and the role of the group modalities. *International Journal of Group Psychotherapy*, 30(1), 7–22.

Bennett-Levy, J. (2018). Why therapists should walk the talk: The theoretical and empirical case for personal practice in therapist training and professional development. *Journal of Behavior Therapy and Experimental Psychiatry*.

Calvert, F., Smith, E., Brockman, R., & Simpson, S. (2018). Group schema therapy for eating disorders: study protocol, *Journal of Eating Disorders*, 6(1).

Cassin, S. E., & von Ranson, K. M. (2005). Personality and eating disorders: A decade in review. *Clinical Psychology Review*, 25, 895–916.

Farrell, J. M., & Shaw, I. A. (2012). *Group Schema Therapy for Borderline Personality Disorder: A Step-by-step Treatment Manual with Patient Workbook*. Chichester: Wiley-Blackwell

Hay, P. (2013). A systematic review of evidence for psychological treatments in eating disorders: 2005–2012. *International Journal of Eating Disorders*, 46(5), 462–469.

Khalsa, A., Portnoff, L., McCurdy-McKinnon, D., & Feusner, J. (2017). What happens after treatment? A systematic review of relapse, remission, and recovery in anorexia nervosa. *Journal of Eating Disorders*, 5, 20.

Reiss, N., Lieb, K., Arntz, A., Shaw, I. A., & Farrell, J. (2014). Responding to the treatment challenge of patients with severe BPD: results of three pilot studies of inpatient schema therapy. *Behavioural and Cognitive Psychotherapy*, 42(3), 355–367.

Rutan, J. S., & Alonso, A. (1982). Group therapy, individual therapy, or both? *International Journal of Group Psychotherapy*, 32(3), 267–282.

Segura-Garcia, C., Chiodo, D., Sinopoli, F., & De Fazio, P. (2013). Temperamental factors predict long-term modifications of eating disorders after treatment. *BMC Psychiatry*, 13, 288.

Yalom, I., & Leszcz, M. (2005). *The Theory and Practice of Group Psychotherapy* (5th ed.). New York, NY: Basic Books.

Zerwas, S., Lund, B., Von Holle, A., Thornton, L., Berrettini, W., Brandt, H., ... Bulik, C. (2013). Factors associated with recovery from anorexia nervosa. *Journal of Psychiatric Research*, 47, 972–979.

# Chapter 16

# Finding and reparenting the *Lonely Child* behind the *Anorexic Overcontroller*

## David Edwards

### Abstract

*This naturalistic clinical case study describes the assessment and treatment of Linda who presented with anorexia nervosa (AN) and major depression. Her early maladaptive schemas (EMSs), including* emotional deprivation, abandonment, defectiveness, *and* failure, *had their origins in a history that featured maternal unpredictability and depression, childhood illnesses and family conflicts. These painful early experiences were shut down by several coping modes, most prominent of which was an overcompensatory eating disordered mode (*Anorexic Overcontroller*). Cognitive-behaviour therapy (CBT) methods alone had limited impact. A schema therapy (ST) conceptualisation and emotion imagery and dialogue work focused on understanding and reparenting her* Vulnerable Child, *and working with the conflict between her* Healthy Adult *and the* Anorexic Overcontroller. *Therapy ended when Linda relocated. It is argued that the ST conceptualisation and the experiential work based on it, created a platform for healing which, had it been followed up, constituted a meaningful path towards further resolution. The clinical material reveals the complexities of the underlying mode structure in an eating disorder. It highlights how automatically the* Anorexic Overcontroller *coping was activated to shut down the emotional pain at the EMS level and points towards ways in which a ST approach can address deeply ingrained automatic patterns.*

## Linda: Developmental origins and diagnostic features

This naturalistic case study of the therapy of Linda (20)[1] demonstrates the underlying mode structure often found in eating disorders (EDs), with a prominent overcompensatory eating disordered mode shutting out painful emotions within various child modes (see Edwards, 2017a and b for a systematic analysis of this case) and shows how steps were taken to access childhood memories and initiate a process of healing. Linda had significant depressive episodes at ages 10 and 13 and first saw a therapist at 17, in her last year of high school after being diagnosed with diabetes mellitus, a condition that increases the risk for developing an ED and also increases treatment resistance (Rodin et al., 2002). She reported feeling too self-conscious to wear a swimming costume and induced vomiting to control her weight. At age 19, after changing courses in her second year at university, far from home, she described the unhappiness she felt as "going through hell". She implemented strict food rules and by the mid-year vacation her body mass index (BMI) had fallen to 16.3. Her parents made it a condition of her continuing at university that she get psychological help. Over the next 15 months, I saw her for 42 sessions while she finished her degree, before moving to undertake postgraduate study in another city.

Linda was born after a long, hard labour, and Linda's mother seems to have been depressed and short tempered subsequently. When the baby was given to her, she "couldn't handle it", and her limited tolerance must have been further stretched by Linda's severe colic. Two years later, after her sister was born, Linda was hospitalised several times with asthma. Her mother continued to experience uncontrolled anger and at times would grab Linda and shake her. At age five, Linda fell out of a tree but when her mother came to help, Linda angrily pushed her away. Around age eight, she recalled compensatory daydreams, for example about "my wedding", and commented, "I lived in this other world". When Linda was nine, her mother, who was also working, started studying again and Linda felt neglected by her. She coped by being responsible, independent and a role model to her peers.

When not under pressure, Linda's mother provided attention, care, appropriate guidance, and support. Their relationship changed when she was 16, and they would regularly chat comfortably together about everyday experiences and concerns. Currently Linda was experiencing her mother as consistently supportive. In childhood, Linda had experienced her father as reliable and stable, "like a rock", but he was strict, gruff, unaffectionate, private and rational, and she was frustrated that he could not give her the affection she longed for. This relationship had also changed. She now recognised that he cared about her, even though he had not expressed it clearly, and they were developing a meaningful relationship.

During the previous two years, Linda had met criteria for bulimia nervosa (BN), but with the increased restricting of food, her BMI had dropped to 16.3 so that she met criteria for AN, purging type. In the two months after, under pressure from her parents and motivated to be allowed to return to her studies, she had gained some weight and her BMI was 17.0 when I assessed her. She also met criteria for major depressive disorder (recurrent, severe) with a score of 46 on the Beck Depression Inventory (BDI-II). She was also highly anxious with a Beck Anxiety Inventory (BAI) of 26 related to worrying about not being able to catch up with her academic work.

## Therapy, phase 1 (S1–S22 and inpatient treatment): Laying a foundation

Linda quickly formed a trusting collaborative relationship with me. She was vulnerable and tearful during most of the second session as we reviewed her life and the history of her ED. Initially, I provided psychoeducation about AN, that included reading on anorexia and the effects of starvation. I introduced a standard CBT approach to address the factors maintaining her behaviour, which she experienced as credible. I gradually introduced a ST conceptualisation from session nine (S9[2]) where I discussed the results of the Young Schema Questionnaire-Short form (YSQ-S). In S16, there was a short chairwork dialogue between two parts. Sad Linda (her *Vulnerable Child: VCh*) was able to say, "I am your sadness and I am hidden away, not able to be expressed. I am hidden so you can be strong, function and carry on." The other part, responded, "I am ashamed of you, afraid of not being normal [if I let you be seen]." We called this "Strong Linda," an overcompensator whose nature would emerge more clearly later. Sad Linda countered that she was "tired of hiding, tired of putting up a facade, of meeting others' expectations. Without me you will lose touch with the feeling side of you." Strong Linda retorted: "You have to function, get your degree…" In S18, her *VCh* was able to say, "Recognize me, I am not selfish," and I could empathise with how lonely, unappreciated, ashamed and scared she felt. During this phase we also identified what seemed to be *Demanding Parent (DemP)* and *Punitive Parent (PP)* voices. There was also a *Rebellious Child (RebCh)* who was "tired of being structured" and rebelled against demands or rules (e.g. by deliberately binging and eating non-diabetic foods), a *Detached Self-Soother (DetSS)* who would comfort eat, a *Healthy Adult (HA)* who could keep a balanced perspective, and a *Happy Child* who could be playful and have fun. I call this the *Authentic Child* as it is the source of spontaneity and self-direction, so it is abbreviated here to "*HAC*."

After 13 sessions focused on assessment and CBT, her depression had largely remitted (BDI-II=11) and her BMI of 21 was normal. But after a break at home for the summer vacation, her depression was again severe (BDI-II=40). She was preoccupied with her appearance, her clothes feeling too tight, afraid to look people in the eye due to shame and inducing vomiting up to seven times daily. I worked with her on reality testing. She recalled photos of herself in her first year having a good time with peers. I encouraged her to deliberately look people in the eye as an anti-shame exercise, and we worked on how the thought that she could vomit was acting as a permission-giving belief for binging. CBT work on controlling the vomiting and restricting had limited impact and she still binged on non-diabetic foods. So, after S22, she voluntarily entered a six-week inpatient program. She benefitted from structured work on meal planning and was able to get control of her vomiting in the hospital and on weekend home visits. On her return her BMI was 24.

## Therapy, phase 2 (S23-S31): CBT and case conceptualisation

S23 to S27 continued the CBT work to consolidate these gains, and chairwork and mode dialogues clarified a ST case conceptualisation. At assessment, there were high scoring items on the YSQ-S on several schemas: *emotional deprivation, abandonment, defectiveness/shame, emotional inhibition, mistrust/ abuse, social isolation, failure, subjugation, insufficient self-control, recognition-seeking, self-punitiveness and unrelenting standards.* These are consistent with her experiences of inconsistency, punitiveness, disappointment and neglect in very early childhood, with her latent sense of unmet needs, and her development of several ways of coping: avoidant, surrender and overcompensating. The mode map in Figure 16.1 was constructed post hoc (at the time I used cards with the names and descriptions of the main modes). It incorporates some insights that emerged from the more intense experiential work in phase three. Subsequently I conducted a formal Interpretative Phenomenological Analysis (Edwards, 2017a, 2017b). Figure 16.1 includes a key to the abbreviations used for each mode.

I was already conceptualising the *Anorexic Overcontroller (A-OC)* as a distinctive mode, that had developed from her *Perfectionist Overcontroller (P-OC)*, with a specialised focus on diet and body mass. It is what I now call a complex composite coping mode, because it is a coherent system that incorporates several distinct elements working together.

Support for this and other aspects of this case conceptualisation came from a dream she reported in S28. In the first scene, her aunt, whom she experiences as very intrusive, and her uncle and female cousin, are present. Her parents are arguing and Linda feels "anxious and very stressed...like it's almost my fault or ...I need to decide and I need to make right decisions...I don't know what I've done or what I did but...sometimes I just think I add to the burden." This dramatised the interpersonal world of self-centred, critical, quarrelsome and competitive family members in which her EMSs formed, a *VCh* subjected to invalidation and experiencing intense distress. She recalled how she had felt she was walking on egg shells when her mother was short-tempered.

In a second scene of the dream, Linda stands on a scale. It starts as "a little black scale and then it just turned into...like a computery thing" with blue flashing lights and a voice that reported her weight and what needed to be done. Her cousin stood on it and was told she was the perfect weight. Linda, by contrast, was told she was overweight and given a list of body parts she must work on. The scale vividly portrayed the composite elements of her *A-OC* mode: the promise that if she could get her weight right she would be perfect/acceptable like her cousin, the self-imposed rules about her body mass and shape, and the punitive self-blaming and shaming that enforced those rules and motivated her to restrict. In S29, she would describe shaming warnings (part of the *A-OC* system): vivid images of various parts of her

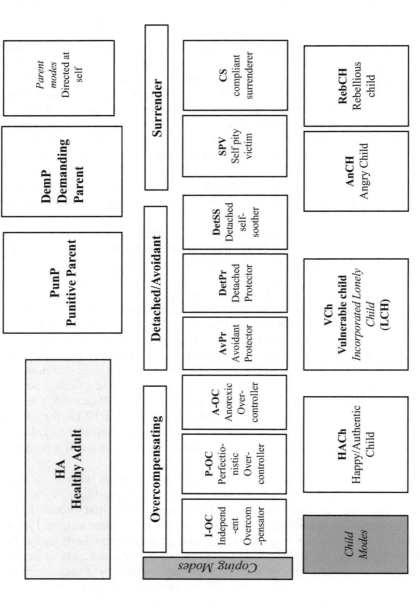

Figure 16.1 Linda's mode map

body that she experienced after binging. These included "extra skin and flab around your stomach and eyes and a double chin", and thighs with "no muscle definition and there's like cellulite build-up". "I can almost see myself not fitting into my clothes", she said.

In a third scene of her dream, her mother told Linda she could take a break from studying or even drop her degree if she wanted to. This was like her mother now, allowing her to make her own decisions and meet her own needs. This represented a path to resolution: an emerging compassionate self-acceptance, something I had been highlighting in the past few sessions.

In S29, Linda reported she was skipping parts of her diet plan and, while studying for a test, could not concentrate, distracted by urges to eat. When she looked at what would happen if she did go and eat, she was afraid of the self-critical and shaming voice (part of the *A-OC mode*). She spontaneously described how she could hear this "police person, yelling and saying, 'How could you let this happen?'" I pointed out that *A-OC* is like a dictator who maintains power by lying to and terrorising people. I encouraged her to find a *HA* voice, but although she could make a *HA* case there was little power or conviction.

Asked to picture these two sides, she saw her *HA*, as a woman who is "just normal, like she's comfortable but well-posed. She stands tall and is proud and...soft and gentle but rational and logical and...she doesn't under-dress or over-dress." By contrast, "The dictator side...is thin...and... always scowling and frowning and with long fingers able to pinpoint... scolding, and sometimes she even has a whip....She's often dressed in black...with high heels or skirts and is over-dressed and very professional and classy,...like a polished look but untouchable." This image portrays the different facets of the *A-OC* including its judgmental punitiveness and contempt for the *VCh*. When I asked how the *Overcontroller* started, she remembered, as a child, having to cope with "fear of not doing stuff right and getting into trouble all the time and getting scolded...You just want to please your parents...but everything you do is either wrong or not appropriate." This raises the question of the relationship between the *A-OC* and the *PP*. Her memories of being scolded are the source of *PP* messages which are understood to be an introject, and therefore not a part of the self. However, these messages can later be recruited by a coping mode to further its objectives as when Linda's *A-OC* scolded her for breaking the food rules. The messages had become part of the self and cannot just be sent away (Edwards, 2017b).

Asked to bridge back from the feeling, she remembered how, aged six or seven, in a conflict, her mother "would always have the last say" and she (Linda) would suppress her anger and hurt (*Angry Child – AnCh; Detached Protector – DetPr*) and walk away (*Avoidant Protector – AvPr*). She also coped by keeping busy (*DetSS*), and being self-sufficient and independent (*Independent Overcompensator – I-OC*). As she put it, anyone looking at her would think, "This girl is strong and is managing everything." But they would also see someone who was "so serious all the time, she can't...have fun, ...can't take a joke." She focused on doing well at school, *P-OC* coping that later provided the basis for the specialised *A-OC*.

She articulated the *A-OC*'s claim, that "if you look...thin, and if you can get everything under control and be strict enough on yourself then you will be pretty or beautiful or acceptable...you will have more fun and other people will want to spend more time with you." When we reality test this, Linda recognised it was untrue. When she had AN, she was desperately unhappy. I asked, "Which of these two [*HA or A-OC*] is going to best take care of you now?" Linda answered, "The *Healthy Adult*. She's just warmer and more inviting. And she's not a pushover, she's strong but she's compassionate as well." I asked if the *VCh* could ask the *HA* for help, and later she reported: "the *Healthy Adult*...takes my [i.e. the *VCh*'s] hand first and leads me and then bends down and hugs me and comforts me, ...and explains to me but listens to me as well. And she goes on one knee and is at eye-level with me and really takes to heart the things that I feel and I have to say because they're important.... And then the control side [*A-OC*] is by herself." In S31 she displayed good insight into her modes and how they functioned in her life as we reviewed them using cards with the names and descriptions of the main ones.

## Therapy phase 3 (S32-S35): Finding and reparenting the *Lonely Child*

In S32, Linda reported eating non-diabetic foods and inducing vomiting to return her blood sugar to a safe level. Her *RebCh* was behind this. She is about five years old, "young enough to be aware of things happening around me – and just wanting time and attention and competing with my sister." Asked to express it, she said, "I want to be noticed. And I want to do what I want, when I want, and I don't want any rules and I...don't even want consequences....I hate having to be responsible...having to think of things in advance." Her *VCh* is scared to disappoint her mother or express her true feelings. She feels unimportant, does not expect her mother to "see things from my angle" and is trying not to be "any kind of burden or inconvenience." This defectiveness/shame had generalised to all her relationships; she expected everyone to think there was something wrong with her and this was being re-enacted as all her friends in the house knew that she had BN.

From her *HA*, she could tell the child she was loved and valued. She said, without prompting, "You have worth, you deserve to be given attention and...taken seriously,...to be loved and...have fun,...and not be yelled at for it, or be scared to have friends over. It's okay to be upset or...confused and you don't have to think of everything all the time in advance...you don't have to be the adult." The caring message evoked her *Authentic Child* (*HAC*), and she saw an image of herself in primary school, a child who was "allowed to be a child" and who felt carefree, "just knowing there's nothing wrong with you at all." I spoke of how, as a little girl, she had tried to make sense of how she was being treated, particularly by her mother, and had concluded that there was something wrong with her. In response to my prompting, Linda spoke to her mother: "I'm only five years old and you are just neglecting me and snapping at me, but actually there's nothing wrong with me as a person." She saw the little girl standing taller.

Her mother appeared relieved and remorseful for not having cared for her properly. I asked if she could forgive her. Linda responded, "I don't agree with the things that you did or how you behaved sometimes or treated us children...I didn't know you were trying to do your best and that you love us, and that you love me, and I can forgive you." The impact of this was remarkable; it seemed to free her to develop her own autonomy. She felt "a lot lighter, almost like separating, like being able to be more independent and to be more free [rather] than having...this tie, this rope between you and your Mom the whole time." After this I sensed her deep sadness, mourning for a childhood lost because of the lack of consistent care. Her mother had told her not to "dwell on the past", but I affirmed that a mourning process is part of letting go of the past, so she could move into the future and into new relationships.

In S33, we looked at several of her modes. When I weighed her, she was angry that her BMI was 22.5: "I'd be much happier if I was thinner." This is an *A-OC* response. On request, she could express an *HA* position: "I can be happy just as I am...learning to be content where I am now; and plus...you're recovering from that. You don't want to go back there [i.e. to having AN]." She also reported being more flexible, relaxing some food rules (e.g. eating cheese). Later, she connected to her *DetSS* mode: "I definitely use food as a soother [for] anything that I want comfort for." This mode "just ignores the responsibility, almost tunes it out for that time." Linda recalled how she learned this as a little girl.

We identified sequences of modes. There's an *Angry Child (AnCh)* – *Avoidant Protector (AvProt)* sequence: annoyed with the other students in the house who were untidy and made accommodation plans for next year without involving her, she withdrew to her room, and worked alone. In hospital, she had fallen behind with her academic work. Her *P-OC* coping set such high standards that her *VCh* who felt alone and hopeless, unable to cope with the responsibility and unmotivated to study. She withdraws socially (*AvProt*) and feels alone (*Lonely Child – LCh*). Her *DetSS* comes to the rescue. It teams up with the *RebCh* and she binges on non-diabetic foods. Then her *A-OC* kicks in with critical, scolding messages and she feels alone and ashamed (*VCh*). This long sequence can be summarised as: *P-OC* – *VCh* (alone, hopeless) –*AvProt* – *LCh* – *DetSS* + *RebCh* (Comfort eat/Binge) – *A-OC* – *VCh* (shamed, lonely).

As we looked at this, I could feel her *LCh* palpably and we considered how the attention she received when she had anorexia nervosa was not the kind that met the *LCh*'s needs. I explained how, in ST, by acknowledging and caring for the *LCh* we could interrupt the shift to the self pity/victim (SPV) and other dysfunctional coping modes. As she learned to do this for herself, she would be building a *HA* that could attend to the needs of the *LCh* and make self-enhancing rather than self-defeating decisions. She understood this. When I asked her, "Can you recover without going back to that Lonely Child and taking care of her?" she replied, "No, because then I'll have those feelings, and I can't move forward without actually feeling it and experiencing it."

This process deepened her connection to the *LCh*. Asked what she was feeling, she said, "It's sore and it hurts my heart...and...all these questions come up...Are you worth love? Why are you alone?" I commented that she felt this because when she was small her mother was depressed and angry, not because there was something defective about her. She had felt as if she was a worthless burden, defective and unlovable. Now she can recognise that this was not her (Linda's) fault. She then expressed her deepest fear, that at core she really was unlovable. "That's why I battle to not only expect love," she says, "but to understand it and to receive it. That someone would love you, does love you [seems incomprehensible]." Flipping into coping modes was a safer and less painful option than exposing the *LCh* to the risk of confirming that she really was unlovable. Now, having faced this fear, she could start to challenge this entrenched belief. In the therapy relationship, she experienced my concern and care as genuine. With her parents, in the new relationships she was developing with them, she was also experiencing their genuine concern and care for her. Thus, there was not only an explicit cognitive shift but also a deep experiential one.

In S34, she said the previous session had made it easier to stay with the experience of the *LCh* and made her "do a lot of thinking". She had eaten non-diabetic foods at a party and could see the role of her *RebCh*. But she was soon in touch with the *LCh* again and I helped her bridge back, expecting a painful childhood memory. Instead, she sees a confident, six year old "playful, happy Linda". But she is in a bubble, and, in response to my questions, Linda recognised that she had shut out the *LCh*. Because this was also a child, what I call a *Protector Child* (*ProtCh*). This kind of early splitting of memory systems is probably the root of the *Pollyanna* mode that is often observed in adulthood (see Chapter 3). I initiated a dialogue beginning with the *LCh* who felt hurt and angry, betrayed by both parents who had been unavailable to meet her needs. She was also angry with the *ProtCh* for not dealing with "this stuff", with the resultant seriousness, shame and withdrawal as she grew older. I invited *HA* Linda to step back and see the two child parts. I asked her to speak to the *LCh*, and modelled empathic and corrective statements such as, "You've nothing to be ashamed of…you're the sensitive and feeling part of me and I need you." Linda repeated them with much feeling and reported that the *LCh* was gaining a new perspective as she came "face-to-face with the facts". I say, "You didn't know how to deal with all this then, but I [Linda] am going to help you deal with it now." This offer of reparenting scared the *LCh*. I empathised with her fear of getting hurt again. I suggested that Linda invite the *LCh* to come a little closer and then stretch out her hand to her. When the *LCh* took her hand, Linda saw herself putting her arm round her. "Draw her close", she said, tearfully and described how "she just like buries her face in you, holds you." I encouraged her to stay with this experience, and Linda reaffirmed "that it's not her fault and she is loved and…she's got so much to give." The child was cautious, though, as this experience is "a new thing, a new concept". Adult Linda also feared she would not be able to care for her properly. I reminded her that she knew how to treat her differently from the way her parents had. When I suggested she visualise putting the *LCh* into her heart, Linda saw her "small and in a corner," and had "to coax her to come out and step into the light and not be afraid". Linda continued, "I think the more love she gets and the more she realises that she can trust it, she won't need to eat so much. She'll have someone to turn to."

Although she had been engaging with imagery and imagery rescripting for several sessions, in S35, I explicitly spelled out how imagery work can bring about change in EMSs and focused on her unrelenting standards and defectiveness/shame. Drawing on the experiential work, I helped her re-evaluate negative beliefs about herself triggered in everyday situations. She realised that the feeling of "being a burden" probably started when she was hospitalised at age three with asthma. I chose a chair for this child and invited her to sit in it. She recalled, "when I was small I had asthma all the time and I was in and out of hospital…[I was] just not a healthy normal child." Then she made the link to her experiences with diabetes and her ED, where her feelings were being amplified by schema-level emotions originating in how she had felt as an infant and toddler, sick with colic and asthma. "Your parents have to pay, and Medical Aid has to pay", she said. "Why can't you just be healthy and normal [so] your parents don't have to keep paying for everything." In rescripting this, I told the *LCh* that, for a long time, grown-up Linda had "been afraid of you and not known what to do with all the pain you feel. But now she's not afraid of you any more – that's why she reached out to you last week and put you in a safe place in her heart – because she's going to need to tell you a lot that she loves you and you're loveable." I continued, "Deep down in your being you're just a lovely human being… even though you're sick. So what you believed then, what you still believe, is wrong."

## Therapy phase 4 (S36-S40): Fighting the *Overcontroller*

During the next four sessions she signed the no-vomiting contract and reported an increasing capacity to resist the urge to induce vomiting. We worked experientially to strengthen the *HA* and protect and care for the *VCh*. But the *A-OC* remained a powerful force. At the start of session 40, I observed that Linda had lost about three kilos in two months. Although not dangerous (BMI = 21.5), it suggested her *A-OC* mode was busy in the background. When I confronted this, she described wanting to get thin to make a good impression on her parents and friends, when she went home for the vacation. From her *HA*, she recognised that she looked attractive as she was (even before she lost the three kilos) and that her parents and friends would be distressed if they saw her restricting and losing weight. But she felt helpless and, through tears, told me it felt like a losing battle. At times with self-talk she could combat "Anorexia" (the *A-OC*) but at others it just took over.

Using chairs, I played the *A-OC*, "Linda you really need to lose a bit of weight now and you are soon going to be home and you really want to create a nice impression on your parents." "My parents don't want to see me lose weight", she said. Rather they want to see her finish the academic year successfully, and look after her health by eating regularly and carefully with respect to her diabetes and "to see me happy and excited about life". Despite this *HA* content, she was becoming increasingly tearful. I continued as the *A-OC*, "It's no good you worrying, I'm in control here; you can trust me. This voice has been here for years and years and I've really helped you. You can't fight me. I'm helping you." Linda fought back tears as she said, "No! You're not helping – you're making me spiral back into an eating disorder where I'm sick and have irrational thoughts and it damages my health." I put on the pressure, "But I'm too strong for you…I've been here too long. I know how to control you." Linda responded forcefully but still speaking through tears, "You don't belong here. And we're going to win this victory. You've had your time and your time is over…I'm on the way to recovery and I am recovering."

I continued as the *A-OC*, urging her to lose a few more kilos. Linda responded, "No, I'm not going to listen to you because then I keep wanting to lose more and more and more…and then I end up in the same place I was." I kept pushing, "Just show what a strong character you are by just not eating so much and showing you can be in control. You'll feel strong if you show that you can resist the urge to eat. You'll feel better, I make you feel better." This proved a crucial point. Linda said pensively, "That's what I battle with – the whole thing of feeling stronger and getting more in control." I continued, "You say you don't need me anymore, but you know you do. I know how to make you feel good." Though tearful, she could still respond, "No! I'm going to learn to take control of my life in other ways and not just by restricting or not eating – being disciplined doesn't have to do with eating alone; it's about being well-balanced and that's a better success."

I shifted my role and modelled an even stronger counter-attack, encouraging her to tell AN, "You're crazy, you're twisted, you're sick, you're destroying me." As she did this, she spontaneously added, "You're a liar...whose end goal is just self-destruction – and loneliness, and miserableness and punishment. And I want to embrace life...and enjoy it and be happy and I can't do that when I follow you." I suggested she say, "I don't want the kind of life you're offering me" and guided her to rehearse positive beliefs about herself. Asked for feedback, Linda said, "It was good," but was tearful as she continued, "I just started off so weak and especially when I feel...her arguments are true and I don't know how to battle them...especially...the last few things she said...'if you listen to her then your life will be more controlled and more disciplined and you will be a success'... Because I feel that when I don't listen to her then I'm not [a success]." I asked if she had to be a success. "I don't know if there's room for failure," she said and her distress intensified. She had accessed a painful Failure schema, a hotspot on the theme of disappointing her parents, letting them down, betraying their trust, wasting their money. Her *Overcontroller* mode offered her a way out of this, first, by helping her achieve by working hard, and then later, as the *A-OC*, offering her the experience of being strong, self-sufficient and in control of her life.

Although we had not systematically reviewed the pros and cons of investing in the *A-OC* versus her new *HA*, she was experientially connected to those pros and cons now. Her parents were now genuinely concerned about her well-being, and her ED maintained the rift between them and her. "What are your parents going to feel about you if you are still going in and out of hospital having anorexia nervosa in ten years time?" I asked. She sobbed deeply, "I can't do that to them. I can't hurt them like that." I said, "She [i.e. *A-OC*] wants you to." Still speaking through tears, she cried, "No, no, no. I have to get better." I helped her review the reality of her current relationship with them. "Do they like being with you? Do they like spending time with you? Do they value you just for who you are?" She said "Yes," with honest conviction. "Or only for your successes?" "No." She now clearly recognised that they could give her now what they couldn't when she was younger.

## Termination (S41–42) and follow up

The University year was ending and Linda would be moving to a university in another city. In the last two sessions, we consolidated these insights and made a maintenance plan. I was sad that we would not work together further. I felt that a good groundwork had been laid but that it would take time and more experiential work to offer the depth of reparenting that Linda needed for her to fully give up the *A-OC* mode.

## Implications for schema therapy theory and practice

This case study shows how coping modes with origins in early childhood contributed to Linda's severe psychological problems in adolescence and young adulthood, and how a case conceptualisation based on a developmental analysis of schemas and modes made sense of the eating dis-ordered behaviour and provided a basis for a meaningful treatment approach. Given the intractability of many EDs, this, in itself, offers hope and direction to clinician and client alike. But the power of the buried pain at the EMS level must not be underestimated. Linda's ED was driven by an *A-OC* mode that had evolved during Linda's adolescence from an existing *P-OC*, and become a formidable force in her life. It can be conceptualised as a complex composite coping mode (Edwards, 2017b) with several elements working together, as por-trayed in the dream image of the computericed scale and her in-session image of the woman in black. This approach opens up more options for experiential dia-logue work than thinking only in terms of clinical perfectionism.

Following the limited impact of standard CBT, the schema work laid a significant foundation. But that took time to establish. Intensive experiential work only took place in the sessions after S30 and mainly focused on mem-ories from around age six. However Linda's EMSs likely had their roots in the experiences of an infant with a depressed and harassed mother, and epi-sodes of such serious asthma that she was hospitalised several times, when only two years old, at a time when she was dealing with the birth of a younger sister and a mother who was still not coping. There was, therefore, still a great deal of early attachment trauma to be addressed. A beginning had been made but another year of weekly therapy working at the experiential level that Linda had reached, would probably have made a considerable difference.

## Notes

1  This is a completely revised version of a chapter entitled "Reparenting in der Schematherapie – eine Fallstudie bei Anorexia nervosa" originally published in C. Archonti, E. Roediger & M. de Zwaan (Eds.) (2016) *Schematherapie bei Essstör-ungen* (pp. 163–191). Weinheim, Germany: Beltz. It is used with permission.
2  Sessions are referred to as S1, S2 etc.

## References

Edwards, D. J. A. (2017a). An interpretative phenomenological analysis of schema modes in a single case of anorexia nervosa: Part 1 – Background, method and Child and Parent modes. *Indo-Pacific Journal of Phenomenology*, 17(1), 1–13. doi:10.1080/20797222.2017.1326728
Edwards, D. J. A. (2017b). An interpretative phenomenological analysis of schema modes in a single case of anorexia nervosa: Part 2 – Coping modes, Healthy Adult mode, superordinate themes and implications for research and practice. *Indo-Pacific Journal of Phenomenology*, 17(1), 1–12. doi:10.1080/20797222.2017.1326730
Rodin, G., Olmsted, M. P., Rydall, A. C., Maharaj, S. I., Colton, P. A., Jones, J. M., …Daneman, D. (2002). Eating disorders in young women with type 1 diabetes mellitus. *Journal of Psychosomatic Research*, 53(4), 943–949. doi:10.1016/S0022-3999(02)00305-7

# Part V

# The future of schema therapy

# Chapter 17

# Schema therapy for eating disorders

## Future directions

*Evelyn Smith and Susan Simpson*

### Abstract

*Preliminary research suggests early maladaptive schemas (EMS) and schema processes play a key role in eating disorder (ED) pathology, indicating a focus on surface level cognitions alone may be insufficient when treating EDs (Gongora, Derkson, & van der Staak, 2004; Hughes, Hamill, van Gerko, Lockwood & Waller, 2006). Although some aspects of the schema model have been investigated, our understanding of the schema mode concept and the interaction between early childhood and adolescent experiences, EMS, schema processes, and ED pathology are at an early stage of development. Further investigations of the schema model are required to build our understanding of the mechanisms for the development and maintenance of ED pathology, thereby highlighting key areas for intervention. Moreover, larger scale trials of both individual and group schema therapy are urgently required, in order to ascertain the effectiveness of this treatment model for those with eating disorders.*

A recent randomised controlled trial (RCT) demonstrated that ST produced equivalent outcomes compared with CBT for bulimic disorders (McIntosh et al., 2016). To reach the strict evidence-based criteria for inclusion in national guidelines, there is a requirement of two RCTs comparing the new treatment to another evidence-based treatment, conducted by separate investigators. To date, ST for EDs does not meet these criteria. Consequently, we suggest that treatments with stronger evidence should be used as the first line of treatment, particularly for adults with a primary diagnosis of bulimia nervosa (BN) and binge eating disorder (BED). However, ST does meet evidence-based Level one for personality disorders (e.g. National Institute for Health and Clinical Excellence, 2009; National Health and Medical Research Council, 2012), and as documented in Chapter 1, around 70% of those with EDs will have a comorbid personality disorder. There is some evidence that avoidant personality disorder can hinder outcomes and increase risk of relapse in standard treatments (Masheb & Grilo, 2008; Zerwas et al., 2013). Indeed, evidence suggests that avoidant personality traits often precede eating difficulties, and xpersist even after successful treatment of the eating symptoms (Casper, 1990; Wagner et al., 2006). Consequently, integrating ST with cognitive behavioural therapy (CBT) for those with comorbid eating and personality disorder is a good option. Those individuals with EDs who do not respond to first line treatment might also benefit from ST. Indeed, there is some suggestion that those with EDs may benefit from a shift from treatment protocols based on ED subtypes, to treatments tailored to specific personality clusters (Wagner et al., 2006). Nevertheless, there is an urgent need for more randomised controlled trials comparing ST to CBT, or comparing ST to CBT for those individuals who are not making progress with CBT after 10–20 sessions. We also hypothesise, based on clinical experience, and on ST trials for personality disorders, that a combination of individual and group therapy is important in this population, providing an opportunity to learn healthy coping and interpersonal connectivity across both settings (Tan et al., 2018).

The research on processes of change throughout ST is in its infancy. As reported in Chapter 2 it seems that schemas do not consistently reduce after short-term treatment, and more research is needed to identify the processes and time needed to facilitate 'trait' level change. However, modes do seem to reduce alongside ED symptoms. This suggests that it may be more useful to place the primary focus of treatment on cultivating change in modes, as state-manifestations of latent schema traits. Since we all have schemas, our treatments should arguably focus on learning how to cope with these, whilst strengthening healthy schemas/modes that facilitate healthy coping and fulfilment. Future research is needed to explore whether teaching people to cope with their schemas has a compounding long-term effect in tolerating and eventually reducing these schemas. In addition, our understanding of the interactions between early childhood experiences and key constructs such as parenting, EMSs, schema processes, and ED pathology are at an early stage of development. We are yet to discover which aspects of ST are the most useful at establishing change. Previous research suggests that experiential and behavioural interventions may have the strongest effect on outcomes (Tan et al., 2018), although this needs further investigation within the context of ED treatment studies.

Although ST for EDs has not reached Level one evidence, it is a possible alternative for those who have not responded to CBT, and those with high comorbidity and traits that interfere with response to standard treatments. We pose an ethical dilemma – given we know that those who respond to CBT generally begin to show behavioural changes within six sessions (e.g. Agras et al., 2000), how long should CBT be delivered without witnessing any change? Although there is no single answer to this question, we propose that if a client is losing interest in therapy, or does not engage with behavioural tasks, it might be time for a new approach. The main benefit of ST, in our opinion, is the level of engagement. Most clients feel a deep level of being understood when delivering the formulation, especially those who have not engaged with CBT. Clinically, even when we are delivering 'pure' CBT we still use ST formulations to facilitate treatment engagement. However, this requires further investigation – what aspects of formulations do clients resonate with most across treatment modalities? Further investigations of the schema mode model are required to build our understanding of the mechanisms for the development and maintenance of ED pathology thereby highlighting key areas for intervention. Specifically, it will be important to identify mode-clusters linked to ED-characterological profiles, in order to develop more nuanced individualised treatment guidelines, that incorporate both eating and comorbid phenomena. This is an exciting time to engage with ST, and we are hoping to collaborate in both clinical and research environments with those with similar interests. Feel free to email us at schematherapybook@gmail.com.

## References

Agras, W. S., Crow, S. J., Halmi, K. A., Mitchell, J. E., Wilson, G. T., & Kraemer, H. C. (2000). Outcome predictors for the cognitive behavior treatment of bulimia nervosa: Data from a multisite study. *American Journal of Psychiatry*, 157, 1302–1308.

Casper, R. C. (1990). Personality features of women with good outcome from restricting anorexia nervosa. *Psychosomatic Medicine*, 52, 156–170.

Gongora, V., Derksen, J., & van der Staak, C. (2004). The role of core beliefs in the specific cognitions of bulimic patients. *Journal of Nervous and Mental Disease*, 192(4), 297–303.

Hughes, M. L., Hamill, M., van Gerko, K., Lockwood, R., & Waller, G. (2006). The relationship between different levels of cognition and behavioural symptoms in the EDs. *Eating Behaviors*, 7(2), 125–133.

Masheb, R. M., & Grilo, C. M. (2008). Examination of predictors and moderators for self-help treatments of binge-eating disorder. *Journal of Consulting and Clinical Psychology*, 76, 900–904.

McIntosh, V., Jordan, J., Carter, J., Frampton, C., McKenzie, J., Latner, J., & Joyce, P. (2016). Psychotherapy for transdiagnostic binge eating: A randomized controlled trial of cognitive-behavioural therapy, appetite-focused cognitive-behavioural therapy, and schema therapy. *Psychiatry Research*, 240, 412–420.

National Health and Medical Research Council (2012). *Clinical Practice Guideline for the Management of Borderline Personality Disorder*. Available at: https://www.nhmrc.gov.au/about-us/publications/clinical-practice-guideline-borderline-personality-disorder

National Institute for Health and Clinical Excellence (2009). *Borderline Personality Disorder: Treatment and Management*. (NICE Guideline 78). Available at: https://www.nice.org.uk/guidance/cg78/evidence/full-guideline-pdf-242147197

Tan, Y. M., Lee, C. W., Averbeck, L. E., Brand-de Wilde, O., Farrell, J., Fassbinder, E., … Arntz, A.(2018). Schema therapy for borderline personality disorder: A qualitative study of patients' perceptions. *PLOS ONE*, 13(11), [e0206039].

Wagner, A., Barbarich-Marsteller, N., Frank, G., Bailer, U., Wonderlich, S., Crosby, R., Henry, S., Vogel, V., Plotnicov, K., McConaha, C., & Kaye, W. (2006).

Personality traits after recovery from eating disorders: Do subtypes differ? *International Journal of Eating Disorders*, 39 (4), 276–284

Zerwas, S., Lund, B., Von Holle, A., Thornton, L., Berrettini, W., Brandt, H., ... Bulik, C. (2013). Factors associated with recovery from anorexia nervosa. *Journal of Psychiatry Research*, 47, 972–979

# Chapter 18

# Appendix 1

Website: http://www.schematherapyscotland.com/st-ed.resources/
  Password: schemasnacks

# Index